HIMMLER'S
BLACK ORDER

HIMMLER'S BLACK ORDER

A HISTORY OF THE SS, 1923—45

ROBIN LUMSDEN

SUTTON PUBLISHING

First published in 1997 in the United Kingdom by
Sutton Publishing Limited · Phoenix Mill
Thrupp · Stroud · Gloucestershire · GL5 2BU

British Library Cataloguing in Publication Data
A catalogue record for this book is available from the British Library

ISBN 0 7509 1396 7

 ALAN SUTTON™ and SUTTON™ are the
trade marks of Sutton Publishing Limited

Typeset in 10/13 pt Sabon.
Typesetting and origination by
Sutton Publishing Limited.
Printed in Great Britain by
Butler & Tanner, Frome, Somerset.

CONTENTS

INTRODUCTION

The SS is one of the best known, yet least understood, organisations in history. To most people, it was simply a brutal arm of the Nazi state which had subjugation by terror as its sole purpose. Consequently, it will forever be equated with concentration camps, torture and mass extermination, and on that basis is fated to be almost universally loathed and detested for generations to come.

Yet this dark side is only part of the SS story. The whole saga is considerably more complex and, in many ways, almost defies belief. In ten years, the SS grew from a small, unpaid bodyguard for a minor politician to a force which dominated the racial, cultural and professional spheres of the most powerful empire mainland Europe has ever seen. All the domestic police agencies of the occupied territories were controlled by the SS, and a network of monopolistic business enterprises gave the organisation's hundreds of factories direct access to their own raw materials, labour and internal markets. People in all walks of life, from farmers and soldiers to academics and members of the aristocracy, flocked to join the SS for their own selfish ends.

At the centre was Himmler, a ruthlessly ambitious idealist. From the day he took command, Himmler was the SS and the SS Himmler. The organisation's progress became bound up with the career of its Reichsführer, who obtained one important post after another until by 1945 he had concentrated more power in his person than any other man except Hitler. Wherever Himmler secured a position, he took the SS with him. The SS became both the basis and the instrument of his strength. At the height of his influence, Himmler was Chief of Police, Reich Minister of the Interior, an NSDAP Reichsleiter, a Member of the Reichstag, Reich Commissioner for the Consolidation of Germanism, Commander-in-Chief of the Home Army, Chief of Military Armament and Commander of Army Groups on the Rhine and Vistula. In effect, he and his SS controlled all forces, military, paramilitary and police, on the German home front during the Second World War.

Yet, with his crippling fascination for genealogy, medievalism and Germanic lore, the Reichsführer-SS exercised total control over a juggernaut which he regarded not as a political vehicle but as a racial Order. So far as Himmler was concerned, the SS was first and foremost a multi-national family, a nordic clan which would eventually unite the Germanic peoples of Europe so that they would never again come into mutual conflict. Himmler planned that after the victorious conclusion of the war, that last great war of extermination in which the SS would prove itself through the achievements of its own battlefield units, he and his successors would build up the Order and produce the leaders to direct industry, agriculture, politics and the activities of the mind in a new pagan Europe, policed and guarded by the SS.

For his part, Adolf Hitler was content to allow his loyal follower's fancies free rein, since he never needed to threaten would-be troublemakers with anything other than being 'handed over to Himmler'. The knowledge that the all-powerful Reichsführer was lurking around as a sort of bogeyman was usually enough to ensure that Hitler received only fawning adulation from all but the strongest willed. As a result, Himmler's personal hopes and dreams for the SS, however unrealistic, were permitted to shape the development of the entire organisation.

In writing this book, I hope to clear up some misconceptions and show that the SS had many more facets than those generally known. Within Germany itself during the Third Reich, the SS held a unique position. It was feared, yet it was also genuinely respected and, in some cases, even revered. SS membership was something to be highly valued, and the carefully designed uniforms and accoutrements intended to set the new élite apart became instant status symbols in the emerging empire. The extremely powerful influence of badges and regalia should never be forgotten when trying to seek answers to the often-asked question of why ordinary, law-abiding citizens happily subscribed to what is now generally regarded as a murderous organisation.

Robin Lumsden
Cairneyhill, March 1997

1. ORIGINS AND EARLY DEVELOPMENT

The origins of the SS are linked inextricably with the events and aftermath of the First World War. This epic conflict had a profound effect upon Adolf Hitler, who, after years of aimless drifting in Vienna and Munich, suddenly found his true vocation fighting on the western front. From the very beginning the German army, unlike that of Great Britain, actively encouraged initiative on the part of its NCOs and private soldiers, so Gefreiter Hitler was more than accustomed to making front-line decisions in his 'deputy officer' capacity. As a trench messenger, he constantly ran the gauntlet of British and French machine guns, receiving the Bavarian Military Cross of Merit 3rd Class and a Regimental Citation for Bravery in the Face of the Enemy. He was wounded twice, gassed, temporarily blinded and emerged with the Iron Cross 1st Class, an unusually high decoration for an enlisted man and one which he wore proudly until the day of his death.

Once the stalemate of trench warfare had set in, Germany was quick to realise the potential of developing élite units of hand-picked infantrymen to act as assault parties and trench raiders. Early in 1915 Major Eugen Kaslow, a pioneer officer, was tasked with evaluating experimental steel helmets, body armour and a new light cannon. To do so, he formed a small assault detachment which came to be known as Sturmabteilung Kaslow. Under his leadership and that of his successor, Hauptmann Willi Rohr, the Sturmabteilung evolved new tactics to break into an enemy trench system. Combat operations in the Vosges mountains that autumn suggested that these ideas were sound and, in January 1916, Sturmabteilung Rohr was duly transferred to Verdun. At that time, the detachment comprised three-man teams called Stosstruppe, or shock troops, whose method of attack involved storming a trench in flank. The first of the trio was armed with a sharpened entrenching tool and a shield made from a machine gun mounting. He was followed by the second man carrying haversacks full of short-fused stick grenades, and the third soldier armed with a knife, bayonet or club. The Stosstruppe technique proved so successful that a number of Sturmkompanie, or assault companies, were soon formed and attached to divisions on a permanent basis. By 1918, most German armies on the western front had expanded units known as Sturmbataillone or assault battalions, each comprising an HQ company, four assault companies, an infantry artillery company armed with the 37 mm Sturmkanone, a machine gun company, a light trench mortar detachment and a flamethrower detachment.

The storm troops, as they became known to their British adversaries, were accorded the status of romantic heroes by the German popular press. Unlike ordinary infantrymen, they spent little time skulking in filthy trenches. Instead, they attacked suddenly then returned to base with the inevitable cache of prisoners. Raids were reported not only at home but also in the front-line newspapers, one of which was even called *Der Stosstrupp* and carried a regular section headed 'Stosstruppgeist', or Shock Troop Spirit. These select soldiers employed a variety of emotive titles, including Sturmtruppe (assault troops), Jagdkommando (hunting groups) and Patrouillentruppe (raiding parties), all of which were tolerated by the High Command. Officially, special insignia for the storm troops was frowned upon, but many varieties of locally adopted badges were worn. These typically featured bayonets, hand grenades and steel helmets. The most popular badge taken up by the Stosstruppe, however, was the Totenkopf or death's head, a skull over crossed bones, which was initially worn by personnel of the 3rd Guard Reserve Pioneer Regiment, an all-volunteer unit created to operate the new flamethrowers. The Totenkopf became representative of a devil-may-care attitude in the face of constant danger and high casualties.

Just as the storm troops were the best the army could offer, so the new élite formations of the emerging German Air Arm were the flights of fast fighters which escorted and protected unwieldy bombers and reconnaissance aircraft. The fighters were sometimes grouped together as aerial shock troops for the purpose of attacking ground targets, but because of their primary role they were given the title of protection squadrons or Schutzstaffeln, Schustas for short. Prominent Schusta members included Hermann Göring and Eduard Ritter von Schleich, the so-called Black Knight, who later commanded the SS-Fliegersturmbann.

Hitler drew on his valuable First World War experiences long after the end of hostilities. In the early days of the Nazi movement, he considered that a front-line combat posting during 1914–18 was an essential prerequisite for any position of leadership in his National Socialist Party, and the regimented organisation and military terminology later used by the NSDAP was directly carried over from its members' army service. The terms Stosstrupp, Sturmabteilung and Schutzstaffel, devised to describe the crack German forces of land and air, were soon adopted by the Nazis for their own paramilitaries and were to take on an entirely new significance in the postwar era.

In November 1918, Germany faced disaster. The war had been lost, the Kaiser had abdicated and the government had collapsed. The armed forces were, in effect, disbanded, and groups of demobilised left-wing soldiers with no prospects roamed the streets calling for a Bolshevik uprising like that which had just taken hold in Russia. The country was also under extreme pressure from the civilian Spartacist revolutionaries, and Polish insurgents threatened to invade Silesia and the eastern Baltic territories of the Reich.

To meet these challenges, new ad hoc Freikorps units were hastily formed by right-wing troops who found themselves anxious to defend their Fatherland and its traditional values, but were without a proper army in which to do so. Such groups traced their ancestry to the Freiwilligenkorps, or volunteer corps, which had been mustered in times of crisis in Germany since the Middle Ages. Still in possession of their wartime uniforms, weapons and transport, they banded together to follow local heroes or well-known military personalities. The usual method of recruitment was simply for an ex-officer to circulate literature or display posters inviting former soldiers to attend at a specified location on a given date and join his Freikorps. In many cases thousands turned up, eager to enlist whether for payment or not. As well as the promise of action, a big attraction was the fact that discipline in the Freikorps was very lax in comparison to that

Freikorps troops in Munich, 2 May 1919. This picture was taken by Heinrich Hoffmann, later Hitler's personal photographer, and shows to good effect the death's head emblem painted on the front of the armoured car.

of the imperial army. Officers were commonly referred to by their forenames and enlisted men saluted only those officers whom they personally respected or admired. The troops paid little attention to formal instructions issued by the weak provisional government and gave their loyalty totally to their Freikorps commander, whom they referred to as their Führer, or leader. To these destitute soldiers, units and comrades became homes and families.

The state was in desperate need of trained military men to assert control and these Freikorps freebooters provided the experienced manpower at just the right time. Dedicated above all to preventing Germany becoming a Bolshevik regime, they smashed riots, kept order in the streets, protected public buildings and became a mainstay of the law until they were dissolved in 1919, at least on paper, by the Treaty of Versailles, which laid down the conditions for the setting up of the Reichswehr, the reconstituted and much-reduced army of the Weimar Republic. Those Freikorps men who were not accepted back into the new army tended to drift into right-wing paramilitary groups such as the Stahlhelm and Reichskriegsflagge of the nationalists, the Jungdeutscher Orden and the Organisation Rossbach. Such men included Himmler himself, and the future SS Generals Kurt Daluege, 'Sepp' Dietrich, Reinhard Heydrich, Friedrich-Wilhelm Krüger, Karl Wolff and Udo von Woyrsch, among many others.

In all, during the period 1919–20, there

were some 250 individual Freikorps units in existence, comprising more than 70,000 men. They created their own range of medals, badges and insignia, and prominent among these were the swastika of the Ehrhardt Brigade and the death's head, borrowed from the imperial storm troops. The following Freikorps are known to have used the Totenkopf on their helmets and vehicles:

(a) *Freikorps Brüssow*
Commanded by Leutnant Hans Brüssow between January and April 1919, this unit had a strength of 1,200 men and later became Reichswehr Infantry Regiment 4.

(b) *Eiserne Division*
One of the most famous of all the Freikorps, this brigade-strength unit under Major Bischoff carried out extensive raids in the Baltic area between November 1918 and February 1920. The following month it was disbanded, together with the Erhhardt Brigade, for its participation in the rightist Kapp Putsch in Berlin. Its veterans were welcomed into the SS a few years later.

(c) *Sub-Units of the Eiserne Division*, in particular:
Beuthener Selbstschutz-Kompanie
Freiwilligen Batterie Zenetti
Freiwilligen Jägerkorps Goldingen
Kurländisches Infanterie-Regiment
Ostpreussisches Jägerkorps
Selbstschutz Bataillon Begerhoff
Selbstschutz Bataillon Generalfeld-marschall von Hindenburg
Selbstschutz Oberschlesien
Freikorps Tilsit

(d) *Freikorps Erlangen*
This battalion-size unit existed from April to June 1919, and was commanded by Generalmajor Engelhardt. It was incorporated into Reichswehr Infantry Regiment 47 and Artillery Regiment 42.

(e) *Freikorps Gerth*
Commanded by Leutnant Gerth between April and June 1919, this formation numbered 625 men and was absorbed into Reichswehr Infantry Regiment 40.

(f) *Minenwerfer Detachment Heuschkel*
A veteran storm troop trench mortar unit, unusually led by an NCO, Feldwebel Heuschkel.

(g) *Freiwilligen Detachment von Schauroth*
A small number of ex-storm troops who banded together under their former commanding officer, Major von Schauroth.

Because of its association with these units, the death's head, already a wartime badge of daring and self-sacrifice, now became a symbol of traditionalism, anti-liberalism and anti-Bolshevism, an ideal totem for the embryonic Nazi élite.

In December 1918, Adolf Hitler was discharged from the military hospital at Pasewalk near Stettin where he had been recovering from a gassing. He volunteered for guard duty at a prisoner-of-war camp at Traunstein, but by January 1919 its last inmate had left. At a loose end, and still in uniform, Hitler made his way to Munich and joined the Bavarian Freikorps which had been formed by the war hero Franz Ritter von Epp to liberate the city from its new Marxist government. This it did with much bloodshed.

Nationalist groups were springing up all over Germany, with the objective of ridding the country of the 'November Traitors' who had brought the disgrace of the dictated peace, and of the communists, whose first loyalty was to Russia. Nationalists came from every level of society, and at the lower end of the Munich social scale was Anton Drexler's tiny German Workers' Party, one of whose meetings Hitler attended as a military observer on 12 September 1919. It was a grouping which brought together racist intellectuals to fight, by means of argument, Marxist influence and 'Jewish infiltration' into the working class. They found the Jews principally responsible for popular Red revolution, citing the fact that all the leaders of the leftist movement, Karl Liebknecht, Rosa Luxemburg, Kurt Eisner and the rest, were Jewish. Hitler found that Drexler's ideas paralleled his own. He joined the party and, through his forceful personality and powers of oratory, virtually took it over from the outset, changing its name to the National Socialist German Workers' Party (Nationalsozialistische Deutsche Arbeiterpartei or NSDAP) and giving it a nationalistic, anti-Semitic, anti-capitalistic programme where, hitherto, it had possessed only a vague set of ideals.

Hitler's speeches soon found a loud echo in the ranks of the Freikorps, and their units provided the new Nazi Führer with his first large followings. Hauptmann Ernst Röhm, von Epp's adjutant, who also headed his own Reichskriegsflagge Freikorps, sent Hitler an incessant flood of officers, NCOs and men. Taking a leaf from the communists' book, Hitler began to hire lorries and had them filled with party members, who drove noisily through the streets to meetings. The difference was that while the communists wore a curious assortment of dress, the Nazis, most of them ex-soldiers, sat bolt upright, wore smart Freikorps uniforms and seemed the very epitome of law and order reinstated. They were invariably cheered as they passed.

Hitler's main aim at this stage was to replace the party's small discussion groups with mass meetings, and the first of these, at the Festsaal of the Munich Hofbräuhaus on 24 February 1920, attracted nearly 2,000 people. The stewards on this auspicious occasion, when the NSDAP programme was laid down, were a squad of Zeitfreiwilligen or temporary volunteers, armed with pistols and clad in the field-grey of the Munich Reichswehr to which they were attached. Such supporters might well have been sympathetic, but they certainly had no undying loyalty to the new movement. So, towards the end of 1920, a permanent and regular Nazi formation called the Saalschutz, or Hall Guard, was set up to protect speakers at NSDAP gatherings. The Saalschutz was short-lived, however, for it was expanded and consolidated into a fresh body, the Sturmabteilung, or SA, during 1921. This was the work of Röhm and an ex-naval Leutnant, Hans-Ulrich Klintzsch, who created the SA as a new Freikorps to hammer the Reds and fend off opponents at political meetings. Whereas the Saalschutz had been designed to defend, the SA was to attack. Yet while the SA was affiliated to the party, it did not initially come under Hitler's personal authority, for its members had little respect for the finesse of politics. It took its orders from its own Führer, the self-appointed Commander-in-Chief Oberstleutnant Hermann Kriebel, who thought that, 'the best thing political blokes could do would be to belt up'. Originally confined to Munich, the SA made its first important foray outside the city when, on 14–15 October 1922, it took part in a 'German Day' at Coburg which resulted in a pitched battle with the communists who controlled the town. The 800 SA men present, almost the entire membership of the Sturmabteilung, succeeded in breaking the hold of the Red Front on Coburg, and press coverage of the incident served to make Hitler's name known to a wider public.

The first national rally of the NSDAP was held on 28 January 1923, when some 6,000

Hermann Göring as Commander-in-Chief of the SA, 1923. Note the Ehrhardt Brigade steel helmet with swastika, and the Order 'Pour le Mérite' at the neck. Rank is denoted by the wide stripes on the armband.

newly recruited SA men paraded before Hitler, who presented standards to the first four full SA regiments, entitled 'München', 'München II', 'Nürnberg' and 'Landshut'. There were sufficient volunteers during the next month alone to form a fifth regiment, and, in an effort to control better the rapidly growing organisation, Hitler appointed a new man of politics, the former air ace Hauptmann Hermann Göring, to lead it. Göring brought with him the prestige of a great wartime hero, the last commander of the von Richthofen squadron, victor of twenty-two aerial dog-fights and holder of Germany's highest gallantry decoration, the

Order 'Pour le Mérite'. However, he was by nature lazy and self-indulgent. The true driving force behind the SA remained Röhm, who continued to use his army and Freikorps connections to supply the SA with arms. So, in spite of Göring's appointment, the SA in 1923 was far from being submissive. Its independence, upheld by the former leaders of the Freikorps, compelled Hitler to set up a small troop of men, from outside the SA, which would be entirely devoted to him. It was in this atmosphere that the SS was born.

In March 1923, Hitler ordered the formation of a Munich-based bodyguard known as the Stabswache, comprising twelve old comrades who swore an oath of loyalty to him personally and owed no allegiance to the leaders of the Freikorps or SA. Two months later, using the Stabswache as cadre, the 100-man Stosstrupp Adolf Hitler was created and fully kitted out with military-style uniforms and two trucks. The Stosstrupp quickly adopted the death's head as its distinctive emblem, and was led by Hauptmann Julius Schreck and Leutnant Josef Berchtold, both veterans of the Ehrhardt Brigade. Its headquarters were located in the Torbräu public house, and there met the first members of Hitler's bodyguard, who were destined to remain faithful to him at all times and follow his way up the political ladder. They included 'Sepp' Dietrich, Ulrich Graf, Rudolf Hess, Emil Maurice, Julius Schaub and Christian Weber.

Hitler quickly recognised that the volatile situation of 1923 was a transient thing, and he resolved to take full advantage of it. He reckoned that his SA and its Freikorps allies might at last be strong enough to seize power in Bavaria and, with luck, march from Munich on Berlin for a final triumph. Similar coups had taken place with varying degrees of success elsewhere in Germany since 1918, and the fascists under Mussolini had just swept to power in Italy after a march on

SA men, in an assortment of military and civilian clothing, muster at Oberwiesenfeld prior to attending the Labour Day parade in Munich on 1 May 1923. Such events usually ended in street fighting between Nazis and communists, hence the distribution of rifles.

The Stosstrupp Hitler leaving for 'German Day' in Bayreuth, 2 September 1923. Josef Berchtold stands leaning on the cab, beside von Salomon and Ulrich Graf. Julius Schreck, with goggles, is seated at the left of the front row.

Rome. At the beginning of November, the 15,000 men of the SA were put on full alert and a suitable opportunity suddenly arose on the 8th of the month. That day, the three most powerful men in Bavaria, Prime Minister von Kahr, local army commander Lossow and police chief Seisser, attended a political meeting in the Munich Burgerbräukeller where they could be handily seized by a strongarm squad. The Reichskriegsflagge Freikorps was having a 'social' in the Augustiner beer cellar when its commander, Röhm, was ordered in his SA capacity to seize the Reichswehr Ministry on the Leopoldstrasse. His troops immediately set off, led by a young former army officer cadet,

Heinrich Himmler, who carried an imperial war flag, the banner of the unit which bore its name. Meanwhile, armed SA men surrounded the Burgerbräukeller and Hitler had von Kahr, Lossow and Seisser arrested and bundled into a side room. They managed to escape, however, and sped off to organise resistance to the Nazi putsch.

On the morning of 9 November, the main force of the SA under Röhm was besieged in the War Ministry by regular army units summoned by Lossow. Hitler and Göring organised a relief column of 2,000 SA men and, accompanied by the former General Erich Ludendorff, marched through the streets of Munich. They ran into the first

A group of the Reichskriegsflagge Freikorps behind the Bavarian War Ministry on 9 November 1923. From left to right in the foreground are: Weickert, Kitzinger, Himmler (with imperial war flag), Seidel-Dittmarsch and Röhm.

cordon of Seisser's police on the Ludwig Bridge, but brushed them aside. A second police cordon on the edge of the Odeonsplatz, however, gave them a different reception. They were in a strategic spot outside the Feldherrnhalle war memorial and were determined not to retreat. Ulrich Graf, who with the rest of the Stosstrupp Adolf Hitler was present to protect his Führer, stepped out and shouted to the police officer in charge, 'Don't shoot! His Excellency Ludendorff is here!'. But this was the police, not the army, and Ludendorff's name had no magic sound. A volley of shots rang out. Josef Berchtold collapsed under a hail of bullets. Andreas Bauriedl, the swastika standard-bearer, was in his death throes, drenching the flag with his blood. The tattered artefact was rapidly gathered up and spirited away, to be piously preserved as the famed Blutfahne, or Blood Banner. Hitler had locked his left arm with the right of his close confidant, Max Erwin von Scheubner-Richter, and when the latter fell mortally wounded he pulled Hitler to the ground with him. Instantly, Ulrich Graf threw himself on his leader and was at once peppered by a dozen bullets which might otherwise have killed Hitler. Somehow, Graf survived it. Sixteen Nazis lay dead and the rest dispersed or were captured, but the Stosstrupp had fulfilled its primary duty – Hitler's life was preserved. The firing outside the Feldherrnhalle finally ended the era of the Freikorps, which had started, five years before to the day, with the revolution of 1918. The time for fighting men had now passed, giving way to the politicians.

The reverse experienced at the Munich putsch and Hitler's subsequent imprisonment, far from harming the cause of the party and its leader, merely served to get them better known. Yet there were still plenty of troubles ahead. Following the putsch, the NSDAP was banned and the SA and Stosstrupp dissolved. Those Nazi leaders who managed to avoid arrest fled to other German states where Bavarian law could not touch them. Refugees from Munich set up personal clandestine SA units under the name Frontbanne, with overall control being exercised by Ludendorff and his deputy, Albert von Gräfe. The largest was Frontbann Nord, centred around Berlin and commanded by Kurt Daluege. Hitler, cooped up in jail with his bodyguards penning *Mein Kampf*, realised that an armed insurrection against a government which enjoyed the loyalty of both the police and the army would be doomed. Henceforth, he determined to employ only legal methods in his struggle for power.

On his release from Landsberg prison on 20 December 1924, Hitler began to rebuild his party, and in February 1925 the NSDAP was reconstituted and the SA reactivated. Hitler the politician now categorically forbade the SA to bear arms or function as any sort of private army. Its purpose was solely to clear the streets of his political enemies, a role hotly contested by Röhm, who envisaged the SA as a citizen army which could bolster and ultimately supersede the Reichswehr. The disagreement between the two became so bitter that Röhm eventually resigned from the party and quit Germany for a military adviser's post in Bolivia. His job as Chief of Staff of the SA fell to the former Freikorps leader Franz Felix Pfeffer von Salomon, but the latter failed to enjoy Hitler's confidence and Röhm was duly reinstated in a stronger position than ever.

In April 1925, Hitler formed a new bodyguard commanded by Schreck, Schaub and his other Stosstrupp favourites. The guard, which came under the auspices of the SA High Command, was known first as the Schutzkommando, then the Sturmstaffel, but on 9 November, probably at the suggestion of Göring, it adopted the old fighter squadron title of Schutzstaffel, which was not subject to any of the governmental prohibitions and

Men of the newly formed SS proudly display an NSDAP Feldzeichen at the end of 1925. Note the wild variety of dress, particularly the strange caps with massive eagle insignia, and the assorted belt buckles.

sown. Applicants had to be between 25 and 35 years of age, have two sponsors, be registered with the police as residents of at least five years' standing, and be sober, disciplined, strong and healthy. Habitual drunkards and gossip-mongers were not to be admitted. The reason for all this was simple. Hitler and his followers were beginning to travel outside Bavaria in their tireless campaigning to increase the membership of the NSDAP. They were now venturing into areas where Nazi allegiance was local, rather than to Hitler himself. The Führer needed a small, hand-picked bodyguard on which he could rely wherever he went. The new SS had its first opportunity to distinguish itself at Chemnitz in Saxony at the end of the year. It was a bold decision to hold a public meeting in this Red territory, but Hitler's audacious stroke proved to be justified. In anticipation of trouble, Schreck gathered fifty SS men from Chemnitz, Dresden, Plauen and Zwickau. They had to face some several hundred counter-demonstrators armed with iron bars and knives. The SS taught them such a lesson in street fighting that Hitler's meetings in that region were henceforth conducted almost without opposition.

In April 1926, Schreck was nominated personal bodyguard and chauffeur to the Führer, and Josef Berchtold re-emerged to take over command of the SS, which then numbered about 1,000 men. On the second anniversary of the Munich putsch, the existence of the SS had been officially proclaimed in a ceremony outside the Feldherrnhalle, and in the spring of 1926 no less than seventy-five Schutzstaffeln were formed right across the country. A new SS-Oberleitung was created and Berchtold adopted the self-styled title of Reichsführer der SS. On 4 July, in a gesture symbolising his intention that the SS should become the true guardian of Nazi values, Hitler solemnly handed over the Blutfahne from the Munich

was not identified with any of the Freikorps traditions. The 'Schutzstaffel der NSDAP' soon commonly came to be known as the SS.

From the start, it was laid down that the SS, unlike the SA, should never become a mass organisation. In September 1925, Schreck sent a circular to all regional groups of the NSDAP asking them to form a local bodyguard, the strength of which was to be fixed at one leader and ten men. This was the beginning of the so-called 'Zehnerstaffeln' or Groups of Ten. Not just anybody could join, for the seeds of élitism had already been

putsch into their safekeeping and appointed Jakob Grimminger from the Munich SS detachment to be official bearer of the Blutfahne at all subsequent special party rituals. Yet despite the extension of its numbers and theoretical prestige, the SS remained a limited organisation subordinated to the SA. When von Salomon attempted to absorb the SS completely in March 1927, Berchtold resigned and was replaced by his deputy, Erhard Heiden, who managed to retain its partial autonomy. However, the SA kept a jealous eye on SS expansion and local SA commanders consistently used the SS under their control for the most demeaning tasks, such as distributing propaganda leaflets and recruiting subscribers to the party newspaper, the *Völkischer Beobachter*. By the end of 1928, morale in the SS was at an all-time low and membership had fallen to 280. On 6 January 1929, a dejected Heiden resigned his titular position as Reichsführer der SS in favour of his timid young deputy, Heinrich Himmler. The SA leadership were cock-a-hoop. This colourless nonentity posed little threat and was just the man to command the SS and to ensure its continued subordination to the SA. They were in for a rude awakening.

There was absolutely no sign of Himmler's future greatness in 1929. The new SS leader was pale, mild-mannered and prim, with spectacles and prematurely receding hair. Born on 7 October 1900, he was a member of the best Bavarian society and was named after his godfather, Prince Heinrich of Bavaria, to whom his schoolmaster father was tutor. He had welcomed the outbreak of the First World War with enthusiasm, and reported for duty as an officer cadet with the 11th Bavarian Infantry Regiment in January 1918. However, he was sent to the front just at the moment when the armistice was signed and never saw action, something he always regretted. On 17 December 1918, Himmler was discharged from the army but he retained his military connections by joining the Oberland Freikorps in 1919. He gained an agricultural degree in 1922, then secured employment as a technical assistant with a fertiliser company, only to see his salary lose half its value to inflation in a single month. In August 1923, Himmler became a member of the NSDAP and two months later enrolled in Röhm's Reichskriegsflagge and participated in the Munich putsch, an act which cost him his job. After the dissolution of the party, he took it upon himself to reorganise the NSDAP in Lower Bavaria in preparation for the elections of 1924. He spent much of his time riding around the countryside on an old motorcycle, indoctrinating the locals. Himmler soon became well known in Nazi circles for his energy, enthusiasm and organising ability, and on 12 March 1925 he was summoned by Hitler who appointed him Gauleiter in Lower Bavaria. He was one of the first to join the SS at the end of the year, and in 1926 became responsible for Nazi propaganda throughout Germany, directly under Hitler's orders. Once he had become the Führer's direct partner, Himmler persisted in putting forward his notion that the SS should become an élite force within the party, and one which would be totally devoted to Hitler. At a time when the SA was becoming increasingly rebellious, the notion appealed and so Hitler approved Himmler's succession to Heiden as Reichsführer der SS.

In April 1929, Himmler persuaded Hitler and von Salomon to approve a recruiting plan designed to create a truly élite body out of the SS. In contrast to the SA, which took all comers, only properly selected candidates would be accepted for the SS, based primarily upon their voluntary discipline. There were none of the racial standards imposed on later recruits, but the early SS men had to demonstrate their willingness to be ready for any sacrifice, in individual rather than group

Protected by SS men, NSDAP Treasurer Franz Xaver Schwarz (left, in overcoat) watches a parade in his home town of Günzburg, September 1929. Himmler stands nearest the camera, his position of seniority as Reichsführer der SS indicated solely by the three white stripes on his armband.

action. At that time, recruits were liable to purchase their own uniforms, which could cost up to 40 marks, an enormous expense for an unemployed man, and that factor alone was enough to deter many. However, high personal standards had a great appeal to ex-soldiers and young nationalists, and veterans of the Freikorps also volunteered in large numbers. By the beginning of 1930, the SS had again grown to 1,000 men, which worried von Salomon. Yet it was still technically subordinated to the SA High Command, despite Hitler's instruction that no SA officer was authorised to give orders to the SS during their day-to-day duties.

Whereas the SS grew steadily, the SA exploded completely. Its sole purpose was to be a mass organisation of pro-Nazi street fighters, and by the time of the first great NSDAP electoral victory of September 1930, 60 per cent of the SA membership were unemployed ruffians who owed allegiance to their local generals, not Hitler. In the north, the SA split down the middle when the new party chief in Berlin, the flamboyant intellectual Dr Joseph Goebbels, arrived to take charge of the city. The Berlin SA began to complain that Hitler and his Bavarian friends were living in the lap of luxury while their comrades in the inner cities were starving. Röhm tried to take charge of the situation, but the SA leaders in Berlin, under SA-Oberführer Walther Stennes, rebelled. On 1 April 1931, Kurt Daluege, now in charge of the SS in Berlin, alerted Hitler that all the Berlin SA had taken sides for Stennes against him. The next day, Stennes' men chased Gauleiter Goebbels out of his office and took over the premises of his newspaper, *Der Angriff*. The revolt spread throughout the whole of northern Germany. The SA Generals in Brandenburg, Hesse, Silesia, Pomerania and Mecklenburg supported Stennes, and Hitler's fall was widely prophesied. However, the uprising lacked organisation and money and died as quickly as it had been born. Göring took a grip of the situation, purging the SA of Stennes' supporters and reorganising the SA throughout the north. Hitler issued his public congratulations to the Berlin SS, which alone had remained loyal to Goebbels and him during the crisis. The devotion of the SS to their Führer had been demonstrated in deeds as well as words. In recognition, Hitler appointed Himmler security chief for the NSDAP headquarters, the Brown House in Munich, on 25 January 1932. In effect, he was now head of the party police.

The SS now grew steadily within the matrix of a rapidly expanding SA and NSDAP. Himmler kept busy, changing and rechanging his unit designations to keep up with the elaborate tables of organisation being constructed by Röhm and his staff. SS membership multiplied five times during 1932, from 10,000 to 50,000, and around 900 officers were commissioned. The SS Stürme had scarcely been numbered when their numbers had to be reassigned to new Standarten. Weak SS companies became even weaker SS regiments, and thirty small SS regiments became tiny SS brigades. The brigade system was then abandoned altogether and light, purely administrative, units known as Oberführer-Abschnitte were interposed between about forty Standarten and the Reichsführer-SS. By now, the political struggle in Germany had taken on the form

'Sepp' Dietrich in 1930, as Standartenführer and head of the SS in Upper Bavaria. He wears an impressive array of decorations, including the Bavarian Military Merit Cross with Crown and Swords, the Iron Cross 1st and 2nd Classes, the Silesian Eagle and the Tank Battle Badge instituted on 13 July 1921. The latter was awarded to the 100 or so surviving combat veterans of the First World War German Panzer Corps, which in its entirety had comprised a total of only twenty A7V tanks and some captured British armoured vehicles. Dietrich served as an NCO on tank no. 560, codenamed 'Alter Fritz', which was blown up the day before the war ended. He wore the Tank Battle Badge with pride throughout his service in the SS and was, in fact, the only recipient known to have been photographed wearing it.

of a civil war. The Communist Party and socialists set up armed militias and the SA and SS responded. The Brüning government ordered the disbanding of paramilitaries and the prohibition of political uniforms, but it then collapsed and the 'Cabinet of Barons' set up under Franz von Papen lifted the ban. Thirteen members of the SS were killed in 1932 and several hundreds wounded during

Julius Schreck in his capacity as Hitler's personal SS bodyguard and chauffeur, April 1932. Political uniforms were banned at the time, hence the civilian clothes.

Hitler on the election trail in the autumn of 1932, accompanied by, from left to right, Julius Schaub, 'Sepp' Dietrich and Kurt Daluege.

street battles with the Red Front. The whole scenario was lapped up by the SS Old Guard, and their catch-phrase, 'Die Kampfzeit war die beste Zeit' ('The fighting days were the best') was frequently repeated as a form of boast to young SS men well into the Third Reich period. As the crucial 1933 elections approached, it suited the Nazis to create the impression that Germany was on the verge of anarchy and that they had the solutions. Order would be restored under Hitler. Deals were done with big business. Jobs would be guaranteed for all. Not surprisingly, the NSDAP won a significant electoral victory and on 30 January the old General-feldmarschall Paul von Hindenburg, Reich President and a sort of 'Ersatz Kaiser' since 1925, entrusted Hitler with the post of Chancellor and the responsibility of forming a government. On 28 February, less than a month after the assumption of power, the Reichstag building was razed to the ground by fire and the communists were blamed. The next day, Hitler issued a decree 'For the Protection of People and State', giving police powers to the SA and SS. Firearms were issued to 25,000 SA and 15,000 SS acting as Hilfspolizei or auxiliary policemen, and left-wing opponents began to be arrested and herded into makeshift prisons and camps. Soon, 27,000 people were being held in protective custody. In March, Himmler became Police President of Munich and opened the first concentration camp, or Konzentrationslager (KL), at Dachau, as a roughly organised labour camp in which to 'concentrate' persons who were deemed to be a danger to the state but had not been legally sentenced to prison by a court of law. Other camps were soon established at Sachsenhausen outside Berlin and at Buchenwald near Weimar. Mean-while, a number of company-sized SS detachments were being armed and put on a full-time paid footing, growing to become

the Leibstandarte-SS 'Adolf Hitler', the Führer's close bodyguard, and the SS-Verfügungstruppe or SS-VT, barracked troops at the special disposal of the new Nazi régime. Another new branch of SS volunteers, the Wachverbände, was recruited to guard the concentration camps and later became known as the Death's Head Units, or Totenkopfverbände (SS-TV), because of their distinctive collar insignia.

While the SS was consolidating its position and controlling its membership and recruitment by a constant purging process, the brown-shirted SA began to throw its weight about noisily. Denied a position in the state to which it felt entitled, the SA talked of a 'Second Revolution' which would sweep away the bourgeois in the party and the reactionaries in the Reichswehr. Among the SS, the SA leaders became known as 'Fleischschnitten' or 'beef steaks', because they were brown on the outside but red on the inside. Röhm, who now commanded a force over forty times the size of the regular army and which included SA cavalry regiments, SA naval battalions and SA air squadrons, demanded the formation of a people's army in which the SA would simply replace the Reichswehr. Röhm, of course, would be Commander-in-Chief. The army Generals called upon Hitler to intervene and the Führer could not refuse their request. Ever since November 1918, the Reichswehr had been the very incarnation of continuity in the state, which had been maintained despite defeat, revolution and civil war. Hitler knew he would never achieve supreme power without the backing of the military, and so decided that the SA would have to be cut down to size. The danger it posed was just too great – not simply the threat of a putsch but the ever-present disorder created by the very men who should have been setting an example of good order. Their incessant brawling, drinking, violence and

SS men prepare to set fire to a collection of placards and flags seized from Berlin communists, March 1933.

SS-Gruppenführer 'Sepp' Dietrich in conversation with Wilhelm Brückner, Hitler's chief adjutant, at the end of 1933. Dietrich has removed the SS armband from his black service uniform, which was a short-term expedient adopted during this period to set the personnel of the infant Leibstandarte apart from the mass of the Allgemeine-SS.

irresponsible conversation, to say nothing of Röhm's homosexual antics, provoked profound discontent in public opinion. The confidence ordinary Germans had in the new régime was in danger of collapsing altogether. On 28 June 1934, Hitler took the final decision to eliminate the SA leadership. Two days later he personally directed operations at Munich and Bad Wiessee, where Röhm and his subordinates had peacefully gathered at their Führer's request. Following a carefully co-ordinated plan, men of the new armed SS formations arrested and executed Röhm and sixteen senior SA commanders. The SS also seized the opportunity to settle its scores with old enemies, such as the former Bavarian Prime Minister von Kahr, Hitler's adversary during the Munich putsch, who was now found dead in a peat bog with his head smashed in. At least 300 victims paid with their lives for their opposition to the SS in this bloody purge, which came to be known as the 'Night of the Long Knives'. The SA suffered a loss of power and influence from which it never fully recovered. The new head of the SA, Viktor Lutze, Police President of Hannover, had an ability to get on with the army and SS which was surpassed only by his obsequious loyalty to Hitler. The rank

THE SS ROLL OF HONOUR

Died		Unit	Died		Unit
16.3.30	Edmund Behnke	1/I/6	2.8.32	Fritz Schulz	2/III/42
5.12.30	Adolf Höh	2/I/30	7.9.32	Josef Lass	3/III/11
7.6.31	Heinz Gutsche	5/III/7	7.9.32	August Assmann	1/II/38
7.6.31	Edgar Steinbach	1/III/7	21.10.32	Johann Cyranka	1/I/28
15.8.31	Heinrich Grobe	2/III/7	22.10.32	August Pfaff	6/I/30
3.9.31	Karl Vobis	1/I/20	1.2.33	Leopold Paffrath	1/II/25
5.10.31	Erich Garthe	1/I/25	5.2.33	Friedrich Schreiber	2/I/20
9.11.31	Karl Radke	1/I/40	12.2.33	Paul Berk	1/I/26
11.11.31	Martin Martens	4/III/40	15.2.33	Franz Müller	2/IV/5
19.1.32	Arnold Guse	2/I/25	20.2.33	Kurt von der Ahe	1/I/6
4.2.32	Fritz Beubler	3/I/14	28.2.33	Josef Bleser	4/II/2
29.2.32	Henry Kobert	1/I/28	28.2.33	Eduard Felsen	1/II/6
8.4.32	Ludwig Frisch	1/III/7	1.5.33	Siegfried Güthling	3/IV/26
20.6.32	Kurt Hilmer	6/II/20	3.5.33	Fritz Kratz	7/I/35
26.6.32	Friedrich Borawski	8/I/30	30.6.33	Gerhard Landmann	1/I/49
24.7.32	Herbert Zimmermann	4/IV/5	28.8.33	Albert Mader	5/II/3
24.7.32	Friedrich Karpinski	4/I/25			

It is noteworthy that eleven (i.e. 33 per cent) of these men were killed *after* the Nazis had actually come to power. On 30 May 1938, they all received posthumous awards of the Blood Order, the highest decoration of the NSDAP.

and file of SA members was reduced from 4 million to just over 1 million of the better elements, and they were stripped of their arms.

On 20 July 1934, in thanks for its actions during the Röhm putsch, Hitler declared the 200,000-strong SS an independent formation of the NSDAP and removed it completely from SA control. Its position of ascendancy was now assured and it entered a period of consolidation in which it developed a new command structure under Himmler, whose rank as Reichsführer-SS for the first time actually meant what it implied and made him directly subordinate to Hitler. He immediately shed some 60,000 SS men who had been recruited at a time when the SS was competing for members with the SA, but who did not now conform to the SS' image of élitism. The Leibstandarte, SS-VT and SS-TV developed their status as separate military branches, eventually amalgamating and expanding during the Second World War under the all-embracing title of Waffen-SS. From the middle of 1934, the traditional non-military SS, the backbone of the organisation, began to be known as the Allgemeine-SS, or General SS, to distinguish it from the armed branches.

During these early years, thirty-three SS men were killed in street fighting with Hitler's political opponents, and were duly recorded on the SS Ehrentafel, or Roll of Honour. In effect, they became SS martyrs. Their names, units and dates of death are shown in the table above.

2. THE ALLGEMEINE-SS

GENERAL ORGANISATION OF THE ALLGEMEINE-SS

During the period 1926–28, the SS-Oberleitung in Munich ran twelve local SS Staffeln, and oversaw six SS-Gau, as follows:

SS-Gau Berlin-Brandenburg, with 2 Staffeln
SS-Gau Franken, with 5 Staffeln
SS-Gau Niederbayern, with 3 Staffeln
SS-Gau Oberbayern, with 4 Staffeln
SS-Gau Rheinland-Süd, with 5 Staffeln
SS-Gau Sachsen, with 4 Staffeln

In theory, each party Gau should have had an SS-Gau but, in fact, only these six were actually set up, and many of their Staffeln dealt directly with the Oberleitung. A large number of early Staffeln were very short-lived.

By 1929–30, an SS-Oberstab had superseded the Oberleitung, and it was split into five distinct divisions, namely:

Abteilung I   – Administration
Abteilung II   – Personnel
Abteilung III – Finance
Abteilung IV   – Security
Abteilung V   – Race

Under the Oberstab were three SS-Oberführer, who ran their own areas, or Oberführerbereiche, as follows:

SS-Oberführerbereich Ost
SS-Brigade Berlin-Brandenburg, with 3 Standarten/7 Stürme
SS-Brigade Schlesien, with 4 Standarten/6 Stürme
SS-Brigade Ostpreussen, with 2 Standarten/6 Stürme

SS-Oberführerbereich West
SS-Brigade Rheinland-Nord, with 4 Standarten/10 Stürme
SS-Brigade Rheinland-Süd, with 4 Standarten/9 Stürme
SS-Brigade Südhannover-Braunschweig, with 3 Standarten/8 Stürme
SS-Brigade Hessen-Nassau, with 3 Standarten/9 Stürme
SS-Brigade Thüringen, with 2 Standarten/7 Stürme

SS-Oberführerbereich Süd
SS-Brigade Baden-Württemberg, with 1 Standarte/4 Stürme
SS-Brigade Franken, with 1 Standarte/3 Stürme
SS-Brigade Niederbayern, with 1 Standarte/3 Stürme
SS-Brigade Oberbayern-Süd, with 3 Standarten/8 Stürme
SS-Brigade Österreich, with 1 Standarte/3 Stürme

Again, in theory, every party Gau was supposed to have an SS-Brigade, each comprising several Standarten, in turn made up of around five Stürme. Since there were at this time thirty Gaue, the SS was obviously spread very thinly around the country. Most units were well under their 'paper' strengths.

Once Himmler had taken control of the SS, things moved apace. Between 1931 and 1933, the whole structure was altered again and again to cope with the increasing administrative and manpower demands placed on the SS command. Two new departments, the SD-Amt and Rasseamt,

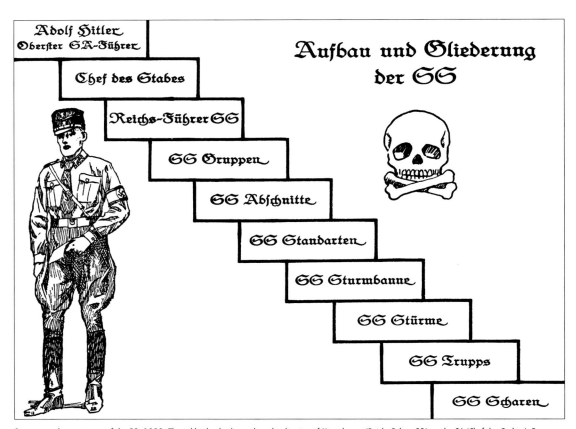

Adolf Hitler
Oberster SA-Führer

Chef des Stabes

Reichs-Führer SS

Aufbau und Gliederung
der SS

SS Gruppen

SS Abschnitte

SS Standarten

SS Sturmbanne

SS Stürme

SS Trupps

SS Scharen

Structure and organisation of the SS, 1933. This table clearly shows the subordination of Himmler, as 'Reichs-Führer SS', to the SA 'Chef des Stabes', Ernst Röhm. (Reproduced from *Die Uniformen und Abzeichen der SA, SS usw.* published by Kolf & Co., Berlin, 1933.)

were established to oversee security and racial matters. A third, the SS-Amt, was the largest of all and was divided into five sections, namely:

I   – Staff Office
II – Personnel
III – Administration
IV – Reserves
V   – Medical

At the next level, the Oberführerbereiche were replaced by five SS-Gruppen, viz. Nord, Ost, Südost, West and Süd, containing fifty-eight Standarten.

Yet despite these internal arrangements, the SS of 1933 was still very much subordinate to the SA and its Stabschef or Chief of Staff, Ernst Röhm. The SS command structure was in no way an independent one, and the most senior SS leaders were all attached to the SA Supreme Command, the Oberste SA-Führung. Until the SS became a separate element in July 1934, Himmler ranked merely as an SS-Obergruppenführer who held the post, not the rank, of Reichsführer der SS. He was, therefore, on an equal footing with any of the other SS or SA generals and, theoretically at least, enjoyed no privileged position. Indeed, his lack of front-line

Himmler and his Old Guard SS leaders in Munich, 1933.

experience during the First World War led to his being despised by many of the old campaigners, who looked upon him as a figure of fun who had weasled his way to the top. The leader of SS-Gruppe Ost, for example, SS-Gruppenführer Kurt Daluege of Stennes putsch fame, had by 1934 acquired considerable powers with Göring's patronage and felt himself to be so strong that he refused to deal with anyone but Hitler and Röhm, and certainly not with 'that Bavarian chicken-breeder Himmler'. He was by no means unique in his attitude. The fall of Röhm, however, altered the situation completely. Himmler's elevation to the newly created rank of Reichsführer-SS, or RfSS, which set him above all others, suddenly made him untouchable.

So far as the armed SS units were concerned, Himmler was soon Reichsführer in name only, for the Leibstandarte, SS-VT and SS-TV came to be regarded not as being in the official employ of the party but as public services of the Reich, on the model of the army. Their expenses were charged to the state, and the Reich Finance Minister, Lutz Graf Schwerin von Krosigk, maintained his impartiality in the allocation of national funds to the armed SS by consistently refusing Himmler's offers of honorary SS rank. In contrast, the Allgemeine-SS always retained its political status as an independent Gliederung, or organisation, of the NSDAP and it was never maintained by the state. Its expenses were paid solely from party funds and its finances were ultimately controlled by the Reichsschatzmeister der NSDAP, or Party Treasurer, Franz Xaver Schwarz, who was renowned as a fist-grasping administrator. However, Schwarz, a veteran of the Munich putsch, was also very close to Himmler, who made him the highest ranking General Officer in the whole SS, second on the seniority list only to the Reichsführer himself. Consequently, the party never actually exercised any close independent supervision over Allgemeine-SS funds. Through his contacts with big business and his mutual back-scratching exercises with Schwarz, Himmler ensured that the Allgemeine-SS got any cash it needed, often at the expense of other party branches such as the NSKK and NSFK. So the Allgemeine-SS, unlike the military side of the organisation, remained totally under the Reichsführer's control until 1945, immune from outside state interference. Himmler's position at the top of the Allgemeine-SS hierarchy was, therefore, unchallenged and his power unbridled by any potential financial constraints. As a result, the highest levels of the Allgemeine-SS organisation centred around him personally.

During the autumn of 1934, Himmler quickly went about the business of once again reorganising his high command structure. The Reichsführung-SS was set up as the supreme authority, comprising two staffs, the Kommandostab RfSS, which was an executive administrative staff at Himmler's personal headquarters, and the Persönlicher Stab RfSS, a much larger and more loosely organised body consisting of a number of advisory officials including the heads of the main SS departments and certain other special offices. The fresh administrative burdens later imposed by the war made it necessary to create a much larger and more complex command structure than had sufficed during peacetime. By 1942, subject to Himmler's controlling authority and that of the Reichsführung-SS, the day-to-day work of directing, organising and administering the SS was carried out by the eight main departments, or Hauptämter, listed below, each of which is duly covered in turn.

In addition, there were a number of minor offices and departments not of Hauptamt status.

The functions of the various Hauptämter were continually adapted to meet new exigencies and by far the greater part of their work during the 1939–45 period concerned

THE SS HAUPTÄMTER

1. Hauptamt Persönlicher Stab RfSS – Himmler's Personal Staff
2. SS Hauptamt – SS Central Office
3. SS Führungshauptamt – SS Operational HQ
4. Reichssicherheitshauptamt – Reich Central Security Office
5. SS Wirtschafts- und Verwaltungshauptamt – SS Economic and Administrative Department
6. SS Rasse- und Siedlungshauptamt – SS Race and Settlement Department
7. Hauptamt SS Gericht – SS Legal Department
8. SS Personalhauptamt – SS Personnel Department

the numerically superior Waffen-SS and the execution of SS policy in the occupied territories. There were ultimately a good many overlapping and conflicting interests as regards their various duties and jurisdictions. By 1945, the Hauptamt system had become a vast and complex network of intertwining bureaucratic empires, each vying for supremacy over the others and for the attention of their Reichsführer. Having said that, there is no doubt that they always functioned effectively, even if not efficiently. The spirit of competition between them, which Himmler actively encouraged, ensured that everything dealt with by each department was recorded, checked and double checked to avoid error. If another Hauptamt had an interest, it too would record, check and double check. The result was the most detailed system of manual files ever compiled, not just on the SS organisation but on every aspect of life in the Third Reich. The SS Personalhauptamt alone housed 150 million individual documents, and the Reichssicherheitshauptamt even maintained secret and potentially incriminating dossiers on Hitler himself and on all the other Nazi leaders, mostly compiled during the 1920s by the security police of the Weimar Republic, whose files were duly inherited by the SS. This attention to detail and ability to come up with all sorts of information gave the impression of an all-seeing, all-knowing command structure which ensured that, right up until the capitulation, the Reichsführung-SS and the SS Hauptämter successfully managed to control and administer the vast SS organisation. That was not an insignificant achievement, considering that, at its peak, the SS operated across an area from the Channel Islands to the Black Sea and from the Arctic Circle to the Mediterranean, with a generally hostile population.

As the core of the Reichsführung-SS, the Personal Staff of the Reichsführer-SS (Pers. Stab RfSS) had its main offices at 8 Prinz-Albrecht-Strasse, Berlin. Its members were designated 'i.P.St.' (on the Personal Staff) and were subordinated directly to Himmler. As more and more high-ranking people inside and outside the SS sought to gain Himmler's ear, the Personal Staff became the focus of influence in the SS command. It consisted of:

1. The heads of the SS Hauptämter, who were ex-officio members
2. SS officials in certain offices and departments integrated into the Pers. Stab
3. SS officials appointed or attached to the staff for special advisory or honorary purposes

Besides being an advisory and co-ordinating body, the Pers. Stab was responsible for all business in which the Reichsführer-SS was concerned that did not come into the province of any of the other SS Hauptämter. In addition, it liaised with government and party offices and controlled various financial and business dealings on Himmler's behalf. The Chief of the Personal Staff was SS-Obergruppenführer Karl Wolff, who served as Himmler's adjutant from 1934. In 1943, 'Wölfchen' was also appointed Supreme SS and Police Commander in Italy, in effect military governor of the country, but he always retained his post as Chief of the Personal Staff and, with it, all the powers and disciplinary prerogatives of a Hauptamtschef.

Much of the administrative work generated by the Pers. Stab was processed through the Kommandostab RfSS which operated during the war on a mobile basis under the title Feldkommandostelle RfSS, or Field Headquarters of the Reichsführer-SS. It was by then organised like a military HQ and accompanied Himmler on his numerous tours of the occupied territories. Together with attached SS units including a signals section, an escort battalion and a flak detachment, the Feldkommandostelle eventually numbered over 3,000 men. Its special train, 'Sonderzug Heinrich', had fourteen carriages.

At various times, the following offices and departments were part of, or directly subordinated to, the Persönlicher Stab RfSS and they give a general idea of the extent of its interests and influence:

1. *Pressestelle RfSS* (Press Office of the RfSS)
   This office handled Himmler's personal press relations and also advised him regarding official SS publications and publicity.
2. *Hauptabteilung Auszeichnungen und Orden* (Main Section for Awards and Decorations)
   This main section advised the RfSS on all awards of orders, medals and decorations to SS men.
3. *Dienststelle 'Vierjahresplan'* (Office for the Four Year Plan)
   This was a liaison office between the RfSS and the economic Four Year Plan under Göring, to deal with those aspects of the Plan which touched upon SS interests and activities.
4. *Abteilung Wirtschaftliche Hilfe* (Section for Economic Assistance)
   This section provided financial and other assistance to SS men who had suffered material loss during the period of the struggle for power. It also loaned money to SS officers to enable them to purchase items of uniform and equipment and, in some cases, liquidated debts incurred by SS members.
5. *Kulturreferat* (Cultural Office)
   This was responsible for the direction of the cultural activities of the SS, including the Nordland Verlag publishing house and the porcelain works at Allach.
6. *Abteilung für Kulturelle Forschung* (Section for Cultural Research)
   This section was concerned with the antiquarian and archaeological aspects of German history. It encouraged expeditions, excavations and research to support with actual historical or archaeological evidence the Nazi account of early German history.
7. *Ahnenerbe- Forschungs- und Lehrgemeinschaft* (Society for the Research and Teaching of Ancestral Heritage)
   This society existed to promote genealogical and biological research.
8. *Hauptabteilung Lebensborn* (Fountain of Life Main Section)
   This main section liaised with the Lebensborn Society, which looked after the welfare of SS mothers and children.

In addition, the following special posts are examples of the types subordinated directly to Himmler. Those officers mentioned held the posts in 1944:

1. *SS Richter beim Pers. Stab RfSS* (SS Legal Officer on the Staff of the RfSS)
   SS-Standartenführer Horst Bender. Dealt with all legal and disciplinary matters coming to Himmler for a personal decision.
2. *Reichsarzt SS und Polizei* (Chief SS and Police Medical Officer)
   SS-Obergruppenführer Prof. Dr Ernst-Robert Grawitz. He was responsible for the general supervision of all the medical services of the SS and police, for medical research and training, and for the control and distribution of medical supplies and equipment.
3. *Chef Fernmeldewesen beim Pers. Stab RfSS* (Chief of Communications on the Staff of the RfSS)
   SS-Obergruppenführer Ernst Sachs. His

function was to supervise the whole field of signals and communications in the SS and police.

4. *RfSS Pers. Stab Beauftragter für Jagd und Forstwesen* (Representative for Hunting and Forestry on the Staff of the RfSS) SS-Brigadeführer Hermann Müller. Müller was also President of the Reich Canine Society and Representative for Service Dogs (SS and Police) on the Pers. Stab.

In short then, all SS activities, and everything which affected the SS, came within the jurisdiction of the Hauptamt Persönlicher Stab RfSS.

The SS Hauptamt or SS-HA, the SS Central Office, was based at 7–11 Douglasstrasse, Berlin-Grünewald, and developed from the SS-Amt which, under SS-Gruppenführer Kurt Wittje, co-ordinated SS operations prior to 1935. It was the oldest of the SS main departments and its bare title of Hauptamt, without further qualification, indicated in itself the fundamental part it originally played in the administration of the SS. As late as 1940, under SS-Obergruppenführer August Heissmeyer, it maintained its supremacy. At that time there were still only three Hauptämter proper, the other two being the Rasse- und Siedlungshauptamt and the Reichssicherheitshauptamt. With the exception therefore of the specialist functions carried out by these two departments, the SS-HA was responsible for all the varied tasks involved in the general administration of the whole SS.

The expansion of the SS as a result of wartime mobilisation, however, made the multiplicity of functions converging on the SS-HA too great a burden for one department, and in August 1940 a major reorganisation of the central administration of the SS took place. Two existing SS-HA branches, the Personalamt (Personnel Office)

and the SS Gericht (Legal Department) were detached and themselves raised to Hauptamt status, becoming the SS Personalhauptamt and the Hauptamt SS Gericht. In addition, two further Hauptämter were created, namely the SS Führungshauptamt and the SS Wirtschafts- und Verwaltungshauptamt, by taking certain responsibilities away from the SS-HA. Several other functions of the SS-HA were also transferred or absorbed elsewhere, an example being the supervision of SS radio communications and signals which was taken over by the Chief of Communications on the Persönlicher Stab RfSS. The result of this reorganisation was that the SS-HA lost eight of its thirteen offices. At one stroke it was completely deprived of the commanding position it had previously enjoyed. The main importance still attaching to the SS-HA under its new chief, SS-Obergruppenführer Gottlob-Christian Berger, was its responsibility for recruitment and the maintenance of records on non-commissioned personnel.

The subsequent recovery of the SS-HA during 1941–45 was almost entirely due to the continued expansion of the Waffen-SS and the extension of the area of Allgemeine-SS influence into occupied territories. From 1941, the Waffen-SS increasingly recruited both individual Germanic volunteers and complete Germanic units from western Europe and Scandinavia. At the same time, efforts were made in Flanders, Holland, Norway and Denmark to raise native Allgemeine-SS formations, the so-called Germanic-SS, to assist in policing these countries. The reflection of this was the creation at the end of 1941 of the Germanische Leitstelle, or Germanic Liaison Office, of the SS-HA, which looked after the welfare of all members of Germanic races who came within the orbit of the SS. These included foreign students at German universities, foreign workers in German factories, and non-German members of the

Allgemeine-SS proper. This aspect of the work of the SS-HA steadily expanded during the war and brought with it a number of allied duties and functions, including the setting up of public exhibitions geared towards the promotion of German culture in western Europe. In addition to these primary concerns, the SS Hauptamt also kept a general watching brief over propaganda, publications, education, sport and physical training for the whole SS and police.

The SS Operational Headquarters or Führungshauptamt (SS-FHA), under SS-Obergruppenführer Hans Jüttner, was located at 188 Kaiserallee, Berlin-Wilmersdorf. It grew from the Operations Department of the SS Hauptamt, becoming a separate entity in August 1940, and developed into the biggest of all the SS Hauptämter, with a staff of 40,000 in 1944. The reason for its rapid growth was the expansion of the Waffen-SS, which imposed a colossal administrative burden on the SS command for which there had been no parallel before the war. However, while the greater operational needs of the Waffen-SS made the administration of that branch by far the most important function of the SS-FHA, the latter was never intended to be the headquarters solely of the Waffen-SS. It was, in fact, the Operational HQ of the Gesamt-SS, or whole SS, and included as one of its departments the Allgemeine-SS Headquarters (Kommandoamt der Allgemeinen-SS) under SS-Gruppenführer Leo Petri, which was responsible for the control and operational deployment of the Allgemeine-SS as well as its general administration, supplies, training and mobilisation. All SS units which were not under the tactical command of the Wehrmacht in the field were entirely subordinated to the SS-FHA for both operational and administrative purposes. It organised the payment of wages and the supply of equipment, arms, ammunition and

vehicles, as well as the maintenance and repair of stocks. The SS-FHA personnel branch was responsible for appointments, transfers and promotions, although questions affecting officer personnel were handled in conjunction with the SS Personalhauptamt, of which the chief of the SS-FHA personnel branch, SS-Obergruppenführer Kurt Knoblauch, was an ex-officio member. In addition, the SS-FHA co-ordinated the training of all SS formations and controlled a large number of training units, schools and camps, while its medical branch supervised SS hospitals. A Movement Control Officer at the SS-FHA was responsible for all matters affecting the transport of the SS and police, including rail, shipping and air transport, and the SS-FHA Field Post Department controlled SS Field post offices and mail censorship. The SS-FHA also oversaw a host of other miscellaneous SS activities, including military geology, war archives and dentistry.

The Reichssicherheitshauptamt or RSHA, the Reich Central Security Office, was set up in September 1939 to bring together the security police forces of both the party and the state. Based at 8 Prinz-Albrecht-Strasse, Berlin, it combined in one command structure the offices of the party-run Sicherheitsdienst or SD (the SS Security Service), and the state-run Sicherheitspolizei or Sipo (Security Police), which itself comprised the Kripo (Criminal Police) and Gestapo (Political Police). Although the RSHA was officially subordinated to Himmler, it quickly became the personal empire of its first chief, SS-Obergruppenführer Reinhard Heydrich, who used its vast resources of information and incriminating dossiers as bargaining counters in his power struggles with the other Nazi leaders until his assassination in 1942. His successor, SS-Obergruppenführer Dr Ernst Kaltenbrunner, a sinister-looking individual and old guard Austrian Nazi, was far less ambitious but still became one of the most feared men in the Third Reich. The RSHA was responsible for both domestic and foreign intelligence operations, espionage and counter-espionage, combatting political and common law crime, and sounding out public opinion on the Nazi régime.

The SS Wirtschafts- und Verwaltungshauptamt or SS-WVHA, the SS Economic and Administrative Department, was formed in 1942. Based at 126–35 Unter den Eichen, Berlin-Lichterfelde, it was headed by SS-Obergruppenführer Oswald Pohl and dealt primarily with the concentration camp system and the financial administration of the SS. It controlled a large number of SS industrial and agricultural undertakings, organised the 'in-house' manufacture of supplies and equipment for SS use, and carried out SS housing and construction programmes.

The SS Rasse- und Siedlungshauptamt or RuSHA, the SS Race and Settlement Department, achieved Hauptamt status on 30 January 1935, having grown from the SS Race and Settlement Office set up at the end of 1931 under SS-Obergruppenführer Richard Walther Darré. It was subsequently commanded by Günther Pancke, who later became Senior SS and Police Commander in Denmark, and finally by Richard Hildebrandt, and had its offices at 24 Hedemannstrasse, Berlin. RuSHA looked after the ideological and racial purity of all SS members. It was the authority for all matters of geneology, and issued lineage certificates and marriage permits within the SS. In addition, it was responsible for executing the policy of settling SS men, especially ex-servicemen, as colonists in the conquered eastern territories, and thus translated into practice the 'Blood and Soil' theories of Darré and the other SS racial teachers.

The Hauptamt SS Gericht or HA SS Gericht, the SS Legal Department, situated at 10 Karlstrasse, Munich, administered the disciplinary side of the special code of laws to which members of the SS and police were subject. It controlled the SS und Polizei Gerichte (SS and Police Courts) in the larger towns of Germany and the occupied countries, and the Strafvollzugslager der SS und Polizei (SS and Police Penal Camps) also came under its jurisdiction. The department was headed by SS-Gruppenführer Paul Scharfe until his death in 1942, when he was succeeded by SS-Obergruppenführer Franz Breithaupt. The Hauptamt SS Gericht was an extension of the older SS Gericht, an office which carried out on behalf of the Reichsführer-SS investigations within the ranks of the SS into disciplinary offences and infringements of the SS code of honour. It prepared and prosecuted cases and was responsible for the remission or reprieve of sentences. In addition, as supreme authority within the SS on matters of law and discipline, it was the channel of liaison between the SS and all other legal bodies of the state and party.

The SS Personalhauptamt, or SS Personnel Department, was based at 98–9 Wilmersdorferstrasse, Berlin-Charlottenburg and co-ordinated the work of the personnel branches of the various Hauptämter. It was the ultimate authority responsible for all questions of SS personnel, but its primary concern was with officers, as the SS Hauptamt retained records concerning NCOs and other ranks. The SS Personalhauptamt had two main offices, one for officer personnel and the other for officer replacements, and it regularly produced and updated the SS Seniority List, or Dienstaltersliste, which recorded details of every serving SS officer. The SS Personalhauptamt was commanded by SS-Obergruppenführer Walter Schmitt until 1942, and thereafter by SS-Obergruppenführer Maximilian von Herff.

In addition to the regular SS Hauptämter,

there were a number of other smaller offices and departments which had their places in the SS command structure. The Hauptstelle der Hauptamt Ordnungspolizei was a department representing the uniformed civil police at Himmler's headquarters. It advised the Reichsführer on all matters concerning the Ordnungspolizei. The Hauptamt Dienststelle Heissmeyer, an office attached to the staff of SS-Obergruppenführer August Heissmeyer in his capacity as the Senior SS and Police Commander for the Berlin District, was responsible for the supervision of the Nationalpolitische Erziehungsanstalten (NPEA or Napolas), the National Political Educational Institutes set up to train the future Germanic élite. The Stabshauptamt der Reichskommissar für die Festigung des deutschen Volkstums, or Hauptamt RKF, Himmler's staff HQ in his capacity as Reich Commissioner for the Consolidation of Germanism, was based at 142–3 Kurfürstendamm, Berlin and commanded by SS-Obergruppenführer Ulrich Greifelt. It had a general interest in all matters affecting the maintenance of the racial qualities of the German population and the protection and enlargement of the German race as a whole. Its principal activity was to promote settlement by Germans of the annexed eastern territories of the Reich. Finally, the Hauptamt Volksdeutsche Mittelstelle or VOMI, the Department for the Repatriation of Racial Germans, operated from offices at 29 Keithstrasse, Berlin and led by SS-Obergruppenführer Werner Lorenz. In contrast to the Hauptamt RKF, its main function was the organised return to the Reich of the descendants of older generations of German colonists and settlers in Russia and south-east Europe.

On a level immediately below the SS Hauptämter were the Oberabschnitte (Oa.) or Regions, the bases of Allgemeine-SS territorial organisation. Initially there were five Oberabschnitte, formed in 1932 from the existing SS Gruppen. By 1944, their number had risen to seventeen within Germany proper and each corresponded almost exactly to a Wehrkreis or Military District. The SS Regions were generally known by geographical names, but it was also customary to refer to them by the Roman numeral allocated to the corresponding Wehrkreis. Each Oberabschnitt was commanded by an SS-Obergruppenführer, Gruppenführer or Brigadeführer designated Führer des Oberabschnittes (F.Oa.). He was usually also Himmler's representative at the military headquarters of the local Wehrkreis and, in addition, held the post of Höhere SS-und Polizeiführer or HSSPf, the Senior SS and Police Commander in the Region. In the few cases where the HSSPf was not the Führer of the corresponding Oberabschnitt it was because the latter, though filling some other active appointment, was allowed to retain the titular leadership of the Oa. on personal grounds. For example, during the war, SS-Obergruppenführer August Heissmeyer found himself appointed HSSPf for Oberabschnitt Spree as the nominal Führer of that Region, 'Sepp' Dietrich, was fully committed with the Waffen-SS on the battlefront.

Directly subordinated to the F.Oa. or HSSPf was the Stabsführer der Allgemeinen-SS (Allgemeine-SS Chief of Staff) who was responsible to him for the general conduct and control of the Allgemeine-SS within the Oa. The Regional Headquarters was staffed primarily by Hauptamtlicher Führer (full-time officers) together with a number of Nebenamtlich (part-time) or Ehrenamtlich (honorary) officials. The full-timers included the Leiter der Verwaltung or Verwaltungsführer (Administrative Officer), the Oberabschnittsarzt (Medical Officer), the Oberabschnittsausbildungsführer (Training Officer), the Oberabschnittspersonalchef (Personnel Officer) and the

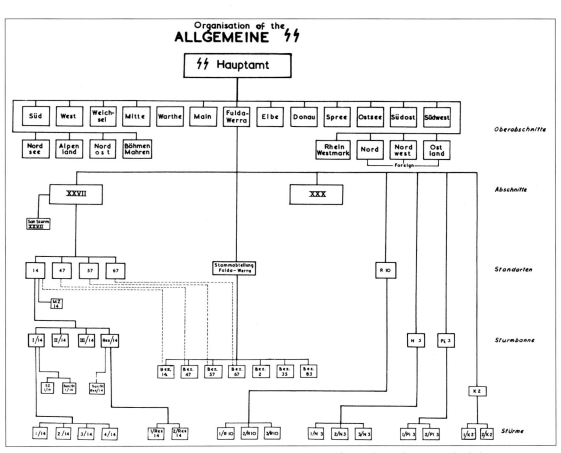

Structure and organisation of the Allgemeine-SS, 1944. This table shows the typical breakdown of units within an Allgemeine-SS Oberabschnitt, using Oberabschnitt Fulda-Werra as an example. (Reproduced from *The General SS*, produced by Allied Counter-Intelligence in 1944.)

Nachrichtenführer (Signals Officer). Parttimers were generally below the rank of Sturmbannführer and were not paid for their services. The seventeen SS Oberabschnitte situated within Germany were named and numbered as follows:

Oberabschnitt	HQ	Wehrkreis
Alpenland	Salzburg	XVIII
Donau	Wien	XVII
Elbe	Dresden	IV
Fulda-Werra	Arolsen-Waldeck	IX
Main	Nürnberg	XIII
Mitte	Braunschweig	XI
Nordost	Königsberg	I
Nordsee	Hamburg	X
Ostsee	Stettin	II
Rhein-Westmark	Wiesbaden	XII
Spree	Berlin	III
Süd	München	VII
Südost	Breslau	VIII
Südwest	Stuttgart	V
Warthe	Posen	XXI
Weichsel	Danzig	XX
West	Düsseldorf	VI

There were no SS Oberabschnitte corresponding to Wehrkreise numbers XIV, XV, XVI and XIX.

Himmler, Wolff and SS-Gruppenführer Heinrich Schmauser, Führer of Oberabschnitt Süd, inspecting men of the 34th SS Fuss-Standarte at Weilheim in December 1934.

In addition to these, there were six foreign Oberabschnitte which evolved during the war, as listed below:

Oberabschnitt	HQ	Region
Böhmen-Mähren	Prague	Czechoslovakia
Nord	Oslo	Norway
Nordwest	The Hague	Holland
Ost	Krakow	Poland
Ostland	Riga	Baltic States
Ukraine	Kiev	Ukraine

Of these six, only Oa. Böhmen-Mähren, which included the Sudetenland, existed long enough to develop an organisation strictly comparable to the Oberabschnitte inside Germany. Oa. Nord and Nordwest co-ordinated police operations and those of the relatively small contingents of Germanic-SS in Flanders, Holland, Norway and Denmark, while Oa. Ost, Ostland and Ukraine directed the miscellaneous security and anti-guerrilla forces in their respective areas.

Each SS Oberabschnitt in turn comprised an average of three Abschnitte or Districts, again distinguished by Roman numerals. They were also referred to by the names of the areas which they covered or by the location of their headquarters. The Abschnitt commander or Führer des Abschnittes (F.Ab.) was generally an officer of the rank of SS-Oberführer or Standartenführer. The first seven Abschnitte covered the entire Reich, and the eighth was for Austria. The ninth and

SS-Oberabschnitte

Nordost	Königsberg
Ostsee	Stettin
Spree	Berlin
Elbe	Dresden
Südwest	Stuttgart
West	Düsseldorf
Süd	München
Südost	Breslau
Fulda-Werra	Arolsen
Nordsee	Hamburg
Mitte	Braunschweig
Rhein-Westmark	Wiesbaden
Main	Nürnberg
Donau	Wien
Alpenland	Salzburg
Weichsel	Danzig
Warthe	Posen
Nordwest	Den Haag
Nord	Oslo
Ost	Krakau
Böhmen-Mähren	Prag
Ostland	Riga
Ukraine	

SS-Abschnitte

I	S	München
II	E	Dresden
III	Sp.	Berlin
IV	Mi.	Hannover
V	W	Duisburg
VI	SO	Breslau
VII	NO	Königsberg
VIII	D	Linz
IX	Ma.	Würzburg
X	SW	Stuttgart
XI	RW	Koblenz
XII	Sp.	Frankfurt (Oder)
XIII	OS	Stettin
XIV	NS	Oldenburg
XV	NS	Hamburg-Altona
XVI	Mi.	Dessau
XVII	W	Münster
XVIII	E	Halle (Saale)
XIX	SW	Karlsruhe
XX	NS	Kiel
XXI	SO	Hirschberg
XXII	NO	Allenstein
XXIII	Sp.	Berlin
XXIV	SO	Oppeln
XXV	W	Dortmund
XXVI	Wei.	Zoppot
XXVII	FW	Weimar
XXVIII	Ma.	Bayreuth
XXIX	SW	Konstanz
XXX	RW	Frankfurt (Main)
XXXI	D	Wien
XXXII	S	Augsburg
XXXIII	OS	Schwerin
XXXIV	RW	Saarbrücken
XXXV	A	Graz
XXXVI	A	Salzburg
XXXVII	BM	Reichenberg
XXXVIII	BM	Karlsbad
XXXIX	BM	Brünn
XXXX	Wei.	Bromberg
XXXXI	Wei.	Thorn
XXXXII	Wa.	Gnesen
XXXXIII	Wa.	Litzmannstadt
XXXXIV	NO	Gumbinnen
XXXXV	SW	Straßburg

SS-Standarten

1.	S	München
2.	RW	Frankfurt (Main)
3.	RW	Nürnberg
4.	NS	Altona
5.	NO	Luxemburg
6.	Sp.	Berlin
7.	E	Plauen
8.	SO	Hirschberg
9.	OS	Stettin
10.	RW	Kaiserslautern
11.	D	Wien
12.	Mi.	Hannover
13.	SW	Stuttgart
14.	FW	Gotha
15.	Sp.	Neuruppin
16.	SO	Breslau
17.	NS	Celle
18.	NO	Königsberg
19.	W	Münster
20.	W	Düsseldorf
21.	Mi.	Magdeburg
22.	OS	Schwerin
23.	SO	Beuthen
24.	NS	Oldenburg
25.	W	Essen
26.	E	Halle (Saale)
27.	Sp.	Frankfurt (Oder)
28.	NS	Hamburg
29.	S	Lindau
30.	W	Bochum
31.	Ma.	Landshut
32.	RW	Heidelberg
33.	RW	Darmstadt
34.	S	Weilheim
35.	FW	Kassel
36.	Wei.	Danzig
37.	D	Linz
38.	A	Graz
39.	OS	Köslin
40.	NS	Kiel
41.	Ma.	Bayreuth
42.	Sp.	Berlin
43.	SO	Frankenstein
44.	Sp.	Eberswalde
45.	SO	Oppeln
46.	E	Dresden
47.	FW	Jena
48.	E	Leipzig
49.	Mi.	Braunschweig
50.	NS	Flensburg
51.	Mi.	Göttingen
52.	D	Krems
53.	NS	Heide
54.	Sp.	Landsberg (Warthe)
55.	NS	Lüneburg
56.	Ma.	Bamberg
57.	FW	Meiningen
58.	W	Köln
59.	Mi.	Dessau
60.	NO	Insterburg
61.	NO	Allenstein
62.	SW	Karlsruhe
63.	SW	Tübingen
64.	Wei.	Berent
65.	SW	Freiburg (Br.)
66.	NO	Bartenstein
67.	FW	Erfurt
68.	Ma.	Regensburg
69.	W	Hagen (W.)
70.	SO	Glogau
71.	Wei.	Elbing
72.	W	Detmold
73.	Ma.	Ansbach
74.	OS	Greifswald
75.	Sp.	Berlin
76.	A	Salzburg
77.	OS	Schneidemühl
78.	RW	Wiesbaden
79.	SW	Ulm
80.	Sp.	Berlin
81.	Ma.	Würzburg
82.	W	Bielefeld
83.	W	Gießen
84.	E	Chemnitz
85.	RW	Saarbrücken
86.	SW	Offenburg
87.	—	Innsbruck
88.	NS	Bremen
89.	D	Wien
90.	A	Klagenfurt
91.	E	Wittenberg
92.	S	Ingolstadt
93.	RW	Koblenz
94.	A	Leoben
95.	BM	Trautenau
96.	BM	Brüx
97.	BM	Eger
98.	BM	Mährisch Schönberg
99.	D	Znaim
100.	BM	Reichenberg
101.	BM	Saaz
102.	BM	Jägerndorf
103.	BM	Aussig
104.	BM	Troppau
105.	NO	Memel
106.	E	Augsburg
107.	BM	Brünn
108.	BM	Prag
109.	Wa.	Posen
110.	Wa.	Hohensalza
111.	Wa.	Kolmar
112.	Wa.	Litzmannstadt
113.	Wa.	Kalisch
114.	Wa.	Leßlau
115.	NO	Zichenau
116.	Wei.	Bromberg
117.	Wei.	Konitz
118.	Wei.	Pr. Stargard
119.	Wei.	Graudenz
120.	Wei.	Kulm
121.	Wei.	Strasburg
122.	SW	Straßburg
123.	SW	Kolmar
124.	SO	Scharley
125.	RW	Metz
	A	Marburg/Drau

SS-Reiterstandarten

R 1	NO	Insterburg
R 2	Wei.	Danzig
R 3	NO	Treuburg
R 4	NS	Hamburg
R 5	OS	Stettin
R 6	W	Düsseldorf
R 7	Sp.	Berlin
R 8	W	Pelkum
R 9	NS	Bremen
R 10	FW	Arolsen
R 11	OS	Breslau
R 12	OS	Schwerin
R 13	RW	Frankfurt (Main)
R 14	SW	Stuttgart
R 15	S	München
R 16	S	Dresden
R 17	Ma.	Regensburg
R 18	D	Wien
R 19	Wei.	
R 20	NO	Tilsit
R 21	Mi.	Hannover
R 22	Wa.	Posen

SS-Nachrichteneinheiten

Na.1	S	München
Na.2	SW	Stuttgart
Na.3	FW	Arolsen
Na.4	W	Düsseldorf
Na.5	Mi.	Braunschweig
Na.6	NS	Hamburg
Na.7	NO	Königsberg
Na.8	Sp.	Berlin
Na.9	E	Dresden
Na.10	SO	Breslau
Na.11	Ma.	Nürnberg
Na.12	OS	Stettin
Na.13	RW	Wiesbaden
Na.14	D	Wien
Na.16	NS	Danzig
Na.17	Wa.	Posen
Na.19	BM	Prag

SS-Pioniereinheiten

Pi.1	S	München
Pi.2	SW	Stuttgart
Pi.3	FW	Arolsen
Pi.4	W	Köln
Pi.5	NS	Harburg-Wilhelmsburg
Pi.6	OS	Stettin
Pi.7	NO	Königsberg
Pi.8	Sp.	Berlin
Pi.9	E	Dresden
Pi.10	SO	Breslau
Pi.12	Mi.	Magdeburg
Pi.13	RW	Frankfurt (Main)/Ludwigshafen/Weilburg
Pi.14	D	Wien
Pi.15	A	Salzburg
Pi.16	Wei.	Danzig

SS-Kraftfahrstürme

K.1	S	München/Augsburg
K.2	FW	Erfurt
K.3	Sp.	Berlin/Senftenberg
K.4	NS	Hamburg/Kiel/Bremen
K.5	W	Düsseldorf/Buer (W.)/Dortmund
K.6	E	Dresden/Chemnitz
K.7	NO	Königsberg
K.8	D	Linz/Wien
K.9	SO	Breslau
K.10	SW	Stuttgart/Karlsruhe/Freiburg (Br.)
K.11	Mi.	Magdeburg/Hannover
K.12	Ma.	Bamberg/Schweinfurt/Nürnberg
K.13	OS	Schwerin/Stettin
K.14	RW	Frankfurt (Main)/Wiesbaden-Biebrich/Pirmasens
K.15	A	Graz/Innsbruck
K.16	Wei.	Danzig/Elbing
K.17	Wa.	Posen/Litzmannstadt
K.19	BM	Asch/Reichenberg/Brünn

Allgemeine-SS unit formations, 1944. This table lists all the Allgemeine-SS Oberabschnitte, Abschnitte, Standarten and specialist units in 1944, with their titles, numbers and locations. (Reproduced from the *SS Dienstaltersliste* of 9 November 1944.)

succeeding Abschnitte made their appearance in 1932, along with Standarten with numbers in the upper forties. The Districts then grew commensurate with the expansion of the SS, and by 1944 the following Abschnitte were listed:

Abschnitt No.	District
I	München/Landshut/Ingolstadt
II	Dresden/Chemnitz/Plauen
III	Berlin-Steglitz
IV	Hannover/Braunschweig/Celle/Göttingen
V	Duisberg/Düsseldorf/Essen/Köln
VI	Breslau/Frankenstein/Glogau
VII	Königsberg/Insterburg/Elbing
VIII	Linz
IX	Würzburg/Nürnberg/Ansbach/Schweinfurt
X	Stuttgart/Tübingen/Ulm
XI	Koblenz/Trier/Darmstadt/Wiesbaden/Bingen
XII	Frankfurt (Oder)/Senftenberg
XIII	Stettin/Köslin/Schneidemühl
XIV	Oldenburg/Cuxhaven/Bremen
XV	Hamburg-Altona/Hamburg-Harburg
XVI	Dessau/Magdeburg/Stassfurt
XVII	Münster/Detmold/Bielefeld/Buer
XVIII	Halle (Saale)/Leipzig/Wittenberg
XIX	Karlsruhe
XX	Kiel/Flensburg
XXI	Hirschberg/Mährisch-Schönberg/Jägerndorf/Troppau

XXII	Allenstein/Memel/Zichenau	XXXVI	Salzburg/Innsbruck
XXIII	Berlin-Wilmersdorf/Neuruppin/	XXXVII	Reichenberg/Trautenau/Brüx/Aussig
	Eberswalde/Potsdam	XXXVIII	Karlsbad/Eger/Asch
XXIV	Oppeln/Beuthen/Kattowitz	XXXIX	Brünn/Iglau/Prag
XXV	Dortmund/Bochum/Hagen	XXXX	Bromberg/Tuchel
XXVI	Danzig/Zoppot/Marienwerder/	XXXXI	Thorn/Kulm
	Marienburg/Neustadt/Elbing	XXXXII	Gnesen/Posen
XXVII	Weimar/Gotha/Gera/Meiningen/	XXXXIII	Litzmannstadt/Kalisch/Leslau
	Erfurt	XXXXIV	Gumbinnen/Memel/Zichenau
XXVIII	Bayreuth/Regensburg/Bamberg	XXXXV	Strassburg/Colmar
XXIX	Konstanz		
XXX	Frankfurt (Main)/Kassel/Giessen		
XXXI	Wien/Krems/Znaim		
XXXII	Augsburg/Lindau		
XXXIII	Schwerin/Greifswald		
XXXIV	Saarbrücken/Kaiserslautern/		
	Heidelberg		
XXXV	Graz/Klagenfurt/Leoben		

It will be noted that the expansion of SS membership in a few towns and cities resulted in their being split between two Abschnitte.

The organisation of the Allgemeine-SS in respect of formation below the level of the Abschnitte was on a more flexible unit, rather

SS men at Hamburg railway station, c. 1934–5. Both styles of death's head are being worn on the cap during this transitional period. The runic collar patch of the man at the left denotes his membership of the Leibstandarte, while the others are from the 48th Standarte.

than territorial, basis, although each unit itself related to, or was recruited from, a particular area. The typical Abschnitt controlled an average of three SS Fuss-Standarten, the equivalent of foot or infantry regiments. As the name suggests, the Standarte was the standard unit of the Allgemeine-SS and had been firmly established as such by 1930, long before the SS regional system fully evolved. The earliest SS Standarten were terribly under-strength, and even in 1931 might comprise only 100 men. Numbers rose steadily, however, with ten new SS Standarten being formed in 1933 and a further fifty in 1934. By 1939, the average Fuss-Standarte comprised around 2,000 men, but corresponding numbers fell to around 1,600 in 1941 and 400 in 1944 due to Allgemeine-SS members being drafted into the Wehrmacht and Waffen-SS. Each regiment was commanded by a Führer des Standartes (F.Sta.), who was assisted by a small staff and part-time headquarters unit. Depending on unit size, the regimental commander could be an SS-Standartenführer, Obersturmbannführer or Sturmbannführer. By 1943, it was common for two of the smaller adjacent Standarten to be placed together under a single acting commander.

Standarten were numbered consecutively from 1 to 127. A select few also bore the names of celebrated SS men who had died, been killed during the 'Kampfzeit', been assassinated and so on, and such 'honour titles' were similarly extended to a number of Stürme or companies within certain Standarten. For example, the 6th Sturm of the 6th Standarte was called 'Eduard Felsen' in memory of its member killed in the street disorder on the night of the Reichstag fire, while the 90th Standarte was awarded the title 'Franz Kutschera' after the latter, one of its officers who rose to command the security police and SD in Poland, who was murdered by partisans on 1 February 1944. The table below lists all of the SS Fuss-Standarten with their regimental numbers and locations and, where applicable, Standarte or Sturm honour titles.

SS FUSS – STANDARTEN

Standarte No.	Location	Standarte Honour Title	Sturm Honour Title
1.	München	'Julius Schreck'	1. 'Karl Ostberg' 2. 'Casella' 5. 'Hellinger' 10. 'Karl Laforce'
2.	Frankfurt (Main)		4. 'Josef Bleser'
3.	Nürnberg		
4.	Hamburg-Altona		
5.	Luxemburg		
6.	Berlin-Charlottenburg		6. 'Eduard Felsen' 8. 'Oskar Goll' 9. 'Kurt von der Ahe'
7.	Plauen	'Friedrich Schlegel'	3. 'Paul Fressonke' 6. 'Paul Teubner'
8.	Hirschberg		
9.	Stettin		

Standarte No.	Location	Standarte Honour Title	Sturm Honour Title
10.	Kaiserslautern		
11.	Wien	'Planetta'	
12.	Hannover		
13.	Stuttgart		
14.	Gotha		
15.	Neuruppin		
16.	Breslau		
17.	Celle		
18.	Königsberg		
19.	Münster		
20.	Düsseldorf	'Fritz Weitzel'	1. 'Karl Vobis'
			3. 'Kurt Hilmer'
			5. 'Werner Hannemann'
			11. 'Friedrich Schreiber'
21.	Magdeburg		
22.	Schwerin	'Friedrich Graf von der Schulenburg'	
23.	Beuthen		
24.	Oldenburg		
25.	Essen		1. 'Garthe'
			3. 'Friedrich Karpinski'
			4. 'Arnold Guse'
			5. 'Leopold Paffrath'
26.	Halle (Saale)		1. 'Paul Berck'
27.	Frankfurt (Oder)		
28.	Hamburg		1. 'Henry Kobert'
			9. 'Hans Cyranka'
29.	Lindau		
30.	Bochum		1. 'Fritz Borawski'
			3. 'August Pfaff'
			11. 'Adolf Höh'
31.	Landshut		4. 'Faust'
			12. 'Andreas Zinkl'
32.	Heidelberg		
33.	Darmstadt		
34.	Weilheim		
35.	Kassel		
36.	Danzig		
37.	Linz		
38.	Graz		
39.	Köslin		
40.	Kiel		1. 'Radke'
			8. 'Martens'

Standarte No.	Location	Standarte Honour Title	Sturm Honour Title
41.	Bayreuth		
42.	Berlin		4. 'Fritz Schulz'
43.	Frankenstein		
44.	Eberswalde		
45.	Oppeln		
46.	Dresden		
47.	Jena		
48.	Leipzig		8. 'Gutsche'
49.	Braunschweig		1. 'Gerhard Landmann'
50.	Flensburg		
51.	Göttingen		
52.	Krems		
53.	Heide		
54.	Landsberg (Warthe)	'Seidel-Dittmarsch'	
55.	Lüneburg		
56.	Bamberg		
57.	Meiningen		
58.	Köln		2. 'Franz Müller'
59.	Dessau	'Loeper'	
60.	Insterburg		
61.	Allenstein		
62.	Karlsruhe		
63.	Tübingen		
64.	Berent		
65.	Freiburg (Br.)		
66.	Bartenstein		
67.	Erfurt		12. 'Fritz Beubler'
68.	Regensburg		
69.	Hagen (Westf.)		
70.	Glogau		
71.	Elbing		1. 'Ernst Ludwig'
72.	Detmold		
73.	Ansbach		
74.	Greifswald		
75.	Berlin		8. 'Edmund Behnke'
76.	Salzburg		
77.	Schneidmühl		
78.	Wiesbaden		
79.	Ulm		
80.	Berlin		
81.	Würzburg		2. 'Hans Purps'
82.	Bielefeld		
83.	Giessen		

Standarte No.	Location	Standarte Honour Title	Sturm Honour Title
84.	Chemnitz		4. 'Grobe' 9. 'Steinbach' 11. 'Ludwig Frisch'
85.	Saarbrücken		
86.	Offenburg		
87.	Innsbruck		
88.	Bremen		
89.	Wien	'Holzweber'	
90.	Klagenfurt	'Franz Kutschera'	
91.	Wittenberg		
92.	Ingolstadt		
93.	Koblenz		
94.	Leoben		
95.	Trautenau		
96.	Brüx		
97.	Eger		
98.	Mährisch-Schönberg		
99.	Znaim		
100.	Reichenberg		
101.	Saaz		
102.	Jägerndorf		
103.	Aussig		
104.	Troppau		
105.	Memel		
106.	Augsburg		
107.	Brünn		
108.	Prag		
109.	Posen		
110.	Hohensalza		
111.	Kolmar		
112.	Litzmannstadt		
113.	Kalisch		
114.	Lesslau		
115.	Zichenau		
116.	Bromberg		
117.	Konitz		
118.	Pr. Stargard		
119.	Graudenz		
120.	Kulm		
121.	Strasburg		
122.	Strassburg		
123.	Kolmar		
124.	Scharley		

Standarte No.	Location	Standarte Honour Title	Sturm Honour Title
125.	Metz		
126.	Marburg/Drau		
127.	Oslo		

It will be noted that a few of the larger towns and cities had more than one Fuss-Standarte.

As well as the Fuss-Standarten, there were twenty-three Allgemeine-SS cavalry units of regimental size, the Reiterstandarten. Each comprised from five to eight Reiterstürme (cavalry companies), a Sanitätsreiterstaffel (medical squad) and a Trompeterkorps (trumpet corps). The Reiterstandarten were never concentrated in their HQ cities, the component companies usually being dispersed among smaller towns of the Abschnitte. They were always basically ceremonial in function, with a distinctly snobbish outlook, and were seldom if ever used to assist the Fuss-Standarten and police in domestic crowd control. The Inspector of SS Cavalry Training was the equestrian SS-Brigadeführer Christian Weber, one of the Old Guard Stosstrupp men and veteran of the Munich putsch. He set up the Main SS Cavalry School, or SS-Hauptreitschule, in Munich which was commanded by Hermann Fegelein until 1939. After the

A kettle-drummer of the SS-Kavallerie-Division in October 1942. The drum cover was made from black velvet with heavy aluminium wire embroidery, and its design had remained unchanged since 1934.

outbreak of war, the majority of members of the Reiterstandarten were conscripted into army cavalry units, or into the hastily mustered SS-Totenkopfreiterstandarten for front-line service. In 1941, the latter amalgamated to form the Waffen-SS Cavalry Brigade which by 1942 had expanded to become the SS-Kavallerie-Division, named 'Florian Geyer' in 1944. All of these formations were commanded during the various stages of their development by Fegelein, whose ever-strengthening position in Nazi circles culminated in his marriage on 3 June 1944 to Gretl Braun, sister of Hitler's mistress. The Allgemeine-SS Reiterstandarten were numbered from 1 to 23, each number being prefixed by the letter 'R' to distinguish them from the Fuss-Standarten. Their headquarters were located as follows:

Standarte No.	HQ
R.1	Insterburg
R.2	Danzig
R.3	Treuburg
R.4	Hamburg
R.5	Stettin
R.6	Düsseldorf
R.7	Berlin
R.8	Pelkum
R.9	Bremen
R.10	Arolsen
R.11	Breslau
R.12	Schwerin
R.13	Frankfurt (Main)
R.14	Stuttgart
R.15	München
R.16	Dresden
R.17	Regensburg
R.18	Wien
R.19	Graudenz
R.20	Tilsit
R.21	Hannover
R.22	Posen
R.23	Pirmasens

Several of these locations were former garrison towns of imperial cavalry regiments and, consequently, had excellent equestrian facilities. Moreover, many nationalist riding clubs were incorporated into the Allgemeine-SS 'lock, stock and barrel' during the 1930s, bringing with them their equestrian expertise. All this meant that the SS Reiterstandarten became the best cavalry formations in the Third Reich, surpassing even those of the army so far as ceremonial was concerned.

Each SS Standarte was composed of three active Sturmbanne or battalions, one Reserve-Sturmbann for men between the ages of thirty-five and forty-five, and a Musikzug or marching band. A Sturmbann was usually commanded by an SS-Sturmbannführer, assisted by an adjutant. The full peacetime strength of a Sturmbann ranged from 500 to 800 men and, as it was considered the basic tactical unit of the Allgemeine-SS, it was planned that the SS Sturmbann would be able to operate as an independent entity in times of strife or revolt. The three active Sturmbanne of a Standarte were numbered in Roman numerals from I to III, for example the third Sturmbann of the 41st Standarte was abbreviated 'III/41'. The Reserve-Sturmbann was distinguished by the prefix 'Res.', in this case 'Res./41'.

Each active Sturmbann was in turn composed of four Stürme or companies, a Sanitätsstaffel (medical squad) and a Spielmannzug (fife-and-drum corps). In 1930, few SS Stürme expanded beyond the original Staffel size of seven to fifteen men. By the mid-1930s, however, the full peacetime strength of a Sturm was 120 to 180 men, under an SS-Hauptsturmführer, Obersturmführer or Untersturmführer. During wartime, one of the four Stürme served locally as a Wachkompanie, or Guard Company, protecting bridges, important buildings and so on. Another stood by as a civil defence Alarmsturm, or Emergency

A detachment from an SS Fuss-Standarte, preceded by its band and traditional musicians' 'Schellenbaum' or 'Belltree' standard, c. 1934.

Company, for use during air raids or ground attacks, and the remaining two were assigned to general patrol duties. A Reserve-Sturmbann generally comprised two Reserve-Stürme, numbered 'Res.1' and 'Res.2', and a Reserve-Sanitätsstaffel. Within each Standarte, the four Stürme of Sturmbann I were numbered 1, 2, 3 and 4. Those of Sturmbann II were numbered 5, 6, 7 and 8, while those of Sturmbann III were numbered 9, 10, 11 and 12. Thus the 1st Sturm of the 2nd Sturmbann of the 3rd Standarte, i.e. the 5th Sturm in the 3rd Standarte, would be referred to within the Standarte as '5/II' and outwith the Standarte as '5/II/3'.

Every Sturm was divided into three or four Truppen (platoons), each composed of three Scharen (sections). A Schar generally numbered ten to fifteen men and was used to patrol blocks of houses within cities and guard official buildings. The Schar itself comprised two or three Rotten (files), the smallest units of the Allgemeine-SS numbering about five men. Depending on their size, Truppen and Scharen were commanded by NCOs of the ranks between SS-Hauptscharführer and Unterscharführer, while Rotten were led by experienced enlisted men known as Rottenführer.

In addition to the regular SS infantry and cavalry units, there were a number of specialist formations intended to act in a support role. Each SS Oberabschnitt was assigned one Nachrichtensturmbann, or Signals Battalion, responsible for SS communications in the Region. These signals battalions were numbered consecutively from 1 to 19, in Arabic rather than Roman numerals, prefixed by the letters 'Na.'. Their headquarters were located as follows:

Sturmbann No.	HQ
Na.1	München
Na.2	Stuttgart
Na.3	Arolsen
Na.4	Düsseldorf
Na.5	Braunschweig
Na.6	Hamburg
Na.7	Königsberg
Na.8	Berlin
Na.9	Dresden
Na.10	Breslau
Na.11	Nürnberg
Na.12	Stettin
Na.13	Wiesbaden
Na.14	Wien
Na.16	Danzig
Na.17	Posen
Na.19	Prag

No records remain of the locations of Nachrichtensturmbanne nos 15 and 18.

Pioniersturmbanne or engineer battalions were again organic components of the Oberabschnitte, and were equipped to carry out emergency construction work such as road and bridge repairs, and maintenance of public utilities including gas, electricity, water and the like. Each Pioniersturmbann was numbered consecutively from 1 to 16, prefixed by the letters 'Pi.'. Their headquarters were located as follows:

Sturmbann No.	HQ
Pi.1	München
Pi.2	Stuttgart
Pi.3	Arolsen
Pi.4	Köln
Pi.5	Harburg-Wilhelmsburg
Pi.6	Stettin
Pi.7	Königsberg

An SS-Unterscharführer reservist, denoted by the 'Reserve' cuff title, c. 1937.

NCOs of the SS-VT signals battalion in October 1935. All wear the 'SS/lightning bolt' collar patch, which from a distance looks like three Sig-Runes side by side, and the blank cuff title sported by personnel of this unit until the introduction of the 'SS-Nachrichtensturmbann' title in 1937.

Pi.8	Berlin
Pi.9	Dresden
Pi.10	Breslau
Pi.11	Nürnberg
Pi.12	Magdeburg
Pi.13	Frankfurt (Main)
Pi.14	Wien
Pi.15	Salzburg
Pi.16	Danzig

The Röntgensturmbann SS-HA, or SS Hauptamt X-Ray Battalion, was formed by SS-Obersturmbannführer Konrad Perwitzschky and was later commanded by SS-Oberführer Dr Hans Holfelder, Professor of Medicine at the University of Frankfurt (Main). It comprised around 350 full-time SS men and toured all the Allgemeine-SS Oberabschnitte, carrying out routine health checks on SS personnel. It utilised portable X-ray equipment and was primarily employed to detect pulmonary diseases among factory workers who were also part-time SS members. The only unit of its kind in Germany, its services could be summoned in times of epidemic by any of the NSDAP Gauleiters and it also co-operated with local officials of the German Labour Front. During the war, the Röntgensturmbann was absorbed into the medical branch of the Waffen-SS.

In addition to the Röntgensturmbann and the Sanitätsstaffel attached to every Sturmbann, each Abschnitt contained at least one Sanitätssturm or medical company. A group of several such Stürme, or a single large Sturm, was often termed a Sanitätsabteilung (medical detachment). These units were referred to by the Roman numeral of the Abschnitt in which they were located.

The SS Kraftfahrstürme, or Motor Transport Companies, were composed of Staffeln, or squads, one Kraftfahrstaffel being allocated to each Abschnitt. They were responsible for the motorised transport of SS personnel within the district. In addition, a motorcycle company was at the disposal of each Oberabschnitt commander to be used for relaying urgent despatches. Kraftfahrstürme were numbered from 1 to 19, prefixed by the letter 'K'. The areas they covered are listed below:

Sturm No.	Area
K.1	München/Augsburg
K.2	Erfurt
K.3	Berlin/Senftenberg
K.4	Hamburg/Kiel/Bremen
K.5	Düsseldorf/Buer/Dortmund
K.6	Dresden/Chemnitz
K.7	Königsberg
K.8	Linz/Wien
K.9	Breslau
K.10	Stuttgart/Karlsruhe/Freiburg
K.11	Magdeburg/Hannover
K.12	Bamberg/Schweinfurt/Nürnberg
K.13	Schwerin/Stettin
K.14	Frankfurt (Main)/Wiesbaden/Pirmasens
K.15	Graz/Innsbruck
K.16	Danzig/Elbing
K.17	Posen/Litzmannstadt
K.19	Asch/Reichenberg/Brünn

No record remains of the location of Kraftfahrsturm no. 18.

The first SS-Fliegerstaffel, or SS Air Squadron, was formed in October 1931 at Munich. It was joined by SS-Fliegerstaffel Nürnberg-Furth nine months later, and both of these units were thereafter renamed SS-Fliegerstürme and consolidated into an SS-Fliegersturmbann under Eduard Ritter von Schleich, the famed 'Black Knight' of the First World War. The SS Air Squadrons were responsible for flying Hitler and other senior Nazi personalities around Germany, and they remained active until absorbed by the Deutscher Luftsport Verband (DLV), the forerunner of the Luftwaffe, in September 1933.

From 1935, each Oberabschnitt commander could form a Streifendienst, or Patrol Service, as and when required. Streifendienst units were fairly small and mobile and their members were specially selected from among the most reliable SS men. They patrolled areas temporarily out of bounds to SS personnel and policed the SS contingents at party rallies. During the annual 9 November celebrations in Munich, for example, only a few SS men in possession of specially issued passes valid for the day could enter the restricted areas around the Feldherrnhalle and Königsplatz where Hitler and his hierarchy congregated. It was the Streifendienst who checked these passes and ensured that no unauthorised SS 'spectators' slipped through. All members of a Streife wore a nickel-plated gorget bearing the legend 'SS Streifendienst' while on duty. This item of regalia was similar to that which identified the military police, and highlighted the fact that the Streifendienst was, in effect, an internal police force of the Allgemeine-SS.

Each Oberabschnitt contained a Sportabteilung, or Sports Detachment, which was responsible for the physical fitness of SS personnel. It also trained with the Hitler Youth and the Allgemeine-SS Reserve. From the outset, sports and physical fitness had been accorded a high priority by both the SA and SS, and indeed the earliest Nazi paramilitaries disguised their true identity by calling themselves Turn- und Sport-abteilungen, or Gymnastic and Sports Detachments. Prior to 1939, SS sports instructors were trained at the SA Sport School in Hamm, Westphalia, but after the occupation of Czechoslovakia an SS Reichssportschule was established at Prague. It duly ran courses for Oberabschnitt sports officers, and issued SS physical training manuals for the reference of all SS personnel.

In addition to the regular and specialist SS units, and the first-line reserve of those between the ages of thirty-five and forty-five, each Oberabschnitt also contained an independent Stammabteilung, or Supple-mentary Reserve Detachment, composed partly of unfit or older men over the age of forty-five, and partly of younger men whose duties to the state or party debarred them from taking an active part in the SS. For example, it was customary for full-time regular police officers to be assigned to the Stammabteilung upon receiving SS membership. The Stammabteilung carried the name of the corresponding Oberabschnitt and was divided into Bezirke or sub-districts, each Bezirk working in conjunction with a Standarte and bearing the Arabic numeral of the latter. As their title indicated, these additional second-line reservists supple-mented the rest of the Allgemeine-SS in the various functions where normal duty personnel and first-line reserves might be overtaxed, as in the case of large national parades and celebrations, or major disasters. They were readily distinguishable by the fact that a reverse colour scheme was employed on their uniform insignia, i.e. a light-grey background to collar patches and cuff titles with black or silver numbers and script. For a short time, members of the Stammab-teilungen also wore light grey rather than black borders on their armbands.

SS Helferinnen, or Female SS Auxiliaries, were first recruited in 1942 to relieve male SS personnel who were more urgently needed at the front. During the war, German women were called to 'do their bit' in all spheres of life, and in this respect the SS was no exception, despite Himmler's view that his Schutzstaffel was essentially an 'Order of German Men'. As more and more SS men were conscripted, their work places were taken over by women. The designation SS Helferin was used only for those who had been accepted as SS members proper and trained at the Reichsschule-SS at Oberehnheim in Elsass, primarily for the communications branches of the Allgemeine-SS and Waffen-SS. All other female auxiliaries engaged by the SS, i.e. those who were not full SS members, were termed Kriegshelferinnen, or War Auxiliaries. Originally, the SS Oberabschnitte were responsible for recruiting SS Helferinnen, but in May 1944 that responsibility was transferred to the SS Hauptamt. Enrolment as an SS Helferin was on a voluntary basis. Official recruiting through newspaper advertisements, radio and cinema was forbidden, since careful selection was necessary. Close co-operation was maintained with the Reichsjugendführung and most of the recruiting was done through the Bund Deutscher Mädel or BDM, the female equivalent of the Hitler Youth. All women between the ages of eighteen and thirty-five were eligible to apply. Upon enrolment, the applicant was interviewed by the Senior SS and Police Commander of the Oberabschnitt in which she resided, in the presence of the BDM Liaison Officer, and a medical examination took place the same day. Next, the applicant signed a statement declaring that she had not observed any signs of pregnancy or serious illness, as well as a statement of her racial suitability. No individual could be accepted until a thorough investigation into her family background had been completed by the Sicherheitsdienst. The

Reichsschule-SS had the task of training the successful applicants as teleprinter operators, telephonists and wireless operators. Instruction was also given in domestic science so that SS Helferinnen would be capable of assuming responsibility for SS nurseries and similar establishments if and when necessary. Upon satisfactory completion of the course, the girls were presented with SS rune insignia to be worn on the left breast of their uniform, and were assigned in groups to the various headquarters of the SS in Germany, France, Luxembourg, Holland, Poland and Russia. During 1943 alone, 422 SS Helferinnen were trained at the Reichsschule.

The strict physical, mental and racial qualifications for entry into the SS meant that not all who desired to do so could become members. However, almost anyone who wished, for public or private reasons, to stand well with the new élite and who could afford to pay for the privilege were allowed to become Fördernde Mitglieder (FM), or Patron Members. The FM organisation developed as a fund-raising body during the mid-1920s, with Hitler himself holding FM membership no. 1. All Aryan Germans of both sexes were eligible to join, and NSDAP membership was not a necessary qualification. When accepted, each patron was presented with an FM membership book and badge, and bound himself or herself to pay a monthly subscription to SS funds. The contribution varied with the income of the member and could be as low as 1 Reichsmark. The money thus levied from bankers, industrialists, businessmen and shopkeepers strengthened the economic base of the SS, and at the same time the contacts secured in German society enlarged SS influence. The FM members themselves were promised the protection of the SS against 'revolutionary tendencies'. In effect, the FM organisation became a sort of 'old boys' network' through which members could

secure business deals, promotion or employment, and in the Third Reich virtually replaced the outlawed Society of Freemasons. By 1935, there were 500,000 Fördernde Mitglieder and there were probably over 1 million in 1943. The practice of appointing selected members of the government or important public figures to high rank in the SS, as Ehrenführer or Honorary Officers, was a natural extension of the FM organisation. While these appointments had no functional significance, they bought for the SS even more extremely influential and well-placed allies who, once they had taken the SS oath in return for the right to wear the prestigious black uniform, suddenly found themselves bound to obey Himmler in terms of the SS discipline code.

The medium which united all these facets of the SS organisation, and kept them in touch with each other, was the SS-Presse. A magazine entitled *Die Schutzstaffel* was published as early as December 1926, but it was short-lived and it was not until 1935 that the Reichsführung-SS began to publish a weekly newspaper called *Das Schwarze Korps* or 'The Black Corps'. Set up on Heydrich's initiative and directed by SS-Standartenführer Gunter d'Alquen, descendant of a Huguenot family, it was printed by the NSDAP publishing house of Eher Verlag, Munich, and had its editorial offices at 88 Zimmerstrasse, Berlin. By 1939, circulation had reached 500,000 copies. *Das Schwarze Korps* was a sharply written paper, very neo-pagan, and specialised in the exposure of those the Reichsführung-SS considered social miscreants whom the courts could not reach. It was the only organ of the German press which was not censored and, although rigorously orthodox at the ideological level, was also the only newspaper that gave any indication of having a critical or non-conformist spirit. From its very first issue, the originality of *Das Schwarze Korps* was emphasised by its aggressiveness to the rest of Goebbels' press. It took sides against leaders of the NSDAP, attacked ministers of state such as Alfred Rosenberg, who had been short-sighted enough to shun Himmler's offers of honorary SS rank, and denounced inadequacies in the administration. Private enterprise and initiative were favoured by the paper because they aided progress, particularly in wartime. After 1939, the publicising of SS and police military heroes became an increasingly important feature, especially when d'Alquen was made commander of the SS War Correspondents' Regiment and Kurt Eggers took over the paper. As the war progressed and the need grew for all sections of the régime to be seen to act as one, the old criticisms of the excesses of the party leaders disappeared. By 1944, *Das Schwarze Korps* and its sister paper for Patron Members, the *FM-Zeitschrift*, had degenerated from lively and controversial publications to propaganda sheets expounding the exploits of Waffen-SS soldiers on the battlefront. In this way, the path of the SS-Presse paralleled that of the entire SS organisation.

SS men guarding Hitler during a speech at Elbing, 5 November 1933. Only the man in the centre sports collar patches: the others are still probationary members.

SS DUTIES AND CONDITIONS OF SERVICE

The first and foremost duty of the entire SS organisation was the protection of Adolf Hitler; at least that was the official line. In 1931, after Hitler had lost the presidential election to von Hindenburg, Himmler described the SS as 'Des Führers ureigenste, erlesene Garde', the Führer's most personal, selected guards. However, while it is true to say that the earliest Stosstrupp and SS men in the 1920s were indeed directly employed only as Hitler's bodyguards and then as 'Rednerschutz' to protect other leading Nazi orators, the vast majority of the Allgemeine-SS in the 1930s and 1940s never even came into the close proximity of members of the

political hierarchy, far less that of the Führer himself, whose protection after 1933 was the responsibility of the Leibstandarte-SS 'Adolf Hitler' alone. Nevertheless, even in later years the primary SS duty of guarding Hitler was still stressed, the Organisationsbuch der NSDAP declaring in 1937: 'It is the fundamental and most noble task of the SS to be concerned with the safety of the Führer'.

After the advent of the Leibstandarte, whose members worked full-time to a rota system and accompanied Hitler on his journeys throughout the Reich, the part-time SS men who had originally been recruited on a local basis to protect Hitler during his trips around Germany found that aspect of their

SS-Standartenführer Julius Schreck after receiving the Golden Party Badge at the end of 1933. Of particular interest are the early pattern collar patches and the Sports Eagle of the National Motor and Air Travel Organisation, the latter being worn below the ribbon bar. Schreck was an expert driver, and frequently chauffeured Hitler around Germany in his open-topped Mercedes tourer at speeds in excess of 100 mph. Co-founder of the Stosstrupp Adolf Hitler, Schreck was constantly at the Führer's side until his death from meningitis in 1936.

work taken from them. Consequently, it was decided that as of 1933 the main day-to-day function of these highly disciplined Allgemeine-SS volunteers would be to bolster the régime by supporting the police in maintaining public order, especially since some of the police themselves were politically unreliable. Their immediate success as Hilfspolizei during the mass arrests of communists and other dissidents after the Nazi assumption of power led to the rapid expansion of the SS organisation and the formation of dozens of new Allgemeine-SS Standarten trained and equipped to combat any internal uprising or counter-revolution which might take place within Germany. It was planned that, in such an event, the Allgemeine-SS Fuss-Standarten and Stammabteilungen would act as police reinforcements in conjunction with the heavily armed SS-Verfügungstruppe and SS-Totenkopfverbände, while the Nachrichtensturmbanne, Pioniersturmbanne and Kraftfahrstürme of the Allgemeine-SS would take over the operation of the post office and national radio network, public utilities and public transport, respectively. Consequently, throughout 1934 particular emphasis was placed on the recruitment of personnel for these specialist SS support units. However, the anticipated civil unrest never came about, and internal party rivalries were crushed during the 'Night of the Long Knives'. As a result, the police duties of the Allgemeine-SS before the outbreak of the war were generally restricted to overseeing crowd control at NSDAP rallies and other celebrations, including national holidays and state visits of foreign dignitaries.

After 1939, members of the Allgemeine-SS who had not been called up for military service took a more active police support role. They were frequently lectured on the work of the police and the SD, and in many cities special SS Wachkompanie and

SS men lining the route for a parade at Bückeberg in 1935, during the annual harvest festival celebrations.

Alarmstürme were detailed to protect factories, bridges, roads and other strategic points and assist the Luftschutz or Civil Defence during air raids. On the borders of the Reich, SS men worked as Auxiliary Frontier Personnel, or Hilfsgrenzangestellte (HIGA), in conjunction with the Customs Service. Others helped with the harvest, supervised foreign labourers and engaged in welfare work among the families and dependants of deceased SS servicemen. During 1944–5, the cadres of the Allgemeine-SS spread throughout Germany were trained to co-ordinate the short-lived guerrilla campaign which took place against Allied occupation troops.

The Allgemeine-SS unit which normally mustered for training purposes was the Trupp or, in more populous districts, the Sturm. Larger musters of the SS were possible only in exceptional circumstances. There were periodic gatherings of the Standarten and occasional conferences of Abschnitte officers, when speeches and propaganda displays helped to foster corporate spirit and preserve SS ideology, but the vast majority of meetings usually took place on a local basis, once or twice a week in the evening or at the weekend. They gave those attending a feeling of 'belonging' and importance which made a welcome break from the humdrum of their daily lives working in the fields and factories of the Reich. In summer, there were route marches, parade and field drill, and manoeuvres. In winter, the routine activity of the Allgemeine-SS comprised instruction in military matters, indoor shooting, specialist and technical training, lectures on propaganda, political topics and Germanic culture, and talks on the general history and work of the SS and NSDAP. At party rallies and assemblies the SS always took a prominent role, and in processions had the place of honour at the end of the parade.

The great reduction in the number of active part-time personnel which resulted from the war and their temporary enlistment in the Wehrmacht and Waffen-SS considerably reduced the day-to-day activities of the Allgemeine-SS. Even among the members still at home in reserved occupations, long working hours and additional war service drastically cut down attendance at company parades. By 1943, it had become the rule to find SS NCOs in command of Stürme and even Sturmbanne, and for duty parades to be confined to one or two hours per week. Under such circumstances, musters were frequently attended by only a dozen or fewer members, and the local Allgemeine-SS administration was run by severely wounded men and those temporarily returned to active duty from the Stammabteilungen. Nevertheless, so far as Himmler was concerned, the Allgemeine-SS was the original and 'real' SS, and he continued issuing orders aimed at reinforcing it well into 1945.

From the day he took charge of the SS in 1929, Himmler set himself the task of creating an aristocracy within the Nazi party, an élite which he later called his 'Deutsche Männerorden' or Order of German Manhood. The qualifications on which he initially based his policy of selection were those of discipline and high personal standards, but after 1933 racial and political attributes became increasingly important. Whosoever possessed the requisite qualities, whatever his background, class or education, could find a place in the SS. The first SS men, the former members of the Freikorps who had fought against communist revolutionaries and Allied occupation troops after the First World War, were followed by an assortment of unemployed labourers, farmers, disillusioned teachers, white-collar workers and ex-officers, all of whom went into the SS during the late 1920s and early 1930s with no aim other than to better their current difficult existence. The turning point so far as SS recruiting was concerned was the spring of 1933, which Himmler called 'the time of the great influx and flood tide of all those opportunists wishing to join the party and its various organisations'. After Hitler's appointment as Chancellor on 30 January that year, everyone suddenly wanted to join the SS and there was a rush at the recruiting offices. Himmler maintained his standards by immediately closing ranks and instituting a vigorous weeding-out process among those already admitted. Between 1933 and 1935 60,000 SS officers and men were expelled from the organisation because of petty criminal convictions, homosexuality, alcoholism, poor health, inadequate physique, questionable racial or political backgrounds or simple lack of commitment. The result was an Allgemeine-SS numbering about 210,000 only 0.4 per cent of whom were now unemployed, which did actually constitute the élite which Himmler required. It was inevitable, because of this policy, that the ordinary SS units were scattered widely throughout Germany. Concentration would have meant a lowering of standards. As a result, the organisation was spread very thinly across all the rural districts of the Reich, so much so that Himmler could proudly boast in 1936: 'Many SS Truppen are recruited from several villages, a single village never having more than its two really best boys in the SS'. Not surprisingly, the majority of these 'best boys' found that their SS membership, while unpaid, had a real and beneficial knock-on effect on their chosen civilian careers.

After 1933, the Hitler Youth (Hitlerjugend or HJ) was the main source of recruitment for the Allgemeine-SS, excepting of course honorary members, specialists and those in affiliated bodies such as the police. Potential SS recruits were singled out by local units while still in the HJ, and boys who had proved themselves in the HJ-Streifendienst were made particularly welcome. Out of every hundred applicants, only ten or so were finally admitted. While no educational qualifications were required, each of these had to demonstrate the good political behaviour of his parents, brothers and sisters, produce a clean police record and an Aryan pedigree dating back to the mid-eighteenth century, and prove that there was no hereditary disease in his family. A Race Commission composed of SS eugenists and doctors supervised the last and most decisive medical tests. They judged not only the shape of head and colour of eyes, but also whether the applicant had the right build. Even if he had attained the prescribed height, which altered periodically but was approximately 5 ft 10 in, he had also to have the correct proportions between the upper and lower leg, and between leg and body. The Commission also considered whether the applicant behaved in a disciplined yet not servile way, and how he answered questions and generally conducted himself. If the applicant satisfied all these requirements of political reliability, racial purity and physique he was officially recognised on his eighteenth birthday as an SS-Bewerber, or SS Candidate, and given a uniform without insignia.

After some preliminary training, the Candidate progressed to the stage of becoming an SS-Anwärter, or Cadet, on the occasion of the annual NSDAP Reichsparteitag celebrations in Nürnberg the following September. At that time he was provisionally enrolled into the ranks of the SS proper, and received his uniform insignia and Ausweis, or membership card. On the following 9 November, the anniversary of the Munich putsch, he and all other SS-Anwärter appointed that year took the organisation's personal oath of allegiance to the Führer, which ran:

> I swear to you, Adolf Hitler, as Führer and Chancellor of the Reich, loyalty and bravery. I promise to you, and to those you have appointed to have authority over me, obedience unto death.

Throughout the next few months, the SS-Anwärter continued with his civilian occupation or apprenticeship during the day and attended the set musters of his local Allgemeine-SS Trupp or Sturm in the evenings or at weekends. Much of his training at this stage in his service revolved around his qualifying for the SA Military Sports Badge and the German National Sports Badge, both of which he was expected to win. Under normal prewar conditions, the SS-Anwärter was thereafter called up for six months' compulsory full-time duty in the Reichsarbeitsdienst or RAD, the National Labour Service which worked on public building programmes, and then for his two-year term of conscription in the Wehrmacht. During that period, he almost completely severed his active ties with the Allgemeine-SS. Subsequently, his labouring and military duties finished, he returned to civilian life and to the SS, still as an Anwärter, to receive his final intensive training and indoctrination. This included ideological schooling in the

SS-Anwärter take the oath of allegiance in front of the Feldherrnhalle in Munich, 9 November 1934. This ceremony, which took place in the most solemn of circumstances at the 'holy shrine' of Nazism, was attended by Hitler, Himmler and the rest of the Old Guard.

fundamental laws and concepts of the SS, marriage orders and the SS code of honour and discipline.

On 9 November following his return from the Wehrmacht to civilian life, the successful Anwärter was received into the SS as a full SS-Mann. On that solemn occasion he took a second oath, swearing that he and his family would always adhere to the principles of the SS, and was thereafter presented with his SS dagger and given the right to use it to defend his honour and that of the Black Order. The confirmed SS man remained in the active Allgemeine-SS until his thirty-fifth year, at which time he was eligible for honourable discharge from the organisation. However, many elected at that stage to apply for acceptance into their local Reserve-Sturmbann, and at the retirement age of

forty-five most of these transferred yet again to the regional Stammabteilung. Long service in this way was recognised by awards of the NSDAP Dienstauszeichnungen, a series of decorations instituted on 20 April 1939 for ten, fifteen and twenty-five years' active membership of any of the Nazi party uniformed bodies.

Recruiting for the Allgemeine-SS, which was the responsibility of the SS Hauptamt, peaked in 1939 then drastically decreased on the outbreak of war. As early as January 1940, Himmler announced that of approximately 250,000 regulars in the Allgemeine-SS at the opening of hostilities, no less than 175,000 had since joined the Wehrmacht and Waffen-SS, the majority going to the army. These men retained their Allgemeine-SS membership throughout the war, but due to the commitments of military service were unable to participate in their normal SS duties. By 1944, the total active strength of the Allgemeine-SS had fallen to 40,000, excluding that part of the organisation represented by the police. Even so, while the purely numerical strength of the Allgemeine-SS declined, its domination of the home front steadily increased, highlighted not only by Himmler's personal concentration of power but also by the ever-expanding influence of the SS hierarchy, reinforced by the police and security services and the patron and honorary membership.

In addition to the general military and political training given to Allgemeine-SS men at local level, at the regular musters of Truppe and Stürme, there were a number of selective and specialist training establishments which members could attend. A batch of NCO and officer candidate schools produced and trained leaders for assignment throughout the whole SS system. As well as the Main Cavalry School at Munich and the Helferinnen Reichsschule at Oberehnheim, there was an SS-Ärztliche Akademie, or SS Medical Academy, at Graz, an SS-Verwaltungsschule, or Administration School, at Dachau, a Kraftfahrtechnische Lehranstalt, or Motor Technical Training Establishment, at Vienna, an SS-Musikschule, or Music College, at Brunswick, a Pioneer and Mining School at Gisleben, and a Signals School and Security Police Training College at Berlin. There were also a number of special SS-Berufsoberschulen, or Higher Technical Schools, set up under the auspices of the SS Hauptamt to teach technical skills to candidates for the Allgemeine-SS and Waffen-SS. All German boys who were apprentices or students in business, trade or agriculture and who attended a trade or technical school could apply for entry to an SS-Berufsoberschule as an SS officer candidate.

Conditions of acceptance were that candidates had to be between fourteen and seventeen years of age and satisfy the general recruitment standards laid down for the SS. The training given qualified students for the Reifeprüfung, or state leaving certificate, in economics, technical subjects or agriculture. Students successful in law, politics, history, forestry, mining and engineering were encouraged to continue their studies either at one of the SS or SD Administration Schools or at a university. In effect, the SS-Berufsoberschulen were designed as a medium for the recruitment and initial training of suitable candidates for the security and administrative branches of the SS.

One of the less well known but important educational offshoots of the SS were the SS Mannschaftshäuser, or SS Men's Halls. These institutions formed a Dienststelle, or branch, of the Allgemeine-SS whose function was to train young officers intending to take up civil and non-political professions. They differed, therefore, from the specialist schools of the SS and police and from the Waffen-SS Junkerschulen in that they were designed for SS men who proposed to make their careers in walks of life that had no official connection with the SS, such as the Civil Service, medicine, the law, art, science, engineering and the academic field generally. The acknowledged object of their training was to infuse the SS spirit into the higher professions.

The SS Mannschaftshäuser originated in 1935 when small groups of ten to fifteen ordinary students, who were united only by their common SS membership, began to live together in a few university and high school towns. As their numbers increased a more careful system of membership selection was practised, qualities demanded being good character, National Socialist beliefs and proven academic or scientific talent. When the number of permanent residents reached

350, Himmler appointed SS-Oberführer Kurt Ellersiek as Chief of the Mannschaftshäuser, with the status and disciplinary powers of a Standarte commander. Life in the Men's Halls before the war included, besides the usual academic studies, an organised series of social occasions at which the students could acquire the ease and conventional courtesies necessary for success in public life. To prevent them from attaching an exaggerated value to the academic and social side of things, however, participation in team sports and athletics, and regular service in an Allgemeine-SS Sturm, was made compulsory for all residents. Each winter the members of all the halls throughout Germany attended a special course at the SS-Junkerschule at Bad Tölz where, for a fortnight, they studied and exercised along with regular SS-Verfügungstruppe officer cadets. In summer, during vacation periods, long marches were organised in northern Germany or in the Alps, during which the students camped out in the open.

The outbreak of war severely checked the growth of the Mannschaftshäuser, as most members were almost immediately conscripted into the Wehrmacht. Only a few discharged or reserved men continued their studies in some of the halls. An official list of Mannschaftshäuser drawn up in May 1944 comprised the following:

Berlin I	Kiel
Berlin II	Köln
Braunschweig	Königsberg
Brünn	Leiden
Danzig	Lublin
Freiburg	München
Graz	Münster
Hamburg	Prag
Halle	Strassburg
Heidelberg	Tübingen
Innsbruck	Wien
Jena	

Of these, however, only four (Berlin II, München, Prag and Wien) were still fully active at that late date.

General propaganda and political education within the SS was the responsibility of the SS Hauptamt, which issued or supervised the issue of a number of related publications. In addition to special pamphlets such as the SS recruiting handbook *Dich ruft die SS* (*The SS Needs You*) and a series of SS Schulungshefte, or educational booklets, the SS-HA put out two periodicals, the *SS Informationsdienst*, a news magazine for the SS and police, and the *SS Leitheft*, an illustrated magazine with stories and articles for more general consumption. The theme of the ideal German family was used extensively throughout this type of publication, and was inevitably slanted to draw comparisons with less favoured ethnic groups. Another much documented subject was the Externsteine, the German equivalent of Stonehenge, which became enshrined in SS mythology. The SS-HA also held political education courses for SS officers and men and, in addition, was responsible for the appointment of Schulungsoffiziere, or Education Officers, to the staffs of the various SS training schools.

So far as advancement for the ordinary SS man was concerned, the sky was the limit. In stark contrast to the imperial army, promotion in the SS depended upon personal commitment, effectiveness and political reliability, not class or education. 'Das Schwarze Korps' continually denounced the old reactionary military system as typifying that 'middle-class arrogance which excluded the worker from society and gave him the feeling of being a third class citizen'. Consequently, the SS cadet schools consciously offered something which those of the Wehrmacht never did – an officer's career for men without a middle- or upper-class background or formal educational qualifications. The SS always encouraged self-discipline and mutual respect rather than a brutally enforced discipline, and its general working atmosphere was more relaxed than that of the army, the relationship between officers and men being less formal. Officers were termed 'Führer', or 'leaders', not 'Offiziere', which had class connotations. On duty, the old military rank prefix 'Herr', implying superiority and dominance, was strictly forbidden and even the lowliest SS-Bewerber would address Himmler himself simply as 'Reichsführer', not 'Herr Reichsführer'. Off duty, junior ranks referred to their seniors as 'Kamerad' (Comrade), or 'Parteigenosse' (Party Colleague) if both were members of the NSDAP.

The SS-Führerkorps or officer corps of the Allgemeine-SS comprised a number of different categories, mainly dependent upon the nature of the officer's employment. Those below the rank of Sturmbannführer were generally Nebenamtlich, or part-time, and unpaid, while higher ranks were usually Hauptamtlich, or full-time, and salaried. The main categories of SS officer were as follows:

1. *Aktive SS Führer* (Active SS Officers)
    All those who held regular part-time or full-time office in the local Allgemeine-SS, SS Hauptämter or other departments, including all officers of the rank of Gruppenführer and above, irrespective of employment.
2. *Zugeteilte Führer bei den Stäben* (Officers attached to Staffs and HQs)
    Officers prevented by reason of their civil, governmental or party posts from taking an active part in the SS. They were normally attached as advisers to the Persönlicher Stab RfSS, or to the staffs of the SS Hauptämter or Oberabschnitte HQs.
3. *Führer in der Stammabteilung* (Officers in the Supplementary Reserve)
    Officers not included in the foregoing

two categories who were obliged by reason of age or infirmity to retire honourably from active service in the SS or first-line SS reserve. The majority of full-time police officers given SS membership were also taken into the Stammabteilungen as they could not readily be absorbed by the active Allgemeine-SS Standarten.

4. *Führer zu Verfügung* (Officers 'on call')
    Officers suspended for disciplinary reasons whom the SS court had put 'on call' for a maximum period of two years, as a term of probation. Within that period, depending upon their behaviour, they were either restored to active service or dismissed from the SS.

Any Allgemeine-SS officer who joined the Waffen-SS during the war retained his Allgemeine-SS status and rank, but usually received a lower Waffen-SS rank until such time as he had gained sufficient military experience to warrant promotion. Thereafter, any promotion he achieved within the Waffen-SS resulted in a simultaneous and level upgrading of his Allgemeine-SS rank.

The undernoted regulations governed promotion within the Allgemeine-SS:

1. Promotion to SS-Gruppenführer and above was decided by Hitler himself, in his technical capacity as Commander-in-Chief of the SS, on the recommendation of the Reichsführer-SS.
2. Promotion to officers below the rank of Gruppenführer was decided by the Reichsführer-SS at the instance of the SS Personalhauptamt. The heads of the SS Hauptämter, acting as Himmler's representatives, could carry out promotions up to and including SS-Hauptsturmführer.
3. Promotion to SS-Hauptscharführer was effected by Oberabschnitte commanders.

4. Promotion to SS-Oberscharführer was carried out by Abschnitte commanders.
5. Other NCOs were promoted by the commanders of the various SS Standarten.
6. Nominations for appointment as SS-Mann, Sturmmann and Rottenführer were made by delegated officers of the Standarten concerned.

Technical, administrative and medical personnel were bound by the same regulations as regards promotion and appointment but, in addition, had to be approved by the SS Wirtschafts- und Verwaltungshauptamt or the Reichsarzt SS und Polizei, whichever was appropriate.

It is noteworthy that, during the early days of the SS, it was not uncommon for some officers to enter the organisation at a high rank, or to skip ranks. For example, 'Sepp' Dietrich enrolled in the SS as a Standartenführer with membership no. 1177 on 18 November 1929, while Julius Schreck, with membership no. 5, skipped from Sturmführer straight to Standartenführer, missing out all ranks in between, on 30 January 1933. Others had a meteoric rise through the ranks, a good example being Karl Wolff, who was promoted in the following way:

Sturmführer	18 February 1932
Sturmhauptführer	30 January 1933
Sturmbannführer	9 November 1933
Obersturmbannführer	30 January 1934
Standartenführer	20 April 1934
Oberführer	4 July 1934

The SS maintained a thorough system of personnel records, based on cards filled out in triplicate in respect of each member. The cards were reddish-brown in colour and contained a host of personal details including date and place of birth, physical measurements, marriage particulars, names and ages of children, SS and NSDAP membership numbers, promotions, decorations and history of RAD and military service. All fixed information was entered in ink and variable information in pencil. Every Sturm maintained a file holding the original cards made out for each officer and man assigned to it. Duplicate cards, which had broad red diagonal stripes on the reverse, were kept at the HQ of the Standarte to which the Sturm belonged. The third set of cards, with dark-green stripes on the back, were filed at the SS Personalhauptamt if they related to officers or at the SS Hauptamt if they referred to NCOs and lower ranks. It was the responsibility of all personnel to ensure that they reported timeously any information relevant to the updating of their records.

Several times a year, the SS Personalhauptamt produced a Seniority List covering all officers in all branches of the SS. As the SS grew so did the List, and by the end of 1944 it comprised several volumes. Known as the *Dienstaltersliste der Schutzstaffel der NSDAP*, it was printed by the government publishers in Berlin and was intended for administrative use only within the offices of the SS. Being classified, it was not for personal issue or distribution to non-SS bodies. Above all, it was not to be made available to the general public. The *Dienstaltersliste* went into great detail about each officer listed. Not only did it state his full name and date of birth, it also gave his SS rank, position of seniority, NSDAP and SS membership numbers, current posting, decorations, and any governmental, military, political or police rank held. It even mentioned if he was on long-term sick leave. In relation to Heinrich Himmler, for example, the 1944 List read as follows:

1. Overall seniority no: 1.
2. Heinrich Himmler. Holder of the Golden Party Badge and Blood Order.

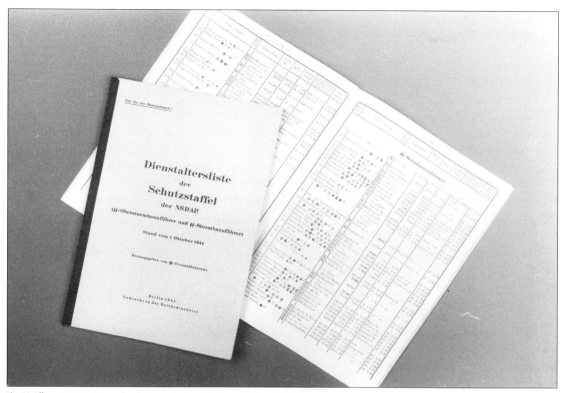

The SS Officers Seniority List, produced in several volumes between 1934 and 1944.

Reichsminister. Reichsleiter. Reichs-kommissar. City Councillor. Member of Parliament.

3. Holder of the SS Sword of Honour and the SS death's head ring.
4. Reichsführer-SS and Chief of the German Police.
5. NSDAP membership no: 14,303.
6. SS membership no: 168.
7. Date of birth: 7 October 1900.
8. Appointed to present position: 6 January 1929.

Further down the first page of the List, the following details were recorded in respect of a member of German royalty, Josias Erbprinz zu Waldeck und Pyrmont:

1. Overall seniority no: 10.
2. Josias, Hereditary Prince of Waldeck and Pyrmont. Holder of the Golden Party Badge, 1914 Iron Cross 1st Class, Cross of Honour 1914–1918, First World War state combat awards, 1918 Wound Badge in Black, 1939 Bar to the 1914 Iron Cross 1st Class, and Second World War combat awards. Member of Parliament.
3. Holder of the SS Sword of Honour and the SS death's head ring.
4. Commander of Oberabschnitt Fulda-Werra and Höhere SS- und Polizeiführer in that Region. General of the Waffen-SS. General of the Police.
5. NSDAP membership no: 160,025.
6. SS membership no: 2,139.

7. Date of birth: 13 May 1896.
8. Appointed to present position: 30 January 1936.

In April 1945, the SS made concerted attempts to destroy all existing copies of the *Dienstaltersliste*, but a few volumes fell into Allied hands and these proved invaluable reference material during the postwar de-Nazification process. Many prominent Germans who were by then vigorously denying all associations with the NSDAP and its affiliated organisations were suddenly confronted with their names appearing on the *Dienstaltersliste* and were forced to admit their intimate involvement in the Nazi régime. One of those was none other than the aforementioned Prince Josias, the only member of a German royal house to be tried for war crimes. As commander of the Oberabschnitt in which Buchenwald concentration camp was situated, he was held to be directly responsible for the conditions which prevailed there and was sentenced to life imprisonment.

Such accountability for their actions was something totally alien to the SS. One of the most important factors to be taken into account when considering the swingeing powers and activities of the various SS and police forces in their role as supreme guardians of law and order during the Third Reich is that they were themselves placed outside and above the normal German legal system. With the foundation of the SS- und Polizeigerichtsbarkeit (Special Jurisdiction of the SS and Police) during 1939–40, SS men were made responsible only to SS disciplinary officers and SS courts for all crimes and offences committed both inside and outside Germany. The very nature of their work meant that SS members frequently had to infringe the common law in the execution of their duties, and so to achieve its ends the SS hierarchy demanded and ultimately achieved the legal independence necessary to ensure that SS men should not be answerable to the civil courts for unlawful acts committed in the line of duty. The significance of this position cannot be overemphasised, as it guaranteed the whole SS organisation immunity from normal prosecution and hence the legal right, according to its own code, to arrest, imprison, ill-treat and ultimately exterminate its political and racial opponents. This was the basis for the often repeated argument after the war that SS men had 'only been obeying orders'. Not only were they simply obeying orders, but they had also been given the legal right to kill, endorsed by the highest courts in the Reich. It was the refusal to obey such orders which was illegal and punishable.

The original decrees and regulations establishing the Special Jurisdiction of the SS and Police continued to be enlarged and supplemented in the years after 1940. On 1 September 1943, the final and definitive SS Disciplinary and Penal Code (Disziplinarstraf- und Beschwerdeordnung der SS, or DBO) came into effect. It was valid for every member of the SS without exception. All SS officers, NCOs and other ranks, male and female, whether Allgemeine-SS, Waffen-SS, full-time, part-time, trainee, auxiliary, inactive or honorary in status, were liable to trial and punishment only by SS courts for all disciplinary and criminal offences they might commit. Where the offences were military ones, they were tried according to military procedures. In the case of criminal offences, the SS legal officials tried the accused by normal German criminal procedure. The jurisdiction of the DBO extended right across Germany and the occupied territories, and the scale of punishment which might be imposed ranged from simple disciplinary measures and expulsion from the SS to penal servitude and death by hanging, shooting or beheading.

Himmler was given the same powers of pardon and commutation of sentences as those held by the Reich Supreme Judge and the commanders of the three branches of the Wehrmacht, and the only course of appeal, and then in very special circumstances, was to the Führer himself.

Only one general exception to this policy of bringing all members of the SS under the stringent penalties of independent SS jurisdiction was ever allowed. By agreement with the Reichsführer-SS, a Wehrmacht regulation published in June 1940 laid down that individual members of the SS and police would become liable to normal military law if they were serving in the armed forces. This exception applied solely to Allgemeine-SS and police men conscripted for regular service in the Wehrmacht, and did not affect independent units and formations of the Waffen-SS, SD and police serving alongside the armed forces. With the advent of the DBO, however, the Wehrmacht regulation ceased to be valid and from 1943 the SS included under its jurisdiction even those of its members temporarily serving in the armed forces.

While in practice most disciplinary matters were disposed of by the competent senior SS disciplinary officers by direct action or courts martial, and most criminal matters by the duly appointed SS courts, full disciplinary powers were attached to Himmler personally, as Reichsführer-SS. He was competent to impose all disciplinary penalties allowed by the DBO, although Hitler usually took a personal interest in rare cases of the punishment of officers from Gruppenführer upwards. In particular, the Reichsführer reserved to himself the rights of:

1. dismissal from the SS, together with demotion or reduction to the ranks, of any SS officer
2. dismissal from the SS of any SS personnel with membership numbers below 10,000 (i.e. the Old Guard)
3. prescribing disciplinary punishments in addition to penal sentences passed by the SS courts

In order to exercise these powers and also for the purpose of considering appeals against disciplinary sentences passed by the heads of the SS Hauptämter, Himmler could order the setting up of a special court, or Disziplinarhof, to hear any particular case and report back to him. In times of absence, he could delegate his disciplinary authority to the Chief of the Hauptamt SS Gericht. In addition, a special legal officer was permanently attached to the Persönlicher Stab RfSS to assist Himmler in dealing with legal matters which came to him for disposal.

The ordinary SS courts were of two types:

1. the Feldgerichte, or Courts-Martial, convened in the normal way by the divisions and higher formations of the Waffen-SS
2. the SS und Polizei Gerichte, or SS and Police Courts, established in Germany and the occupied territories

By 1943 there were over forty of these SS und Polizei Gerichte. Outside the Reich they were set up in the capitals and larger towns of conquered countries. Inside Germany there was one in every Oberabschnitt, normally but not invariably at the seat of the Oberabschnitt HQ. They were numbered in Roman figures which, unlike the Oberabschnitte, did not follow Wehrkreis numbering but corresponded to the chronological order in which they were set up. Each SS and Police Court was competent to try all cases which occurred within its area. In addition, there were two other special courts, both based in Munich, which deserve mention. The first of these was the Oberstes SS und Polizei Gericht,

A jovial Himmler broadcasts to the nation on 'German Police Day', 28 January 1939. By this time he had amassed awesome legal powers as head of the police, and his discipline code ensured total obedience from the SS. During the war he was to boast: 'Thank God – we have not had a single case of treason from our ranks'.

the Supreme SS and Police Court, presided over by SS-Oberführer Dr Günther Reinecke. It tried cases of particular gravity, for example treason, crimes against the state and espionage. It was also the only competent tribunal for the trial of SS and police generals of the rank of Brigadeführer and above. The second of the special courts was the SS und Polizei Gericht z.b.V., or Extraordinary SS and Police Court. It was attached directly to the Hauptamt SS Gericht and was a secret tribunal which dealt with delicate and difficult cases which it was desired to keep from the general knowledge even of the SS itself.

During the war, the various SS und Polizei Gerichte were made competent to try non-SS personnel and civilians, which was a major development in their powers and a particularly efficient weapon in the general security system of the SS. Initially, civilians could be tried and condemned by SS courts only in respect of crimes committed in SS and police buildings or similar establishments, or crimes committed in conjunction with other persons who were themselves subject to SS jurisdiction. As the war progressed, however, this competence to try cases affecting the general interests of the SS was extended and the SS und Polizei Gerichte eventually came to be used for all serious security trials, including cases involving sabotage, illegal propaganda and traffic with an enemy power. The great majority of those tried in this way were sentenced to terms in concentration camps or to death by firing squad.

In common with the other formations and affiliated organisations of the NSDAP, the SS had its own code of honour enforced by special Courts of Honour, or Schiedshofe. This code had two primary objectives: firstly to protect the general repute of the SS against the scandal of internal dissension and quarrels, and secondly to provide its individual members with a formal method of defending their honour with weapons. In dealing with cases which came into the first category, the Courts of Honour had only limited powers, their main function being to reconcile differences by means of arbitration. As regards cases in the second category, their purpose was to see that 'affairs of honour' were settled according to due form. In principle, all SS men were entitled to demand satisfaction with pistol or sword for affronts to their honour and integrity. However, the Schiedshofe usually intervened to prevent matters proceeding to an actual duel, particularly since Hitler had long set his face against the practice. Minor and Major Courts of Honour (Kleine und Grosse Schiedshofe) could be convened by the Reichsführer and by commanders of the Oberabschnitte, Abschnitte and SS Hauptämter. The minor courts carried out preliminary examinations of disputes and the major courts proceeded to actual adjudications.

A special class of SS legal officers or SS Richter existed to administer SS law. Full-time officials held their commissions directly from the Führer and their status and independence were guaranteed by the Reichsführer-SS. Their main duty was to prepare cases and conduct proceedings in court. These SS Richter were helped, and on occasion represented, by assistant legal officers or SS Hilfsrichter. SS protocol officers and NCOs (SS Beurkundungsführer und Unterführer) dealt with the preparation of documents, and examining officers (Untersuchungsführer) interviewed witnesses. All of these officers were subordinated to the Hauptamt SS Gericht. Their initial training and subsequent examinations took place at the Hauptamt and all appointments and promotions were issued from there.

As soon as the Special Jurisdiction of the SS and police was legally established, measures were taken to provide the SS organisation with facilities for carrying out sentences imposed by its courts. For this purpose punishment camps for the SS and police (Straflager der SS und Polizei) were set up at Dachau, near to the concentration camp, and at Karlsfeld. Moreover, prison camps (Strafvollzugslager) were instituted at Danzig and Ludwigsfelde. Minor periods of detention were generally completed in the relatively comfortable surroundings of the prison quarters of the SS barracks at Munich. Longer terms of imprisonment were served in one of the Strafvollzugslager. Execution of such sentences might at any time be postponed and the prisoner remitted to a Straflager, which represented an intensification in the severity of the sentence in that conditions at the punishment camps were much worse than those in the prisons, and the period served in the Straflager did not count towards the legal term of imprisonment still pending.

For men dismissed from the SS during the war, and simultaneously sentenced to a term of imprisonment, another possibility was open. They might choose to be handed over to one of the following two special formations of the Waffen-SS, in an attempt to redeem themselves while working out part of their sentence:

1. The Rehabilitation Detachment (Bewährungs Abteilung) at Chlum in Bohemia. After a period of initial training

there, the men were sent to units employed as fighting troops in the front line.

2. The Labour Detachment (Arbeits Abteilung) based at Debica in Poland. Members of that unit did not normally bear arms but were employed on heavy and dangerous work at the front, including bridge repair and minefield clearance.

For men dismissed from the police there was a similar formation attached to the SS-Police-Division, officially entitled the Sondereinheit der SS-Polizei-Division but colloquially known as the 'Verlorene Haufen' or VH, the 'Lost Souls'. Members of these special units did not rank as SS or police men and did not wear SS or police insignia on their uniforms.

While the SS punished its wrongdoers, those who conformed to the ideals of the Black Corps were very well cared for. The Reichsarzt SS und Polizei, or Chief SS and Police Medical Officer, SS-Ober-gruppenführer Prof. Dr Ernst-Robert Grawitz, was responsible for the general supervision of all the medical services of the SS and police, for medical research and training, and for the control and distribution of medical supplies and equipment. He was assisted by two senior officials, the Chief Medical Quartermaster, SS-Gruppenführer Dr Carl Blumenreuter, and the Chief Hygiene Officer, SS-Oberführer Prof. Dr Joachim Mrugowsky. Grawitz was also Business President of the German Red Cross and used that position to ensure that the SS kept up to date with all the latest international medical developments. Moreover, Himmler purposely gave senior SS rank to many German doctors of renown, including Karl Gebhardt, head of the famous Hohenlychen Orthopaedic Clinic, and Leonardo Conti, the Reich Minister of Health. In this way, the SS was kept at the forefront of medical technology, and the

Sanitätsstürme and Sanitätsstaffeln attached to the Abschnitte and Sturmbanne were able to provide the best treatment possible to ailing SS members and their families.

The whole relationship between the SS and most medical men came to be soured during the war, however, when Himmler was persuaded by his hard-pressed Waffen-SS battlefield surgeons and certain military scientists to allow live research to take place among condemned inmates of concentration camps. Those inmates who agreed to take part in potentially fatal experiments, and who survived them, would have their death sentences commuted to life imprisonment, albeit 'life' in a concentration camp after 1942 probably meant a few months at most. The Luftwaffe doctor Sigmund Rascher was one of those 'researchers' with the most sinister reputation. He carried out meaningless medical experiments at Dachau on the effects of decompression on prisoners, and thereafter turned his attention to the problems of survival in cold conditions, then survival in extreme heat. Rascher was continually 'sucking up' to Himmler. The following extracts from letters give an indication of the spirit of these times:

Dr Rascher to Camp Commandant Weiss, Dachau, 10 October 1942
The Russian prisoner of war Chonitsch, born 24 May 1920, was transferred to me on 28 September for experimental purposes. Chonitsch is a Russian who was to be executed. As the Reichsführer-SS had ordered me to use persons sentenced to death for dangerous experiments, I wanted to conduct an experiment on this Russian which I was absolutely sure he would not survive. I reported at the time that you could be assured that the Russian would certainly not survive the experiment and would be dead by the time of his scheduled execution date. Contrary to all

expectations, the Russian in question survived three experiments which would have been fatal for any other person. In accordance with the Reichsführer's order that all test subjects who are sentenced to death but survive a dangerous experiment should be pardoned, I beg to take the appropriate steps. I regret that the wrong assumption on our part has given rise to extra correspondence work. With many thanks and Heil Hitler! RASCHER.

Camp Commandant Weiss, Dachau, to the Reichsführer-SS, 20 October 1942
Highly esteemed Reichsführer! Will you please clarify the following case as soon as possible. In your letter of 18 April 1942, it is ordered that if prisoners in Dachau condemned to death live through experiments which have endangered their lives, they should be pardoned to life-long concentration camp imprisonment. I respectfully ask if this order applies to Poles and Russians, as well as to non-Slavs. Heil Hitler! WEISS.

SS-Obersturmbannführer Brandt, Reichsführung-SS, to Weiss, 21 October 1942
Weiss. Please inform SS-Untersturmführer Dr Rascher that the instruction given some time ago by the Reichsführer-SS concerning the pardoning of experimental subjects does not apply to Poles and Russians. Heil Hitler! BRANDT.

It can be assumed, therefore, that the unfortunate Chonitsch was duly killed. Eventually, the SS concluded that Rascher was nothing more than a dangerous charlatan evading front-line service, and sentenced him to death in April 1945.

However, not all medical studies carried out at the camps were of such a fantastic nature. One of the benefits others provided was the development of haemostatic and coagulant products which did much to help wounded men in the Wehrmacht during the Second World War and, indeed, injured soldiers of all nations thereafter. Nevertheless, even the ordinary doctors of the Allgemeine-SS, whose only concern was the welfare of their men and who had nothing whatsoever to do with these matters, eventually came to be tarred with the same brush as Rascher and his accomplices in the minds of the postwar public.

Medicine apart, the main welfare activities of the Allgemeine-SS were administered by the Rasse- und Siedlungshauptamt and financed from the private funds of the SS. The concept of the SS as 'one big family' resulted in considerable care being devoted to the provision of financial help for those members in need of it. Even in the early days of the organisation, before the profits of office and established position put the finances of the SS on a sound footing, a special Economic Assistance Section was set up under the auspices of Himmler's headquarters to provide help to SS men who had suffered material loss during the struggle for power. In November 1935, the Reichsführer put the matter on a more businesslike basis by instituting a savings fund to which all future SS recruits in employment and all serving full-time officers and men were to contribute according to their means. In this way, the SS was able to build from its own resources the necessary financial reserve from which assistance could be given or loans made to its members.

All commanders of Oberabschnitte, Abschnitte, Standarten and Sturmbanne had a general duty to look after the welfare of their subordinates and particularly of the widows and orphans of deceased SS men. Each Abschnitt and Standarte had a welfare official or Fürsorgereferent, usually an NCO, who was the primary local authority to which

SS men and their relatives could appeal. Questions outside his competence were referred to the Sippenpflegestelle (Family Welfare Office) of the Oberabschnitt and, if required, could be passed on up yet again to the Sippenamt, or Family Office, of the Rasse- und Siedlungshauptamt for a decision. Where an SS man died or was killed on active service and left a widow and children, the Oberabschnitt appointed a suitable SS man as Berater, or family adviser. He gave as much personal advice and help as was possible, assumed responsibility for the education of the children and, when necessary, called in the assistance of the welfare official.

In addition to the private SS welfare system, members of the Allgemeine-SS serving in the Wehrmacht also enjoyed all the advantages of the statutory welfare system established for the armed forces. Moreover, the SS Hauptamt controlled a number of rest homes for SS and police servicemen and provided mobilised SS units with light entertainments such as films, concert parties, radio sets, books and magazines.

Since it had long been recognised that the prevention of illness was as important as curing it, sport and physical fitness were given great emphasis in the day-to-day training programmes of the Allgemeine-SS, and there were many local SS sports clubs. Members were eligible to win not only the SA Military Sports Badge and the German National Sports Badge, which they strove for during their term as SS-Anwärter, but also the Achievement and Championship Badges of the National Socialist Physical Training League, the Heavy Athletics Badge, the German Motor Sports Badge, ski competition badges, and the various national equestrian awards. Many of these decorations had to be competed for annually, i.e. holders had to pass the set qualification tests at least once every year in order to retain the right to wear the badges concerned, so training was a continual and ongoing process.

The SS Hauptamt was charged with the overall responsibility for SS physical training. In August 1942, a decree of the Reichsführer-SS enlarged and consolidated that function as follows:

1. The organisation and control of all physical training for the whole SS, including routine training, competitive events and military sports, was the responsibility of the SS Hauptamt.
2. The Chief of the SS Hauptamt, Obergruppenführer Berger, was appointed Inspector of SS Physical Training and Deputy Leader of the SS Sports Clubs (Inspekteur für die Leibeserziehung der SS und stellvertretender Führer der SS Sportsgemeinschaften e.V.).
3. Amt V of the SS Hauptamt was made the competent department for the physical training of the whole SS, with the title of Amt für Leibesübungen.
4. The former office of the Inspector and Central Directorate of SS Sports Clubs was incorporated into Amt V.
5. The Chief of Amt V was appointed Deputy Inspector of SS Physical Training.
6. The SS Central School of Physical Training in Prague, which taught SS sports instructors, was directly subordinated to the Chief of the SS Hauptamt.

In March 1943, a slight extension of the functions of the SS Hauptamt in this respect took place. By an agreement between the Reichsführer-SS and the German Life Saving Society (Deutsche Lebensrettungs-gemeinschaft e.V., or DLRG), the SS and police formed a special section of the Society under the title of 'Landesverband SS und Polizei der DLRG', with offices at 18 Bülowstrasse,

Disabled servicemen competing on the games field during their convalescence, 28 March 1942. The man on the right wears SS sports kit.

Berlin. The Chief of the SS Hauptamt or his deputy acted as representative of the SS and police at the central headquarters of the Society. The function of the Landesverband was to promote lifesaving and artificial respiration techniques and, thereafter, hold examinations and grant relevant proficiency certificates. It took in all formations of the Allgemeine-SS, Waffen-SS, SD, security police and uniformed police, and instruction was given in conjunction with physical training.

The Reichssportführer, or National Sports Leader, was an SA-Obergruppenführer, Hans von Tschammer und Osten, and consequently the SA tended to organise most of the paramilitary competitive sports events during the Third Reich. At these domestic competitions, however, the SS and police teams always figured prominently and invariably dominated the scene. In February 1937, for example, the SS won the Führer's Prize at the NSDAP Ski Championships at Rottach-Egern, and Himmler and von Tschammer und Osten were present to award it. Internationally, too, SS men made their mark. Hermann Fegelein led Germany's equestrian squad in the 1936 Olympics, and the SS motorcycle team of Zimmermann, Mundhenke, Patina and Knees, all wearing green leathers emblazoned with the SS runes, won the Six Day Trial at Donnington in England in July 1938. Later the same year, an SD team headed by Heydrich himself and comprising von Friedenfeldt, Hainke, Liebscher and Losert, all graduates of the SS-

Fechtschule, or SS Fencing School, at Bernau, emerged victorious from the International Sabre Competition in Berlin. Finally, in April 1940, Italy's famous Gran Premio di Brescia motor racing event was won by the SS driver von Manstein in a BMW 328 coupé. Not surprisingly, SS physical training establishments attracted outstanding talent, and at one time eight out of the twelve coaches at the Junkerschule at Bad Tölz were national champions in their events.

Conditions of service in the Allgemeine-SS were therefore very good in terms of the society in which the organisation grew and developed. Members' duties were not onerous, at least prior to the war, and there were excellent promotion prospects, fine medical and welfare facilities, and the very best sporting opportunities. Moreover, the SS man was placed above the law. He and his family were accorded special status, as the physical and racial élite of the new Germany.

THE RACIAL ELITE

In January 1935, Himmler addressed an audience of senior Wehrmacht officers on his vision of the Third Reich. 'I am,' he said, 'a convinced supporter of the idea that the only thing which really matters in the world is good blood. History teaches us that only good blood, in particular the blood engaged in military activity and, above all, Nordic blood, is the leading creative element in every State. I have always approached my task from this angle, and will continue to do so.' It is perhaps surprising, given the generally non-Nazi nature of the audience, that such a statement was accepted at face value, as a valid and realistic opinion to expound. However, it is important to appreciate that this Nazi form of racism was nothing new in Germany. The notion that the Germanic master race or Herrenvolk had somehow been endowed with an inherent superiority, contrasting particularly sharply with the corrupt characteristics of Slavs, Latins and Jews, had enjoyed widespread support in Germany since the mid-nineteenth century. Theories were regularly propounded that stronger peoples had a natural right to dominate or even exterminate weaker nations in the general struggle for survival, and various versions of the message, often supported by the claims of scientific research, appeared in German, British and other European journals over the years.

One of the early twentieth-century proponents of racial ideology was Alfred Rosenberg, born the son of an Estonian shoemaker in 1893. Rosenberg studied in Russia, and received a degree in architecture from the University of Moscow. Having fled to Germany after the Russian Revolution, he settled in Munich and joined the Thule Society, whose members specialised in anti-Bolshevik and anti-Semitic philosophy. In 1920 he enrolled in the Nazi party with membership number 18, and immediately won Hitler's attention with the publication of the first of his many books attacking Judaism. In 1923, Rosenberg was nominated by the Führer as editor of the NSDAP newspaper, the *Völkischer Beobachter*, which thereafter vigorously denounced communists, Jews, Freemasons and Christians. Rosenberg ultimately proposed a new religion which would counter the weak doctrine of Christian love with a strong ideal of racial superiority. In 1930 he produced his masterpiece, *The Myth of the Twentieth Century*, a massive tome which concluded that any given culture would always decay when humanitarian ideals obstructed the right of the dominant race to rule those whom it had subjugated. The latter were degraded in the book to the level of Untermenschen, or sub-humans. According to Rosenberg, the mixture of blood, and the sinking of the racial standard contingent upon it, was the primary cause for the demise of all cultures. Although over 20 million copies of *The Myth of the Twentieth Century* were eventually sold, few people could be found who actually had the stamina to wade through it from cover to cover. Hitler himself had to admit to 'giving up' half way through the book.

One who did read and admire Rosenberg's theories, however, was Richard Walther Darré, a First World War artillery officer who turned to agriculture after 1918 and whose consuming enthusiasm was the peasantry. In 1929 he wrote a book entitled *Blood and Soil – The Peasantry as the Life Source of the Nordic Race*, which called for an energetic programme of selective breeding to ensure the increase of Nordic peasant stock and their domination of the Jews and Slavs. In Darré's view, blood alone determined history, ethics, law and economics, and the blood of the German farmer was related to the ground he worked. The argument ran like this. The farmer who toiled the land would be buried in the same soil, therefore the farmer's daily bread was, in fact, the blood of his forefathers, which fertilised the earth. German blood would be passed on from generation to generation by means of the soil. Himmler loved Darré's book, befriended its author, and took him into the SS to pursue his research with official sanction and financial backing. At Hitler's request, Darré later prepared an agricultural policy for the NSDAP which favoured Aryan farmers and re-established the medieval hereditary system by which no farmland could ever be sold or mortgaged.

Heavily influenced by Darré, Himmler now began to use agricultural metaphors to justify his new SS recruitment policy of racial selection. In 1931 he wrote: 'We are like a plant-breeding specialist who, when he wants to breed a pure new strain, first goes over the field to cull the unwanted plants. We, too, shall begin by weeding out people who are

Introductory page to a series of prints by the renowned German artist Wolfgang Willrich, commissioned by Himmler in 1936 to illustrate the racial purity of the SS.

not suitable SS material'. Applicants for the SS were soon being categorised according to their racial characteristics, from I-a-M/1 (racially very suitable) to IV-3-c (racial reject). Himmler's rapidly increasing obsession with racial purity began to motivate more and more of his schemes during the 1930s. At his behest, the SS kept a genealogical register of its members, and the Reichsführer often pored over it like a horse-breeder examining a stud book. He ordered elaborate investigations into his own ancestry and that of his wife, to gather irrefutable evidence of their pure German lineage, and he dreamed of a new feudal Europe, cleared of Untermenschen, in which model farms would be operated by a racial élite. The spearhead

Willrich print depicting the ideal SS soldier.

of that élite was to be the SS, an 'Orden nordischer Rasse', or Order of Nordic Men, of the purest selection, acting as guardians of the German people. The SS would become a 'Blutgemeinschaft', a blood community. To paraphrase Himmler, they would 'march onward into a distant future, imbued with the hope and faith not only that they might put up a better fight than their forefathers but that they might themselves be the forefathers of generations to come, generations which would be necessary for the eternal life of the Teutonic German nation'. As late as 1943, when SS manpower shortages were desperate, the discovery of even minor racial blemishes ('borderline type – eighteenth-century Jewish ancestor') resulted in a swift removal of SS officers from their positions.

As foretold in *Mein Kampf*, Hitler's Nürnberg Laws of 1935 deprived Germany's Jews of Reich citizenship, the vote and eligibility for appointment to state offices. Marriage or extra-marital relations between Jews and Germans was forbidden, and Jewish businesses closed down. By 1938, the Nazis were raising an international loan to finance the emigration of all German Jews and their resettlement on some of Germany's former colonies overseas. When war broke out, however, Jews began to be moved instead to ghettos in occupied Poland, which was a cheaper and more expedient alternative. This racial fanaticism reached its ultimate and infamous conclusion at the end of 1941, when it became clear that an easy victory would not be won and that the Second World War might drag on for years. The complex prewar plans for the peaceful removal of Jews and Slavs from Reich territory were now shelved. Einsatzgruppen in the east had been executing Jews and suspected partisans on an ad hoc basis since the invasion of Russia, but the actual process of killing was random and had to be accelerated. On 20 January 1942, Heydrich convened a meeting of representatives of the various government ministries at the pleasant Berlin suburb of Wannsee, and they decided upon a much simpler and irrevocable 'Final Solution' to the problem. All the Jews and Slavs of Europe and western Russia were to be rounded up and transported to specified locations to be worked to death, then cremated. Those who were unfit for work would be killed on arrival by gassing. To that end, large Vernichtungslager, or extermination camps, were established at Auschwitz, Belzec, Chelmno, Majdanek, Sobibor and Treblinka, all in Poland, and minor ones were set up at Kaunas, Lwow, Minsk, Riga and Vilna. Naturally, all were placed under the control of the Reich's racial warriors, the SS. By the end of 1943, most of the death camps had completed their horrific work and had been closed down and demolished. The gas chambers at Auschwitz and Majdanek, however, continued almost until the arrival of the Soviet army. Those still alive in the slave labour barracks at Auschwitz and Majdanek as the Russians approached were force-marched westwards, to Dachau and Belsen, where tens of thousands died of starvation. In 1946, the Nürnberg indictment concluded that these camps witnessed the deaths of 5,700,000 Jews, Slavs and gypsies between 1942 and 1945, in the Nazi drive towards the 'racial purification of Europe'.

At Auschwitz, the main extermination camp complex, which comprised twenty labour camps and four massive gas chambers, racial experiments were carried out in the same way that Rascher engaged upon military medical experiments at Dachau. Skeletons of victims were collected for racially-based 'scientific measurements'. Skulls and skin types were compared, eyes and noses categorised, brains weighed and hair graded. An assortment of SS eugenists from Ahnenerbe strove to prove by their research that humans could be bred exactly like animals, with full pedigrees. The most infamous of them all was Josef Mengele, a Doctor of Philosophy (Munich) and a Doctor of Medicine (Frankfurt/Main), who was rabidly inspired by the hope of eliminating all racial impurities and physical abnormalities from the German people. He served as a medical officer with the Waffen-SS in France and Russia, and in 1943 was appointed Chief Doctor at Auschwitz, with *carte blanche* from Himmler and an unlimited supply of human guinea-pigs at his disposal. At once, he began a study of deformities. All prisoners who were in any way malformed were immediately butchered upon their arrival at Auschwitz so that Mengele and his team could examine the bodies in a special dissection ward. No twins, dwarves or hunchbacks escaped his scalpel. He even sewed normal twins together to create

artificial Siamese twins, and injected the brown eyes of living patients in an effort to turn them blue. These racial experiments caused untold agonies and had little or no practical benefits, unlike some of the purely medical experiments carried out in other camps.

Modern apologists for the Waffen-SS have consistently put forward the argument that the horrors which took place in concentration and extermination camps during the war must have been unknown to ordinary SS soldiers fighting at the battlefront, on the basis that the camps had nothing at all to do with the Waffen-SS. However, the fact is that from April 1941 the camps were classified by Himmler as an integral part of the Waffen-SS system. From that time on, during the worst atrocities, camp officers and guards wore Waffen-SS uniforms with distinctive brown piping and carried Waffen-SS paybooks. The permanent camp administrative staffs of older Totenkopf NCOs were reinforced by substantial numbers of wounded and recuperating personnel transferred in on a temporary rota basis from various battlefield SS units, of which the Totenkopf-Division was only one. For example, Feldgendarmerie elements of the Leibstandarte and men from the 13th SS-Division were stationed at Buchenwald and Gross-Rosen camps in 1943, while 'Wiking' Division troops found themselves in the unfortunate position of manning Belsen when it was liberated by the British. Karl Gebhardt, supervisor of medical and racial experiments at the camps, had formerly been a front-line surgeon with SS-Division 'Das Reich', and Richard Glücks, the man in daily charge of the whole concentration camp system, was a Waffen-SS general as well as being Inspekteur der Konzentrationslager. The Waffen-SS men who transiently staffed the camps took their directions from the permanent cadre of Totenkopfverbände veterans, and were

Security policemen searching Jews in the Warsaw Ghetto, November 1939.

An SS medical officer, from Mengele's staff, examining a newly arrived consignment of Jews at the railway sidings at Auschwitz-Birkenau in 1944. Those deemed unfit for work in the SS factories were despatched for immediate gassing.

assisted by foreign auxiliaries, selected prisoners, and even a few factory guards, SA and Wehrmacht personnel in 1944–5. So while the WVHA administered the camps and the RSHA decided who was to be incarcerated in them, members of the Waffen-SS effectively ran them and were certainly not exempt from practising the Final Solution at grass-roots level. It is still a common misconception that 'the black-uniformed Allgemeine-SS staffed the concentration camps'.

Under Himmler, the SS came to regard itself not merely as a temporary political association but as a 'Sippe', i.e. a tribe or clan. The same racial qualities looked for in

the SS man were therefore also required of his wife. The Engagement and Marriage Order of the SS, one of the oldest fundamental laws of the organisation, was issued by Himmler on 31 December 1931, and read as follows:

1. The SS is an association of German men, defined according to their Nordic blood and specially selected.
2. In conformity with the National Socialist conception of the world, and recognising that the future of our people is founded on selection and the preservation of good German blood, free from all taint of hereditary disease, I now require all members of the SS to obtain the

Young German girls from a Lebensborn home, their heads garlanded with flowers in pagan style, give the Nazi salute at Nürnberg in 1938.

authorisation of the Reichsführer-SS before marriage.

3. Consent to marry will be given solely on the grounds of racial or physical considerations, and with a view to congenital health.

4. Any SS man who marries without seeking the prior authorisation of the Reichsführer-SS, or who marries in spite of being refused such authorisation, will be dismissed from the SS.

H. HIMMLER.

To administer the racial and marriage procedures, Himmler created the SS Race and Settlement Office on the same day the order was issued, and placed it under Darré, his racial guru.

The main objects looked for in adjudging the marriage applications of SS men were, firstly, racial purity and, secondly, physical compatibility between the two partners likely to result in a fertile union. Thus an application to marry an elderly woman, or a woman markedly bigger or smaller than the intended husband, was likely to be rejected. The prospective bride and her family had to prove their Aryan ancestry back to the mid-eighteenth century, uncontaminated by the presence of Jewish or Slavonic ancestors. She further had to demonstrate that she was free from all mental and physical disease and had to submit to an exhaustive medical examination, including fertility testing, by SS doctors. Only after a couple had successfully completed all these tests could an SS marriage take place. More than a few members found the marriage regulations impossible to live with, and in 1937 alone 300 men were expelled from the SS for marrying without approval.

Christian weddings were replaced in the Allgemeine-SS by pseudo-pagan rites presided over by the bridegroom's commander. Marriages no longer took place in churches, but in the open air under lime trees or in SS buildings decorated with life runes, sunflowers and fir twigs. An eternal flame burned in an urn in front of which the couple swore oaths of loyalty, exchanged rings and received the official SS gift of bread and salt, symbols of the earth's fruitfulness and purity. A presentation copy of *Mein Kampf* was then taken from a heavy oak casket carved with runes, and handed over to the groom. Finally, as the couple departed from the ceremony, they invariably passed through a sombre arcade of saluting SS brethren.

During the war, the position as regards Allgemeine-SS men serving in the Wehrmacht became fairly unclear, for a decree published in Army Orders on 27 October 1943 stated that the decision on the marriage of such persons to foreigners rested with the Reichsführer-SS. Requests for permission were to be forwarded through official service channels to the competent High Command which would then transmit the request to RuSHA for a final decision. The implication, at least, of this decree was that marriage between SS men in the Wehrmacht and females who were Reich German nationals no longer required the authorisation of the Reichsführer-SS.

The SS maintained colonies for the convenience of its married personnel. Eight of these existed in 1944. Four (Auschwitz, Buchenwald, Dachau and Oranienburg) were located at the large SS settlements which grew up around or near concentration camps, and the remainder (Berlin, Graz, Radolfzell and

Wien) were in the neighbourhood of main SS headquarters, barracks or schools. In addition, three colonies specifically for married officers of the Allgemeine-SS were established at Bad Frankenhausen, Jüterbog and Klagenfurt.

It is interesting to note that the marriage rules applied not only to male members of the SS but also to female employees and auxiliaries. In the case of the latter, if they were already married when they applied for appointment with the SS, they were obliged to produce on behalf of their husbands records and genealogical charts going back to the grandparents, for examination by RuSHA.

The SS demanded that its racial élite should breed quickly and multiply, to compensate for the catastrophic losses of manpower suffered between 1914 and 1918. In 1931, Himmler announced that it was the patriotic mission of every SS couple to produce at least four children, and where that was not possible the SS pair were expected to adopt racially suitable orphans and bring them up on National Socialist lines. To show the interest the SS had in its children, the organisation created a range of official gifts for them. At the birth of their first child, Himmler sent each set of SS parents a ribbon and bib of blue silk, symbolising the unity of birth, marriage, life and death, and a silver beaker and spoon representing eternal nourishment. During the subsequent pagan naming ceremony, which replaced the traditional christening in SS circles, the child would be wrapped in a shawl of undyed wool embroidered with oak leaves, runes and swastikas, while both parents placed their hands on the baby's head and pronounced names such as Karl or Siegfried, Gudrun or Helga, and, of course, Adolf or Heinrich. The Reichsführer served as nominal godfather to all SS children born each year on the anniversary of his birth, 7 October, and on

The future SS: new pupils on parade at the Potsdam NPEA, 1938.

the birth of a fourth child he sent the happy parents a letter of congratulations and a Lebensleuchter, a silver candlestick engraved with the words, 'You are a link in the eternal racial chain'.

However, the SS birthrate during the 1930s remained average for the country as a whole. Wages were low, and children were expensive. On 13 September 1936, in a further desperate attempt to encourage SS families to have more offspring, the Reichsführer established a registered society known as Lebensborn, or the Fountain of Life. Senior full-time SS officers were expected to make financial contributions so that the Society could provide maternity homes to which both married and unmarried mothers of SS children could be admitted free of charge. Although affiliated to RuSHA,

Lebensborn was directly subordinated to SS-Standartenführer Max Sollmann of the Hauptamt Persönlicher Stab RfSS. Its stated objectives were:

1. to assist in sustaining large racially valuable families
2. to look after pregnant women of good race
3. to care for the children of racially suitable unions

Maternity homes were quickly set up at Hohehorst, Klosterheide, Polzin, Steinhöring and Wienerwald, and Himmler took an intense personal interest in them. Every detail fascinated him, from the shapes of the noses of newly born infants to the volume of milk produced by nursing mothers, the most prolific of whom received Mothers' Crosses and other special recognitions. Any babies appearing with mental or physical handicaps were smothered at birth and, so far as the mothers were concerned, were said to be 'still-born'. Despite the contemporary salacious rumours about brothels and 'SS stud farms', only a small percentage of children appearing from the Society's homes in peacetime were illegitimate. The establishment of the Lebensborn homes was a genuine attempt by Himmler to provide free but high-quality maternity care for the poorer SS families.

The outbreak of war in 1939 stimulated the Reichsführer to remind all members of the SS that it was now their most urgent duty to become fathers. On 28 November, he issued the following instruction:

Order to the SS and Police.
Every war involves a shedding of the purest blood. A multitude of victories will mean a great loss of it, but the death of our best men will not in itself be the ultimate consequence. What will be worse will be the absence of children who have not been procreated by the living during the war, and who most certainly cannot be procreated by the dead after the war. Regardless of the civil law and normal bourgeois customs, it must now be the duty of all German women and girls of good blood to become mothers of the children of SS soldiers going to the front. Official guardians will take over the wardship of all legitimate and illegitimate children of good blood whose fathers have fallen in the war, and the Chief of the RuSHA and his staff will observe discretion in the keeping of documentation relating to the parentage of illegitimate children. SS men must see clearly that, in complying with this order, they will perform an act of great

importance. Mockery, disdain and non-comprehension will not affect us, for the future belongs to us!

H. HIMMLER

It was the same concern to ensure the future of the race which was behind Himmler's subsequent 'Special Order' of 15 August, 1942. It indicated that when an SS family had only one son left, and he was of military age, he would be withdrawn from the battlefield and sent home for anything up to a year, or at least long enough to find a mate and make her pregnant, so as to 'preserve his lineage'. Therefore, no justification could exist for SS men to fall short of their biological duty. In fact, failure to carry it out hampered their careers. By virtue of a Himmler memorandum issued in February 1944, all recommendations for the promotion of married SS officers had henceforth to include details of their date of marriage, age of wife, number of children and date of birth of the last child. Where the last child was born more than two years previously, and where the wife was not over forty years of age, an explanation had to be added as to why no more children had been conceived. If there was no sufficient explanation, the application for promotion would be rejected. In a similar vein, a forty-four-year-old bachelor, SS-Hauptsturmführer Franz Schwarz, was threatened in 1943 that if he had not married within the year, he would be dismissed from the SS!

The Lebensborn Society continued to operate until the end of the war, and new SS maternity homes were opened up in Oslo, Schwarzwald, Schloss Wegimont in Belgium, and Taunus. Suitable foreign children, usually war orphans and even infants who had been torn from their Polish, Czech or Russian families by VOMI officials because they were recognised as being of Nordic descent, were accepted into Lebensborn homes to be adopted by childless SS couples. Ultimately, more than 80,000 non-German children were thus 'Germanised' by the SS.

As SS racial policies expanded and developed, so too did the departments charged with their administration. Darré's Race and Settlement Office achieved Hauptamt status on 30 January 1935, as the SS Rasse- und Siedlungshauptamt or RuSHA, the SS Race and Settlement Department. It was therefore one of the three oldest Hauptämter in the Reichsführung-SS, and by 1937 consisted of the following seven ämter:

I – Organisation & Verwaltungsamt (Organisation & Administration)
II – Rassenamt (Race)
III – Schulungsamt (Education)
IV – Sippen- und Heiratsamt (Family & Marriage)
V – Siedlungsamt (Settlement)
VI – Amt für Archiv und Zeitungswesen (Records & Press)
VII – Amt für Bevölkerungspolitik (Population Policy)

In the general reorganisation of the SS administration which took place in 1940, RuSHA, like the SS Hauptamt, lost some of its functions and retained only the Rassenamt, Sippen- und Heiratsamt, Siedlungsamt and Verwaltungsamt. It was thus stripped down to the bare essentials for continuing the work indicated by its title. Nevertheless, in spite of this restriction in its field of activity, the volume of work undertaken by RuSHA necessarily increased with the progress of the war. That was due partly to the physical expansion of the SS, and partly to the repatriation of racial Germans from Russia and the Balkans and their resettlement in Germany and the occupied areas of Poland.

The main duty of RuSHA was to translate into practice the general racial theories of SS ideology. To assist in the execution of its policy it had a special officer (Führer im Rasse- und Siedlungswesen) on the staff of each Oberabschnitt, and Family Welfare Offices (Sippenpflegestellen) set up in the larger towns of Germany and the occupied territories. With the racial laws of the SS as a basis, it was the task of RuSHA and its agencies to supervise the selection and breeding of SS men and to foster the general well-being of the SS in accordance with its code of 'tribal solidarity'. RuSHA was the only competent authority for checking the racial and genealogical records of SS recruits. In peacetime, and in wartime so far as the Allgemeine-SS was concerned, these checking procedures were strictly adhered to. With the rapid expansion of the Waffen-SS after 1940, however, the racial rules became something of a dead letter for its 750,000 rank and file. During the war, the hard-pressed RuSHA authorities were content to accept a signed declaration of Aryan descent from enlisted German and west European Waffen-SS men, which could be investigated later when the opportunity presented itself. RuSHA was also responsible for issuing one-year marriage permits, or Heiratserlaubnis, on behalf of the Reichsführer-SS, granting his approval for SS personnel to wed. Another of its functions was to keep the Sippenbuch, or Family Book of SS members, and it compiled a register of all SS men willing and suited to become colonists in the occupied territories. In addition, RuSHA was responsible for SS and police welfare, particularly the maintenance of orphans and widows of SS and police men killed in the war, and the care of families and dependants of SS men serving in the Wehrmacht and Waffen-SS in all cases of distress, hardship or private difficulty. By 1944, RuSHA had absorbed the Hauptfürsorge und Versorgungsamt der Waffen-SS und Polizei (HFVA), the Waffen-SS and Police Welfare und Pensions Department. The rehabilitation and retraining for civil or administrative posts of war-disabled SS men formed a further part of the work of RuSHA, and for that purpose it controlled two training schools at Schleissheim and Mittweida and a craft school at Bernau near Berlin. Moreover, there was a very close co-operation between RuSHA and Lebensborn in view of the overlapping nature of their work and, while Lebensborn was technically subordinated to the Hauptamt Persönlicher Stab RfSS, RuSHA was the normal channel through which it received its instructions from Himmler.

Darré headed RuSHA until February 1938, when he quarrelled with Himmler and left to concentrate on his government career as Minister of Agriculture. He was succeeded by Obergruppenführer Günther Pancke, later HSSPf in Denmark, and in July 1940 by Obergruppenführer Otto Hofmann, subsequently HSSPf in Oberabschnitt Südwest. The last chief of the Rasse- und Siedlungshauptamt was Obergruppenführer Richard Hildebrandt, who took over in April 1943. Although Hildebrandt had an active appointment abroad as HSSPf Black Sea during 1943–4, he did not relinquish his post as Chef RuSHA. His deputy, SS-Gruppenführer Dr Harald Turner, covered for him during his absence in Russia.

A cornerstone of SS racial policy was the desire to reunite the Volksdeutsche with their German relations. When the Nazis came to power, millions of these Volksdeutsche, or ethnic Germans, were living in central and eastern Europe. Ever since the Middle Ages, their ancestors had moved eastwards from their original German territories to find new lands and livelihoods. Settling in an enormous region stretching from the Baltic states in the north to the Volga and the Caucasus in the south, these migrants formed closely knit communities that remained independent of their neighbours and retained strong ties of kinship with the old 'Heimat'. They had their own association, the League for Germans Abroad, or Volksbund für das Deutschtum in Ausland (VDA), which was taken over by the NSDAP in 1930 and put under the direction of Werner Lorenz, a former First World War pilot who owned a vast estate near Danzig and had the reputation of being something of a *bon vivant*. Lorenz joined the SS in 1931, and his sophisticated lifestyle, combined with his unique ability to be equally at ease with diplomats and peasant farmers alike, soon brought him to Himmler's attention.

From the outset, the Nazis were counting on ethnic Germans to augment their new Reich's depleted population and help in its ultimate expansion eastwards. Himmler in particular vowed to take German blood from wherever it could be found in the world, and to 'rob and steal it' whenever he could. To that end, an agency of the NSDAP known as the Büro von Kursell was formed in March 1936 to co-ordinate attempts to encourage the return of the Volksdeutsche to Germany. In 1937 it was renamed the Volksdeutsche Mittelstelle or VOMI, the Department for the Repatriation of Racial Germans, and put under the direction of Lorenz, now an SS-Obergruppenführer. Under Lorenz, VOMI performed so efficiently that in July 1938 Hitler increased its power by allowing it to absorb the VDA and similar agencies, bring together rival factions in the ethnic German communities, and generate money to build recreational facilities and hospitals and spread Nazi propaganda. As an SS-inspired aside, VOMI also investigated the politics of individual ethnic Germans, and began compiling files on those suspected of opposition to the Führer. Although VOMI was not formally incorporated into the Allgemeine-SS structure until 1941, Himmler very quickly made it his own instrument. He infiltrated SS men into the department from its earliest days, and persuaded its existing staff to join the SS. The Reichsführer also installed as Lorenz's deputy an SS colleague, Gruppenführer Dr Hermann Behrends of the SD, by which means Heydrich was soon using VOMI to plant SD officials in far-flung communities of ethnic Germans in eastern Europe.

Himmler first exercised his new-found authority in foreign affairs in Czechoslovakia. Created after the old Austro-Hungarian empire was carved up in 1919, Czechoslovakia was home to more than 3 million people of German descent. Most of these Volksdeutsche lived in the country's western part, the Sudetenland, and their presence became a wedge by which Hitler began to splinter the Czech republic in 1938. He used VOMI and the SS to continuously penetrate Sudeten communities. SD *agents provocateurs* played upon the grievances of the Sudeten Germans, who had been hard hit by the depression and felt mistreated by the Czech government, and SS funds subsidised the pro-Nazi Sudeten German Party under Dr Konrad Henlein. Heydrich won the allegiance of Henlein's deputy, Karl Hermann Frank, and VOMI helped form a secret fifth column to subvert the Czech government in the event of a German invasion. However, the mere threat of armed conflict was sufficient for the Czechs to cede the Sudetenland to Germany as of 1 October 1938. Henlein became Gauleiter of the area, and both he and Frank were rewarded by Himmler with the rank of SS-Gruppenführer.

The emergence of the SS as a force in foreign policy had relegated von Ribbentrop's diplomats to a back seat during the Sudeten crisis, and Hitler again looked to VOMI and the SS as he plotted to take over the rest of Czechoslovakia. Late in January 1939, the Führer assigned Heydrich and other leading members of the SD key roles in the final dismemberment of the country. Hitler's plan hinged upon provoking trouble in the eastern provinces of Slovakia, where nationalist feelings had been stirred by the events in the Sudetenland. A team of SS men led by Gruppenführer Wilhelm Keppler set off bombs in Bratislava and put the blame on the Slovaks. VOMI organised street demonstrations and SD groups led by Heydrich's troubleshooter, Alfred Naujocks, carried out further acts of provocation. On 15 March, rather than risk war, the Czechoslovakian President agreed to German 'protection' of the provinces of Bohemia and Moravia, while Slovakia became a German puppet state and Hungary grabbed the easternmost and last remaining province, Ruthenia. Late in August 1939, Hitler turned to the SS once more to provide his excuse for invading Poland. Heydrich dreamed up scores of incidents which could be attributed to Polish extremists and thus justify a German attack. These were played out by a dozen teams of SD men and police officers under the Gestapo chief, Heinrich Müller. The most important of the bogus raids, codenamed 'Operation Himmler', was launched by Alfred Naujocks against a German radio station at the border town of Gleiwitz on 31 August. The following day, citing the Gleiwitz incident as the reason for his actions, Hitler declared war on Poland.

During September 1939, the advances of the Red Army into eastern Poland in accordance with the Nazi-Soviet Pact brought some 136,000 Volksdeutsche under Russian occupation. In discussions with Berlin, however, the Soviets agreed to let these people leave. Moreover, the Reich also negotiated for the transfer of another 120,000 ethnic Germans living in the Baltic states. Throughout the winter of 1939–40, the first 35,000 east European Volksdeutsche were evacuated from Wolhynia. The provisions of the Russo-German Resettlement Treaty had to be completed by November

1940, and during October alone some 45,000 rapidly uprooted men, women and children made the long and so-called 'final trek' from Bessarabia and northern Bukovina to VOMI reception camps in Pomerania, East Prussia and the Warthegau before leaving for permanent resettlement in the incorporated Polish territory. By mid-1941, 200,000 ethnic German repatriates had been given possession of 47,000 confiscated Polish farms comprising a total of 23 million acres, in the two new Reichsgaue of Danzig-West Prussia and Wartheland.

As the Reich expanded further eastwards into the Ukraine after 1941, masses of Volksdeutsche were moved out from Romania, Hungary, Albania and Yugoslavia for resettlement in the newly occupied lands under the Eastern Ministry of Alfred Rosenberg. Each family was permitted only 50 kilogrammes of personal possessions or two horse-drawn wagon loads, and some wagon trains travelled as many as 2,000 miles in scenes reminiscent of the American frontier era. All arrivals were probed by SS doctors and racial examiners from RuSHA to confirm that they were suitable to be reclassified as Reichsdeutsche and given German citizenship, but long stays in VOMI's 1,500 resettlement and transit camps left many Volksdeutsche feeling disappointed, embittered and hopeless. By 1945, VOMI had forcibly moved as many as 1,200,000 ethnic Germans, the bulk of whom became displaced persons at the end of the war.

While VOMI dealt with the transportation of Volksdeutsche repatriates and RuSHA supervised their racial purity, their actual resettlement was the responsibility of a third SS organisation, the Reichskommissariat für die Festigung des deutschen Volkstums, or RKFDV, the Reich Commission for the Consolidation of Germanism. It was created on 7 October 1939, with Himmler as its Reichs-

kommissar, and he immediately established a Berlin staff HQ, the Hauptamt RKF, directed by SS-Obergruppenführer Ulrich Greifelt. To administer the financing of its operations, a Land Bank Company was set up under SS-Obersturmbannführer Ferdinand Hiege and money poured in from the sales of confiscated Jewish and Polish property. Himmler intended that not only repatriated ethnic Germans but also crippled SS ex-servicemen and returned veterans should eventually be settled in the eastern territories as 'Wehrbauern' or 'peasant guards', to provide a buffer between the Reich proper and the unconquered wilderness beyond the Urals. From 1940, SS recruiting propaganda laid considerable stress on the opportunities which would be open to all SS men after the war, with the promise of free land in the east, and a number of SS soldiers invalided out from the services were employed on preparatory settlement work with the so-called 'SS-Baueinsatz-Ost'. In the words of SS-Obergruppenführer Otto Hofmann of RuSHA, the east would 'belong to the SS'.

In May 1942, SS-Oberführer Prof. Dr Konrad Meyer of the Hauptamt RKF finished drawing up the great resettlement plan on behalf of Himmler. Under its terms, the Baltic states and Poland were to be fully Germanised. The occupied east would be carved up into three huge provinces or Marks, namely Ingermanland, Narev and Gotengau, under the supreme authority of the Reichsführer-SS, who was to be their new liege lord. He would direct the settlers to the areas provided for them and grant them lands of varying types depending on their service, including 'life fiefs', 'hereditary fiefs' and 'special status properties'. Provincial headmen appointed by Himmler were to supervise the Marches of the new SS empire. After a 25-year period of racial purification, it was calculated, their population would be

50 per cent Germanic. There would be a direct autobahn linking Berlin with Moscow, and a 4 metre-wide railtrack between Munich and Rostov. A system of twenty-six eastern strongpoints consisting of small towns of about 20,000 inhabitants, each surrounded by a ring of German villages at a distance of about three miles, would guard the intersections of German communications arteries. The villages themselves were to comprise thirty to forty farmhouses and have their own SS 'Warrior Stürme' to which all male inhabitants would belong. Working along Viking lines, it was to be the greatest piece of continental colonisation the world had ever seen, designed to protect western civilisation from the threat of Asiatic invasion.

From the beginning, however, Himmler and the RKFDV encountered insurmountable obstacles set up not by the enemy but by competing Nazi satraps in the occupied lands, each intent upon securing his own niche of influence in the new empire. Neither Hans Frank, Governor-General of Poland, nor Alfred Rosenberg, Minister for the Occupied Eastern Territories, were SS men and they owed no allegiance to the Reichsführer. Several Gauleiters, particularly Erich Koch, Reichskommissar in the Ukraine, and Wilhelm Kube, Reichskommissar in Byelorussia, fought consistently to hinder the resettlement programme in their areas, which they saw as an SS impingement on NSDAP authority. Even Albert Forster, the Gauleiter of Danzig-West Prussia, who was an SS-Obergruppenführer and had been a member of the SS before Himmler himself, was so antagonistic to the prospect of taking Volksdeutsche settlers into his domain that ships carrying repatriates from Estonia to Danzig had to be re-routed.

In the end, the practicalities consequent upon the turn of the tide of war smashed Himmler's dream of an eastern Germanic empire run by the SS. The Reichsführer clearly viewed the Second World War as the final war of racial extermination which would secure the future of the Germanic peoples once and for all. The fairly modest racial policies of the early SS, which centred around its recruiting standards, had exploded out of all recognition by the spring of 1942, with the mass killings of the Einsatzgruppen and the commencement of the 'conveyor belt' destruction of human life at Auschwitz. Had the war gone in Germany's favour, there is little doubt that the Jews, gypsies and Slav races would have been depleted to extinction in Europe. However, from 1943 Hitler felt that their labour, and that of the repatriated ethnic Germans, could be better used in solving Germany's pressing domestic manpower shortage, and Himmler had little choice but to listen and agree. Thereafter, Volksdeutsche were brought 'home to the Reich' only to work in the thriving armaments industry and to staff factories and farms that had been sorely affected by Wehrmacht recruitment. In so doing, these ethnic Germans toiled alongside Poles, Russians and other imported labourers whom they were supposed to have replaced in the east. Ironically, huge numbers of anti-communist Slav volunteers in the Schutzmannschaft and Wehrmacht, technically Untermenschen by SS standards, were by that time being relied upon to bolster and defend the Nazi régime in the occupied territories, and had even been accorded the honour of their own range of medals and decorations. Many were employed as auxiliaries by the SS itself.

Heinrich Himmler had attempted to do too much too quickly, to reverse the developments of a thousand years in a single decade, and the whole racial programme had come crashing down about his head.

GUARDIANS OF THE STATE

Himmler's intention that his racial élite should eventually police and guard occupied Europe stemmed from the fact that the most important achievement of the SS from the earliest days of the Third Reich had been its dominance of the security apparatus within Germany itself, and the power and influence which that entailed. The failure of the Munich putsch in 1923, which was smashed by the police rather than the army, brought home to Hitler the realisation that unrestricted control of the police would be an essential element in the successful foundation of a long-term Nazi state. Consequently, the period immediately following the assumption of power on 30 January 1933 witnessed a concerted effort by the Führer to have his most trusted lieutenants nominated to senior police positions in the governments of the various provinces, or Länder, which existed under the Weimar Republic. Foremost among these men was Hermann Göring, one of the first Nazis elected to the Reichstag and its President since 30 August 1932, who received ministerial duties in both the national and Prussian governments. As Prussian Minister of the Interior, he became responsible for policing the Reich capital and two-thirds of the land area of Germany. Göring appointed Kurt Daluege, head of the Berlin SS, as his Chief of Prussian Police and Rudolf Diels, his cousin's husband, as Deputy Chief. He then moved swiftly to separate the Prussian Political Police, which dealt with subversives, from the rest of the organisation. On 27 April 1933 he created a new political department staffed by thirty-five men, to be called the Secret State Police or Geheime Staatspolizei (Gestapo), and assigned Diels to head it. The Gestapo was instructed that it could disregard the restrictions imposed by Prussian state law, and it was removed from the control of the Prussian Ministry of the

Portrait photograph of Heinrich Himmler, circulated to all police stations in 1936 after his appointment as Chef der Deutschen Polizei. It was produced and distributed by the German Police Officers' Association, and bore an appropriate stamp on the reverse.

Interior to new offices at 8 Prinz-Albrecht-Strasse, Berlin, and made an independent force responsible to Göring personally. By mid-1933, therefore, Göring had a firm grip on the largest provincial police force in Germany and launched it and the SA against the communists and other opponents of the New Order.

Diels, however, soon became a problem. He was a professional policeman, not a Nazi, and at once went to war against all extremists and law-breakers, regardless of political persuasion. His fledgling Gestapo, armed with machine-guns, regularly surrounded ad hoc SA and SS detention centres in Berlin and forced the Brownshirts to surrender and release their severely beaten political prisoners. Daluege and some SS men who worked their way into the Gestapo began to campaign viciously for the downfall of Diels and his faction, and such infighting developed that it eventually became commonplace for members of the Gestapo to arrest one another. Daluege even plotted to invite Diels to a meeting and then throw him out of an upper-storey window! But Diels continued to enjoy Göring's patronage and friendship, and retained his command of the Gestapo.

While Göring was the first official of the Third Reich to assert a measure of personal authority over the regular provincial police, it remained for Himmler to realise that ambition on a national scale. When the Gauleiter of Munich-Upper Bavaria, Adolf Wagner, became Bavarian Minister of the Interior at the beginning of March 1933, his natural choice as Police President of Munich was Himmler, who had been Head of Security at the NSDAP headquarters in the city for over a year. On 1 April, Himmler was appointed Commander of the Political Police for the whole of Bavaria, a position which gave him the power to challenge Göring's Prussian supremacy. He found an ally in the Reich Minister of the Interior, Dr Wilhelm Frick, a former Munich policeman who was a confirmed opponent of the autonomy of the Länder and an old enemy of Göring. With Frick's support, Himmler was nominated Chief of Police in province after province until only Prussia remained out of his reach.

In January 1934, Frick laid before Hitler a Bill for the Administrative Reorganisation of the Reich. As a result of its acceptance, all the provincial police forces were to be amalgamated to form the first national German Police Force, officially termed 'die Deutsche Polizei', under the Reich Minister of the Interior. Swift changes were made, including the incorporation of the eagle and swastika into the design of existing police uniforms.

Göring stood fast for a time in Prussia, and he might have frustrated the unification process entirely were it not for the growing dread of Röhm and the SA. The Stabschef was hungry for power and eager to trample on anyone who stood in his way. The menacing presence of the SA, and the fact that the SS was the only reliable body which could capably oppose it, finally persuaded Göring to compromise. He ousted his beleaguered protégé Diels on 20 April 1934 and appointed Himmler as Chief of the Prussian Gestapo, with SS-Brigadeführer Reinhard Heydrich as his deputy. Only two months later, the Göring/Himmler/Heydrich triumvirate successfully decapitated the SA in the 'Night of the Long Knives'.

During 1935, the intrigues continued and Himmler took his turn at coming into conflict with Frick. The latter was anxious to pursue his aim that all German police forces should ultimately be subordinated to him alone, as Reich Minister of the Interior. To that end he sought the support of Daluege, still head of the uniformed police in Prussia, against Himmler. Frick proposed that Daluege should be nominated Chief of the German Police on the understanding that he would take his instructions only from the Ministry of the Interior. Not surprisingly, Daluege expressed interest, but both he and Frick were outmanoeuvred by Himmler and Heydrich, who had got wind of the plot to undermine them. On 9 June 1936, Heydrich approached Hitler direct and presented a strong case for giving Himmler the rank of Minister and title Chief of the German Police. The crux of Heydrich's argument was that Himmler's efficiency and personal loyalty to the Führer were beyond question, and he would cut out the 'middle man', Frick. Frick retaliated but was successful only in his objection that Himmler should not be given ministerial rank. On 17 June 1936, the Reichsführer-SS was appointed to the newly created government post of Chief of the German Police in the Reich

From 18 to 22 February 1939, Himmler paid a fact-finding visit to Warsaw as a guest of the chief of the Polish Police. His next visit, seven months later, was to inspect and congratulate SS troops who had participated in the conquest of Poland.

Ministry of the Interior (Chef der Deutschen Polizei im Reichsministerium des Innern), answerable only to Hitler. Heydrich was rewarded for his efforts by being put in charge of the security police, and Daluege accepted command of the uniformed police. The entire system was reorganised around these two major divisions and, with the introduction of a series of new police uniforms, all vestiges of the old Länder forces finally disappeared.

Basking in his impressive new title, which had to be abbreviated in official corres-pondence to RfSSuChdDtPol, Himmler was now the undisputed head of two important but separate organisations: the SS and the national police. The police, however, by far the more powerful and intrusive agency, affecting the daily lives of the entire German population,

consisted of individuals who were not racially screened and, more importantly, not always politically reliable. Consequently, one of Himmler's first actions on assuming command was to expel twenty-two police colonels, hundreds of junior officers and thousands of NCOs who were considered to have socialist sympathies. The end result, in terms of lost experience, was catastrophic. Those dismissed had been professionals, and totally outclassed the SS men brought in to replace them. Many had to be reinstated after a hastily arranged programme of Nazi indoctrination.

The Nazification of the existing police membership was a short-term expedient, however. Himmler now began to formulate his greatest project, the complete merger of the SS and police into a single Staatsschutzkorps, or

The Berlin Schutzpolizei parade along the Wilhelmstrasse past Daluege, Himmler and Hitler, 20 April 1939.

State Protection Corps, so that the conventional police forces could be done away with altogether. This was to be achieved first by reorganisation and then by the absorption of police personnel into the SS. Acceptable members of the uniformed police would join the Allgemeine-SS, forming interim SS-Police units in the major cities, while security policemen who fulfilled the various racial and ideological requirements of the SS would enrol in the SD. In autumn 1936, as the first stage in this process, various SD leaders were appointed Inspectors of Security Police and charged with promoting the gradual fusion of the Gestapo, Kripo and SD. A year later, the SS Oberabschnitte commanders became the first Höhere SS- und Polizeiführer, assuming responsibility for all SS and police formations in their regions. Most important of all, a great recruiting drive was set in motion at the beginning of 1938 to encourage young members of the Allgemeine-SS to join the police as a full-time career. The ultimate intention was to replace the older and retiring police officers with 'new blood' so that, through a progression of selective recruitment, accelerated promotion and natural wastage, the Staatsschutzkorps would be in full operation and the police disbanded by 1955.

With the object of picking only the most reliable serving members of the police for acceptance into the SS, Himmler issued a

Rank Parity Decree on 26 June 1938, which laid down the following provisions:

(i)   Members of the police could, on application, be accepted into the SS provided that:

    (a) They fulfilled general SS recruiting conditions; and

    (b) They had been members of the NSDAP or any of its organisations before 30 January 1933, or

    they had been Patron Members (FM) of the SS before 30 January 1933, or they had served for at least three years in the police under RfSS command and had proved themselves satisfactory.

(ii)   The Reichsführer-SS reserved to himself the right to authorise the acceptance of any further categories of persons, including most Police generals who would normally have been rejected by the SS on account of their age.

(iii)   Acceptance into the SS would take place according to the police rank held.

(iv)   Police civilian employees could be incorporated into the SS with SS rank corresponding to their Civil Service grade.

(v)   Rank parity promotions would take place from case to case, as required.

The effect of provision (i) of the decree was that only racially and physically suitable and politically reliable members of the police would be accepted into the SS and, thereafter, into the intended Staatsschutzkorps. However, provisions (ii) to (v) threatened to swamp the Allgemeine-SS with police officials who were to be automatically given SS ranks corresponding to their status in the police, even though they had never held any junior SS positions before. For instance, a police Oberwachtmeister would enter the SS as a Hauptscharführer, an Inspektor as an Obersturmführer, an Oberst as a Standartenführer, and so on. Consequently, a practical ceiling had to be put on the number of police men who could be incorporated into the SS each year, and competition for places became fierce. Successful applicants were normally taken into the SS Stammabteilungen, without any real powers of operational SS command, and were permitted to wear the SS runes embroidered on a patch below the left breast pocket of the police tunic.

The outbreak of war in 1939 dealt a mortal blow to the steady progression towards a Staatsschutzkorps, for the majority of the finest potential police recruits from the Allgemeine-SS were suddenly swallowed up by the Wehrmacht. Nevertheless, the acceptance of serving police men into the SS organisation continued apace. During October 1939, no less than 16,000 members of the uniformed police were called up *en masse* to form the Polizei-Division, a combat unit affiliated to the Waffen-SS, which fought on the western front and in Russia. Its soldiers were not obliged to pass the SS racial and physical requirements and so were not initially considered to be full SS men, although by February 1942 they had distinguished themselves sufficiently in battle to be completely integrated into the Waffen-SS. Over 30 heavily armed police regiments also served under SS command as occupation troops throughout Europe, and in February 1945 an SS-Polizei-Grenadier-Division was raised with cadre personnel from the police school at Dresden. The Staatsschutzkorps idea was ultimately overtaken by events and never came to fruition. However, while the German police always managed to retain its position as a technically separate entity, its operational independence was rapidly eroded in real terms through continual SS

Kurt Daluege in the uniform of SS-Oberst-Gruppenführer und Generaloberst der Polizei, 24 August 1943. From this time on, he was continually ill and was, in fact, only semi-conscious when hanged at the end of the war.

Dietrich. The following year he was made Deputy Reichsprotektor of Bohemia and Moravia, and the day-to-day running of Orpo fell to SS-Obergruppenführer Alfred Wünnenberg, formerly commander of the SS-Polizei-Division. By that time, the Allgemeine-SS had permeated every aspect of the uniformed police system. SS-pattern rank insignia were sported by police generals, SS-style swords were worn by police officers and NCOs, and SS-type flags and standards were carried by police units on ceremonial occasions. A department known as the Hauptstelle der Hauptamt Ordnungspolizei had been set up within the Reichsführung-SS to advise Himmler on all matters concerning the uniformed police and, as Chef der Deutschen Polizei, he made policy decisions regarding its operations and deployment. In effect, the massive Orpo organisation had become subordinate to, and took its instructions from, the leadership of the Allgemeine-SS.

By the end of the war, the Ordnungspolizei had expanded to include a large number of distinct police formations, each with its own purpose and often its own series of uniforms. These groups are listed below.

1. THE SCHUTZPOLIZEI

The Schutzpolizei, or Protection Police, comprised the regular municipal 'beat bobbies' of the Third Reich and numbered around 200,000 men in 1943. This branch was itself subdivided into the Schutzpolizei des Reiches, whose jurisdiction extended throughout Germany, and the Schutzpolizei des Gemeinden, who operated only within their own towns. In addition, companies of Schutzpolizei were organised into Kaserniertepolizei or Barracked Police, equipped with armoured cars, machine guns and grenades. Their function was to act as a mobile reserve to back up the local police when additional manpower was needed in

infiltration. By the end of the war, Himmler had inevitably succeeded Frick as Reich Minister of the Interior, and he and his SS generals completely dominated all branches of both the uniformed and security police forces across the Reich.

By far the larger of the two main divisions of the German police was the Ordnungspolizei or Orpo, the so-called 'Order Police', which comprised all uniformed civil police personnel. From its inception in 1936, Orpo was commanded by Kurt Daluege, whose powerful position qualified him to become one of the first three SS-Oberst-Gruppenführer in April 1942, the other two being Franz Xaver Schwarz and 'Sepp'

times of mass demonstrations or similar events. After 1936, recruits for the Schutzpolizei were taken primarily from the Allgemeine-SS and the Wehrmacht. Their initial training by SS lecturers emphasised political indoctrination and was followed by specialised instruction at one of the thirty police schools scattered across Germany, the main ones being at Berlin-Köpenick and at Fürstenfeldbruck near Munich. The Inspector-General of Police Schools was an SS-Gruppenführer, Adolf von Bomhard.

2. THE GENDARMERIE

The Gendarmerie or Rural Police, under SS-Gruppenführer August Meyszner, covered landward districts and small communities of less than 2,000 inhabitants. They were particularly adept at combatting poaching, detecting black market slaughtering of animals, and the like. In those areas of the Reich, including the occupied territories, that were of a mountainous nature or prone to heavy snowfall, members of the Gendarmerie skilled in skiing and mountaineering were employed. They had to undergo rigorous training at the Hochgebirgs Gendarmerie Schools at Oberjoch bei Hindelang, Sudelfeld am Wendelstein and Kitzbühel in the Tirol. In January 1942, a separate branch of the Gendarmerie known as the Landwacht or Rural Guard was set up by Himmler to supervise prisoners-of-war engaged in agricultural work. It was recruited from older policemen and disabled SS ex-servicemen. After 20 July 1944, military prisoner-of-war camps themselves were put under the administration of the SS and police, with responsibility for running them being placed in the hands of SS-Obergruppenführer Berger.

3. THE VERWALTUNGSPOLIZEI

The Verwaltungspolizei, commanded by SS-Obergruppenführer August Frank, was the administrative branch of Orpo, units of which were attached to each police headquarters. Their various duties included record keeping, the enforcement of statutory regulations affecting theatres, factories and shops, the registration of foreign nationals, and the issuing of firearms licences, travel permits, etc. This administrative force took in the former Gesundheitspolizei (Health Police), Gewerbepolizei (Factory and Shops Police) and Baupolizei (Buildings Police). Many Verwaltungspolizei employees were civilians, who had been given extensive periods of training at the SS and police administrative schools.

4. THE VERKEHRSPOLIZEI AND MOTORISIERTE GENDARMERIE

The Verkehrspolizei, or Municipal Traffic Police, consisted of specially trained units of men who were stationed alongside the Kaserniertepolizei in all major German cities. They regulated traffic and patrolled the main roads in their areas, and were well versed in the field of traffic law. The Verkehrspolizei was responsible for the prevention of traffic accidents, piecing together and recording the causes of accidents, and escorting abnormal loads, ambulances and other emergency vehicles. The Motorisierte Gendarmerie was formed to cope with the increase in traffic on rural roads and the new network of autobahn – or motorways being built across Germany. Unlike the Verkehrspolizei, their jurisdiction was not limited by geographical divisions. They were organised into Bereitschaften or mobile reserves containing three or four platoons of men and vehicles, each located in barracks at strategic points on the German highway system. The wail of their sirens could often be heard as they provided high-speed escorts for NSDAP leaders travelling throughout the Reich.

5. THE WASSERSCHUTZPOLIZEI

The Wasserschutzpolizei, or Waterways Protection Police, was responsible for policing and patrolling all navigable inland rivers and canals, regulating waterborne traffic, preventing smuggling, enforcing safety and security measures and inspecting waterways shipping. It was supplemented during the war by special units of the Allgemeine-SS known as Hafensicherung-struppen, or Port Security Troops, which patrolled the waterfronts and major ports of the coastal SS Oberabschnitte in co-operation with the police authorities and the SD. In addition, by a proclamation of SS-Ober-gruppenführer Karl Kaufmann, Gauleiter of Hamburg and Reich Commissioner for Ocean Navigation, all ships which were operating for Germany's war effort in the Baltic and North Sea areas, and which were manned partially or entirely by Danes, Dutchmen, Norwegians and other non-Germans, had on board so-called SS-Bordschutzmannschaften. These SS Shipboard Security Crews were assigned by the Führer of the Oberabschnitte from whose ports the vessels sailed, and they were used to man flak guns and generally assist the German officers in maintaining order on the ships.

6. THE BAHNSCHUTZPOLIZEI

The Bahnschutzpolizei, or Railway Police, recruited primarily from Deutsche Reichsbahn employees who held part-time membership of the Allgemeine-SS or SA, were armed with rifles and machine-guns and were charged with protecting railway property, preventing espionage and sabotage, and maintaining law and order on trains and at stations. They were assisted by the Reichsbahn Wasserschutzpolizei which patrolled railway facilities associated with harbours, canals and inland waterways.

7. THE POSTSCHUTZ

The Postschutz, or Postal Protection Service, had the responsibility of protecting and maintaining the security of all post offices and other postal establishments, together with mail, telephone and telegraph services throughout the Reich. Prior to 1942 the 4,500-strong Postschutz was under the control of the Postmaster-General, NSKK-Obergruppenführer Dr Wilhelm Ohnesorge, but in March of that year, upon the directions of Hitler, it was completely incorporated into the Allgemeine-SS and redesignated as the SS-Postschutz. From then on, SS collar patches were worn with the Postschutz uniform.

8. THE FEUERSCHUTZPOLIZEI

All of Germany's provincial fire brigades were incorporated into the Ordnungspolizei in 1938 under the title Feuerschutzpolizei, or Fire Protection Police, which thereafter directed fire-fighting and fire prevention across the Reich. The size of the Fire Protection Police was fixed in accordance with the local population, and in those towns with more than 150,000 residents auxiliary fire brigades known as Freiwillige Feuerwehren were established on a voluntary basis to assist the regulars. At the height of the wartime air raids on Germany, the fire-fighting services numbered over 1,700,000 men and women, all of whom were technically under the command of SS-Gruppenführer Dr Johannes Meyer, the Inspector-General of the Feuerschutzpolizei.

9. THE LUFTSCHUTZPOLIZEI

Germany's civil defence system comprised three main bodies. The first was the Reichsluftschutzbund or RLB, which engaged in the widespread civil defence training of the civilian population. The second was the Luftschutz Warndienst or LSW, which acted like Britain's Royal Observer Corps in alerting the local populace to impending air attacks. The third body was the Sicherheits- und Hilfsdienst or SHD, the Security and Assistance Service, a highly mobile rescue organisation which rendered immediate help to trapped and injured air raid victims. The equipment used in their dangerous work included hydraulic jacks, cutting machines and wrecking tools. During the war, the RLB and the LSW came under the direct control of the various NSDAP Gauleiters, whose responsibilities included civil defence in their Gaue. The SHD, however, was absorbed into the police in May 1942, renamed the Luftschutzpolizei and issued with police insignia. Members were housed in barracks on a rotating basis, i.e. they were allowed to sleep at home every second night, and were exempt from conscription into the Wehrmacht as service with the Luftschutzpolizei was a reserved occupation. Consequently, those who were also in the Allgemeine-SS could keep up their normal SS activities, air raids permitting.

10. THE TECHNISCHE NOTHILFE
The Technische Nothilfe, or TeNo, was a Technical Emergency Corps founded initially as a strike-breaking organisation by the government in September 1919, and used later as a technical reserve in cases of natural disaster. In 1937, it was incorporated into the Ordnungspolizei and set the task of dealing with breakdowns in public services and utilities such as gas, water and electricity, particularly after air raids. A second and more remote purpose was to meet potential revolutionary conditions in the 'Theatre of War Inner Germany', as Himmler liked to call the home front where the majority of his forces operated. In addition to this domestic work, units known as TeNo Kommandos laboured with the Wehrmacht on front-line construction and repair. From 1943 the 100,000 members of TeNo were authorised to wear SS-style rank badges. The wartime Chef der TeNo was SS-Gruppenführer Hans Weinreich, later succeeded by Willy Schmelcher.

11. THE SS-FUNKSCHUTZ
In 1941, the Allgemeine-SS assumed responsibility for the protection of radio stations because of their vulnerability to sabotage in wartime. To that end, an SS-Funkschutz, or Radio Guard, was established. It ultimately policed all the official radio stations, or Reichssender, raided illicit radio stations and detected illegal listening to foreign stations. Members wore standard Allgemeine-SS uniform with the addition of a gorget bearing the legend 'SS-Funkschutz' while on duty.

12. THE WERKSCHUTZPOLIZEI
Members of the Werkschutzpolizei, or Factory Protection Police, were stationed at important industrial concerns to act as factory guards and watchmen, and were under the command of the Führer of the SS Oberabschnitt in which their factory was sited. They were generally kitted out with surplus black Allgemeine-SS uniforms and outdated Prussian-blue fire service uniforms, to which they attached their own insignia.

By 1943 therefore, through his continued absorption of uniformed police responsibilities, Himmler had succeeded in achieving ultimate control of all conventional German police forces, the fire brigade, railway and post office guards, rescue and emergency services, and even night watchmen. Moreover, the corresponding domestic police forces in the conquered territories also came under his authority. The active Allgemeine-SS proper was by that time a relatively small organisation in its own right, and numerically far inferior to the Waffen-SS. However, its leaders directed the operations of hundreds of thousands of uniformed policemen throughout the Greater German Reich, and had access to their intimate local knowledge. In that way, the oft-maligned and faceless bureaucrats of the Allgemeine-SS hierarchy exercised a power and influence more widespread and effective than anything contemplated by their fighting comrades in the Waffen-SS, who naturally received all the propaganda publicity during the war.

Just as the German police network could be split into two distinct groupings, the uniformed police and the security police, so the security police forces themselves comprised two entirely separate divisions prior to September 1939, namely those of the Nazi party and those of the state. The principal party force was the Sicherheitsdienst des RfSS, or SD, the SS security service, which absorbed all other intelligence services of the NSDAP in June 1934. The state force was known as the Sicherheitspolizei, or Sipo (Security Police), a general administrative term used to cover both the traditional Kriminalpolizei, or Kripo (Criminal Police),

and the more recently formed Geheime Staatspolizei, or Gestapo (Political Police). In 1939, all of these groups were united as part of the Staatsschutzkorps programme to become departments of a single newly created SS Hauptamt, the Reichssicherheitshauptamt, or RSHA (Reich Central Security Office). These main security police bodies are best described in turn, to indicate their wide-ranging responsibilities and the power which the SS obtained by taking them over under Himmler's authority.

1. THE SD

In June 1931, Himmler accepted Reinhard Heydrich, a former naval communications officer, into the SS as a Sturmführer and set him the task of organising an SS intelligence service to keep watch on the political opposition. Initially known as Department Ic of the SS-Amt, or the Ic-Dienst, then as the Press and Information Service, it was finally renamed the Sicherheitsdienst des Reichsführers-SS (Security Service of the Reichsführer-SS), or SD, in June 1932. By that time, Heydrich had been promoted to SS-Sturmbannführer and with a staff of seven civilians established his small SD headquarters in Munich. When the Nazis came to power at the beginning of 1933, the SD had no more than 200 personnel, most of whom were attached to the various Abschnitte HQs throughout Germany. During the 1933–4 period, however, the service was expanded and many doctors, lawyers and other academics who applied to join the Allgemeine-SS were advised that their best prospects for advancement within the organisation lay with the SD branch. As soon as Himmler took over the Gestapo in April 1934, Heydrich, by then a Brigadeführer, reorganised it and placed as many of his SD men as possible in positions where they could observe the activities of the political police and gain valuable experience. However,

SS-Gruppenführer Reinhard Heydrich at his desk in 1937. The SS death's head ring can be seen clearly on his left hand.

although the SD continued as a separate entity, it had neither the manpower nor the expertise to replace the existing political police altogether. Himmler's original plan to incorporate all members of the Sipo into the SD was continually frustrated, and by January 1938 the SD still had only 5,000 full-time and honorary members across the Reich. In fact, with the formation of the RSHA the following year, the SD eventually became superfluous and was itself almost completely absorbed into the security police. Its continued existence as a separate branch of the Allgemeine-SS was due solely to Himmler's desire to retain his SD's unique position as the only intelligence agency of the NSDAP.

The remit of the SD gradually expanded from purely political intelligence to social, economic and religious matters, and became somewhat 'airy-fairy'. Its members made detailed studies of communism, Judaism, the doctrine of papal supremacy, Freemasonry, astrology, religious sects and the forces of reaction generally. They were concerned not so much with actual and current security problems as with perceived ideological questions. They delved into the influence of Bolshevism on Masonic circles abroad, and looked at the symbolism of top hats at Eton. They studied Jewish economics and the black market in currency. They propounded the theory that by 1960 communism would become a religion centred in Asia, designed to destroy the whole white world. By the time war broke out, many members of the SD had become something of a laughing stock among their colleagues in the Sipo who were engaged in the real day-to-day struggle against criminals, saboteurs and active enemies of the state.

The connotations of dread and horror which later attached themselves to the SD in occupied Europe and Russia stemmed from the fact that all members of the security

Security Police storming a suspect's house in Warsaw, November 1939. Note the 'Pol', i.e. 'Polizei', prefix on the registration plate of their vehicle.

police serving in the conquered territories, whether or not they were members of the SS or SD, were instructed to wear the grey SS uniform with a combination of SD collar and sleeve insignia and police shoulder straps, to give them the protection of military status yet at the same time distinguish them from other uniformed SS, police and Wehrmacht personnel. During the early days of the war, security policemen, who were detested by the fighting services, had worn civilian clothing and there had been occasions when they had been conveniently 'mistaken for resistance people' and shot by German soldiers! The uniform was therefore intended to protect them as much from their own side as from the enemy. The atrocities carried out by some of these Sipo men, particularly those attached to extermination squads in the east, reflected directly on the SD proper, the majority of

NCOs of the Sipo uncovering a cache of hidden weapons in Warsaw, November 1939.

whose members were engaged almost exclusively in academic research, intelligence-gathering and policy formulation. In fact, while the death squads which penetrated deep into Soviet territory in 1941 killing communists, partisans and Jews as they went were entitled 'Einsatzgruppen der Sicherheitspolizei und des SD', only 3 per cent of their members were actually SD men. The greater number were Waffen-SS (34 per cent), army (28 per cent) and uniformed police (22 per cent), assisted by Gestapo (9 per cent) and Kripo (4 per cent).

2. THE GESTAPO

When the Gestapo was established by Göring in 1933, it had thirty-five members with a budget of 1 million Reichsmarks. Two years later, its membership had risen to over 600 and its budget exceeded 40 million Reichsmarks. As the political police of the Reich, the Gestapo was responsible for gathering information on all subversive individuals and organisations, carrying out plain-clothes surveillance operations and raids, and effecting arrests on a grand scale. It also decided who was to be interned in concentration camps. At its Berlin headquarters, the known enemies of the régime, from Jehovah's Witnesses to fanatical anti-Nazis, were categorised into one of the following three groups:

A1 – those to be imprisoned in case of probable mobilisation

A2 – those to be imprisoned in case of certain mobilisation

A3 – those to be closely supervised in time of war because of their political apathy

While the SD simply amassed intelligence, the Gestapo had real power to act on the information contained in its files. It was the Gestapo which organised the 'dawn raids' and the infamous 'three o'clock knock'. The SD and Gestapo inevitably expended a great deal of energy competing with one another until their amalgamation under the RSHA.

3. THE KRIPO

The Kripo comprised regular police detectives who carried out standard criminal investigation work. Like the Gestapo, they operated in civilian clothes before being ordered to wear the SD uniform during the war. Their main duties were the investigation of serious statutory offences and common law crimes such as murder, rape, fraud and arson, and the interrogation of suspects. They attended at break-ins, took fingerprints, collected material evidence and prepared relevant reports. The Kripo was the most stable and professional of all the security police forces, and was a favoured recruiting ground for the Reichssicherheitsdienst or RSD (not to be confused with the SD), an élite force which provided small bodyguard detachments for Himmler and leading Nazis. Its commander was SS-Brigadeführer Hans Rattenhuber.

4. THE RSHA

In October 1936, Inspectors of Security Police (Inspekteur der Sicherheitspolizei or IdS) were appointed in each SS Oberabschnitt to improve co-ordination between the SD, the Gestapo and the Kripo. Liaison and interdepartmental co-operation improved thereafter, and on 27 September 1939 the

A Security Police Hauptscharführer, c. 1941. The blank right collar patch is clearly evident, as are the military-style shoulder straps which gave way to police versions in January 1942. This official may well have been a member of one of the Einsatzkommandos responsible for rounding up potential partisans following the invasion of Poland and Russia. His kindly countenance belies the unspeakable atrocities in which he may have been involved.

Sipo and SD were brought together to form adjacent departments of a single, all-embracing SS Hauptamt, the Reichssicherheitshauptamt or RSHA. Once again, a governmental or state office, the Chief of the Security Police, and a Nazi party office, the Chief of the Security Service, were merged into a single post, Chief of the Security Police and Security Service (Chef der Sicherheitspolizei und des SD, or CSSD). Needless to say, the first CSSD was SS-Gruppenführer Reinhard Heydrich. The RSHA (often abbreviated to 'RSi-H' in SS correspondence to avoid confusion with

Sipo and SD officers who participated in a course at the Italian Colonial Police School in Rome from 9 to 16 January 1941 are saluted by the Italian Colonial Minister, Teruzzi.

RuSHA) was divided into seven departments, or ämter, as follows:

Amt I   *Personnel.* This department dealt with all security police and SD personnel matters and was led by SS-Gruppenführer Dr Werner Best, a senior jurist and Heydrich's deputy until 1940. He was succeeded by Bruno Streckenbach, Erwin Schulz and finally Erich Ehrlinger. Streckenbach went on to command the 19th Division of the Waffen-SS, and Schulz ended the war as security police leader in Salzburg.

Amt II   *Administration.* This effectively ran the RSHA and was also initially headed by Best, then by Dr Rudolf Siegert, and finally by Josef Spacil, an SS-Standartenführer on the staff of Oberabschnitt Donau.

Amt III   *SD (Home).* An information service, led by SS-Gruppenführer Otto Ohlendorf, which collated data relating to politics and counter-espionage within Germany. It financed the 'Salon Kitty', a high-class brothel in Berlin popular with senior Nazis and wealthy locals. The salon was wired for sound and, depending on what they said during their romps, the clients often found themselves being blackmailed by the SD or arrested by the Sipo shortly thereafter. The prostitutes were in fact female agents of the security police, and went out of their way to entice anti-Nazi remarks from their partners.

Amt IV *Gestapo.* Under SS-Gruppenführer Heinrich Müller, the Gestapo continued in its set task of eliminating the enemies of the Nazi régime.

Amt V *Kripo.* This active department retained its executive powers in dealing with common crime. Its long-time commander, SS-Gruppenführer Arthur Nebe, was hanged in 1945 for his complicity in the attempt to assassinate Hitler the previous year.

Amt VI *SD (Abroad).* An intelligence-gathering service directed against foreign countries, which also organised espionage in enemy territory. It was led first by SS-Brigadeführer Heinz Jost, then by Walter Schellenberg.

Amt VII *Ideological Research.* This department was headed by SS-Oberführer Prof. Dr Franz Six, and sounded out general public opinion on a range of subjects. Working in conjunction with the Ministry of Propaganda, it monitored the progress of the Nazi indoctrination of the German people. Dr Six was the officer selected to command the security police and SD in occupied Britain – a post which he never took up!

The activities of the RSHA were extremely varied, ranging from the defamation of Tukachevsky and other Soviet generals, which led to Stalin's purge of the Russian officer corps, to the liberation of Mussolini by Skorzeny's commandos. They encompassed anti-terrorist operations, assassinations,

control of foreigners in Germany, and the collation of political files seized from the police forces of the occupied countries. When the Gestapo took over the administration of the Customs Service from the Reich Ministry of Finance, border controls and the combatting of smuggling also came under the jurisdiction of the RSHA. As CSSD, Heydrich controlled one of the most complex and all-embracing security police systems the world had ever seen, and in 1940 his standing on an international level was recognised with his nomination to the post of President of Interpol.

A surprisingly high percentage of senior SS officers were attached to the RSHA, since the very nature of its work and the expertise required for many of its operations necessitated that it should be a 'top heavy' organisation so far as rank was concerned. Taking into account every section of the SS, including the vast Waffen-SS, almost a quarter of all officers holding the rank of SS-Sturmbannführer in 1944 (i.e. 714 out of 3,006 or 23.8 per cent) worked with the RSHA. Corresponding figures for higher ranks were as follows:

Obersturmbannführer 240 out of 1,199 (20%)
Standartenführer   95 out of 623 (15.2%)
Oberführer   41 out of 274 (15%)
Brigadeführer   31 out of 270 (11.5%)
Gruppenführer   7 out of 94   (7.4%)
Obergruppenführer   4 out of 91   (4.4%)
Oberst-Gruppenführer   0 out of 4   (0%)

These statistics are remarkable, and serve to indicate the size and extent of the security police network in 1944, for they show that no less than one-fifth of all SS majors and colonels at that time were Sipo or SD men. Ultimately, there were some 65,000 junior security police officials stationed across Europe and Russia, fed by over 100,000 local informers.

Kurt Daluege accompanies Lina Heydrich at her husband's funeral. Karl Hermann Frank stands saluting at the right, beside the puppet President of Bohemia and Moravia, Dr Emil Hácha.

On 27 May 1942, Heydrich, then Deputy Reichsprotektor of Bohemia and Moravia, was blown up by Czech agents in Prague and he died a week later. Upon his death, he was awarded the Blood Order (the last posthumous bestowal of that revered decoration) and he became only the second ever recipient of the Deutscher Orden or German Order, a new Nazi version of the medieval Teutonic Order. Heydrich's assassination caused shockwaves throughout the Nazi hierarchy and stunned Himmler, as it emphasised his own vulnerability to attack. His heavily armed personal escort battalion, the Begleitbataillon RfSS, was immediately

doubled in size. On 1 January 1943, after some considerable anxiety and indecision, Himmler finally appointed SS-Ober-gruppenführer Dr Ernst Kaltenbrunner to fill the combined posts of Chief of the RSHA and CSSD, as Heydrich's successor.

It was inevitable that sooner or later the RSHA would clash with the Abwehr, the Wehrmacht intelligence service under Admiral Canaris, but it was not until Canaris was implicated in the 20 July 1944 plot against Hitler that the Abwehr was finally absorbed by ämter IV and VI of the RSHA, leaving the German armed forces as the only major European military organisation

Hitler pays his last respects to Reinhard Heydrich at the Wagnerian state funeral service held for him in the Mosaic Chamber of the new Reich Chancellery, 9 June 1942. Karl Wolff and SS-Gruppenführer Gauleiter Dr Friedrich Rainer are among the guard of honour, drawn from the SS, police, NSDAP, army, navy and Luftwaffe. Despite all of his Security Police responsibilities, Heydrich still found time to fly over sixty operational missions as a fighter pilot on the Russian front, being shot down behind enemy lines and winning the Iron Cross 1st Class.

without its own intelligence network. As the war drew to a close, Sipo and SD men furnished themselves with false papers and scurried underground, only to be rooted out again to face trial for their wartime activities or, more often, to continue in their old specialist roles as agents of the Americans or Russians, as East and West prepared for what then seemed an almost unavoidable confrontation.

One part of the police organisation was engaged in more active combat duties than the rest of Orpo and Sipo. During the period 1940–2, a large number of younger members of the Ordnungspolizei, supplemented by Allgemeine-SS conscripts, were transferred to thirty newly created independent Police Regiments comprising around 100 battalions, each of 500 men. They were organised and equipped on military lines and served as security troops in the occupied countries. In February 1943, these German formations were officially designated SS-Police Regiments, to distinguish them from the recently formed native 'Police Rifle' units, and they subsequently gained a reputation for extreme brutality and fanatical loyalty to Himmler and the Nazi régime. Relatively few SS-Police Regiments were garrisoned in the west. The 4th, 14th, 19th and 29th went to

Soldiers of the Polizei-Division, distinguished by their use of a combination of army, police and SS uniform insignia, during mortar training, April 1940.

France, and the 26th and 27th to Norway, while Denmark was allocated only two police battalions. In Belgium, no German police deployment at all was felt necessary. The Italian situation was somewhat more volatile, with widespread partisan activity after 1943, and necessitated the presence of the 10th, 12th and 15th SS-Police Regiments and several local units.

The vast majority of SS-Police Regiments were posted to Russia, eastern Europe and the Balkans, where roaming partisan bands of brigade strength or even larger caused constant havoc behind the German lines. In 1942, Himmler was made responsible for all counter-guerrilla operations, and he appointed SS-Obergruppenführer Erich von dem Bach, formerly head of Oberabschnitt Nordost, as his Chief of Anti-Partisan Units (Chef der Bandenkampfverbände). It quickly became apparent that the territories to be controlled, particularly in Russia, were so vast that the SS-Police needed additional support. Consequently, various pro-German local militias and home guard units composed mainly of Balts, Cossacks and Ukrainians

DIE POLIZEI IM FRONTEINSATZ

This postcard, produced for 'German Police Day' in 1942, depicts members of the Ordnungspolizei and Sicherheitspolizei on joint patrol on the eastern front. Its symbolism emphasises the close ties between the SS and the police, and the fact that both organisations were fully involved in combat.

While he was HSSPf in Serbia, SS-Gruppenführer August Meyszner (left) was responsible for all counter-guerrilla operations in the country. Here he confers with SS-Obergruppenführer Artur Phleps of the 'Prinz Eugen' division during the spring of 1943. Of particular note are the differing patterns of collar patch and the puttees worn by both men.

were consolidated into an auxiliary police force known as the Schutzmannschaft der Ordnungspolizei, or Schuma, later expanded to include a Schutzmannschaft der Sicherheitspolizei. Members of the Schuma were generally nationalists at heart, whose main aim was the defeat of communism, and they viewed the Germans as liberators. Moreover, on a practical level, their service in the Schuma ensured that they and their families received favourable treatment from the Nazis. Schuma units often committed terrible atrocities against their own compatriots, in an effort to prove that their loyalty to the Reich was beyond question and that they were 'more German than the Germans'.

In Poland, twelve SS-Police Regiments supported the Wehrmacht in maintaining order, backed up by the Polish police and twelve Schuma battalions. Fourteen SS-Police Regiments served in Byelorussia, as did seven Police Rifle Regiments, which were mixed German-Russian units, and a vast number of

Schuma battalions. In Estonia, twenty-six Schuma battalions were formed, being redesignated 'Estonian Police Battalions' in May 1943 and issued with German police uniforms on account of their reliable record. An estimated 15,000 Latvians and 13,000 Lithuanians served in sixty-four other Schuma battalions which were deployed right across the eastern front, from the Ostland to Yugoslavia, while the Ukraine alone supplied 70,000 volunteers to staff a further seventy-one Schuma battalions. In Croatia, pro-Nazis set up a regimental-sized 'Einsatzstaffel', based on the Allgemeine-SS and dressed in quasi-SS uniform, and 15,000 more went into a multi-national 'German-Croatian Gend-armerie' of thirty battalions. On a smaller scale, the Serbians produced ten auxiliary police battalions, and the Albanians two Police Rifle Regiments. All of these native auxiliary formations (and there were many more than those mentioned briefly here) were completely separate from the foreign legions of the Wehrmacht. They were police organisations directly subordinate to the local Orpo and Sipo commanders and, ultimately, took their orders from Himmler through his HSSPfs. In effect, they were remote extensions of the Allgemeine-SS, operating in the occupied territories.

Each Oberabschnitt commander normally held the post of Höhere SS- und Polizeiführer or HSSPf, the Senior SS and Police Commander in the region. He acted as Himmler's representative and had technical jurisdiction over all SS and police formations based in the Oberabschnitt. The close relationship between the SS and police subsequently resulted in a joint admin-istration at regional level, and this amalgamation was particularly convenient in newly occupied territories where it was necessary rapidly to set up tried and tested administrative structures for both the SS and the police. In the conquered countries,

therefore, as in Germany itself, SS headquarters and police command posts were usually established in the same building, with frequent interdepartmental transfers of staff. During 1943–4, Hans Prützmann became Höchste SS- und Polizeiführer (Supreme SS and Police Commander) in southern Russia, and a similar post was held by Karl Wolff in Italy, making these two officers the highest ranking of all the HSSPfs.

Subordinate to the HSSPfs, a number of local SS- und Polizeiführer and Poliz-eigebietsführer directed SS and police operations in areas particularly troubled by partisans and other civil insurgents. In addition, each major city across Germany and the occupied territories had its Befehlshaber der Ordnungspolizei (BdO) and its Befehlshaber der Sicherheitspolizei und des SD (BdS), whose authorities were restricted to their local uniformed police and security police forces, respectively.

In practice, the ultimate authority of the Senior SS and Police Commanders was increasingly challenged during the war by the Chiefs of the SS Hauptämter, who felt that they should have supremacy in all matters relating to the functioning of their departments, and also by Waffen-SS generals, who demanded total autonomy of action in deploying their troops. In so doing, they went against Himmler's direct orders, for the HSSPf system was devised as an essential administrative step in the Reichsführer's planned progression towards the Staats-schutzkorps, and he bolstered it to the end. He regularly issued decrees confirming the jurisdiction of his HSSPfs over all SS and police officials in their regions, without exception, specifically including members of the Allgemeine-SS, Waffen-SS, Orpo, Sipo and SD, and representatives of the Hauptamt RKF and VOMI. However, as the Reich began to fall back on all fronts, the HSSPfs in previously occupied territories had their fiefdoms snatched away from them by the advancing Allies, and the struggle for survival overtook the grand notion of the State Protection Corps. By 1945, the HSSPfs had become figureheads with little or no means of actually directing the vast forces still technically under their command.

THE INDUSTRIAL EMPIRE

As well as being a great consumer of goods and materials, the SS was also a large-scale producer of them. Before the war, Himmler indulged in limited productive economic enterprises, or SS Wirtschaftsunternehmungen, such as the Apollinaris mineral water works at Bad Neuenahr. Great publicity was given to the SS porcelain factory at Allach, a satellite of Dachau concentration camp, which manufactured top quality decorative pieces as well as basic ceramic utensils for kitchen use. The sword smithy at Dachau, which kept alive the tradition of making high-grade damascus steel edged weapons, was another example of the acceptable face of the SS economy, with workers being very well treated to protect their precious skills. The war, however, and the acquisition of large fertile territories, greatly enlarged the scope of these activities. Farming and stockbreeding in Poland, and lumbering, mining and fishing in Russia, all entered the field of SS economics. Ad hoc SS Economic Operations Units, or Wirtschaftskommandos, were formed to co-ordinate local entrepreneurial projects, and between 1941 and 1944 the SS exploited the wealth, resources and population of the conquered East on a massive scale.

In wartime Germany itself, an equally great range and even greater ambition of SS economic activity was apparent. Just as the SS achieved a fair measure of independence in the sphere of military supply, so it sought and attained independence in the more general production field. The concentration camp system gave the SS a virtually inexhaustible source of cheap expendable labour, and where it was not expedient in any given case to set up an SS enterprise the camp workers could be farmed out to private firms or used on sub-contract work, for which the SS received payment. The projects thus directly or indirectly carried out by the SS ranged from tailoring to armaments and from quarrying to aircraft construction, and nearly 2 million labourers of both sexes were 'employed' on Himmler's business. By 1944, the SS had developed its own comprehensive and widespread economic system in which was found the raw materials, the factories which processed them, the workers who handled them, and finally the consumers who absorbed them. It ultimately controlled more than 500 manufacturing plants, and produced 75 per cent of Germany's non-alcoholic beverages and practically all of the country's furniture. Moreover, by virtue of this economic activity, the SS maintained influential representatives and contacts at many points throughout normal German industrial life. Indeed, Hitler often joked that Himmler was Germany's biggest industrialist!

For his part, the Reichsführer attached supreme importance to making the best possible use of all available concentration camp labour. It was planned that the building projects of the SS after the war would be on such a large scale that the creation of a camp reserve of 5,000 stonemasons and 10,000 bricklayers was ordered in 1942. These workers would be employed to deliver to the state at least 100,000 cubic metres of granite per year, more than was ever produced by all the quarries in the old Reich. Since there were only 4,000 skilled stonemasons in the whole of Germany before the war, an extensive training programme was instigated. Camp commandants were directed to ensure that the efficiency of prisoners selected for

The munitions factory within the confines of Dachau concentration camp, showing inmates working on the production of rifle components for the Waffen-SS and police.

Rifle grenades, signals flares and other explosives were manufactured in large numbers by prisoners at Dachau. Trusted inmates were employed by the SS as inspectors, to ensure that quality control was maintained. There was an automatic death sentence for any inmate found sabotaging production.

training was increased through the provision of suitable food and clothing, and willing trainees were given rewards as an example to the indifferent. One of the biggest incentives was that inmates successfully undergoing training were exempt from transfer to other less humane camps – or to extermination camps.

For construction and building purposes, Germany was subsequently divided into four great SS Work Inspectorates, the SS-Bauinspektion Reich, with headquarters at Berlin, Dachau, Posen and Wiesbaden. The wartime activities carried out by their workers included road making and the building of barracks and training grounds. Plans to lay the foundations of a large SS town, the so-called 'SS-Stadt', around Wewelsburg Castle had to be shelved until after the war. Instead, SS construction brigades, or SS-Baubrigaden, drawn from unskilled concentration camp inmates assisted in clearing up bombed areas. A large number of prisoners were detailed to build the extermination camps, to construct various experimental rocket sites and to transfer vital war production plant to secret underground locations in Germany, before being 'permanently silenced'. In occupied territories it was customary to use for general construction purposes formations known as SS Front Labour Units, or SS-Frontarbeiterunternehmen, composed chiefly of foreign workers, while building equipment stores, or SS-Bauhöfe, holding reserve stocks of equipment, were maintained in most large towns.

All this industry was co-ordinated and directed by the SS Wirtschafts- und Verwaltungshauptamt or WVHA, the SS Economic and Administrative Department. Commanded by SS-Obergruppenführer Oswald Pohl, the WVHA was formed in March 1942 by amalgamating three existing offices:

1. the old Verwaltungsamt (Administrative Office) of the SS Hauptamt
2. the Hauptamt Haushalt und Bauten (Department of Finance and Building)
3. the office of the Inspekteur der Konzentrationslager (Inspectorate of Concentration Camps)

Its creation recognised the potential which the SS and police system had for generating its own income, and solved the problem of conflicting interests and divided authority over such questions as the allocation of prison and concentration camp labour.

As with the other SS Hauptämter, the province of the WVHA covered the whole SS. The Allgemeine-SS was, for the most part, an unpaid and only lightly equipped organisation, so the administration of both supply and finance for that branch did not require a very extensive or complicated machinery. Nevertheless, the employment of full-time Allgemeine-SS staff, the upkeep of Allgemeine-SS property and the supervision of stocks of weapons, uniforms and equipment at regional level all fell within the scope of the WVHA. The Waffen-SS and police imposed much larger claims upon it, including the overseeing of administrative units of the Waffen-SS, the provision of Waffen-SS clothing, and the undertaking of engineering and construction work. Moreover, a WVHA Wirtschaftsführer or Economics Official was attached to the HSSPf in each occupied territory to co-ordinate the joint administration of the SS and police. When the National HQ of the uniformed police was bombed out in February 1944, it moved most of its departments to the premises of the WVHA, which thereafter carried out services on behalf of the Ordnungspolizei not only in the occupied territories but also in the Reich proper. In addition to these activities, the WVHA was the supreme financial authority for the SS and ran the vast range of SS economic undertakings. To a large extent, the day-to-day work of the WVHA was decentralised and carried out by administrative departments of the various SS Hauptämter, the administrative officers attached to the HSSPfs, and administrative sections at Oberabschnitt and Abschnitt level. Even so, the WVHA remained in charge of the general supervision of all SS and police administration, and appointed administrative personnel. It had to approve the promotions of administrative officers in the SS and police, and acted in close liaison with the SS Führungshauptamt regarding administrative training courses, for which it maintained two specialist schools at Arolsen and Dachau. The SS Verwaltungsdienst, or Administrative Service, included for its enlisted ranks the posts of accountant, baker, billeting official, butcher, clerk, cook, paymaster and storekeeper, while officer grades specialised in agriculture, engineering, forestry and mining, as well as general administrative duties. The SS maintained its own system of supply distinct from that of the Wehrmacht, for which purpose a large network of depots and stores was built up in Germany and the occupied territories. Operationally, these came under the control of the SS Führungshauptamt, but the actual responsibility for supply was divided between the Führungshauptamt and the WVHA. Broadly speaking, the former dealt with arms, ammunition and other technical equipment, while the latter was responsible for rations, clothing, wood, coal, fodder and personal items. The WVHA also engaged in the bulk purchase of leather and textiles, although all other raw materials were acquired for the SS by a special Rohstoffamt (Raw Materials Office) attached to the Persönlicher Stab RfSS.

By 1945, the WVHA had developed to incorporate five distinct branches, or Amtsgruppen, with general allocation of functions as follows:

Amtsgruppe A	Finance, Law and Administration (SS-Brigadeführer Heinz Fanslau)
Amtsgruppe B	Supply, Billeting and Equipment (SS-Gruppenführer Georg Lörner)
Amtsgruppe C	Works and Buildings (SS-Gruppenführer Dr Hans Kammler)
Amtsgruppe D	Concentration Camps (SS-Gruppenführer Richard Glücks)
Amtsgruppe W	Economic Enterprises (SS-Gruppenführer August Frank)

Pohl proved to be a very capable administrator of the entire system, and by the end of the war the WVHA had attained a nationwide economic imperium for the SS.

Amtsgruppe W was subdivided into eight distinct departments or ämter at the end of 1944. These are detailed in the table on p. 104, together with the main activities coming under their jurisdiction, to show the immense variety of SS enterprises being undertaken at that time. Due to its very nature, Amtsgruppe W was considerably decentralised, with each of its ämter located away from the WVHA headquarters.

The massive concentration camp industry was supervised on the ground by only a few junior SS officers and NCOs, assisted by a large number of foreign auxiliary troops and senior inmates known as ältesten. These inmates acted as works foremen or Kapos, and were free from all other camp duties. Political prisoners and hardened habitual criminals were usually entrusted with such jobs since they often wielded great influence over their comrades. Many clerical positions

AMTSGRUPPE W – THE SS ECONOMIC ENTERPRISES

AMT I   *Deutsche Erd- und Steinwerke GmbH, or D.E.St.* (German Clay and Brickworks Co., Ltd) under SS-Obersturmbannführer Karl Mummenthey.
Section 1: Brickworks.
These were located at Sachsenhausen, Neuengamme, Buchenwald and Stutthof concentration camps.
Section 2: Quarries.
This section supervised granite quarries at Mauthausen, Gross-Rosen, Flössenburg and Natzweiler; stone quarries at Rotau and Linz; masonry at Oranienburg; gravel dredging at Auschwitz; and an oil shale research distillery at Natzweiler.
Section 3: Pottery and Porcelain Works.
These were in operation at Allach, Dachau and also in Bohemia.

AMT II   *Baustoffswerke und Zementfabriken* (Building Materials and Cement Factories) under SS-Obersturmbannführer Dr Hanns Bobermin.
Section 1: Building Materials.
These plants made plasterboard, insulation, roofing tiles, etc. and were sited in Posen, Bielitz and Zichenau.
Section 2: Cement Factories.
The main enterprise under this Section was the Golleschau Cement Works at Auschwitz.
Section 3: Eastern Works.
Dealt with the large number of Russian building companies which the SS took over 'lock, stock and barrel' during 1941–2.

AMT III   *Ernährungs Betriebe* (Food Industry) under SS-Oberführer Karl Möckel.
Section 1: Mineral Water.
There were three SS soft drinks factories which went under the trade names of Sudetenquell, Mattoni and Apollinaris, and an associated SS bottling plant, the Rheinglassfabrik.
Section 2: Meat Processing.
This was carried out at Auschwitz, Dachau and Sachsenhausen.
Section 3: Bread Making.
SS bakeries operated at Auschwitz, Dachau, Sachsenhausen, Herzogenbusch, Lublin and Plaszow.

AMT IV   *Deutsche Ausrüstungswerke, or D.A.W.* (German Equipment Works) under SS-Sturmbannführer Dr Hans May.
Section 1: Military Armaments.
SS involvement in the armaments and munitions industry increased as the war progressed, not only for the purpose of supplying the Waffen-SS but also to assist conventional arms manufacturers by furnishing them with cheap labour. The SS made many of its own weapons and technical instrumentation at Auschwitz, Neuengamme, Ravensbrück, Sachsenhausen, Stutthof, Lublin and Plaszow,

maintained an ordnance testing and repair shop at Stutthof, and melted down scrap cable at Dachau. In addition, aircraft parts assembly was carried out at Flössenburg, Mauthausen and Natzweiler on behalf of the Messerschmitt and Junkers companies. Heinkel contracted the SS to produce hangars for them at Sachsenhausen, gun carriages were repaired at Mauthausen, hand grenades assembled at Sachsenhausen, and industrial diamonds cut at Herzogenbusch and Belsen.

Section 2:   Carpentry and Cabinet Making.
              Almost every concentration camp had a furniture workshop, making articles for both military and civilian consumption.

Section 3:   Weaving.
              The vast majority of SS and police uniforms were manufactured at so-called SS-Bekleidungswerke or clothing factories in the concentration camps, with a central store at Dachau. In addition, the SS made webbing and braid for the Wehrmacht on sub-contract to the Schwarz Company of Hamburg.

Amt V   *Land-, Forst- und Fischereiwirtschaft* (Agriculture, Forestry and Fisheries) under SS-Obersturmbannführer Heinrich Vogel.

Section 1:   Nutrition and Food Research.
              This section purchased both live and dead animals such as guinea-pigs, mice and rats for experimental use in the research institutes of the SS. It also bred Angora rabbits at Auschwitz and maintained medicinal herb and spice gardens in many other camps.

Section 2:   Forestry.
              Administered the economic use of forests situated on SS property.

Section 3:   Fisheries.
              The SS operated a fish processing company under the trade name of Anton Loibl GmbH.

Amt VI   *Textil- und Lederverwertung* (Re-processing of Textile and Leather Goods) under SS-Obersturmbannführer Fritz Lechler.
              There were textile and leather works at Dachau and Ravensbrück which upgraded old uniforms, belts, boots, etc. for re-issue to combat units of the Waffen-SS and police. They also processed clothing confiscated from concentration camp inmates, which was then forwarded to the SS-Bekleidungswerke to be made into uniforms.

Amt VII   *Buch und Bild* (Books and Pictures) under SS-Sturmbannführer Dr Alfred Mischke.
Section 1:   Nordland-Verlag.
              The SS publishing house which produced books and magazines on Germanic history and culture for general public consumption.

Section 2:   Bauer & Co.
              An SS picture restoration company, employed by major European art galleries, which also confiscated valuable paintings for display at Wewelsburg or in the House of German Art in Munich.

Amt VIII   *Kulturbauten* (Cultural Monuments) under SS-Obersturmbannführer Horst Klein.

Section 1:   Society for the Maintenance of German Monuments.

Looked after the upkeep and improvement of historical buildings including the SS castles at Wewelsburg, Kranichfeld and Sudelfeld. Many of the tapestries, wood carvings and the like used to embellish these institutions were manufactured by craftsmen at Buchenwald and other concentration camps. This section also supervised the SS Damascus School at Dachau.

Section 2:   Memorial Foundations.

This section was principally concerned with the King Heinrich Memorial Trust and the Externsteine Foundation, the latter looking after a sanctuary situated among a group of rocks in the Teutoberg Forest.

within the camps were also held by selected inmates, and there was a high degree of prisoner self-administration. Employment of inmates on desk work also provided the camp officials with an opportunity to play the prisoners against one another, and make them scapegoats for thefts and other petty crimes committed by some of the SS men. The permanent SS contingent at each camp was usually fairly small, Dachau, for example, having just 300 Totenkopf veterans, all over forty years of age, to oversee 17,000 inmates

SS men guarding Hungarian Jews at Auschwitz railway terminal, summer 1944. This candid photograph was found in Czechoslovakia at the end of the war, among the possessions of a dead Waffen-SS soldier who had previously served at the camp. Himmler expressly forbade the taking of such souvenir snapshots, realising that they might well eventually be used in evidence against the SS.

in 1943. However, most camps also had Waffen-SS training grounds sited nearby from which extra men were regularly drafted in on a rota basis, and from which emergency reinforcements could be summoned if required.

During the second half of the war, the working hours of most prisoners were raised considerably. By 1944, an eleven-hour day had become the rule, even during the winter months, with only Sunday afternoons set aside for rest. Debility and mortality increased rapidly, and the productivity of inmates remained far below Himmler's and Pohl's high expectations. Consequently, more and more had to be employed to maintain even a static output. Anti-social elements and petty criminals were soon being transferred *en masse* by the RSHA from conventional German state prisons to the concentration camp factories, and according to a WVHA report of 15 January 1945 the number of inmates incarcerated at that time had reached an all-time high of 715,000, including 200,000 women. Probably as many as one-third of those subsequently lost their lives in the exhausting evacuation marches organised in the face of Allied advances on the camps. The total number of prisoners who died during the war from weakness and disease while labouring for the SS in the concentration camps and industrial complexes of the Reich was estimated by the Nürnberg tribunal at half a million.

The Nazi party in general, as a nationalist and anti-socialist movement, was supported from its infancy by big business. The SS was particularly attractive to major industrial groupings such as I.G. Farben, whose directors shared Himmler's opposition to the costly protection of the old Junker landholders, and his goal of building German hegemony in Europe, in a closed economic bloc independent of American capital and the world market. During the spring of 1934,

A typical concentration camp guard, February 1945. This is one of only three known photographs showing the double-armed swastika collar patch being worn. It was used from September 1944 to identify full-time concentration camp guards who had been compulsorily transferred in from the Wehrmacht, SA, Werkschutz or similar non-SS organisations. Such men, who had little to do with the horrors of the camp system, bore the brunt of Allied reprisals when the camps were liberated.

Himmler befriended Wilhelm Keppler, one of I.G. Farben's managers, and bestowed upon him the honorary rank of SS-Gruppenführer. In return, Keppler was instrumental in the creation of the so-called Freundeskreis RfSS, or Circle of Friends of the Reichsführer-SS, a group of wealthy industrialists and business advisers. They agreed to make regular financial contributions towards the cultural, social and charitable activities of the SS, in return for Himmler's patronage and protection. While Keppler was the instigator of the Freundeskreis, its leading member was the renowned financier Kurt Freiherr von Schröder, whose Cologne Bank maintained the special account, codenamed 'S', which held Freundeskreis donations. Other prominent members of the Circle included:

Foreign Minister Joachim von Ribbentrop in his uniform as an honorary SS-Brigadeführer, early 1936. At this stage in his career, von Ribbentrop had just been appointed Hitler's ambassador to Great Britain.

Dr Rasche, Director of the Dresden Bank; Dr Lippert, Oberbürgermeister of Berlin; Dr Ritter von Halt, Director of the Deutsche Bank; and Gottfried Graf von Bismarck. Heavy industry was represented by, among others: Director-General Röhnert of the Lüdenscheid Metal Works; Steinbrinck of the Flick Steel Consortium; Bingel of the Siemens electrical combine; Bütefisch of I.G. Farben; and Walz of the Bosch chemical concern.

Throughout the life of the Third Reich, the Freundeskreis deposited vast sums into the coffers of the SS, and a special office was set up under SS-Brigadeführer Fritz Kranefuss to administer donations received from the Circle. For its part, the SS was able to award lucrative contracts in the conquered territories to the companies concerned, and supply them with cheap concentration camp labour. In September 1943 alone, over 1 million Reichsmarks went into Account 'S', 200,000 of them from von Schröder personally, who wrote that he was very happy to be able to help Himmler perform his 'special tasks'. There is no doubt that these pillars of German society played a most important part in oiling the wheels of the SS economic machine.

THE SS SOCIETY

Besides the acknowledged and logical development of the SS as regards its fusion with the police and security services, the organisation enlarged its position and range of influence in more insidious ways. By means of an unobtrusive but thorough policy of infiltration, the SS furnished itself with representatives in every branch of official and semi-official German life. It became, in effect, the archetypal 'state within the state', a closely knit and powerful group of men and women governed by a rigid set of rules, the chief of which was loyalty to Himmler and unquestioning obedience of orders.

Membership of the SS was always

Members of the Reichstag saluting Hitler in 1937. SS uniforms are evident everywhere, and prominent SS personalities in the group include Schaub, von Ribbentrop, Lammers, Otto Dietrich, von Neurath, Darré and Seyss-Inquart.

attractive after 1933, offering a steady and lucrative job in the agency of the most influential body in Germany, with the chance of a quick lift on the road to economic, political, professional or even artistic success. Consequently, the Allgemeine-SS soon outgrew its origins as a group of guardsmen and came to represent a very carefully organised racial élite composed of intellectuals as well as ex-soldiers, shopkeepers and peasant youths. In May 1944, no less than 300 of the 1,200 leading personalities in Germany, including industrialists, financiers and academics, held SS membership. By that time, SS domination throughout the Reich had become total.

A starting point in the study of SS personalities can be made with the immediate entourage of the Führer. Hitler surrounded himself with SS men, the principal of whom were his secretary, SS-Obergruppenführer Philipp Bouhler, and his personal adjutant, SS-Obergruppenführer Julius Schaub, both constant companions and confidants since the old Stosstrupp days. The Führer's chief medical officer, Prof. Dr Karl Brandt, was a Gruppenführer; his personal pilot, Hans Baur, was a Brigadeführer in the RSD; and his chauffeur, Erich Kempka, was a Sturm-bannführer. In addition, the majority of Hitler's young valets and aides, including Fritz Darges, Otto Günsche, Wilhelm Krause,

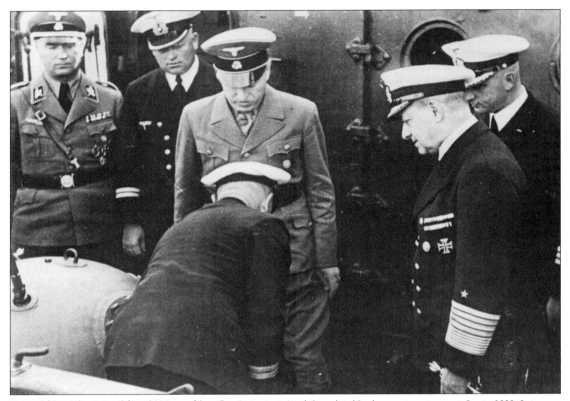

SS-Brigadeführer Arthur Greiser (left) and SS-Gruppenführer Albert Forster (centre) with Grossadmiral Raeder on an inspection tour in Danzig, 1939. Greiser, a former navy pilot, wears the pale-grey Allgemeine-SS uniform while Forster sports a personalised political tunic, without insignia, in his other capacity as the local NSDAP Gauleiter. Greiser, then Forster's deputy, later became an SS-Obergruppenführer and Gauleiter of Wartheland.

Heinz Linge, Hans Pfeiffer, Max Wünsche and the brothers Hans-Georg and Richard Schulze, were junior SS officers.

As it was with the head of the party, so it was with the NSDAP itself. One of the key posts at the top of the Nazi hierarchy, that of Party Treasurer, was held by SS-Oberst-Gruppenführer Franz Xaver Schwarz, who controlled the whole financial policy of the NSDAP. Below him were three SS-Obergruppenführer: Walter Buch, the Supreme Party Judge; Max Amann, Chief of the Party Press Office; and Martin Bormann, Head of the Party Chancellery. To quote only two more examples, SS-Brigadeführer Erich

Cassel was Chief of the NSDAP Racial Department, and SS-Brigadeführer Bernhard Ruberg was Deputy Gauleiter of the Foreign Section of the NSDAP, which co-ordinated all party activities abroad.

Control of access to Hitler and domination of the NSDAP by the SS could perhaps be expected, but the same penetration was also evident in the machinery of the state. Some of the most important posts in the Cabinet were held by SS generals. Obergruppenführer Dr Hans Lammers was Head of the Reich Chancellery, while Constantin Freiherr von Neurath and Joachim von Ribbentrop both served as Foreign Minister. In the various

SS-Obergruppenführer Karl Fiehler, Lord Mayor of Munich, unveiled the city's Freikorps Memorial on 9 May 1942.

Reich Ministries, thirty-nine key positions were occupied by SS men from the ranks of Obergruppenführer down to Obersturmbannführer. In the Foreign Office alone, ten posts were held by SS officers, including Wilhelm Keppler, Walther Hewel and Prof. Dr Werner Gerlach, who were heads of departments. Brigadeführer Kurt Freiherr von Schröder, of the Freundeskreis RfSS, and the giant Dr Alexander Freiherr von Dörnberg, Chief of Protocol, were ministerial directors. SS-Oberführer Prof. Dr Franz Six, Chief of Amt VII of the RSHA, was also Head of the Foreign Office Cultural Department. Ribbentrop is known to have fought hard to maintain the independence of the Foreign Office and Diplomatic Service against the encroachments of the SD, so it is all the more significant that so many SS men held influential posts in the sphere of activity which he controlled.

In view of Himmler's position after 1943 as Reich Minister of the Interior, it was inevitable that the SS were well represented in that branch of the government. SS-Obergruppenführer Oswald Pohl of the WVHA was a ministerial director, and Obergruppenführer Dr Wilhelm Stuckart was a Secretary of State. Moreover, SS-Gruppenführer Prof. Dr Friedrich Weber, SS-Brigadeführer Dr Anton Kreissl and SS-Oberführer Hans Rüdiger were heads of departments. The special significance of the Ministry of the Interior, however, extended beyond the mere list of SS personalities holding office within it. Not only was it the

Himmler in conversation with SS-Obergruppenführer Dr Hans Lammers, Head of the Reich Chancellery, who is wearing the white summer tunic. The chief administrators of the Party, the Wehrmacht and the state (Bormann, Keitel and Lammers) were known as the 'Gang of Three'. Two of them (Bormann and Lammers) were SS generals, and so were directly under the influence of Himmler.

central authoritative ministry in all matters concerning the home front, but from it Himmler was able to keep control of the vast German bureaucracy. The power of appointment, promotion and dismissal which he enjoyed as Minister of the Interior was one of the greatest reinforcements to its infiltration policy which the SS achieved.

At Goebbels' Ministry of Propaganda, the Chief of the Reich Press, Dr Otto Dietrich, was an SS-Obergruppenführer. Other SS officers of high rank included: Alfred-Ingemar Berndt, the Controller of Broadcasting; Karl Cerff, a departmental

head; Dr Werner Naumann, Secretary of State for Propaganda; and Dr Toni Winkelnkemper, Head of the Foreign Broadcasting Department. As with the Foreign Office, this SS infiltration into the Propaganda Ministry was one of particular significance since Goebbels was no friend of Himmler and can scarcely have welcomed the presence of SS men among his subordinates. There is no doubt that this aspect represented a deliberate attempt by the SS to gain control of the German press and the nationwide machinery of propaganda.

At the Ministry of Labour, the Head of the Reich Inspectorate of Manpower was SS-Gruppenführer Prof. Rudolf Jung, while SS-Brigadeführer Prof. Wilhelm Börger was head of a department and SS-Oberführer Kurt Frey was Reich Inspector of Labour. In the Justice Ministry, SS-Gruppenführer Leo Petri was a member of the People's Court and SS-Oberführer Karl Engert was a Ministerial Director. The Ministry of Agriculture and Food was headed by SS-Obergruppenführer Walther Darré until 1942, when he was succeeded by SS-Obergruppenführer Herbert Backe. SS-Gruppenführer Werner Willikens was a Secretary of State at the Ministry, and SS-Obersturmbannführer Ferdinand Hiege of the Hauptamt RKF was a departmental head. The Minister of Health, Dr Leonardo Conti, was an SS-Obergruppenführer and the Ministries of Economics, Finance and Education all had their share of SS permeation. SS-Gruppenführer Dr Franz Hayler and SS-Gruppenführer Otto Ohlendorf, both important SD officials, were at the first, SS-Brigadeführer Otto Heider at the second, and SS-Standartenführer Prof. Dr Albert Holfelder at the last, to name only a sample.

In local government, the tale was the same. Provincial State Ministers and Secretaries, Presidents and Vice-Presidents of state governments, were but a few of the men

SS-Obergruppenführer Dr Otto Dietrich, Chief of the Reich Press, addressing the first Congress of the Union of National Journalists' Associations at the Doge's Palace in Venice, 9 April 1942.

whose high SS rank was not always the most publicised feature of their careers. Further down the scale, in municipal affairs, at least six cities had senior SS officers as their Lord Mayors, including the Stosstrupp veteran Karl Fiehler, Oberbürgermeister of Munich. Emil Maurice, Ulrich Graf and their Old Guard comrades were invariably installed as local city councillors, in addition to their national appointments.

Turning to industry, Paul Körner, Secretary of State for the Four Year Plan, and Wilhelm Meinberg, Commissioner for Fuel, were both SS generals. In other spheres such as armaments, shipping, banking and the motor and textile industries, the SS was again well represented. For instance, SS-Stand-artenführer Dr August Schwedler was Director of the Reichsbank; SS-Brigadeführer Hans Kehrl was leader of the Textiles Economics Group; SS-Oberführer Jakob Werlin was Reich Inspector of Motor Traffic and Director-General of the Mercedes firm; and SS-Oberführer Rudolf Diels, first chief of the Gestapo, headed the Hermann Göring Shipping Company.

The same was true of the military aristocracy, and some parts of the *SS Dienstaltersliste* read like a 'Who's Who' of German nobility. In addition to those mentioned elsewhere in this book, aristocratic members of the Allgemeine-SS included General Friedrich Graf von der Schulenburg, Generalmajor Anton Edler Kless von

Drauwörth, Kuno Freiherr von Eltz-Rübenach, Oberst Friedrich Freiherr von der Goltz, Oberstleutnant Rolf von Humann-Hainhofen, Carl Reichsritter von Oberkamp, Wilhelm Freiherr von Holzschuher, Rittmeister Erasmus Freiherr von Malsen, Friedrich Erbgrossherzog von Mecklenburg, Carl Graf von Pückler-Burghaus, Friedrich Freiherr von Reitzenstein, Hildolf Reichsfreiherr von Thüngen, Paul Baron von Vietinghoff-Scheel, and Generalmajor Gustav Adolf von Wulffen. The list went on and on. One of the more renowned of their number during the Second World War was Oberst Hyazinth Graf Strachwitz, who won the Knight's Cross of the Iron Cross with Oakleaves, Swords and Diamonds while serving as an army Panzer commander on the eastern front. He was one of a mere twenty-seven recipients of the coveted decoration, and the only man ever to wear it with the black Allgemeine-SS uniform.

The widespread influence of the SS was not confined to the Reich, for in every occupied territory SS men held some of the most important administrative posts. For example, Brigadeführer Dr Wilhelm Kinkelin was leader of the Section for Colonisation Policy in Rosenberg's Eastern Ministry. In Poland, SS-Gruppenführer Dr Otto Wächter was Governor of Galicia and SS-Gruppenführer Dr Richard Wendler Governor of the Lublin District, while two more key positions in Krakow were held by Brigadeführer Prof. Dr Heinrich Teitge and Brigadeführer Dr Harry von Craushaar. In Bohemia and Moravia, SS-Obergruppenführer Karl Hermann Frank was Minister of State, with Brigadeführer Dr Walther Bertsch as his Minister of Economics and Labour. In the west, Obergruppenführer Dr Werner Best was German Plenipotentiary in Denmark and Obergruppenführer Dr Arthur Seyss-Inquart was Reich Commissioner for the Netherlands. Under them were many SS officers at the head of the civil administration, and all this was in addition to the normal machinery of the SS and police set up in the conquered countries.

The realms of education, culture and charitable organisations were no more closed to the ubiquitous SS than were the high governmental circles or heavy industry. Many university professors were SS officers of high rank and SS-Gruppenführer Johannes Johst was President of both the Reich Chamber of Literature and the German Academy of Poets. SS-Sturmbannführer Hermann Müller-John, bandmaster of the Leibstandarte, was on the Council of the Reich Chamber of Music. Even the German Red Cross Society, under the leadership of SS-Obergruppenführer Prof. Dr Ernst-Robert Grawitz, was permeated with SS officials. Similarly, the head of the Nazi People's Welfare Organisation was SS-Gruppenführer Erich Hilgenfeldt, who was also in charge of the annual Winter Charities Campaign, the Winterhilfswerk. One of his close WHW colleagues, the Reich Women's Leader Gertrud Scholtz-Klink, was the wife of SS-Obergruppenführer August Heissmeyer. The SS likewise dominated the sporting world with, for example, Standartenführer Hans Hieronymus as Secretary of the German Boxing Federation.

This SS penetration into all parts of German life was steadily achieved in two ways. Firstly, in the early days of the Nazi movement, before the SS was in a position to appoint or arrange the appointment of its own men to influential offices, the main method used was the practice of awarding honorary SS rank to important public figures. The new members felt their authority enhanced by the black uniform and semi-military status, while Himmler secured well-placed allies bound to him by the oath of loyalty which could be backed up if necessary by the SS discipline code. Initially, there were two categories of honorary officer: the Rangführer and the Ehrenführer. The term

Rangführer was used for honorary ranks up to and including Obersturmbannführer, while Ehrenführer covered Standartenführer and above. Both groups wore distinctive ivory-coloured cuff titles. After the separation of the SS from the SA in 1934, the Rangführer grade and the special insignia were abolished, and from that time there was nothing to outwardly distinguish the SS-Ehrenführer from active SS officers.

The second method of SS infiltration reached its full efficiency only after the consolidation of the Nazi régime, and was the direct promotion of SS men to high positions in the state. A marked feature of the German governmental hierarchy was the pluralism of offices held by leading SS figures, which enabled a few men to exercise a disproportionately large influence. The best example was that of Himmler himself, who eventually controlled all military, para-military and police forces on the home front, as well as two entire Army Groups in the field. He was able to appoint his lieutenants to correspondingly high positions in both the state and, after the July 1944 bomb plot, the Wehrmacht. By the end of 1944, SS-Obergruppenführer Hans Jüttner was Chief of Staff of the Home Army as well as being head of the SS Führungshauptamt, while SS-Gruppenführer August Frank of the WVHA and Verwaltungspolizei had also been appointed Chief of Administration for the Army High Command. That last bastion of the old traditional Germany, the army, had finally fallen to the SS.

The primary function of the SS was to protect Hitler and his régime, and it operated all the more efficiently having placed its representatives and contacts in all sections and at all levels of the society which it guarded. The part it played in preserving the general security of the Third Reich and in strengthening Himmler's position against his rivals from within the NSDAP cannot be overemphasised. In short, there was nothing in Nazi Germany which was not political, and nothing political with which the SS was not concerned.

NOBLE ANCESTORS

Himmler's plans for the SS were in many ways dominated by his genuine belief that the Black Order constituted a brotherhood which was spiritually descended from the heroes of pagan and medieval Germany. This view of a mythical Germanic past linked to the present by invisible bonds of race and will was not unique to Himmler, and was shared by many of his contemporaries. During the nineteenth century, Germany had witnessed a resurgence of nationalism and in the progression towards a unified Reich there had grown a tremendous interest in medieval history and ancient Teutonic legend. The general fascination was fired by the operatic works of Richard Wagner (1813–83), a rabid anti-Semite whose heroes such as Parsifal and Lohengrin were the epitomes of knightly chivalry, continually battling against the forces of evil. Wagner's last and epic work, however, entitled *Der Ring des Nibelungen* (*The Ring of the Nibelung*), was set in the murky world of Dark Age fables. Its four great interconnected operas, *Rheingold*, *Die Walküre* (which includes a Valkyrie named Siegrune!), *Siegfried* and *Götterdämmerung*, were acted out in a land of gods, giants, dragons, supermen and slavish sub-human dwarves, where a magical ring and enchanted sword bestowed limitless power and invincibility upon their owners. The Ring Cycle had a timeless message about the human desire for influence and wealth at the expense of all other things, but the moral of the tale was soon lost in its telling, as the operas with their sublime music captivated and bewitched those who attended them, and instilled in the audiences a feeling of racial

Over 120,000 Germans enjoyed an impressive neo-pagan summer solstice celebration in the Berlin Olympic Stadium on 21 June 1939. The event was organised jointly by the SS and the Ministry of Propaganda.

unity and national identity which seemed to extend back to the beginning of mankind. Hitler himself was inspired in his youth by Wagner's music, and it was while he was entranced by it that he conceived his great plans for the future of Germany. He said years later, 'For me, Wagner was someone godly and his music is my religion. I go to his concerts as others go to church'.

Exalted by the works of Wagner and by the writings of the philosopher Friedrich Nietzsche (1844–1900), whose *Man and Superman* divided the world into masters and slaves and foresaw the coming of a great leader who would build a new order of 'Übermenschen', a number of German nationalists founded the Thule Society in Berlin in 1912. The Society took its name from the legendary 'Ultima Thule' or 'Land at the End of the World', supposedly the birthplace of the Germanic race, and its primary purpose was to serve as a literary circle for the study of ancient German history and customs. After 1918, it became fanatically anti-Bolshevik and anti-Semitic, and eventually propounded the aim of unifying Europe under the leadership of a Great Germanic Reich. Significantly, the symbol of the Thule Society was a sunwheel swastika.

The Bavarian branch of the Society was small, but its membership was hand-picked and included Himmler, Hess and Röhm. The nobility, the judiciary, higher academics,

116

leading industrialists and army and police officers were all represented, to the virtual exclusion of the lower classes. Thule conducted open nationalistic propaganda through its own newspaper, the Munich *Völkischer Beobachter,* edited by Dietrich Eckart (who later coined the Nazi battle-cry 'Deutschland Erwache!' or 'Germany Awake!'), and set up a secret intelligence service which infiltrated communist groups. It maintained and financed three Freikorps units, i.e. Oberland, Reichskriegsflagge and Wiking, and to win popular support to its cause promoted the German Workers' Party under 'front-man' Anton Drexler in 1919. When Drexler's party was taken over by Hitler and expanded under its new name as the NSDAP, it completely absorbed the Thule Society, together with its newspaper, nationalist programme and racist policies.

Through his association with Thule, Himmler became obsessed with pagan Germanic culture, an obsession which grew ever stronger as the years went by and one which came to influence his entire way of life and that of the SS. During the early 1930s, the Reichsführer established an SS-sponsored Society for the Care of German Historic Monuments and acquired a publishing house, Nordland-Verlag, to spread his ideas to the general public. Plans for the systematic creation of a cultural framework to replace Christianity, referred to as the Development of the German Heritage, were worked out between Himmler's personal staff and selected academics in 1937. A new moral philosophy based on the supposed beliefs of the old Germanic tribes was formulated, and two pagan rites, the summer and winter solstices, were revived to replace Christian festivals. The summer event centred around sporting activities and the winter one, the Yule, was a time devoted to the honouring of ancestors. God became 'Got' in SS circles (allegedly the old Germanic spelling), to distinguish the pagan SS god from the conventional Christian 'Gott', a suggestion which came from Karl Diebitsch during his preparation of new SS wedding and child-naming ceremonies.

What distinguished Himmler from Rosenberg, Darré and the other blood mystics was the flair he brought to the practical task of realising his vision of a pagan Germanic Reich. The Reichsführer was considered a persuasive speaker, with his light Bavarian accent, and, more importantly, he clearly believed in everything he said at the moment he said it. No man looked less like his job or appeared more normal than the SS chief. He successfully convinced ultra-traditionalists that they were the vanguard of the new Germany, while at the same time providing the young with the glamour of a dark and secret Order sworn to a pagan creed running counter to the rules of bourgeois Christian society. He also appealed to most women, tracing as he did the origin of the subjugation and undervaluation of women to the teachings of the Christian Church. The Church leadership, he asserted, had always been nothing more than a glorified homosexual male fraternity which on that basis had terrorised the people for a thousand years, to the extent of burning 150,000 good German women (not men, he emphasised) as witches. Far better to be pagan than Christian, he declared over the radio in 1937. Far better to worship the certainties of nature and ancestors than an unseen deity and its bogus representatives on earth. For a Volk which honoured its ancestors, and sought to honour itself, would always produce children, and so that Volk would have eternal life. It is evident that Himmler truly saw himself as founder of a new Pagan Order which would eventually spread across Europe and last at least as long as the German millennium being ushered in by Adolf Hitler. As late as 1944, Himmler spoke of the paganisation of Europe being a 'never-ending task which will fully occupy the tenth or twentieth Reichsführer after me'.

While paganism dominated the spiritual side of his adult life, Himmler's first historical love was medievalism. As a child the young Heinrich had followed in his father's footsteps by collecting small and inexpensive medieval artefacts. At school, he read avidly about the arrival of Vikings in the Lake Ladoga area around the year 700, their adoption of the name Rus, and how their descendants, the Norse tribe known as Russians, repelled the Mongols and settled all across the east from the Baltic to the Black Sea. He was also fascinated by the tale of Rurik the Dane, founder of Novgorod and Kiev around 856, and the story of the Saxon king Heinrich I, 'The Fowler', elected King of All Germany in 919, who had checked the incursions of Bohemians and Magyars from the east and laid the basis of the German Confederation of Princes which became, under his son Otto, the Holy Roman Empire. The aspect of medieval history which captured the boy Himmler's imagination completely, however, was that of the Order of Teutonic Knights, or Deutsche Ritterorden, founded by Heinrich Walpot von Bassenheim in 1198. Like the other hospital Orders of the time, i.e. the Knights of St John and the Templars, it was established to aid western knights who had been wounded or fallen sick during the Crusades. However, unlike the others, the Teutonic Order was distinguished by the fact that it was exclusively Germanic in its recruitment. In 1211, the Golden Bull of Rimini entrusted to its knights the colonisation of the Slavonic lands to the east of the Elbe. Under its Grand Master, Hermann von Salza, the Order immediately undertook a programme of German expansion, extending domination over Prussia and the Baltic states. It reached its height in the second half of the fourteenth century, but was brought to a sudden end in 1410. On 15 July that year, the Teutonic Knights were crushed at Tannenberg by a coalition of Poles, Lithuanians and Mongols. The power of the Order was broken, but the memory of its valorous deeds under the badge of the black cross never ceased to haunt German dreams thereafter.

It seemed to the adolescent Himmler that all of German medieval life had centred around the constant struggle between Norseman and Mongol, between Teuton and Slav, and he longed to continue the historic mission of his forefathers. Even as a nineteen-year-old student, he wrote in his diary that he hoped one day to live his life in the east and to fight his battles 'as a German far from beautiful Germany'. Himmler eventually harnessed this romantic view of history to provide an attractive integrating factor for his SS, recruited as it was from all walks of life. It was not by chance that the SS colours, black and white, were those formerly worn by the Teutonic Knights, who simply handed them down to Prussia. And when Himmler later talked about blood as the symbol of honour and fidelity, he was again appealing to medieval tradition. The mysticism of the Blutfahne itself harked back to the chivalric initiation ceremony by which the feudal suzerain was linked to his vassal by sword, fire and blood. For the SS, the Führer was their liege lord.

When his power was consolidated in 1934, Himmler's early medieval fantasies could be realised and given free rein. Obsessed by the old legend that a Westphalian castle would be the sole survivor of the next Slavonic assault from the east, the Reichsführer scoured western Germany until he found the ruined mountain fortress of Wewelsburg near Paderborn, named after the robber knight Wewel von Büren, which had been a focus of Saxon resistance to the Huns and had been rebuilt in triangular form in the seventeenth century. Following the example of the Grand Master of the Teutonic

Order who built his headquarters at Marienburg, Himmler determined to convert Wewelsburg into the stronghold of the SS. The castle was duly purchased and the architect Hermann Bartels, a Standartenführer on the Persönlicher Stab RfSS, was given 12 million Reichsmarks and set to work creating a ceremonial retreat for his master.

Entering the finished complex in 1937 was like stepping back in time. A grand staircase was bordered by a banister of forged iron, decorated with runic motifs, and the walls of the entrance hall were hung with huge tapestries depicting Germanic and rural scenes. All the woodwork was of oak and everywhere stood marble statues of Heinrich I, Friedrich von Hohenstaufen and other German heroes. Each room was furnished in medieval style. The 100 × 145 ft dining room held a massive circular Arthurian table in solid oak, around which Himmler and his twelve senior SS Obergruppenführer of the day regularly held conferences seated on high-backed pig-skin chairs bearing the names of their owner knights. A fire crackled in the monumental chimney, and behind each general hung his SS coat of arms, specially designed by Karl Diebitsch. The dining room stood above a stone basement with 5 ft thick walls, from which a flight of steps led down to a well-like crypt housing twelve granite columns and known as the 'Realm of the Dead'. The idea was that when each of the twelve SS lords died, his body would be cremated and his ashes entombed in one of these obelisks. Himmler's private apartments within the fortress were particularly sumptuous and adjoined a gold and silver strongroom, a hall for his extensive collection of medieval weaponry, a library with more than 12,000 books and an awesome chamber where the Extraordinary SS and Police Court could be convened in special circumstances. There were also magnificent guest rooms set aside for Adolf Hitler, who never appeared at

Oak carving featuring a sword, shield, steel helmet and runes, typical of the pseudo-medieval wall decorations which adorned Himmler's castle at Wewelsburg.

the castle, giving rise to the local village rumour that one day the Führer would be buried there. Himmler intended that Wewelsburg should ultimately be used as a Reichshaus der SS-Gruppenführer or SS Generals' Residence, but the outbreak of the war saw its conversion to SS-Schule Haus Wewelsburg, a staff college for senior SS officers. Its commandant was SS-Obergruppenführer Siegfried Taubert, who was formerly Heydrich's chief of staff and was father-in-law of Ernst-Robert Grawitz, the SS medical chief.

A large section of Wewelsburg Castle was dedicated to the Saxon ruler Heinrich I. The Reichsführer approved of the fact that his men nicknamed him 'King Heinrich', and came to see himself as the spiritual reincarnation of The Fowler and the embodiment of his aims to consolidate Germany against the hordes from the east. On 2 July 1936, the thousandth anniversary of the King's death, Himmler inaugurated a solemn remembrance festival at Quedlinburg, once Heinrich's seat, and in 1938 he founded the King Heinrich Memorial Trust to revive the principles and deeds of The Fowler.

Numerous SS badges were subsequently struck to commemorate Heinrich as 'Ewig das Reich' or 'The Eternity of the Reich'. To instil a general feeling of knighthood in all his junior officers and men, the majority of whom never even saw the splendour of Wewelsburg, Himmler rewarded them with the three less grandiose trappings of dagger, sword and ring. That mystical combination, harking back to a warrior aristocracy and the legend of Nibelung, was to symbolise the Ritterschaft of the new SS Order, at one and the same time both new and yet rooted in the most ancient Germanic past.

Himmler's crippling enthusiasm for German history, the ideals of which were to form the basis of the new era, led to his

Himmler delivering a eulogy on Heinrich I in Quedlinburg Cathedral, 2 July 1936. Behind him, from left to right, stand Frick, Daluege, Bouhler, Darré and Heydrich.

foundation of the Ahnenerbe- Forschungs-
und Lehrgemeinschaft, usually abbreviated to
Ahnenerbe, the Society for the Research and
Teaching of Ancestral Heritage. Its first
President was Dr Hermann Wirth, a
university lecturer known for his
controversial work on the Middle Ages and
Germanic antiquity. Wirth had joined the
NSDAP in 1925, left in 1926, and re-enrolled
in 1933. His book, *What is the German
Soul?*, was dismissed as claptrap by
Rosenberg, but Wirth managed to seduce
Himmler with the promise that he could
study and research Nordic history for the
purpose of verifying National Socialist and SS
theories by scientific proof. Obergruppenführer Darré of RuSHA also became
interested in the scheme, and his assistance
was of enormous value since, as Minister of
Agriculture, he had huge financial resources
at his disposal. It was he who actually paid
for the setting up and commissioning of the
Society in July 1935, under the auspices of his
Ministry.

The following year, however, differences of
opinion appeared between Himmler, who saw
the German as a nomadic warrior ever in
search of new lands, and Darré, who saw him
as sedentary and firmly rooted to his own
soil. This conceptual argument was to have a
profound effect on Ahnenerbe. In November
1936 it was integrated into the Abteilung für
Kulturelle Forschung (Section for Cultural
Research) of the Persönlicher Stab RfSS, and
a few months later, when the split between
Himmler and Darré reached breaking point,
the Reichsführer appointed SS-Standartenführer Bruno Galke as a special
representative to the Society to undermine
Darré's influence. One of Galke's first
measures was totally to discredit Wirth, who
was Darré's eyes and ears in the Society.
Wirth was subsequently dismissed and
replaced as President of Ahnenerbe by Prof.
Dr Walther Wüst, Dean of Munich

After his speech (see p. 120) the Reichsführer laid a wreath on the King's tomb.

University, who occupied the Chair of Aryan
Culture and Linguistics and who had a much
larger audience in academic circles. He was
also an SS-Oberführer, whose first loyalty
was to Himmler.

With Wirth gone and Darré's power over
Ahnenerbe cancelled out, the Reichsführer-SS
proceeded to restructure the Society during
the summer of 1937, establishing its new and
independent headquarters at 16 Pückler-
strasse, Berlin-Dahlem. Himmler reserved
overall control for himself, with the title of
Curator, but the day-to-day management was
carried out by Wüst, Galke and SS-
Standartenführer Wolfram Sievers of the
Persönlicher Stab RfSS. Wüst was responsible
for the direction of scientific activity, Galke
was the Treasurer, and Sievers took charge of
general organisational matters. The latter was
one of the most talented administrators in the

Himmler salutes 'The Fowler' after the wreath-laying ceremony depicted on p. 121, with Karl Wolff, Gauleiter Rudolf Jordan and Reinhard Heydrich behind. The blank collar patch worn by the SS officer on the left indicates in this case not membership of the SD, as often erroneously assumed, but his attachment to the Reichsführer's Personal Staff.

Reich, and had many influential contacts among financiers and industrialists as well as access to the Sipo and SD. He soon established a foundation of companies which were prepared to make massive monetary contributions to the Society. Other funds were found from the coffers of the Sicherheitsdienst, thanks to Sievers' friendship with SS-Oberführer Prof. Dr Franz Six, who was responsible to the SD for overseeing university policies.

At the end of 1937, Himmler defined the purpose of the reconstituted Ahnenerbe. It was to carry out research into ancient history

by studying facts from a scientific and ideological point of view, in an objective manner and without falsification. It was also to be responsible for the setting up in each SS Oberabschnitt of educational and cultural centres devoted to German greatness and the Germanic past. The first such centre was duly established at Sachsenhain by Verden, with the reconstruction of a prehistoric Saxon village which included in its displays a 5,000-year-old plough and runic inscriptions carved in stone. The whole idea was to show every German that the wealth of his land and culture were the makings of his own ancestors, not things which had been brought in by the Romans or other outsiders.

All of Germany's archaeological excavations were soon put into the hands of the Society. Their overall direction was entrusted first to SS-Obersturmbannführer Dr Rolf Höhne, who was personally responsible for researches at Quedlinburg to find the remains of Henry The Fowler, then to Obersturmbannführer Prof. Dr Hans Schleif, who organised digs in the Teutoburg Forest where the Germans of Arminius (or Hermann) had crushed the Roman legions of Quintus Varus in AD 9. Schleif later teamed up with Obersturmbannführer Prof. Dr Herbert Jankuhn to excavate the Viking site of Haithabu in Schleswig, a wall built by King Godfred in the ninth century to defend the Danes against the incursions of the Carolingian Franks. In time, Ahnenerbe organised similar excavations in Austria, Croatia, Czechoslovakia, Greece, Poland, Serbia and southern Russia, and sponsored associated expeditions to the Near East and Tibet to look for signs of an ancient Nordic presence in these areas.

From 1939, the remit of Ahnenerbe was considerably enlarged. Himmler was no longer content to be restricted to Dark Age history and Middle Age heraldry. He now hoped to prove by scientific means the racial hypothesis of National Socialism. In conjunction with the SD, the Society would also look into other matters, such as astronomy, control of the weather, the extraction of petrol from coal, the occult and herbal remedies (Himmler's wife being a qualified homoeopath). Ahnenerbe expanded to include more than fifty departments, employing over thirty university professors. The Reichsführer showed evidence of quite a surprising amount of liberalism in their appointment, and drew a fairly vague line between research ability on the one hand and political reliability on the other. However, the

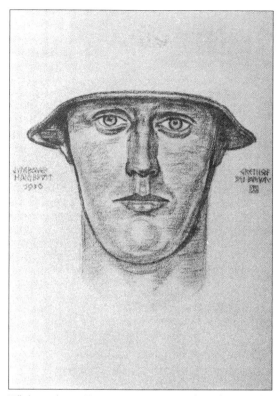

Willrich print showing SS-Mann Hans Brütt, a peasant farmer from Grethof. The frontal style of this drawing is intentionally reminiscent of medieval Viking and Norman sculpture. Note also the pseudo-runic caption to the portrait.

contract he required his academics to sign stipulated that their findings could never be published if they turned out to be contrary to SS ideology.

One of the most controversial figures among the new researchers was SS-Sturmbannführer Dr August Hirt, Professor of Anatomy at the University of Strasbourg, where SS students were particularly numerous. With Himmler's support, it was Hirt who collected thousands of human skulls at Auschwitz for the purpose of making comparative anthropomorphic measurements. He later toured various battlefronts where the Wehrmacht's foreign volunteers were deployed, to study the

In July 1938, an SS-sponsored parade celebrating '2000 Years of German Culture' was held in Munich. Pseudo-medieval and Nazi symbolism mingled on an awesome scale throughout the event.

performance and behaviour of combatants as a function of their racial categories. Other anatomical specialists from Ahnenerbe occupied themselves by examining body parts of different races, while SS-Sturmbannführer Dr Ernst Schäfer was commissioned to develop a special breed of horse on the Russian steppes for military use in extremely cold weather.

The war's principal sector of scientific research, that of secret weapons, fell under the authority of Ahnenerbe in 1944. Up to the middle of that year, the V1 and V2 rocket development programmes at Peenemünde had been directed by Prof. Dr Wernher Freiherr von Braun, who was loyal first and foremost to the Wehrmacht even though he was an SS-

Sturmbannführer on the staff of Oberabschnitt Ostsee. Himmler knew that the Reich was by then laying all its hopes on secret weapons, and after the army plot to assassinate Hitler on 20 July 1944 he took personal control of the Peenemünde operation from von Braun and placed it under SS-Gruppenführer Dr Hans Kammler. The V1 and V2 programmes fully occupied the best minds of Ahnenerbe for the remainder of the war.

Towards the end of the war, when Himmler was overwhelmed by his military and police responsibilities, he said that reading Ahnenerbe reports was his only real pleasure and his only relaxation. He revelled in the discourses on ancestral tombs,

A series of plastic badges sold for the benefit of the Nazi Charities Campaign, organised by SS-Gruppenführer Erich Hilgenfeldt. They reproduce finds from SS archaeological digs in Germany, Rome and Greece, and portray the use and development of the swastika in antiquity. Such projects were dear to Himmler's heart.

Germanic customs and marriage ceremonies. In a long and critical letter to Wüst and Sievers dated 17 August 1944, he referred to the tradition of newly married couples copulating on the tombs of their ancestors at the time of the new moon, and suggested that research on wild animals might prove whether or not the new moon was particularly favourable to fertility. Himmler wrote:

> No good blood must be allowed to die without having been fruitful. Our SS must be sufficiently strong and vigorous so that each generation can, without argument, offer up two or three sons per family on the field of battle without exhausting the torrent of Germanic blood. We are going to create the chance for the Germanic people and for Europe as a whole, directed by the Germanic people, to build an Order which will, for generations, be able to fight victoriously against all Asiatic aggression. Woe to us if the Germanic people cannot win this battle. It will be the end of beauty, of culture and of creative thought on this earth. We struggle for that future only so that we can maintain the heritage of our most noble ancestors. I consider it necessary for the life of our people to teach all this to our grandsons, so that they may understand the difficulties of their ancestors and willingly enter into the SS way of life.

THE NEXT GENERATION

Himmler realised only too well that it was essential that the best minds among the youth of Germany should be cultivated to ensure a continual pool of talent willing and able to fill the highest positions in the hierarchies of the SS and National Socialist state. University lecturers and school teachers were actively encouraged to join the Allgemeine-SS, and

Fritz Wächtler, the head of the NS-Lehrerbund or Nazi Teachers' League, was given the rank of SS-Obergruppenführer. The ultimate aim was that the most selective schools and colleges should be dominated by the SS.

On 20 April 1933, Dr Bernhard Rust, Reich Minister for Science, Education and Culture, set up the first of a series of special residential schools to train the future Germanic élite. They were termed National Political Educational Institutes, or Nationalpolitische Erziehungsanstalten, commonly abbreviated to NPEA or Napolas, although the latter term was unpopular because it sounded too Italian. Three were opened during the course of 1933, at Plön in Schleswig-Holstein, Potsdam in Berlin and Köslin in Pomerania. Five more (Spandau, Naumburg, Ilfeld, Stuhm and Oranienstein) followed in 1934, with a further eight (Bensburg, Ballenstedt, Backnang, Rottweil, Klotzsche, Neuzelle, Schulpforte and Wahlstatt) the next year. Favourite locations were old army cadet schools, requisitioned monasteries or refurbished castles.

The motto of the NPEA was 'Mehr sein als scheinen', which is perhaps most meaningfully translated as 'Be Modest, but Always Excel'. The end product of these schools was to be a political soldier who could be entrusted with the leadership of any type of public service activity. Each establishment received an average of 400 applications for admission annually, of which around 100 were successful. A comprehensive academic education encompassing history, geography, music, the arts, languages, politics, mathematics, biology, physics and chemistry was provided for boys between the ages of ten and eighteen years, and there was also a strong emphasis on physical training. Specialisation, both academic and sporting, was encouraged. Some Napolas aimed at producing scientists, others linguists, and a number of pupils were allowed to concentrate on developing their skills in rowing, boxing, fencing, riding, skiing, yachting, gliding, and so on. The boys came from all walks of life, and where parents could not afford payment of tuition the fees were usually waived.

One of the more original features of the NPEA was the importance placed on practical education. The younger boys had to spend six to eight weeks of each year working on a farm, while the older pupils served down mines or in factories. The idea was that they should discover the 'nobility of manual labour' and avoid the temptations of class exclusiveness. The knowledge and experience gained found their practical application in spring and autumn paramilitary exercises, holiday hikes and organised travel abroad. The structure of each school was patterned after the military. Some establishments carried on the traditions of certain famous German army regiments, and the teachers lived in the schools with the pupils. NPEA boys were known as Jungmannen, and were divided into Hundertschaften, or companies, of one hundred. Each of these was sub-divided into three Züge, or platoons, with about thirty boys. In turn, each Zug was split into three Gruppen of about ten boys apiece. The Hundertschaftsführer, Zugführer and Gruppenführer were pupils who fulfilled the combined functions of a school prefect and a military academy Cadet NCO. NPEA graduates were highly sought after by the Wehrmacht as potential officers, and those who went on to university could rely on the NSDAP to assist them financially.

From the outset, control of the NPEA schools was hotly contested by various party bodies. The original mentor of the NPEA system, Joachim Haupt, was an SA officer, and he fell from favour after the 'Night of the Long Knives' in June 1934. Dr Robert Ley, head of the Labour Front, then tried openly to attract the Napolas into his own sphere of influence, but his project encountered such

Two schoolboys from NPEA Naumburg taking pictures during the winter solstice celebrations in 1941. Note the SS-inspired Sig-Rune insignia worn on the left arm.

strong opposition from the Ministry of Education that he relented and set up the rival Adolf Hitler Schools with the support of Baldur von Schirach, leader of the Hitler Youth. As always, Heinrich Himmler acted unobtrusively but with the utmost skill. From the time of the first public festivities organised by the NPEA in 1934, he took pains to be invited along and presented to the staff as an honoured guest. In July of that year, the Reichsführung-SS volunteered to assume the responsibility of paying for Napola clothing and equipment, and also began to provide scholarships and tuition fees for ethnic German students. On 9 March 1936, SS commitment to the schools was

Proficiency Badge for ten- to fourteen-year-olds in the Deutsche Jungvolk, the junior branch of the Hitler Youth. The SS influence on the runic design of this award is unmistakable.

replaced by the study of pagan Germanic rites. The celebration of Julfest, the SS Christmas, brought the pupils together to worship the Child of the Sun, arisen from his ashes at the winter solstice. New school songs commemorated the struggle between day and night, and praised the eternal return of light. The night of 21 June became the Night of the Sun, when the boys mounted a 'Joyous Guard' awaiting the sun's triumphal reappearance. Lectures were given on racial superiority and SS ideology, and emphasis was placed on duty, courage and personal obligation. The SS influence on the NPEA was also apparent in its dress, with the adoption of SS-style daggers and insignia. After 1940, a new scheme of ranks which was entirely SS in form was introduced for NPEA staff, as follows:

NPEA-Untersturmführer	Probationary teacher
NPEA-Obersturmführer	Teacher
NPEA-Hauptsturmführer	Senior Teacher
NPEA-Sturmbannführer	Deputy Head of Department
NPEA-Obersturmbannführer	Head of Department
NPEA-Standartenführer	Deputy Headmaster
NPEA-Oberführer	Headmaster
NPEA-Brigadeführer	Local School Inspector
NPEA-Gruppenführer	National School Inspector

rewarded with the appointment of SS-Obergruppenführer August Heissmeyer as Inspector-General of the NPEA. He set up his own HQ, the Hauptamt Dienststelle Heissmeyer, and subsequently required all NPEA personnel to enrol in the Allgemeine-SS. By 1940, the SS had completely taken over the Napolas, with full powers of decision in matters relating to curriculum and staff appointments. The selection of new Jungmannen was determined by RuSHA, and the NPEA commandants and teachers were subjected to SS discipline.

The rhythm of Napola life was thereafter based on that of the SS. Conventional religion was abolished from the curriculum and

With the needs of Lebensborn and similar SS organisations in mind, the first all-girl NPEA school was opened in 1941 at Achern in Baden, to be followed shortly thereafter by two more. Some of the previously all-male schools subsequently admitted female pupils and staff. No less than twenty-seven new Napolas were founded between 1941 and 1942, and with the enormous expansion of the NPEA programme during the war SS influence became paramount. For example, VOMI ensured that the school at Rufach included a substantial number of young Volksdeutsche from Bessarabia and Bukovina in the student body. Three schools known as NPEA Reichsschulen were set up in the occupied western territories specifically to take in non-German Nordic pupils, the future leaders of the Germanic-SS. The Reichsschule Flandern at Kwatrecht in Flanders, opened in September 1943, was equipped to accommodate some 800 boys, although it never managed to enrol more than 120, all under the age of fourteen. It was commanded by SS-Obersturmführer Paul Steck. The Reichsschule Niederlande für Jungen at Valkenburg in Holland took Dutch boys and was 'twinned' with its nearest German counterpart, the NPEA Bensburg, with regular exchanges of students and staff between the two establishments. The closely associated all-female Reichsschule Niederlande für Mädchen was located at nearby Heithuijsen, and was run by a pro-Nazi Dutch baroness.

In December 1944, by virtue of his successes with the NPEA and Reichsschulen, and his position as Commander-in-Chief of the Home Army, Himmler was appointed by Hitler to be supervisor of all schools from which future Wehrmacht and Waffen-SS officers could be recruited. In theory, that put him in charge of almost every educational establishment in the Third Reich and conquered countries!

Himmler's long-term plans made it desirable that the SS should control not only junior and secondary schools, but also the centres of higher learning. Nazi students' groups had been formed at some German universities as early as 1922, but these were simply gatherings of students who had enrolled in the NSDAP. It was not until February 1926 that a separate student organisation, the National Socialist German Students' League (Nationalsozialistische Deutsche Studentenbund or NSDSt.B), was established at Munich University under Baldur von Schirach. He organised the NSDSt.B into ten districts, each under a Kreisführer, and membership was extended to include students at Technical Colleges, Trade Schools and Business Colleges. Ultimately, the proportion of NSDSt.B members at university was lower than that of those attending the other centres of further education. They were encouraged to join the SA and take part in military sports, but less than half did so, many balking at the thought of associating with the party's rougher elements. By January 1933 the NSDSt.B still had only 6,300 male and 750 female members. Even after the Nazi assumption of power, enrolment in the organisation was not made obligatory for all students. On the contrary, membership was deliberately selective and restricted to 5 per cent of the student body. As the NPEA accepted only the cream of German school pupils, so the NSDSt.B would take on only the best and most reliable students in further education. Each university or institute of higher learning had an NSDSt.B Stamm-Mannschaft, or regular company, limited to not more than sixty individuals, all of whom had already to be members of the NSDAP, SA, SS, NSKK or HJ. They signed on for at least a year, and their task was to act as political leaders among their fellow students.

Both Himmler, who had a degree in agriculture, and the NSDAP Deputy Führer Rudolf Hess, a history graduate and SS-Obergruppenführer, took a keen interest in NSDSt.B matters. Hess spoke of it as 'a sort of intellectual SS', and Himmler hoped that it would furnish the future élite of the party. They saw it as a natural extension of the NPEA system, which would continue to oversee those boys and girls from the Napolas who had proved themselves capable of further education. The two were instrumental in the setting up of a new office, the Reich Student Leadership (Reichsstudentenführung or RSF), in November 1936. It had ultimate control over both the NSDSt.B and the ordinary German Student Association (Deutsche Studentenschaft or DSt.) to which all German students automatically belonged. Command of the RSF was given to SS-Obergruppenführer Dr Gustav-Adolf Scheel, who was nominated Reichsstudentenführer. From that time on, student affairs began to be heavily influenced by the SS. NSDSt.B members were soon kitted out in a dark-blue uniform derived from the garb of the Allgemeine-SS and the Hitler Youth. Scheel set up the NS-Altherrenbund der Deutschen Studenten, a new Nazi alumni organisation, and forced the existing associations of former students to affiliate with it on pain of otherwise being barred from further participation in student affairs. Only the Catholic alumni bodies refused to capitulate, and they were subsequently outlawed by Himmler. As a result, all financial contributions and legacies from 'old boys' had to be channelled through the Altherrenbund, and so were controlled by the RSF and, ultimately, the SS.

After 1939, most NSDSt.B leaders departed to join the Wehrmacht and Waffen-SS, thus leaving political indoctrination of students in the hands of less committed individuals. Moreover, the actual composition of the student body was altered radically. Whereas before the war only a small percentage of students had been women, by 1943 they accounted for more than 35 per cent of the student population. That factor alone greatly reduced the influence of the SS, still basically a male organisation, over student life. Himmler actively encouraged potential Germanic-SS leaders from Flanders, Holland, Norway and Denmark to study at German universities and technical colleges through the Langemarck Scholarship scheme, which commemorated

the young German student volunteers who had fought so heroically at the Battle of Langemarck near Ypres in November 1914. However, the second half of the Second World War saw Nazi interest in, and dominance over, the universities fall away, and in some cases they even became staunch centres of anti-Nazi resistance.

While the majority of ordinary German youngsters never had any associations with the NPEA or NSDSt.B, most either belonged to, or had friends in, the Hitler Youth (Hitlerjugend or HJ) and its female equivalent the League of German Girls (Bund Deutscher Mädel or BDM). After 1933 the HJ was a main source of recruitment for the Allgemeine-SS, and as the power and prestige of the SA declined so those of the SS and HJ increased. In 1936 it was decreed that the whole of German youth was to be 'educated, outside the parental home and school, in the HJ, physically, intellectually and morally, for service to the nation and community'. The HJ initially found it hard to meet the great demands made upon it, and for that reason obligatory membership was delayed for several years. Even so, voluntary enlistment resulted in the number of Hitler Youths reaching 8 million (i.e. 66 per cent of those eligible to join) at the end of 1938. Compulsory HJ service for all male seventeen-year-olds was introduced on 25 March 1939, and in September 1941 membership finally became obligatory for both sexes from the age of ten onward. Many of the activities, trappings and insignia of the HJ were derived from those of the SS, with much anti-Semitism, neo-paganism and use of runic symbolism, and co-operation between the SS and the HJ became ever closer until by the end of the war the two had merged their interests almost completely. By that time, the ultimate aim of every Hitler Youth was acceptance into the SS.

The élite branch of the Hitler Youth organisation was the HJ-Streifendienst, or Patrol Service, created in December 1936. It

Volunteers for the 'Hitlerjugend' Division swear an oath of loyalty before the Sig-Runes, flanked by Hitler Youth flags, in 1944. The smart M36 uniform of the helmeted officer contrasts sharply with the more basic M43 dress worn by the recruits.

A 'Hitlerjugend' MG42 team alongside a 'Panther' tank in Normandy, June 1944. All wear standard helmet covers and smocks, with baggy Italian-pattern camouflage trousers. The panzer's number, '326', denotes the 6th tank of the 2nd platoon of the 3rd company, 12th SS-Panzer Regiment.

was in effect an internal police force for the HJ, and kept order at Hitler Youth rallies and camps, controlled transport movements, supervised HJ hostels and counteracted juvenile crime. Each member was issued with a special pass and an SS-style cuff title and, as needs demanded, a small calibre rifle. In August 1938, under an agreement between Himmler and von Schirach's Reichsjugend-führung, the HJ-Streifendienst was reorganised as a sort of preparatory school for the SS. Its training was placed entirely in SS hands, and boys were expected to graduate into the SS or police after leaving the service.

Another HJ formation closely associated with the SS was the Landdienst or Land Service, the purpose of which was to provide voluntary agricultural assistance, particularly in the eastern provinces of the Reich. The Landdienst was formed in 1934 and sent urban HJ volunteers on to farms for one year, the so-called Landjahr, to give them agricultural experience. At the outbreak of war, the service had 26,000 members. In February 1940, the Siedlernachwuchsstelle Ost, or Eastern Young Settlers Office, was created under a joint agreement between the SS and HJ to train youngsters as Wehrbauern, peasant guards who would populate and defend the conquered east. Volunteers were racially scrutinised by RuSHA and had to register with the RKFDV. To further this aim,

During their first week of action in Normandy, these three soldiers of the 'Hitlerjugend' Division won the Iron Cross.

the Landdienst concept was extended in 1942 to include youths from the Nordic countries of Flanders, Holland, Norway and Denmark, who volunteered for employment with the newly created Germanic Land Service, or Germanischer Landdienst. Its badge was the Odal-Rune, and its motto was 'Schwert und Scholle' ('Sword and Soil'). With the turn of the tide of war, however, the Germanic Land Service was officially wound up in March 1944 and many of its male personnel were transferred to the Waffen-SS.

From 1936, the HJ ran weekend courses in field exercises (Geländesport) and rifle shooting. Initially it relied on its own personnel and the Wehrmacht to furnish instructors, but increasingly the SS became involved in Hitler Youth paramilitary training. In 1939 toughening-up camps, or Wehrertüchtigungslager (WE-Lager), were established in which boys between the ages of sixteen-and-a-half and eighteen were put through a three-week course culminating in an award of the K-Schein, or War Training Certificate. By 1943 there were around 150 such camps, which included among their trainees and instructors volunteers from Flanders, Holland, Norway, Denmark and Latvia. There was a sound practical reason why the SS took a great interest in the WE-Lager system, for it furnished Himmler with a means of circumventing the Wehrmacht's monopoly on military recruitment. The Waffen-SS possessed no powers of direct conscription among German nationals, but if a young man could be persuaded to volunteer for the Waffen-SS before reaching his twentieth year, the normal age for conscript service, his preference for that branch of the fighting forces was normally respected. The SS therefore strove to persuade WE-Lager boys to volunteer for service in one of its combat divisions after they had obtained their K-Schein.

In February 1943, following the loss of the 6th Army at Stalingrad, manpower shortages became so acute that Hitler authorised a programme to encourage voluntary enlistment of seventeen-year-olds, boys who would not have been subject to conscription until 1946. The SS saw this as a golden opportunity to build up its own forces. Negotiations between Himmler and the Reichsjugendführer, Artur Axmann, began at once, as a result of which it was decided to raise an entirely new Waffen-SS division from Hitler Youths who had completed their courses at the WE-Lager. By mid-summer the required number of 10,000 volunteers had been mustered. In October the division was officially named 12th SS-Panzer Division 'Hitlerjugend' and it went into action following the Allied invasion of Normandy. The fanatical young soldiers, keen to demonstrate their worthiness to wear the honoured SS runes, threw themselves into battle without regard for losses, which were devastating. Over 8,500 of their number were either killed or wounded, and by the end of the war a single tank and 455 men were all that remained of one of Germany's foremost armoured divisions.

The SS also made use of HJ volunteers on the home front. By the middle of 1943, there were some 100,000 young Germans in the Auxiliary Flak organisation, run by the Luftwaffe, but the demand for anti-aircraft gunners and searchlight operators was such that Göring and Axmann approached Alfred Rosenberg in March 1944 with a request that the youth of the occupied eastern territories should also be enrolled as Flak Helpers. This would apply, as in Germany, to boys and girls from their fifteenth birthday until they were old enough to be drafted into their respective ethnic legions. Since these foreign legions were controlled by the SS, the youngsters from the east likewise came under Himmler's jurisdiction. Over 16,000 boys and 2,000 girls were eventually recruited from the Baltic states, Byelorussia and the Ukraine. They were first called SS-Helfer, then Luftwaffen-Helfer, and finally SS-Luftwaffen-Helfer, and were required to operate throughout the Reich. Service in the Flak batteries was fully combatant, with over forty foreign Flak auxiliaries being killed in action and two winning the Iron Cross. Each youngster wore the SS runes on a black triangle on the upper left arm, in the manner of the standard HJ district insignia.

The other area where SS and Hitler Youth came into close contact was fire fighting. In June 1939, SS-Gruppenführer Dr Johannes Meyer, commander of the Feuerschutzpolizei, met HJ leaders to discuss the participation of the Hitler Youth in fire defence. The HJ-Feuerlöschdienst (HJ Fire Fighting Service) was subsequently established, and the following December it was integrated into the HJ-Streifendienst. In March 1941 its official designation was altered to HJ-Feuerwehrscharen (HJ Fire Defence Squads), and the HJ uniform was replaced for members by a modified version of that of the Feuerschutzpolizei. As the war progressed, the distinction between the specially trained HJ-Feuerwehrscharen and other HJ units became blurred. By 1943, age restrictions had been jettisoned and all members of the youth services acted as volunteer helpers in air raids. In mid-1943 there were 700,000 boys engaged in fire defence, and in the course of that year alone thirty-two were killed, 607 wounded and 300 decorated with the Iron Cross or War Merit Cross.

Late in February 1945, when the advancing Russian Army was closing in on Berlin, special units of saboteurs and partisan guerrillas were formed from the German populace for the purpose of harassing the approaching enemy. In the event of the capture of the capital, members of these units, known as 'Wehrwolf' or the 'Freikorps Adolf Hitler', were to function behind Allied lines in the occupied zones creating what havoc they could. It fell to Himmler, as Commander-in-Chief of the Home Army, to set up the Wehrwolf organisation and he put it under the command of SS-Obergruppenführer Hans Prützmann, with SS-Brigadeführer Karl Pflaumer as his deputy. However, with all able-bodied personnel already at the front line or in the Volkssturm, Wehrwolf had to rely on very young members of the HJ and BDM to make up its numbers. A variety of duties was entrusted to these boys and girls, including the salvaging and concealment of arms and ammunition, minor acts of sabotage such as puncturing tyres, and the conveying of messages and distribution of Nazi propaganda. Older Wehrwolves seconded from the Waffen-SS and All-gemeine-SS set up secret radio transmitters, took part in assassinations and infiltrated enemy headquarters. Without doubt, the Wehrwolf organisation inflicted substantial damage and, even after the surrender, marauding groups of SS and Hitler Youth participated in acts of sabotage against the American, British, French and Russian occupation authorities.

By its indoctrination of youth through interaction with the NPEA, NSDSt.B, HJ and BDM, the SS ensured that the ideals of Himmler and Hitler survived long after their demise.

THE GERMANIC-SS

Possessed as he was by the desire to attract all the Nordic blood of Europe into the SS, Himmler envisaged the ultimate creation of a new Germanic province to be called Burgundia, grouping the Netherlands, Belgium and north-east France, which would act as a buffer protecting Germany from invasion. Burgundia would eventually be policed and governed by the SS, and to that end the Reichsführer established native replicas of the Allgemeine-SS in Flanders, Holland and Norway soon after the conquest of these countries. At the end of 1942, these formations were removed from the influence of their own national, collaborationist political leaders and amalgamated to become a new 'Germanic-SS' under Himmler's direct orders. With the raising of a Danish branch in 1943, the Germanic-SS grew to encompass a total active membership of almost 9,000 men, whose primary task was to support the local police by rooting out partisans, subversives and other anti-Nazi elements. Members retained their own languages and customs, but there was no question that Germany pulled the strings. From the outset, Himmler told his western volunteers:

Be certain of this. There will be in all Europe just one SS – the Germanic-SS under the command of the Reichsführer-SS. You can resist, but that is a matter of indifference to me for we will create it in any case. We do not ask you to turn against your country, nor to do anything repugnant to anyone proud of his country, who loves it and has his self-respect. Neither do we expect you to become Germans out of opportunism. What we do ask is that you subordinate your national ideal to a superior racial and historical ideal, that of the single and all-embracing Germanic Reich.

General responsibility for the supervision of the Germanic-SS and its forerunners rested with the SS Hauptamt, which assisted in the foundation and expansion of the new body. Personnel were soon kitted out with surplus black Allgemeine-SS uniforms imported from Germany, to which suitable national insignia were attached. A special Germanic Liaison Office, or Germanische Leitstelle, was set up, with headquarters at 20 Admiral von Schröder Strasse, Berlin, and branches in The Hague, Oslo and Copenhagen. The function of these outposts was to oversee the whole political propaganda and recruiting activity of the SS in the respective areas of western Europe and Scandinavia. After a time, it became apparent that the Germanic recruits often needed special handling and indoctrination before they could be fully accepted into the SS, and to meet this requirement a Germanic-SS Training Department was established, with four main training camps at Sennheim in Alsace, Schooten in Belgium, Hovelte in Denmark and Avegoor in Holland. The emphasis in the camps' curriculum was on games, sport and political education. In addition, there was a Germanic-SS Officers' School (Führerschule der Germanischen-SS) at Hildesheim, the purpose of which was to provide general training for future political leaders in the Germanic-SS. In fact, the vast majority of applicants to join the Germanic-SS were immediately redirected towards the Waffen-SS, particularly the 'Wiking' and 'Nordland' Divisions, for combat service. Each of the four national formations which came to make up the Germanic-SS had its own distinct history, and these are now covered in turn.

So far as Belgium was concerned, the Nazis had always drawn a clear distinction between its two peoples, at first favouring the Flemings of Flanders, who were Germanic in language and race, as against the Walloons of Wallonia, who were French-speaking and of Romanic origin. From 1940, Hitler played upon the long-standing resentment felt by Flemings against the Walloon-dominated state of Belgium, which had been created only 110 years before. He encouraged nationalist dissension in the country, supporting the Vlaamsch Nationaal Verbond or VNV (Flemish National Union) of Gustave 'Staf' de Clercq, which saw Flanders as a natural part of the Netherlands rather than of Belgium, and which soon absorbed all collaborationist parties in Flanders. The VNV had its own version of the German SA, called the Dietsche Militie Zwarte Brigade, and a network of other organisations which paralleled the HJ, NSKK, RAD and NSDAP political leadership.

In September 1940, two pro-German Flemings, Ward Hermans and René Lagrou, set up a Flemish equivalent of the Allgemeine-SS in Antwerp. Hermans was a prominent member of the VNV, and began by enrolling 130 of his party colleagues into the corps, which he called the Algemeene Schutsscharen Vlaanderen, or Flemish General SS. By March 1941 there were 1,580 active members with a further 4,000 Patron Members or Beschermende Leden, who contributed financially, like the German Fördernde Mitglieder. However, due to the constant loss of its men to the German armed forces, particularly the 'Westland' and 'Nordwest' Regiments and Flemish Legion of the Waffen-SS, the strength of the Algemeene-SS Vlaanderen fell away considerably during 1941, although it was never less than 300. In 1942, veterans returning from their voluntary service on the eastern front again built up the numbers of the Flemish SS. That October, in accordance with Himmler's policy of bringing all Germanic General SS formations within a single German orbit, the body was renamed the Germaansche-SS in Vlaanderen, or Germanic-SS in Flanders. Those who were too old or not up to the physical requirements of the Germaansche-SS could

Badge worn by Patron Members, or Beschermende Leden, of the Germanic-SS in Flanders.

enrol in its reserve unit, known as the Vlaanderen-Korps. The policy of the Flemish SS was very much at odds with the cautious pro-Dutch attitude of the VNV, and it used its own newspaper, *De SS Man*, openly to advocate total German control over Flanders.

The nominal strength of the Flemish SS in June 1944 was 3,500. However, 1,600 of these were on military service with the Waffen-SS, 940 were with the NSKK and 500 were in the Vlaanderen-Korps, leaving only 460 active General SS members in Flanders, of whom 100 were still probationers. By the end of the year, most of Belgium had been liberated. There was only one significant exception – the important port of Antwerp, birthplace of the Flemish SS, which remained in German hands. The Senior SS and Police Commander in Belgium, SS-Gruppenführer Richard Jungclaus, linked the remnants of the Germaansche-SS in Vlaanderen and the paramilitaries of the VNV into a Security Corps, or Sicherheitskorps, of some 2,500 men. A battalion of this corps fought alongside the German defenders of Antwerp in a battle which lasted throughout September–November 1944. It was one of the rare examples of western European SS being used to fight against the British and Americans, most of their colleagues seeing combat service only in Russia.

So far as Holland was concerned, over 50,000 Germans lived and worked there before the Second World War so it is not surprising that a number of pro-Nazi groups sprang up in the Netherlands during the formative years of the Third Reich. The most important of these was the Nationaal-Socialistische Beweging or NSB, the National Socialist Movement of Anton Adriaan Mussert. The NSB was a highly organised and fully uniformed party with its own paramilitary section, the Weer Afdeelingen or WA, and in 1940 it was granted a political monopoly in the Netherlands under the controlling authority of the country's Reichskommissar, SS-Obergruppenführer Dr Arthur Seyss-Inquart. In November 1940, following the Flemish example, the NSB took the bold step of establishing its own SS within the framework of the party. The initiative came from the former leader of Mussert's personal bodyguard, Johannes Hendrik ('Henk') Feldmeijer, who created what was known simply as the Nederlandsche-SS. In October 1942, the Dutch SS ceased to be a paramilitary formation of the NSB. It was renamed the Germaansche-SS en Nederland and became a part of the greater Germanic-SS under Himmler's orders. Mussert's control over it came to an end, and all Dutch SS men had to swear a personal oath of loyalty to Adolf Hitler.

The Germaansche-SS en Nederland had, on paper, a strength of five regiments plus an SS-Police regiment, in addition to 4,000 Patron Members, or Begunstigende Leden. It also supported its own journal, the *Storm SS*. However, its nominal active membership of 3,800 was constantly depleted by voluntary enlistments in the Waffen-SS. An affiliated guard unit set up by the HSSPf Nordwest, SS-Obergruppenführer Hanns Rauter, after the

Tunic of an Opperschaarleider, 2nd Standaard (Arnhem), Germanic-SS in the Netherlands, c. 1944. This is a non-regulation item, probably converted from a Dutch police jacket at a time when black SS service uniform tunics were in short supply.

disbanding of the 'Nordwest' Regiment, took the title SS-Wachbataillon Nordwest. It had four companies, one of which was used largely for ceremonial duties at SS Headquarters in The Hague. The others acted as guards at the concentration camps which were established at Herzogenbusch, Vught and other parts of the Netherlands. The SS-Postschutz in Holland also employed a number of over-age Dutch volunteers.

In addition to bringing in their own police, the German occupation authorities in Holland set about reorganising the Dutch police, and the SS were inevitably involved in the process. A new body, the Communal Police, replaced the various municipal forces and was trained under SS direction at the Police School at Schalkhaar. Members were kitted out in a uniform based upon that of the Allgemeine-SS but with a closed collar, and any Dutch policeman who was also a member of the Germanic-SS could wear the SS runes below the left breast pocket of his tunic. In March 1943, the NSB set up the Landwacht Nederland (Dutch Home Guard), in which all party members between the ages of seventeen and fifty were required to serve. The following October, it was renamed Landstorm Nederland and taken over by the SS. Members initially wore WA or Germanic-SS uniform, but later went into field-grey. The Landstorm fought primarily against the Dutch resistance, but was also engaged against the British airborne forces around Arnhem in September 1944. Two months later it absorbed the SS-Wachbataillon Nordwest, the staffs of various training establishments and around 3,000 Dutchmen brought back from working in Germany, and became the SS-Grenadier Division 'Landstorm Nederland'. The division saw minor defensive fighting before it surrendered in May 1945.

Unlike the other occupied western countries, Norway had only one collaborating party of any importance, the uniformed Nasjonal Samling or NS (National Unity) movement of Vidkun Quisling. Quisling attempted to assume power immediately after the German invasion, but was ordered to step down and it was not until February 1942 that Hitler appointed him President of Norway, the only collaborator ever to achieve such high office in a German-occupied country. However, he was not entrusted with exclusive power. The real ruler of Norway was his arch-rival, Reichskommissar Josef Terboven, who operated a ruthless régime from his fortress at Castle Skaugum in Oslo. In April 1941, Jonas Lie, Chief of the Norwegian Police, and Axel Stang, Minister of Sport and Chief of Staff of the Rikshird (the NS version of the German SA), saw service in Yugoslavia with the

Waffen-SS Division 'Reich'. Both received the Iron Cross 2nd Class. After his homecoming as a war-decorated hero, Lie at once set about intriguing with Terboven against their mutual foe, Quisling. With German complicity, Lie founded the Norges-SS, a Norwegian equivalent of the Allgemeine-SS recruited from the cream of the Rikshird. Quisling, who had not been consulted or forewarned, was furious but there was little he could do, for Himmler had given the Norwegian SS his blessing. The Reichsführer arrived in Oslo to preside over the oath-taking ceremony, and duly appointed Lie to command the unit with the rank of SS-Standartenführer. Before the Norges-SS could complete even its basic training, however, Hitler invaded Russia and 85 per cent of its membership immediately volunteered for service with the Norwegian Legion in the east. The rest went into a Police Company under Jonas Lie, which took part in the siege of Leningrad.

In July 1942, many veterans returned from Russia and the Norges-SS was reactivated. A few months later, in accordance with Himmler's policy, it became the Germanske-SS Norge. The former Rikshird insignia was abandoned and a common scheme of ranks, based on those of the Allgemeine-SS and the other Germanic-SS formations, was adopted. The Germanic-SS in Norway severed all connections with its Rikshird parent and it was henceforth forbidden for members to belong to both organisations. A new oath of allegiance was taken, to Hitler rather than Quisling, and the German-inspired motto 'Min Aere er Troskap' ('My Honour is Loyalty') was authorised. No Germanic-SS unit in Norway attained sufficient size to be regarded as a Standarte. The largest that could be mustered was a Stormbann or battalion, of which there were twelve in various parts of the country. It is possible that at least five of these existed only on paper and that all the others were consistently

Himmler inspecting Norwegian volunteers for the SS-Standarte 'Nordland', 9 February 1941.

under-strength. This was not the result of a lack of volunteers so much as the fact that the Germanic-SS in Norway, as elsewhere, was part-time and often merely a stepping stone into the Waffen-SS or other branches of the Wehrmacht. So many Germanic-SS men did, in fact, volunteer for full-time Waffen-SS service that they were able to contribute an entire company to the 'Nordland' Regiment in the spring of 1943. At the same time, the Germanske-SS Norge established the SS-Wachbataillon Oslo, which recruited another 500 Norwegians to act as guards at various installations in the city and elsewhere. The concept of Patron Members, or Stottende Medlemner, was introduced into Norway as in the other Germanic countries. Official figures published in *Germaneren*, the Norwegian SS paper, in September 1944 gave the strength of the Germanic-SS in Norway as 1,250 of whom 330 were on combat duty with the Waffen-SS and 760 in police units, including SS-Wachbataillon Oslo. That left only 160 Norwegians in the active Germanic-SS, so many units must have existed in a skeleton form only. At the same time, there were 3,500 Patron Members.

The other Germanic country, Denmark, had several pro-Nazi political parties before the Second World War, the main one being the Danmarks National-Socialistiske Arbejder Parti, or DNSAP, under Frits Clausen. The DNSAP was highly organised, with its own Corps of Political Leaders, Youth Section, Labour Service and SA, which it called the Storm Afdelinger. In December 1939 the Danish SA could muster only 900 men, but by the beginning of 1941 this had risen to

2,500, many of whom were later sent on training courses to the Germanic-SS camp at Sennheim. In April 1941, 200 Danes volunteered for service with the Waffen-SS 'Nordland' Regiment, and after the invasion of Russia a further 1,200 joined the hastily raised Freikorps Danmark to fight in the east. The Freikorps was commanded by Christian Frederick Count von Schalburg, a Danish aristocrat of Baltic-German origin and one-time leader of the DNSAP Youth, who had until recently been serving as an SS-Sturmbannführer with the 'Wiking' Division. The unit went into battle in May 1942 attached to the SS-Totenkopf-Division, and took part in the celebrated action at Demjansk where von Schalburg was killed on 2 June. He was given a state funeral by the Nazi authorities in Denmark. The Freikorps ultimately suffered over 20 per cent casualties, and was officially disbanded a year later.

Most of the Freikorps veterans were transferred, without much regard for their personal wishes, to the Waffen-SS division 'Nordland'. A few, however, including SS-Obersturmbannführer Knud Martinsen, the last commander of the formation, returned to their homeland to set up what amounted in all but name to a Danish branch of the Allgemeine-SS. In April 1943, with German support, Martinsen established the Germansk Korpset (Germanic Corps), which he shortly thereafter renamed the Schalburg Korpset or Schalburg Corps in memory of the Freikorps hero. Several eastern front veterans formed themselves into the cadre of the new unit, which opened its ranks to all young Danes of Nordic blood. The Corps was divided into two main groups, namely the active uniformed personnel, in five companies, and the non-regular patrons who gave moral and financial support. The latter came to be known as the Dansk-Folke-Vaern, or Danish People's Defence, and practised the use of small arms.

The Schalburg Corps adopted the same techniques as the partisan groups which it fought, and responded to each resistance assassination with one of its own. It was said that every act of sabotage provoked one of 'Schalburgtage'. A so-called 'Schalburg Cross' bearing the Corps motto 'Troskab vor Aere' ('Our Honour is Loyalty') was instituted and, according to the Corps journal Foedrelandet, at least one posthumous award was made to a Schalburg man killed by partisans. After a general strike in Denmark in July 1944, the Schalburg Corps was moved to Ringstad outside Copenhagen and incorporated into the Waffen-SS as SS-Ausbildungsbataillon (Training Battalion) Schalburg. Members were taught to use heavy weapons, in preparation for their defence of Denmark against the impending Allied invasion. Six months later the unit became SS Vagtbataillon Sjaelland, or SS Guard Battalion Zealand. It never saw front-line combat, however, and was disbanded in February 1945.

The Efterretnings Tjenesten, or ET, the Intelligence Service of the Schalburg Corps, was withdrawn from its parent body in April 1944 and placed under the direct control of the HSSPf in Denmark, SS-Obergruppenführer Günther Pancke. On 19 September, as a consequence of what the Germans regarded as unreliable behaviour during the general strike, the traditional Danish police organisation was stood down in its entirety and Pancke ordered the ET to form a new auxiliary police force in its place. This body, known by the Germans as the Hilfspolizeikorps, or Hipo, quickly acquired an ugly reputation and was responsible for the murder of at least fifty resistance suspects and the torture of hundreds more. In effect, it became a Danish branch of the Gestapo. Some members wore a black uniform similar to that of the Schalburg Corps, but the majority operated in civilian clothes.

Initially, SS personnel from Flanders, Holland, Norway and Denmark were entitled to compete for and wear the paramilitary sports badges awarded by their domestic pro-Nazi parties, the VNV, NSB, NS and DNSAP. However, the consolidation of the Germanic-SS at the end of 1942 all but severed such links with home and consequently a new all-embracing award was called for. On 15 July 1943, SS-Obergruppenführer Berger of the SS Hauptamt drew up draft regulations introducing just such a badge for the Germanic-SS. It was to take the form of two Sig-Runes, symbolic of victory and long the emblem of the German SS, superimposed over a sunwheel swastika which was associated with the west European Nazi movements. The design was therefore representative of the union between the German SS and the Germanic-SS. Approved and instituted by Himmler on 1 August 1943, the award was named the Germanische Leistungsrune, or Germanic Proficiency Rune. It came in two grades, bronze and silver, and the tests leading to an award were on a par with those undergone by Germans in the SS to qualify for the German National Sports Badge and SA Military Sports Badge. As well as athletics and war sports such as shooting and signalling, proficiency in National Socialist theories had to be demonstrated. Over 2,000 members of the Germanic-SS presented themselves for the first tests in January 1944, but only 95 passed. The Allied invasion of France and the ensuing battles undoubtedly prevented widespread distribution, and it is believed that total awards numbered fewer than 200. As the only nationally recognised decoration instituted by Himmler, the Germanic Proficiency Rune holds a unique place in the history of the SS.

In addition to the Germanic-SS formations proper, the Allgemeine-SS established its own Germanische Sturmbanne or Germanic

The Germanic Proficiency Rune was, in Himmler's words, intended for those who 'distinguished themselves in sports, the use of weapons and spiritual maturity, demonstrating a voluntary desire to attain the Germanic joint destiny'. While technically open to 'all German and Germanic men', no German ever won it.

Battalions in the areas of the Reich where there were large concentrations of workers imported from the Nordic countries. These foreigners numbered several hundred thousand by the end of 1942, and posed a major problem for German internal security. To assist in their control, Flemish and Dutch SS officers and men, most of them fresh from front-line service in the east, were employed by German firms to engage upon a propaganda campaign in the factories. They succeeded in persuading such a large number of their compatriots to join the local Allgemeine-SS that seven Germanic Battalions were set up in Berlin, Brunswick, Dresden, Düsseldorf, Hamburg, Nürnberg and Stuttgart. Service in the Germanische Sturmbanne was voluntary and unpaid, and was performed either during after-work hours or at weekends.

By the end of 1944, the Germanic-SS in

Germany was fully organised as an integral but distinctive part of the regular Allgemeine-SS. Membership peaked at around 7,000 and SS-Obersturmbannführer Max Kopischke held the post of Chef der Germanischen-SS in Deutschland (Chief of the Germanic-SS in Germany). Subordinated to him were several Reichsreferenten, officials for the various national groups into which the Germanische Sturmbanne were divided. Their Sonderstäbe, or special staffs, worked from the headquarters of the Oberabschnitte in which the battalions operated. The cultural centre of the Germanische Sturmbanne was the Germanische Haus, or Germanic House, in Hannover, set up by the Germanische Leitstelle of the SS Hauptamt in May 1943 and subsequently moved to Hildesheim under the title of Haus Germanien. It also served the social needs of associated Nordic workers, students and young people employed or holidaying in Germany, organising visits from their own national orchestras, singers, film stars and other celebrities. Copies of *Das Schwarze Korps* were distributed widely by the House, along with *De SS Man*, *Storm SS*, *Germaneren* and *Foedrelandet*. As the war situation worsened, the House placed more emphasis on extolling the virtues of Germanic-SS men at the front, and by the end of 1944 it had become little more than a glorified recruiting office for the Waffen-SS.

Symbolism and Regalia of the Black Order

From 1934, the SS was consciously promoted as not only a racial élite but also a dark and secret Order. To that end, symbolic insignia and carefully designed uniforms were created, and these proved to be fatal attractions which drew thousands of ordinary citizens into the web-like structures of Himmler's empire.

Of all SS uniform trappings, the one emblem which endured throughout the history of the organisation and became firmly associated with it was the death's head or Totenkopf, an eerie motif comprising a skull and crossed bones. The death's head was the only badge common to all SS formations, whether Allgemeine-SS, Germanic-SS or Waffen-SS, German or non-German. It has often been assumed that the Totenkopf was adopted simply to strike terror into the hearts of those who saw it. However, that was not so. It was chosen as a direct and emotional link with the past, and in particular with the élite military units of imperial Germany.

Medieval German literature and romantic poems were filled with references to dark forces and the symbols of death and destruction, a typical example being the following short excerpt from an epic work by the fifteenth-century writer, Garnier von Susteren:

> Behold the knight
> In solemn black manner,
> With a skull on his crest
> And blood on his banner . . .

That verse could have been composed with the SS uniform in mind! In 1740, a large right-facing jawless death's head with the bones lying behind the skull, embroidered in silver bullion, adorned the black funeral trappings of the Prussian king, Friedrich Wilhelm I. In his memory, the Leib-Husaren Regiments Nos 1 and 2, élite Prussian Royal Bodyguard units which were formed the following year, took black as the colour of their uniforms and wore a massive Totenkopf of similar design on their pelzmützen or busbies. The State of Brunswick followed suit in 1809 when the death's head was adopted by its Hussar Regiment No. 17 and the third battalion of Infantry Regiment No. 92. The Brunswick Totenkopf differed slightly in design from the Prussian one, with the skull

The German death's head was first used by Prussian cavalry regiments in the eighteenth century. The Totenkopf featured on the tall mirliton caps of the 5th Hussars (the 'Black' or 'Death' Hussars), while the mirlitons of the 9th Hussars bore a reclining skeleton which led to their being called the 'Total Death' Hussars. This busby dates from around 1910 and was worn by a member of the 1st Leib-Husaren Regiment based at Danzig-Langfuhr.

facing forward and situated directly above the crossed bones. During the First World War, the death's head was chosen as a formation badge by a number of crack German army units, particularly the storm troops, flamethrower detachments and tank battalions. Several pilots of the Schutzstaffeln, including the air ace Georg von Hantelmann who had served in the Death's Head Hussars, also used variants of it as personal emblems. Almost immediately after the end of hostilities in 1918 the death's head could be seen again, this time painted on the helmets and vehicles of some of the finest and most famous Freikorps. Because of its association with these formations it became symbolic not only of wartime daring and self-sacrifice, but also of postwar traditionalism, anti-liberalism and anti-Bolshevism. Nationalist ex-servicemen even had death's head rings, cuff links, tie pins and other adornments privately made for wear with their civilian clothes.

It is not surprising, therefore, that members of the Stosstrupp Adolf Hitler eagerly took the Totenkopf as their distinctive emblem in 1923, initially acquiring a small stock of appropriate army surplus cap

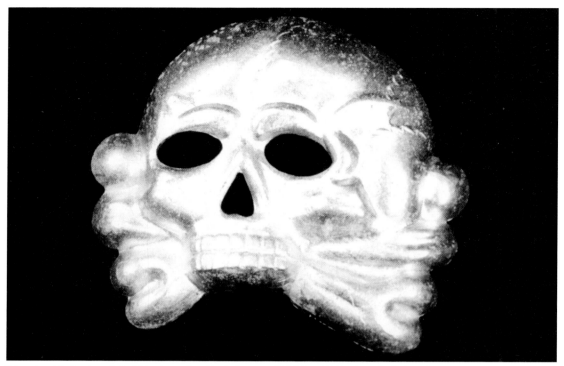

This version of the Prussian-style death's head was adopted by the Stosstrupp Adolf Hitler in 1923 and worn by the SS until 1934.

The 1934-pattern SS death's head. This particular example was produced by the firm of Deschler in Munich.

badges. Their successors in the SS thereafter contracted the firm of Deschler in Munich to restrike large quantities of the Prussian-style jawless death's head which they used on their headgear for the next eleven years. As Hitler's personal guards, they liked to model themselves on the imperial Bodyguard Hussars, who had become known as the 'Schwarze Totenkopfhusaren', and were fond of singing their old regimental song, with its emotive verse:

> In black we are dressed,
> In blood we are drenched,
> Death's Head on our helmets.
> Hurrah! Hurrah!
> We stand unshaken!

In 1934, when the Prussian-style Totenkopf began to be used as an élite badge by the new army Panzer units which were, after all, the natural successors to the imperial cavalry regiments, the SS devised its own unique pattern of grinning death's head, with lower jaw, which it wore thereafter.

The 1934-pattern SS Totenkopf ultimately took various forms, right-facing, left-facing and front-facing, and appeared on the cloth headgear of all SS members and on the tunics and vehicles of the SS-Totenkopfverbände and Totenkopf-Division. It was the centrepiece of the prestigious SS death's head ring and could be seen on dagger and gorget suspension chains, mess jackets, flags, standards, drum covers, trumpet banners and the SS and police Guerrilla Warfare Badge. Moreover, because of its direct associations with Danzig, where the Prussian Leib-Husaren regiments had been garrisoned until 1918, it was selected as the special formation badge of the SS-Heimwehr Danzig and the Danzig Police. Himmler wanted his men to be proud of their heritage and there is no doubt that the honourable associations of the German death's head were well used to that

end. It became an inspiration to those who were granted the privilege of wearing it.

Alongside the Totenkopf, the SS Runen, or SS runes, represented the élitism and brotherly comradeship of the organisation, and were elevated to an almost holy status. Indeed, as SS men marched off to war in 1939, they sang their hymn 'SS Wir Alle' ('We are all SS') which included the line: 'Wir alle stehen zum Kampf bereit, wenn Runen und Totenkopf führen' ('We all stand ready for battle, inspired by runes and death's head'). The word 'rune' derives from the Old Norse 'run', meaning 'secret script'. Runes were characters which formed the alphabets used by the Germanic tribes of pre-Christian Europe for both magical and ordinary writing. There were three major branches of the runic alphabet and a number of minor variants, and some runes doubled as symbols representative of human traits or ideals, much as the Romans used oak and laurel leaves to denote strength and victory. In AD 98, in his work *Germania*, the historian Cornelius Tacitus described in detail how the Germans engaged in divination by runes.

In the nineteenth and early twentieth centuries, runes began to be re-examined by the fashionable 'Völkisch' or 'folk' movements of northern Europe, which promoted interest in traditional stories, beliefs and festivals. The Thule Society was among these groups, and through his association with its activities Himmler began to look back to the mystical Dark Age Germanic period for much of his inspiration. He had always had a fascination for cryptic codes and hidden messages, so it was doubly appropriate that he should tap many of the ideas in pagan symbolism and adopt, or at least adapt, certain runes for use by his SS. All pre-1939 Allgemeine-SS Anwärter were instructed in runic symbolism as part of their probationary training. By 1945, fourteen main varieties of rune were in use by the SS, and these are described on pp. 146–7 and seen in the accompanying illustration.

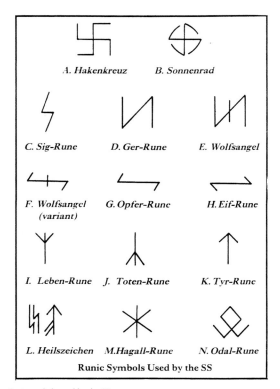

A. Hakenkreuz B. Sonnenrad

C. Sig-Rune D. Ger-Rune E. Wolfsangel

F. Wolfsangel (variant) G. Opfer-Rune H. Eif-Rune

I. Leben-Rune J. Toten-Rune K. Tyr-Rune

L. Heilszeichen M. Hagall-Rune N. Odal-Rune

Runic Symbols Used by the SS

Runic symbols used by the SS.

A. *The Hakenkreuz*

The Hakenkreuz, or swastika, was the pagan Germanic sign of Donner (or Thor), the god of adventurers. During the nineteenth century it came to be regarded as symbolic of nationalism and racial struggle, and in the post-1918 period was adopted by several Freikorps units, primarily the Ehrhardt Brigade. As the senior badge of the Nazi party and state, it inevitably featured on many SS accoutrements, either static (i.e. standing flat) or mobile (i.e. standing on one point to give the appearance of an advancing movement). An elongated version of the mobile swastika was used by the Germanic-SS in Flanders.

B. *The Sonnenrad*

The Sonnenrad, or sunwheel swastika, was the Old Norse representation of the sun, and was taken up as an emblem by the Thule Society. It was later used as a sign by the Waffen-SS Divisions 'Wiking' and 'Nordland', many of whose members were Scandinavian nationals, and also by the Schalburg Corps. It formed the main part of the design of the Germanic Proficiency Rune, and was worn by the Norwegian SS.

C. *The Sig-Rune*

The Sig-Rune (also known as the Siegrune) was symbolic of victory. In 1931, SS-Sturmführer Walter Heck, who was a graphic designer employed by the badge manufacturing firm of Ferdinand Hoffstätter in Bonn, drew two Sig-Runes side by side and thus created the ubiquitous 'SS Runes' insignia widely used by all branches of the organisation after 1933. The SS paid him 2.50 Reichsmarks for the rights to his design! Heck was likewise responsible for the 'SA Runes' badge, which combined a runic 'S' with a Gothic 'A'.

D. *The Ger-Rune*

The Ger-Rune was symbolic of communal spirit, and featured as a variant divisional sign of the Waffen-SS Division 'Nordland'.

E. *The Wolfsangel*

The Wolfsangel, or wolf hook, was originally a pagan device which supposedly possessed the power to ward off wolves. It then became a heraldic symbol representing a wolf trap, and as such still features to this day on the coat-of-arms of the city of Wolfstein. Adopted as an emblem by fifteenth-century peasants in their revolt against the mercenaries of the German princes, the Wolfsangel was thereafter regarded as being symbolic of liberty and independence, although it was also referred to as the 'Zeichen der Willkür' or 'Badge of Wanton Tyranny' during the Thirty Years War. The Wolfsangel was an early emblem of the Nazi Party, and was later used as a sign by the Waffen-SS Division 'Das Reich'.

F. *The Wolfsangel* (variant)
A squat version of the Wolfsangel with hooked arms was the emblem of the Germanic-SS in the Netherlands and was later adopted by the Waffen-SS Division 'Landstorm Nederland', which comprised Dutch volunteers.

G. *The Opfer-Rune*
The Opfer-Rune symbolised self-sacrifice. It was used after 1918 by the Stahlhelm war veterans' association and was later the badge which commemorated the Nazi martyrs of the 1923 Munich putsch. It also formed part of the design of the SA Sports Badge for War Wounded, which could be won by disabled SS ex-servicemen.

H. *The Eif-Rune*
The Eif-Rune represented zeal and enthusiasm. It was the early insignia of specially selected SS adjutants assigned personally to Hitler and, as such, was worn by Rudolf Hess in 1929.

I. *The Leben-Rune*
The Leben-Rune, or life rune, symbolised life and was adopted by the SS Lebensborn Society and Ahnenerbe. It likewise featured on SS documents and grave markers to show date of birth.

J. *The Toten-Rune*
The Toten-Rune, or death rune, represented death, and was used on SS documents and grave markers to show date of death.

K. *The Tyr-Rune*
The Tyr-Rune, also known as the Kampf-Rune or battle rune, was the pagan Germanic sign of Tyr, the god of war, and was symbolic of leadership in battle. It was commonly used by the SS as a grave marker, replacing the Christian cross, and a Tyr-Rune worn on the upper left arm indicated graduation from the SA-Reichsführerschule, which trained SS officers until 1934. It was

later the specialist badge of the SS recruiting and training branch, and an emblem of the Waffen-SS Division '30 Januar' which comprised staff and pupils from various SS training schools.

L. *The Heilszeichen*
The Heilszeichen, or prosperity symbols, represented success and good fortune, and appeared on the SS death's head ring.

M. *The Hagall-Rune*
The Hagall-Rune stood for unshakable faith, which was expected of all SS members. It featured on the SS death's head ring as well as on ceremonial accoutrements used at SS weddings. It was also chosen as the sign of the SS-Polizei-Division, since it resembled the traditional 'Police Star' badge.

N. *The Odal-Rune*
The Odal-Rune symbolised kinship and family and the bringing together of people of similar blood. It was the badge of the SS Rasse- und Siedlungshauptamt and emblem of the Waffen-SS Division 'Prinz Eugen', which comprised mainly Volksdeutsche from the Balkans.

The symbolism of death's head and runes was brought together in one of the most potent yet most obscure of all SS uniform accoutrements, the Totenkopfring der SS, or SS death's head ring, instituted by Himmler on 10 April 1934. The ring was not classed as a national decoration since it was in the gift of the Reichsführer. However, it ranked as a senior award within the SS brotherhood, recognising the wearer's personal achievement, devotion to duty and loyalty to Hitler and his ideals. The concept and runic form of the ring were undoubtedly adopted by Himmler from Germanic mythology, which related how the god Thor possessed a pure silver ring on which people could take oaths (much as Christians swear on the Bible), and how binding treaties were carved in runes on

The Sig-Runes collar patch, initially restricted to members of the Leibstandarte but eventually worn by all German formations of the Waffen-SS.

Wotan's spear. The Totenkopfring comprised a massive band of oakleaves deeply engraved with a death's head and a number of runes. The award document presented with each ring described the latter and interpreted them thus:

The Sig-Rune in a triangle represented membership of the SS
The swastika in a square stood for Nazi philosophy
The Heilszeichen in a circle stood for prosperity
The Hagall-Rune in a hexagon denoted unshakable faith.

However, these were much diluted meanings in comparison to those initially drawn up by SS-

Brigadeführer Karl-Maria Wiligut-Weisthor, an expert on runes and their coded symbolism, who designed the ring for Himmler. Wiligut-Weisthor's interpretations are given below and, meeting with the Reichsführer's approval, give an interesting insight into the workings of Himmler's mind at the time he was planning the future of his Black Order:

The Sig-Rune in a Triangle
The triangle means life is eternal. The three sides stand for birth/development/death, or past/present/future. Each death is the way to a new life and the triangle symbolises the eternal cycle of creation. The Sig-Rune represents the sun and good health. It was also the pagan symbol of victory. Hence it encompasses both the greeting ('Heil' or

A unique oil painting of Heinrich Himmler by the Third Reich's court artist, Conrad Hommel, *c.* 1943. (Courtesy of the US Army Captured War Art Collection.)

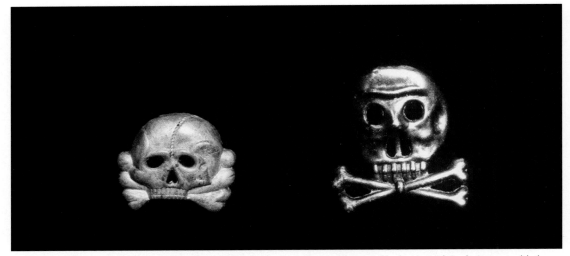

Death's heads were not worn solely by the SS during the Third Reich. The Prussian style on the left was used by the army's 5th Cavalry Regiment, while the Brunswick pattern, right, was sported by members of the 17th Infantry Regiment. Panzer units, the Naval Kustenschütz Danzig and the Luftwaffe's Schleppgruppe 4 and Kampfgruppe 54 all chose the Totenkopf as their distinctive emblem.

An Austrian 1916-pattern steel helmet with hand-painted death's head, as worn by various Freikorps formations c. 1919–20.

Himmler prized the plain and simple Blutorden, or Blood Order, above all his other decorations. This medal, also known as the 'Ehrenzeichen vom 9. November 1923', recognised NSDAP members who had participated in the Beer Hall putsch or rendered outstanding services to the Nazi party during its formative years. The award became steeped in a deliberately cultivated mystique which guaranteed the wearer special privileges wherever he went.

Black service uniform as worn by an SS-Oberscharführer in the 12th Sturm, 3rd Sturmbann, 88th SS Fuss-Standarte (Bremen), *c.* 1935. The 'swallow's nests' at the shoulders denote his position as a member of the unit's drum corps, and his decorations, including the Turkish War Star, indicate extensive First World War service.

The SS newspaper *Das Schwarze Korps* alongside copies of *FM-Zeitschrift*, the magazine for SS Patron Members, and *Storm SS*, the periodical of the Germanic-SS in the Netherlands.

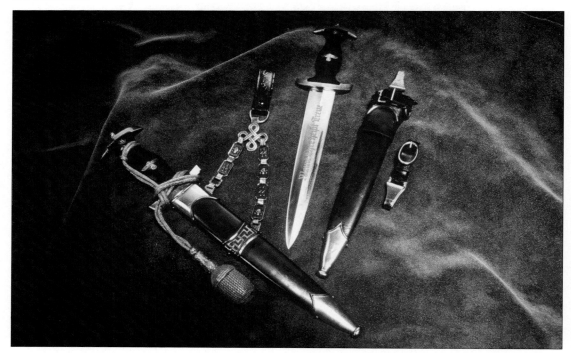

The 1936-pattern SS chained dagger was an ornate item of dress weaponry, and is depicted here alongside the 1933-pattern with hanging strap. Every facet of their design harked back to the medieval and Dark Age Germanic past.

The SS death's head ring. This particular example was awarded to SS-Hauptsturmführer Kurt Taschner on 9 November 1942. Taschner, an administrative officer in both the Allgemeine-SS and the Waffen-SS, served at various times in the 61st SS Fuss-Standarte (Allenstein), the 11th SS-Totenkopf Regiment, 'Das Reich', 'Deutschland', the WVHA and finally the Latvian SS Brigade.

Three unofficial rings, bearing death's heads and runes. These were popular among SS officers and men, and are known to have been manufactured to order by concentration camp inmates who were jewellers by trade.

An oak casket carved with Sig-Runes, a swastika, a Hagall-Rune, oakleaves and acorns. The symbolism apparent on this artefact is akin to that used on the SS death's head ring. The casket was employed at SS wedding ceremonies as a container for the presentation copies of *Mein Kampf* which every newly married couple received.

The SS Cavalryman was one of Allach's equestrian subjects. It could not be purchased on the open market, but was reserved for presentation by Himmler to notable personalities of the Third Reich.

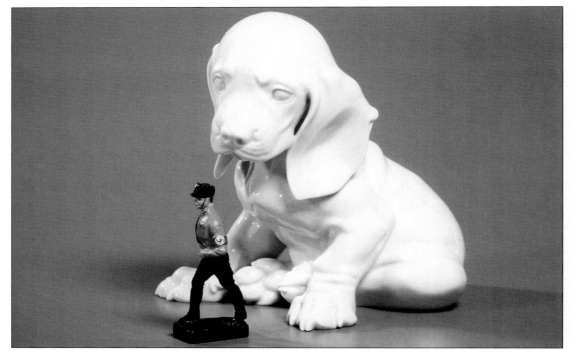

This exquisitely formed Dachshund puppy was a typical product of the SS porcelain factory at Allach, and is shown here overlooking a model SS man in traditional uniform. A range of Nazi toy soldiers of this type, made from a sawdust and glue mixture, were manufactured by the firms of Elastolin and Lineol for the mass market during the 1930s.

Allgemeine-SS man's peaked cap, *c.* 1935. It sports the 1929-pattern NSDAP eagle over a 1934-pattern SS Totenkopf.

The rectangular belt buckle for SS NCOs and other ranks, alongside the circular version for officers. These were designed personally by Hitler, who was also responsible for the SS motto 'Meine Ehre heisst Treue'.

This ornate wine cooler in hammered silver plate was given to a member of the signals platoon, 2nd battalion, 3rd SS regiment as a twenty-seventh birthday present from eight of his colleagues. The SS runes have been finely engraved into the central body of the piece.

Typewriters with special runic keys were introduced during the first half of 1936 for use in SS offices. This portable example bears the mark of a Dutch retailer but was reputedly 'liberated' by a British officer from Buchenwald concentration camp in 1945. Presumably, the original owner was transferred from Holland to the camp, taking his typewriter with him.

A selection of documents including Allgemeine-SS identity cards, a Waffen-SS Soldbuch and an FM membership book. The two 'death cards' at lower right commemorate SS men killed in battle, and were distributed by their families to friends and acquaintances as keepsakes. Of particular note is the use of the Toten-Rune on the card relating to Gustav Kräter.

Documents signed by Himmler, his adjutant Wolff and Heydrich are displayed beside a sheet of the Reichsführer's official headed notepaper and a New Year card from Adolf Hitler to SS-Oberführer Ulrich Graf, who saved Hitler's life during the Munich putsch.

This unique version of the M42 steel helmet, in black with white stencilled insignia, is the only known surviving example of its kind. It may have been worn unofficially by a section of the Germanic-SS, or by Allgemeine-SS Alarmstürme units engaged in front-line defence fighting with the Volkssturm during the spring of 1945. It is certainly a late war item, bearing a hitherto undocumented form of the SS runes badge.

The Germanic Proficiency Rune in Bronze, less than ten of which are still known to survive. The striking design is finely executed in plated zinc and enamelled bronze, and typifies the high quality of Nazi decorations even during the latter stages of the war.

Police field service uniform as worn by a Hauptmann of Gendarmerie, c. 1944. This outfit features breast runes denoting full membership of the SS. It also sports the Old Campaigner's Chevron, adjutant's aiguillette, the German National Sports Badge in Silver, War Merit Cross and, interestingly, the basic NSDAP membership badge pinned to the left breast pocket, a fairly common practice among the civil police during wartime.

MED WAFFEN-SS OG DEN NORSKE LEGION MOT DEN FELLES FIENDE.....

MOT BOLSJEVISMEN

Recruiting poster for the Norwegian Legion, dating from 1941. It reads: 'With the Waffen-SS and the Norwegian Legion against the common enemy – against Bolshevism'. Such exhortations persuaded 6,000 Norwegians to sign up with the SS for combat service on the eastern front.

M42 Waffen-SS steel helmet, clearly showing the regulation SS runes decal and distinctive sharp silhouette. The Leibstandarte motorcycle registration plate below again features the SS runes, and dates from around 1938. Such registration numbers eventually ran into hundreds of thousands, with the plate 'SS – 1' being reserved for Himmler's personal heavily armoured staff car.

1940-pattern tunic with field-grey collar, as worn by an artillery Rottenführer of the 'Götz von Berlichingen' division, spring 1944. The ribbons are those of the Iron Cross 2nd Class and Russian Front Medal, and the General Assault Badge and Wound Badge in Black are also displayed. The dress bayonet and knot were carried when walking out.

BEVO-pattern woven cuff title introduced in 1943 for men of the 16th SS-Panzergrenadier Division 'Reichsführer-SS', named in honour of Himmler. Since SS units were normally called after dead, rather than living 'heroes', Himmler's rank was used in preference to his actual name. The division is best remembered for its massacre of 1,200 Italian civilians at Marzabotto in September 1944, in reprisal for the activities of a partisan brigade in the Apennines.

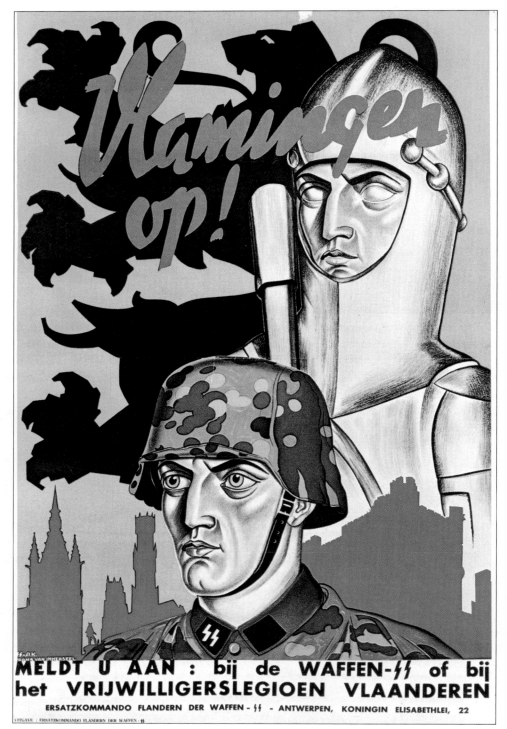

Recruiting poster for the Flemish Legion, declaring 'Flemings Rise Up!' It depicts a Waffen-SS soldier as the direct descendant of a national hero, a theme common to recruiting drives in the Germanic countries.

The other ranks' 1940-pattern Schiffchen field cap, or 'Feldmütze neuer Art', with machine-woven eagle and death's head.

SS subjects featured on a number of postage stamps during the Third Reich. The red example on the left depicts a Waffen-SS mortar crew in action, while the black one was issued in the Protectorate of Bohemia and Moravia to commemorate the assassinated Reinhard Heydrich. It shows Heydrich's death mask, by the sculptor F. Rotter, alongside the SS runes.

The field-grey fez with dark-green tassel was issued to members of the Muslim SS divisions 'Handschar' and 'Kama' instead of the Einheitsfeldmütze. Traditionally, Muslim troops wore the peakless fez, and even brimless steel helmets during the First World War, so that they could press their foreheads to the ground during prayer without removing their regulation headgear.

The Guerrilla Warfare Badge in Bronze, one of the most symbolically potent of all Nazi decorations.

1944-pattern camouflage drill tunic, as worn by an infantry Obersturmführer of the Waffen-SS. It was not uncommon for full rank insignia and decorations to be worn on the camouflage tunic, contrary to regulations. Most notable here are the Knight's Cross of the Iron Cross at the neck and the Close Combat Clasp above the ribbon bar.

This Waffen-SS recruiting poster by O. Anton was the best known German poster of the Second World War, being printed in a number of different languages and displayed prominently in public places throughout the occupied territories.

A Waffen-SS officer's classic 'old style' or 'crusher' field cap, which was custom-made in Italy in 1943. It bears the trade mark 'Successori Fare – Milano/Roma/Toreno/Modena', and features a leather peak and narrower than usual black velvet band. This pattern of cap came to be the mark of the veteran Waffen-SS officer.

Sturmbannführer Hermann Buchner of the SS-Totenkopf-Division was one of the 'heroes' of the Waffen-SS, winning the following awards before he was killed in action outside Warsaw in November 1944: (a) Knight's Cross of the Iron Cross; (b) German Cross in Gold; (c) Iron Cross 1st and 2nd Classes; (d) Close Combat Clasp in Gold; (e) Wound Badge in Gold; (f) Infantry Assault Badge in Silver; (g) Demjansk Shield; (h) War Merit Cross 2nd Class with Swords; (i) Russian Front Medal; (j) Czech Occupation Medal with Prague Castle Bar.

Close-up of the Sig-Runes key which featured on SS typewriters from 1936. SS documents and printed publications invariably used the Sig-Runes instead of the usual Roman letters 'SS'.

'Good Health') and the battle-cry ('Sieg' or 'Victory') of the Germanic ancestors of the SS. (This combination of ancient greeting and battle-cry gave the Nazis their 'Sieg Heil'.)

The Swastika in a Square
The swastika comprises four 'U'-Runes. The 'U'-Rune represents the path of the sun and is symbolic of fertility. A split or halved swastika results in the 'G'-Rune or Gibor-Rune, which means handing down to one's descendants. The total symbolism of this rune is man being at one with god and eternity.

The Heilszeichen in a Circle
In the circle are two Sig-Runes and one combined Tyr-Rune and Os-Rune. The circle stands for the circulation of divinity in nature, which forged the human spirit. It is the circle of life. The Sig-Runes stand for the SS and prosperity. The Tyr-Rune is the spear of Tyr, the Norse god of war. This all means that death is powerless and should not be feared. Those who fight bravely to ensure the prosperity of their Volk shall be forever remembered.

The Hagall-Rune in a Hexagon
All eighteen runes derive from the hexagon. Carrying this symbol gives strength over adversity as it encompasses the total power of all the runes. The overall interpretation of this rune is to believe in yourself and you will become the master of everything.

It is clear that Himmler personally believed in all the foregoing, and he treated the ring with extreme reverence. Initially, the Totenkopfring was reserved for those Old Guard veterans with SS membership numbers below 3,000. In effect, this meant that the ring was restricted to officers, for on 20 April 1934 Himmler commissioned as Sturmführer all SS men with membership numbers below 3,000 who were not already officers. All of these thousand or so individuals had joined the SS prior to September 1930, when the Nazis scored their first notable election success. Qualification for award of the ring was gradually extended, until by 1939 most SS officers with three years' service were entitled to wear it. Entitlement could be postponed or withdrawn for anything between three months and three years if the holder had been punished under the SS discipline code. Rings were bestowed on set SS and NSDAP festival dates, namely 20 April, 21 June, 9 November and 21 December, and all awards were recorded in the *Dienstaltersliste*. When a ring holder died, his ring had to be returned to the SS Personalhauptamt, which arranged for its preservation in a special shrine at Himmler's castle at Wewelsburg. In the spring of 1945, these returned rings were blast-sealed into a mountainside near Wewelsburg, to prevent their falling into Allied hands. To this day, they have never been found.

The SS death's head ring. The first such rings were presented by Himmler to the SS Old Guard on 24 December 1933, four months before publication of the order which elevated the Totenkopfring to the status of an official SS award. It is noteworthy that those who eventually qualified for the ring had to apply for it through the usual SS channels. This explains why many officers entitled to the ring never received it – they simply forgot to apply for it, or chose not to do so. Fewer than twenty death's head rings are known to survive in private collections.

Between 1934 and 1944, around 14,500 death's head rings were awarded. As at 1 January 1945, 64 per cent of these had been returned to the SS on the deaths of their holders (i.e. those to be buried at Wewelsburg), 10 per cent had been lost on the battlefield, and 26 per cent were either still in the possession of ring holders or otherwise unaccounted for. That would mean that, in theory, about 3,500 rings might have been in circulation at the end of the war. The Totenkopfring became so sought after an honour that many SS and police officers and men not entitled to wear it had a variety of unofficial 'skull rings' produced in gold or silver by local jewellers and even concentration camp inmates. However, these lacked the runic symbolism and were rather vulgar representations of the real thing.

The powerful and symbolic SS uniform of the late 1930s and early 1940s developed from very humble origins. The earliest Nazis wore normal civilian clothing and were distinguished only by their crudely homemade Kampfbinde, or swastika armbands, worn on the left upper arm. With the advent of the paramilitary SA in 1921, however, it became necessary to evolve a uniform specifically for its members. At first, their dress lacked any consistency and was characteristically Freikorps in style, generally taking the form of field-grey army surplus double-breasted windcheater jackets, waist belts with cross-straps, grey trousers, trench boots, steel helmets and mountain caps. Many SA men simply retained the uniforms they had worn during the 1914–18 war, stripped of badges. The swastika armband was the only constant feature, sometimes bearing a metal numeral or emblem to indicate unit identity and a metal 'pip' or cloth stripes to denote rank. The Commander of the 1st Company of SA Regiment 'München', for example, wore a Brunswick-style death's head over the numeral '1' and a single pip on his armband. In 1923, members of the Stosstrupp Adolf Hitler wore similar garb with the addition of a Prussian-pattern Totenkopf on the cap, usually surmounted by the 'Reichskokarde', a circular metal cockade in the imperial colours of black, white and red. After the failure of the Munich putsch and the banning of the SA and Stosstrupp, the men continued to wear their old uniforms as members of the Frontbanne, adding a steel helmet badge to the centre of the swastika armband.

At the end of 1924 Leutnant Gerhard Rossbach, formerly one of the most famous of the Freikorps and SA leaders, acquired a bargain lot of surplus German army tropical brown shirts in Austria. These items, which had been destined for the Reich's colonies in Africa, were not in fact shirts at all, but blouses with collars and pockets which were worn over an ordinary collarless shirt. When the NSDAP was reconstituted and the SA reactivated in February 1925, Hitler kitted his men out with these readily available shirts and had ties, breeches and kepis made to match. Thus by chance circumstances rather than design, brown became the adopted colour of the SA and the Nazi party in general. When the SS was formed in April of the same year, its members too were issued with brown shirts. To distinguish them from the SA, however, they retained their Stosstrupp death's heads and wore black kepis, black ties, black breeches and black borders to the swastika armband. By the end of 1925, the brown shirt with black accoutrements was firmly established as the 'traditional uniform' of the SS. The vast majority of SS men, who were also members of the NSDAP, wore the Nazi party badge on their ties.

On 9 November 1926, the rapidly expanding SA introduced collar patches or Kragenspiegel to indicate unit and rank, replacing the badges and stripes formerly denote rank and unit. As with the SA, rank was shown on the left patch, or both patches for Standartenführer and above, with unit markings on the right patch. However, the SS system was much more simple than that of the SA. All SS collar patches were black in colour with white, silver or grey numerals, pips, bars and oakleaves. Moreover, the unit collar patches were restricted to indicating Standarte, specialist or staff appointment.

To show Sturmbann and Sturm membership, the SS devised their own complicated system of cuff titles or Ärmelstreifen, narrow black bands worn on the lower left sleeve. Within every Fuss-Standarte, each Sturmbann was assigned a colour which bordered the upper and lower edges of the cuff title. The prescribed Sturmbann colours were:

Sturmbann I	Green
Sturmbann II	Dark Blue
Sturmbann III	Red
Sturmbann IV (Reserve)	Light Blue

The number and, if appropriate, honour name of the wearer's Sturm appeared embroidered in grey or silver thread on the title. Thus a member of the 2nd Sturm, 1st Sturmbann, 41st SS Fuss-Standarte would wear a green-bordered cuff title bearing the numeral '2' in conjunction with the number '41' on his right collar patch. A man in the 11th Sturm, 'Adolf Höh', 3rd Sturmbann, 30th SS Fuss-Standarte would sport a red-edged cuff title with the legend '11 Adolf Höh', and regimental numeral '30' on the right collar patch. All members of the Allgemeine-SS cavalry units had yellow-edged cuff titles, while those of signals and pioneer formations had their titles bordered in brown and black, respectively. A relatively small number of cuff titles bore Roman numerals or designations relating to staff or specialist appointments.

The plain SS traditional uniform as worn by Himmler in 1929 (see p. 12).

worn on the armband. The right patch bore unit numerals and the left patch a Stahlhelm-type system of rank pips, bars and oakleaves. By contrasting the colour of the patch with that of the numerals, an attempt was made to reflect the state colours of the district in which the unit concerned was located. For example, Berlin SA men wore black and white patches, Hamburg SA men red and white, Munich men blue and white, and so on. This arrangement proved difficult to sustain and the colour combinations ultimately underwent a number of changes. SA unit patches were particularly complex, accommodating not only Standarte, specialist and staff appointments, but also Sturmbann and Sturm designations. In August 1929, the SS likewise introduced collar patches to

Early SA belt buckle, worn by the SS until 1931.

During the autumn of 1929, at the same time as the new SS collar patches and cuff titles were being manufactured and distributed, a small sharp-winged eagle and swastika badge, or Hoheitsabzeichen, was introduced for wear on the SA and SS kepi in place of the Reichskokarde. SS bandsmen's uniforms were further modified by the addition of black and white military-style 'swallow's nests' worn at the shoulder.

At the end of 1931, the SS adopted the motto 'Meine Ehre heisst Treue' ('My Honour is Loyalty') following a well-publicised open letter which Hitler had sent to Kurt Daluege after the Stennes putsch, declaring in his praise: 'SS Mann, deine Ehre heisst Treue'. Almost immediately, a belt buckle incorporating the motto into its design was commissioned and produced by the Overhoff firm of Lüdenscheid to replace the SA buckle hitherto worn by all members of the SS. The new belt buckle was circular in form for officers and rectangular for lower ranks, and continued in wear unchanged until 1945. In May 1933, shoulder straps, or Achselstücke, were devised for wear on the right shoulder only. These straps were adornments to be used in conjunction with the collar insignia already in existence and indicated rank level only (i.e. enlisted man or NCO/junior officer/intermediate officer/ senior officer) rather than actual rank. In February 1934, a silver Honour Chevron for the Old Guard (Ehrenwinkel für Alte

Red-edged cuff title indicating membership of the 12th Sturm, 3rd Sturmbann of an SS Fuss-Standarte.

Kämpfer) was authorised for wear on the upper right arm by all members of the SS who had joined the SS, NSDAP or any of the other party-affiliated organisations prior to 30 January 1933. Qualification was later extended to include former members of the police, armed forces or Stahlhelm who fulfilled certain conditions and transferred into the SS. The traditional brown shirt uniform of the SS therefore developed almost continually over eleven years and incorporated many additions or alterations at specific times. These can be of great assistance in dating period photographs. The traditional uniform was gradually phased out after the Nazi assumption of power and was not generally worn after 1934, except on special ceremonial occasions by members of

the SS Old Guard. At such events, some of the Alte Kämpfer even sported their homemade armbands from the 1921–2 era.

A major change to SS uniform was made in 1932, in response to a governmental demand that the SA and SS should adopt a more 'respectable' outfit as a condition of the lifting of the ban on political uniforms. On 7 July, a black tunic and peaked cap, harking back to the garb of the imperial Leib-Husaren, were introduced for the SS to replace the brown shirt and kepi. These items were made available first to officers, then lower ranks, and were worn side-by-side with the traditional uniform during 1933 while all members were being kitted out. By the beginning of 1934, sufficient quantities of the black uniform had been manufactured for it

SS men in formalised traditional uniform mount a guard of honour over their comrade Fritz Schulz, killed in street fighting in Berlin, August 1932.

to be in general use. During the remainder of the 1930s, the black service uniform was developed as the SS organisation expanded. Greatcoats were produced and a series of specialist arm diamonds, or Ärmelraute, devised for wear on the lower left sleeve. On 21 June 1936 a new and larger SS cap eagle replaced the old 1929-pattern, and white shirts were authorised for wear under the tunic, instead of brown shirts, on ceremonial occasions. For evening functions such as parties, dances and so on there were black mess jackets for officers and white 'monkey suits' for waiters, all bearing full SS insignia. As from 27 June 1939, officers were provided with an all-white version of the service uniform for walking out during the summer period, officially defined as 1 April to 30 September each year.

Full-time SS men were regularly issued with items of uniform and equipment. So far as part-timers were concerned, however, all uniform articles had to be purchased by the SS members themselves at their own expense. The only exceptions were replacements for items lost or damaged during the course of duty, which were provided free of charge. If an SS man wished to acquire a new tunic, for example, he could either buy it direct from a tailoring shop which was an approved sales outlet of the Reichszeugmeisterei der NSDAP, i.e. an authorised dealer in Nazi party uniforms and equipment, or else place a pre-paid order with his local Trupp or Sturm

SA and SS men parading during the ban on political uniforms in 1932.

which would, in turn, arrange to requisition a tunic on his behalf from one of the clothing stores run by the SS administrative department. The latter regularly produced price lists which were circulated to all SS formations for the attention of would-be buyers. The following small selection of prices is taken from the extensive Allgemeine-SS price list of January 1938, and gives a general idea of the cost of items for sale at that time:

Item	Price in Reichsmarks
Black service tunic	34.80
Black breeches	18.00
Black trousers	19.90
Black overcoat	45.40
Peaked cap for NCOs and lower ranks	4.90
Peaked cap for officers	7.50
Peaked cap for generals	7.80
Field cap	2.30
Steel helmet	12.30
White tunic	30.00
Waiter's jacket	18.90
Athletic vest with SS runes	3.75
Brown shirt	5.50
Black tie	0.85
Riding boots	27.50 per pair
Marching boots	23.70 per pair
1933 service dagger	7.10
1936 chained dagger	12.15
Belt buckle for NCOs and lower ranks	0.50
Belt buckle for officers	1.25

An Allgemeine-SS Schar on parade, 1933. Note the mixture of traditional and black uniforms.

Shoulder strap	0.33
Collar piping	0.05 per metre
Collar patch	0.60
Swastika armband	0.80
Cuff title	0.75
Sleeve diamond	0.55
Old Guard chevron	0.10
Eagle for peaked cap	0.25
Death's head for peaked cap	0.10
Vehicle pennant	1.20
Command flag	47.40

The reduction in the number of active part-time Allgemeine-SS men because of the enhancement of conscription at the outbreak of war, led to a surplus of black uniforms building up in SS stores after 1939. In 1942, the police collected most of the unwanted black Allgemeine-SS uniforms in Germany

Sig-Runes embossed in gold under the celluloid sweat shield of an Allgemeine-SS peaked cap, indicating that it was manufactured to comply with SS uniform regulations and supplied through SS channels.

Dienst- und Paradeanzug der Allgem. ᛋᛋ
ᛋᛋ-Oberscharführer

Traditionsanzug der ᛋᛋ
ᛋᛋ-Unterscharführer

Dienstanzug, Mantel
ᛋᛋ-Rottenführer

Ausgehanzug mit Regenmantel
ᛋᛋ-Sturmbannführer

Styles of Allgemeine-SS uniform. From left to right: standard 1932-pattern black service and parade uniform for SS-Oberscharführer; 'traditional uniform' for SS-Unterscharführer. This was the first formalised SS uniform, worn by all ranks until 1932–4, and donned on selected ceremonial occasions thereafter by members of the Old Guard; service uniform with overcoat for SS-Rottenführer; walking out uniform with raincoat for SS-Sturmbannführer. The raincoat was unpopular and was soon replaced by a heavy leather coat. (Reproduced from the *Organisationsbuch der NSDAP*, 1937 edition.)

and sent them east for distribution to Schuma units, or west for issuing to the Germanic-SS. Those destined for the Schuma had their SS badges removed and distinctive bright green lapels, shoulder straps, pocket flaps and cuffs added. Similarly, the Germanic-SS attached their own special insignia to these uniforms. As a result, very few black Allgemeine-SS tunics survived the war with their original German badges intact.

In 1938, the Allgemeine-SS introduced a very elegant pale-grey uniform for its full-time staff, thus bringing the SS into line with the general war footing of the other uniformed services. The new outfit was identical in style to the black uniform, but bore an SS-pattern shoulder strap on the left shoulder as well as one on the right, and replaced the swastika armband with a cloth version of the 1936-pattern SS eagle. The idea was to give the appearance of a military rather than political uniform, thus lending some authority to full-time Allgemeine-SS officers who were, by the nature of their employment, exempt from service in the Wehrmacht. The pale-grey uniform was issued first to Hauptamt personnel and thereafter to others qualified to wear it. The 40,000 or so active part-time members of the Allgemeine-SS, who were almost exclusively

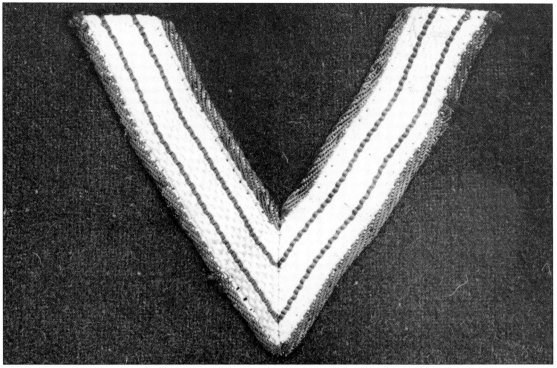

The Honour Chevron for the Old Guard. This came to be regarded as the badge of the 'die-hard' Nazi, even though an eighteen-year-old SS recruit in 1939 would have been entitled to wear it had he been a ten-year-old Hitler Youth in 1931.

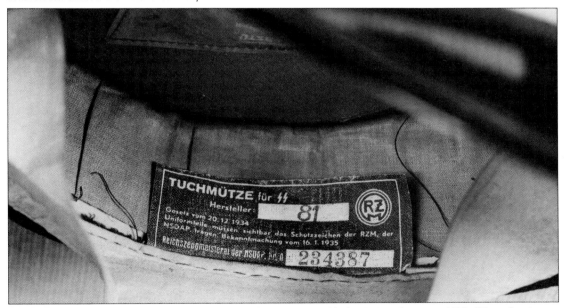

RZM label inside an Allgemeine-SS peaked cap, indicating that the manufacturer was approved by the NSDAP. As of 16 January 1935, all Nazi uniform items were obliged by law to carry these tags. Unauthorised production of NSDAP equipment was strictly forbidden, and there were severe penalties for non-compliance with the regulations. The RZM had the authority to close down offending firms, and the owners were liable to be imprisoned.

RZM label on the reverse of an SS armband. It can be decoded as follows: RZM — approved by the RZM; SS — approved by the SS; D — 'Dienstkleidung' or service uniform division of the RZM; A4 — cloth insignia manufacturer; 275 — maker's number, allocated by the RZM; A No. 293333 — serial number of the armband, allocated by the RZM.

engaged in reserved occupations, were never issued with grey outfits and continued to wear the black uniform proudly while on duty in Germany. By 1945, however, that most impressive of all uniforms, which had been such a status symbol in the prewar days, had become an object of derision since its wearers were increasingly thought of as shirking military service.

Although the SS became one of the most complex of all Nazi paramilitary organisations, its rank structure remained relatively stable and underwent few major alterations.

Until 1930 there were basically only two SS ranks, namely SS-Mann and SS-Staffelführer. That year, with the evolution of Stürme and Sturmbanne, nine grades began to be employed by the SS, based on those of the SA. These were:

SS-Mann
SS-Scharführer
SS-Truppführer
SS-Sturmführer
SS-Sturmbannführer
SS-Standartenführer

Himmler wearing the elegant pale-grey Allgemeine-SS uniform introduced in 1938.

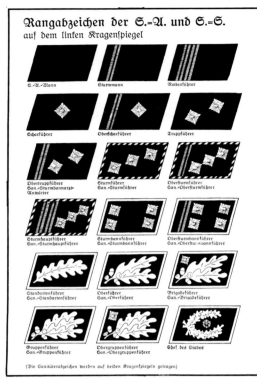

Rangabzeichen der S.=A. und S.=S.
auf dem linken Kragenspiegel

Rank badges of the SA and SS, c. May 1934. At this stage, lower ranks had white piped collar patches while junior officers' patches were piped in black and silver and those of senior officers in plain silver. Early terms such as Sturmhauptführer still feature, and there is no special insignia for Himmler who, even though he held the post of Reichsführer der SS, was ranked simply as an SS-Obergruppenführer. (Reproduced from *Die Uniformen der Braunhemden*, 1934.)

SS-Oberführer
SS-Gruppenführer
SS-Obergruppenführer

On 19 May 1933, a further eight ranks were created to accommodate the general expansion of the SS, namely:

SS-Sturmmann
SS-Rottenführer
SS-Oberscharführer
SS-Obertruppführer
SS-Obersturmführer

SS-Sturmhauptführer
SS-Obersturmbannführer
SS-Brigadeführer

In August 1934, Himmler was elevated to the new rank of Reichsführer-SS and given insignia unique to his position, replacing the SS-Obergruppenführer badges he wore prior to that time.

On 15 October 1934, further revisions were made to the SS rank system:

SS-Bewerber was added as the lowest rank
SS-Anwärter was added as the second lowest rank
SS-Scharführer became SS-Unterscharführer
SS-Oberscharführer became SS-Scharführer
SS-Truppführer became SS-Oberscharführer
SS-Obertruppführer became SS-Hauptscharführer
SS-Sturmführer became SS-Untersturmführer
SS-Sturmhauptführer became SS-Hauptsturmführer

Rank insignia remained unchanged from that point until 7 April 1942, when new collar patches were introduced for:

SS-Oberführer
SS-Brigadeführer
SS-Gruppenführer
SS-Obergruppenführer

At the same time, a new and senior rank of SS-Oberst-Gruppenführer was created.

The final and definitive Allgemeine-SS rank system, dating from April 1942 and lasting until the end of the war, was as follows:

Mannschaften (Other Ranks)

SS-Bewerber	Candidate
SS-Anwärter	Cadet
SS-Mann	Private
SS-Sturmmann (Strm.)	Lance Corporal
SS-Rottenführer (Rotf.)	Senior Lance Corporal

Unterführer (NCOs)

SS-Unterscharführer (Uschaf.) — Corporal

SS-Scharführer (Schaf.) — Sergeant

SS-Oberscharführer (Oschaf.) — Staff Sergeant

SS-Hauptscharführer (Hschaf.) — Sergeant-Major

Untere Führer (Junior Officers)

SS-Untersturmführer (Ustuf.) — 2nd Lieutenant

SS-Obersturmführer (Ostuf.) — Lieutenant

SS-Hauptsturmführer (Hstuf.) — Captain

Mittlere Führer (Intermediate Officers)

SS-Sturmbannführer (Stubaf.) — Major

SS-Obersturmbannführer (Ostubaf.) — Lieutenant-Colonel

Höhere Führer (Senior Officers)

SS-Standartenführer (Staf.) — Colonel

SS-Oberführer (Oberf.) — Senior Colonel

SS-Brigadeführer (Brigf.) — Brigadier

SS-Gruppenführer (Gruf.) — Major-General

SS-Obergruppenführer (Ogruf.) — Lieutenant-General

SS-Oberst-Gruppenführer (Obstgruf.) — General

Reichsführer-SS (RfSS) — Supreme Commander

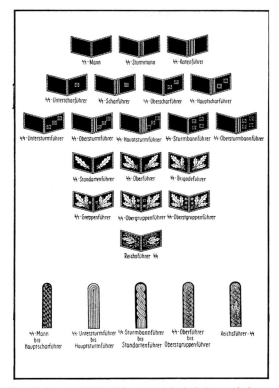

SS rank badges, *c.* April 1942. This illustration includes the final pattern of collar patches worn by SS and police generals, whose badges were altered when the new rank of Oberst-Gruppenführer was created. Shoulder straps for the Allgemeine-SS are also depicted. (Reproduced from the *Organisationsbuch der NSDAP*, 1943 edition.)

As with all NSDAP formations, Hitler was ultimately Commander-in-Chief of the SS and held the personal title of 'Der Oberste Führer der Schutzstaffel'.

During the war, where an Allgemeine-SS member temporarily serving in the Wehrmacht attained a military rank higher than his rank in the SS, the Wehrmacht rank generally preceded that of the SS so far as ordinary day-to-day affairs were concerned. However, in official SS correspondence and publications the Allgemeine-SS rank always took precedence over all other designations, even governmental titles. For example, 'Das Schwarze Korps' constantly referred to the German Foreign Minister by his honorary position as 'SS-Obergruppenführer von Ribbentrop' rather than by his ministerial appointment. Similarly, Allgemeine-SS ranks took precedence over those of the Waffen-SS and police. In April 1941, Himmler arranged for a blanket appointment of all HSSPfs to the ranks of Generalmajor, Generalleutnant or General der Polizei and,

The 1933-pattern SS dagger, showing the single strap hanger (left) and the vertical hanger (right).

after 20 July 1944, the HSSPfs were also made generals of the Waffen-SS. So a man who was nominated to be a general in the Allgemeine-SS, the police and the Waffen-SS would be entitled 'SS-Obergruppenführer und General der Waffen-SS und Polizei', in that order.

The symbolic uniforms and exclusive ranks and titles of the SS were further enhanced by the Black Order's use of decorative edged weaponry. The SS service dagger, or Dienstdolch, was introduced along with its SA counterpart by the interim Chief of Staff of the SA and Himmler's then superior, Obergruppenführer von Krausser, under SA Order No. 1734/33 of 15 December 1933. Black and silver in colour, it bore the SS motto etched on the blade and runes and eagle on the grip, and its general design was based on that of a seventeenth-century German hunting dagger known as the 'Holbein', which bore a representation of Holbein's painting 'The

Dance of Death' on its scabbard. Worn by all ranks of the Allgemeine-SS with service and walking out dress, the SS dagger was presented to its owner only at the special 9 November ceremony when he graduated from SS-Anwärter to SS-Mann. It was not issued at any other time, or *en masse* like the daggers of the plebian SA. Each SS-Anwärter paid the full cost of his dagger, usually in small instalments, prior to its presentation.

On 17 February 1934, SS-Gruppenführer Kurt Wittje, Chief of the SS-Amt who was dismissed the following year for homosexuality, forbade the private purchase or 'trading in' of SS daggers on the open market. Henceforth, daggers could be ordered only from manufacturers through the SS-Amt, for issue via the three main SS uniform distribution centres at Munich, Dresden and Berlin, which regularly processed requisitions received from the various Oberabschnitte headquarters. Moreover, it was made a disciplinary offence for an SS man to dispose of or lose his dagger, on the grounds that it was a symbol of his office. In that way, it was assured that no unauthorised person could buy or otherwise acquire an SS dagger. As of 25 January 1935, members dismissed from the SS had to surrender their daggers, even if they were personal property paid for from their own funds. In cases of voluntary resignation or normal retirement, however, daggers could be retained and the person in question was given a certificate stating that he was entitled to possess the dagger.

The SS dagger was suspended at an angle from a single leather strap until November 1934, when Himmler introduced a vertical hanger for wear with service dress during crowd control. However, the vertical hanger, while more stable, was too reminiscent of the humble bayonet frog and in 1936 the single strap was reintroduced for both the walking out and service uniforms. Thereafter, the vertical hanger was restricted to use on route marches and military exercises.

In September 1940, due to national economies, the 1933-pattern dagger was withdrawn from production for the duration of the war.

A more ornate SS dagger, to be worn only by officers and by those Old Guard NCOs and other ranks who had joined the organisation prior to 30 January 1933, was introduced by Himmler on 21 June 1936. Generally known as the 'chained dagger', it was very similar to the 1933-pattern but was suspended by means of linked octagonal plates, finely embossed with death's heads and SS runes, and featured a central scabbard mount decorated with swastikas. The dagger could be worn only with the black uniform until 1943, when Waffen-SS and security police officers were permitted to sport it with their field-grey walking out dress, and were allowed to attach knots in the army style. Production of the chained dagger had to be discontinued at the end of 1943 because of material shortages, and its wear was subsequently forbidden for the duration of the war.

In addition to the standard 1933-pattern and 1936-pattern SS daggers, several special presentation variants were also produced. The first of these was the so-called Röhm SS Honour Dagger, 9,900 of which were distributed in February 1934 by SA Stabschef Ernst Röhm to members of the SS Old Guard. It took the form of a basic 1933-pattern dagger with the addition of the dedication 'In herzlicher Kameradschaft, Ernst Röhm' ('In heartfelt comradeship, Ernst Röhm') etched on the reverse of the blade. Following the 'Night of the Long Knives', 200 similar daggers, etched 'In herzlicher Kameradschaft, H. Himmler', were presented by the Reichsführer to SS personnel who had participated in the bloody purge of the SA. A very ornate and expensive SS honour dagger, with oakleaf-decorated crossguards, leather-covered scabbard and Damascus steel blade, was created by Himmler in 1936 for award to high-ranking officers in recognition of special achievement. When one was presented to the NSDAP Treasurer, Franz

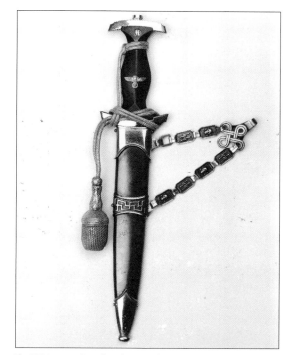

The 1936-pattern chained SS dagger, with regulation portepee knot authorised in 1943 for wear by officers of the Waffen-SS, Sipo and SD.

Xaver Schwarz, he responded by secretly commissioning the Eickhorn firm to produce an even more elaborate example, with fittings and chain hanger in solid silver, which he then gave to Himmler as a birthday present!

During the 1933–6 era, SS officers and NCOs engaged in ceremonial duties were permitted to wear a variety of privately purchased army-pattern sabres, often with silver rather than regulation gilt fittings. In 1936, however, a series of standardised swords in the classic straight-bladed 'Degen' style, was introduced specifically for members of the SS and police, emphasising the close relationship between the two organisations. There were minor differences between Degen for officers and those for NCOs, while SS swords featured runes on the grip and police examples the police eagle. Policemen who were also members of the SS could sport the SS runes on the pommel of their police sword. Personnel attached to SS Reiterstandarten retained the traditional curved sabre for use on horseback.

The SS officer's sword, which was referred to as the Ehrendegen des Reichsführers-SS, or Reichsführer's Sword of Honour, was given an elevated status and could not be worn automatically by every SS officer. It was bestowed by Himmler only upon selected Allgemeine-SS commanders and graduates of the Waffen-SS Junkerschulen at Bad Tölz and Braunschweig. Each presentation of the Ehrendegen was accompanied by a citation in which the Reichsführer instructed the recipient: 'Ich verleihe Ihnen den Degen der SS. Ziehen Sie ihn niemals ohne Not! Stecken Sie ihn niemals ein ohne Ehre!' ('I award you the SS sword. Never draw it without reason, or sheathe it without honour!'). Awards of the officer's sword, like those of the death's head ring, were recorded in the *Dienstaltersliste*, which reveals that only 86 per cent of even the most senior SS commanders were entitled to wear it. That percentage can be broken down as follows:

Standartenführer	58%
Oberführer	83%
Brigadeführer	90%
Gruppenführer	91%
Obergruppenführer	99%
Oberst-Gruppenführer	100%

Manufacture of the Ehrendegen ceased on 25 January 1941.

Still more exclusive were the so-called 'Geburtstagsdegen', or 'birthday swords', given by Himmler to SS generals and other leading Nazi personalities as birthday presents. They were made to order by Germany's master swordsmith, Paul Müller, Director of the SS Damascus School at Dachau, and featured hallmarked silver fittings and blades of the finest Damascus steel with exquisitely raised and gilded personal dedications from Himmler. The sword gifted to von Ribbentrop on his birthday in 1939, for example, bore the golden legend 'Meinem lieben Joachim von Ribbentrop zum 30.4.39 – H. Himmler, Reichsführer-SS' set between two swastikas. Hitler received a similar weapon, the blade inscription of which extolled the virtues and loyalty of the entire SS officer corps. Müller continued producing Geburtstagsdegen on commission from Himmler until 1944.

The regalia of the Allgemeine-SS also included an extensive range of flags and banners. From 4 July 1926, the SS had the distinction of keeping the most revered flag in the Third Reich, the Blutfahne, which had been carried at the head of the Nazi Old Guard during the Munich putsch when they were fired upon by the police. It was splattered with the gore of those shot during the encounter and was thereafter considered to be something of a 'holy relic'. SS-Mann Jakob Grimminger from the Munich SS detachment, a veteran of the First World War Gallipoli campaign and participant in the 1922 'Battle of Coburg', was accorded the honour of being appointed the

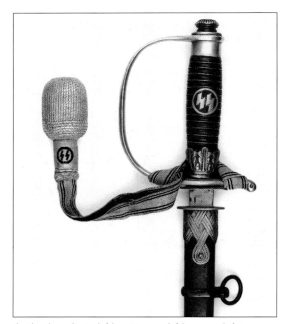

The Ehrendegen des Reichsführers-SS, or Reichsführer's Sword of Honour.

first official bearer of the Blutfahne and he retained that position throughout his career. Grimminger was a wood-carver by trade, and had no particular qualification as the Reich's 'number one standard-bearer', other than the fact that he had been a 'tail-end' marcher when the shooting started at the Feldherrnhalle. By April 1944, when the Blutfahne made its last public appearance at the funeral of Adolf Wagner, Gauleiter of Munich-Upper Bavaria, Grimminger had attained the rank of SS-Standartenführer, his association with the mystical flag having assured him a steady succession of promotions.

Every Allgemeine-SS Standarte was represented by a banner, or Feldzeichen, which was itself known as the regimental 'Standarte'. Somewhat reminiscent of the ancient Roman vexillum banner, it took the form of a wooden pole surmounted by a metal eagle and wreathed swastika, below which was a black and silver boxed nameplate. The plate bore the SS area name (e.g. 'Kassel' or 'Giessen') or regimental honour title (e.g. 'Julius Schreck' or 'Loeper') on the front and the initials 'NSDAP' on the back. From the box was suspended a red silk flag with a black static swastika on a white circle. The motto 'Deutschland Erwache' ('Germany Awake') was embroidered in white thread on the obverse, with 'Nat. Soz. Deutsche Arbeiterpartei – Sturmabteilung' on the reverse. The whole item was finished off with a black/white/red fringe and tassels. Apart from the black name box, the SS Feldzeichen was identical to that of the SA. When an SS unit achieved roughly regimental proportions, it was awarded a

Himmler placing a wreath at the Feldherrnhalle on the eleventh anniversary of the Munich putsch, 9 November 1934. The Blood Banner, held by Jakob Grimminger in traditional brownshirt uniform, stands in the background. A 'Mahnmal' or Martyrs' Monument was erected at this spot, and every member of the public walking past it was obliged to give the Nazi salute. Two SS men guarded the monument in perpetuity.

Feldzeichen in a mass pseudo-religious ceremony known as the Fahnenweihe which took place each September as part of the annual NSDAP celebrations at Nürnberg. During the proceedings, Hitler would present many new standards to regimental commanders and touch them with the Blutfahne which Grimminger was carrying alongside, so linking in spirit the most recent SS members with the martyrs of the Munich putsch. The table below shows all the area names which featured on Allgemeine-SS infantry Feldzeichen (i.e. those not bearing honour titles or the name of the regimental HQ town) and the Standarten to which they referred.

SS Reiterstandarten carried similar but distinctive Feldzeichen which had the 'Deutschland Erwache' flag hanging from a wooden bar fixed at right angles to the standard pole. In place of the name box, these cavalry standards featured a black patch, or Fahnenspiegel, on the flag cloth, bearing crossed lances and the unit numeral in silver.

Each SS Sturmbann was represented by a Sturmbannfahne, or Battalion Flag, in the form of a swastika flag with black and silver twisted cord edging. In the upper left corner

Allgemeine-SS standards. Top: The 'Deutschland Erwache' standard or Feldzeichen, of the 1st SS Fuss-Standarte 'Julius Schreck'; bottom left: battalion flag of Sturmbann III of the 1st SS Fuss-Standarte; bottom right: cavalry standard of the 15th SS Reiterstandarte. (Reproduced from the *Organisationsbuch der NSDAP*, 1938 edition.)

STANDARTE AREA NAMES

Area Name	SS Fuss-Standarte No.	Area Name	SS Fuss-Standarte No.
Alt Bayern	92	Kärnten	90
Baden	32	Lippe	72
Brandenburg	15	Marienburg	64
Braunschweig	49	Masuren	61
Burgenland	11	Mecklenburg	22
Charlottenburg	6	Mittelfranken	73
Dithmarschen	53	Mosel	5
Franken	56	Neisse	45
Friedland	66	Niederbayern	31
Gothaland	14	Niedersachsen	12
Gross-Beeren	80	Niederschlesien	8
Hanauer Land	86	Nordschleswig	50
Hart	51	Ob der Enns	37
Hessen	2	Oberbayern	34

Area Name	SS Fuss-Standarte No.	Area Name	SS Fuss-Standarte No.
Oberfranken	41	Schwaben	29
Oberhessen	83	Schwarzwald	65
Oberpfalz	68	Stedingen	88
Oberschlesien	23	Tempelhof	75
Obersteiermark	94	Thüringen	14
Ostfriesland	24	Thüringer Wald	57
Ostmark	27	Tirol	87
Ostpommern	39	Uckermark	44
Ostpreussen	18	Unter-Enns	52
Ostsee	74	Unterelbe	16
Pfalz	10	Wartburg	67
Pommern	9	Weichsel	71
Rhein-Hessen	33	Weser	55
Ruhr	25	Westfalen-Nord	19
Saale	84	Westfalen-Süd	30
Sauerland	69	Württemberg	13
Schleswig-Holstein	4	Württemberg Süd	63

The Feldzeichen and Sturmbannfahne of the SS-VT on display at Nürnberg, September 1937. All the standard-bearers wear gorgets and bandoliers.

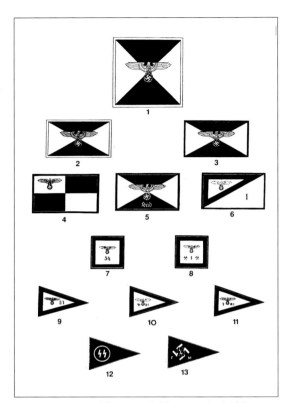

Allgemeine-SS command flags. 1. Reichsführer-SS; 2. heads of the SS Hauptämter; 3. head of the Persönlicher Stab RfSS; 4. heads of SS Ämter; 5. Führer of SS Oberabschnitt Süd; 6. Führer of SS Abschnitt I; 7. Führer of the 34th SS Fuss-Standarte; 8. Führer of the 1st SS Reiterstandarte; 9. Führer of Sturmbann I of the 1st SS Fuss-Standarte; 10. Führer of SS Pioniersturmbann 1; 11. Führer of SS Nachrichtensturmbann 1; 12. SS officers; 13. officials of the FM Organisation. (Reproduced from the *Organisationsbuch der NSDAP*, 1943 edition.)

or canton, a black Fahnenspiegel was embroidered in silver thread, with the Sturmbann and Standarte numbers in Roman and Arabic numerals, respectively.

Command flags, or Kommandoflaggen, in the shape of rigid pennants on flag poles, were carried as unit markers at large parades or, in smaller versions, were flown from the front nearside mudwing of staff cars. They were square, rectangular or triangular in form depending upon designation, and were made of black and white waterproof cloth with rustproof silver thread. Command flags were usually covered in a transparent celluloid casing during inclement weather. Each SS Oberabschnitt was required to keep on hand one official vehicle flag and one command pennant for the Reichsführer-SS, for use in the event of a 'flying visit' by Himmler. Other Kommandoflaggen included those for the heads of SS Hauptämter, SS Oberabschnitte and Abschnitte com-manders, the leaders of Standarten, Reiterstandarten, Sturmbanne, SS stores and inspectorates, and senior members of the FM organisation.

In 1934, Himmler noted: 'A sworn oath is not enough. It is essential that every SS man be committed to the very roots of his being'. The symbolism and regalia of the Allgemeine-SS went a long way to achieving that end, instilling a feeling of superiority and 'belonging' in every member of the Black Order.

3. THE WAFFEN-SS

ORIGINS AND ORGANISATION OF THE WAFFEN-SS

When Hitler assumed the Chancellorship on 30 January 1933, he felt that he could not rely entirely on the traditional Reichswehr and police guards appointed by the state to protect him. Consequently, he quickly issued instructions for the formation of a new full-time armed SS unit whose sole function would be to escort him at all times, whether in Berlin or on his official journeys throughout Germany. The task of forming the unit was entrusted to 'Sepp' Dietrich, who by that time had risen to the rank of SS-Gruppenführer through his position as one of Hitler's closest personal friends.

By 17 March 1933, Dietrich had handpicked 120 loyal SS volunteers, including a few former members of the Stosstrupp Adolf Hitler, to become the nucleus of a new headquarters guard called the SS Stabswache Berlin. They were armed with rifles and initially quartered in the Alexander Barracks on Friedrichstrasse, not far from Hitler's official residence, the Reich Chancellery. In May, the Stabswache was enlarged and reformed as the SS Sonderkommando Zossen, with three training companies which had their instructors drawn from the army and police rather than the Allgemeine-SS. In addition to guard duties, this 'Special Force' could now also be used for armed police and anti-terrorist tasks. The following month, three new companies were recruited as the SS Sonderkommando Jüterbog, and at the NSDAP party rally in September 1933 both detachments were merged into a single formation and renamed the 'Adolf Hitler Standarte'. On 9 November, in front of the Munich Feldherrnhalle, the Standarte took a personal oath of loyalty to its Führer and was renamed the Leibstandarte-SS 'Adolf Hitler', or LAH, which may best be translated as the 'Adolf Hitler' Life Guards, invoking memories of the famed Imperial Royal Bodyguard Regiments. There could now be no doubt that these men, unlike the soldiers of the Reichswehr, were Hitler's personal troops.

As an SS unit, the Leibstandarte theoretically came under Himmler's overall control. However, in practice, Hitler considered himself to be the ultimate director of its actions. That fact, combined with Dietrich's friendship with Hitler, which the guard commander exploited to the full, ensured that the Leibstandarte enjoyed a fair measure of independence within the SS organisation. Indeed, the prewar Leibstandarte, which was on the national budget rather than that of the NSDAP, ultimately became in Himmler's own words 'a complete law unto itself'. Dietrich frequently argued with the Reichsführer, whom he addressed as an equal, a luxury enjoyed by very few SS officers.

At the end of 1933, the LAH moved into quarters at Berlin-Lichterfelde from where squads of troops were sent to the Reich Chancellery on a rota basis to provide a smart, impressive and effective bodyguard for the Führer. They were given their own, then very distinctive, insignia of un-numbered SS

Fanfare trumpeters of the Leibstandarte at the opening ceremony of the Berlin Horse Show in 1934. The banners were produced between September and November 1933, when the unit was called the 'Adolf Hitler Standarte'. It is noteworthy that the man in the foreground has attached the banner to his trumpet the wrong way round, making the death's head appear to face backwards rather than forwards.

Leibstandarte sentries at the courtyard entrance to the new Reich Chancellery, November 1938. The LAH, being a guards regiment, spent much of its prewar time on ceremonial duties for which distinctive white leather equipment comprising waist belt, cross-strap, ammunition pouches, bayonet frog, pistol holster and pack straps, was introduced in stages from 1936. The police wore similar white leathers on parade.

runes on the right collar patch and a cuff title bearing the name 'Adolf Hitler'. The Leibstandarte came to be in exclusive prominence around Hitler, its men serving not only as his guards but also as his adjutants, drivers, servants and waiters. Their ceremonial activities ultimately became almost legendary, and their performance on the drill square and at Nazi rallies, where they consistently held the place of honour at the end of the parade, was second to none.

By 6 March 1934, the Leibstandarte comprised 986 men, of whom 45 were not members of the Nazi party, having been recruited directly from the military or police. The unit also included a number of non-Germans, such as thirty Austrian Nazis whose political beliefs had obliged them to leave their homeland for Germany. On 24 May, Himmler agreed to Dietrich's request that the LAH should use army, rather than SS, terminology to describe its constituent components. Thus 'Bataillon' and 'Kompanie' began to replace 'Sturmbann' and 'Sturm'. On 30 June 1934, the Leibstandarte helped to quell the Röhm putsch and was largely responsible for the killing of many of Hitler's enemies in the 'Night of the Long Knives'.

Most of those arrested were taken to the Lichterfelde Barracks which became a clearing house for unwanted people and corpses. It is not known precisely how many 'enemies of the state' were shot by the Leibstandarte firing squads, but it is thought that some forty executioners were involved. The shooting finally ended on 2 July, and the Leibstandarte's first action was over. It had carried out Hitler's orders to the letter. The Führer promoted Dietrich to SS-Obergruppenführer and also upgraded by one rank all members of the Leibstandarte who had played an active part in the Röhm affair. The 'Night of the Long Knives' saw a dramatic change take place, not only between the SA and the SS, but between the Allgemeine-SS and the armed SS detachments. One of the first outward signs of this shift was the changing of the guard outside Gestapo HQ, where the SA-Feldjägerkorps and Allgemeine-SS sentries were replaced by men of the LAH. Similar changes took place at other important locations across the Reich.

Early in October 1934, it was decided that the Leibstandarte should be motorised, a rare honour in days when most of the Reichswehr was still horse-drawn. By the beginning of 1935, the strength of the LAH had risen to 2,551 men, and it became a regiment in fact as well as in name, divided into:

1 × staff
3 × motorised infantry battalions
1 × motorcycle company
1 × mortar company
1 × signals platoon
1 × armoured car platoon
1 × regimental band

It was a relatively short step from being equipped and trained for anti-terrorist police duties to being organised for military activities and the Leibstandarte was soon wearing field-grey. Given its largely ceremonial background, it is surprising just how quickly the LAH developed into a first-class military unit and how far it assimilated itself within the rest of the armed SS. On 1 March 1935 the 5th Company, under SS-Hauptsturmführer Wilhelm Mohnke, marched into Saarbrücken on the return of the Saarland to Germany. Three years later, the Leibstandarte took a prominent part in the annexation of Austria. It moved through Linz, where it provided a guard of honour for Hitler, and on to Vienna, taking part in the triumphal celebrations there. The Austrian operation saw the LAH covering no less than 600 miles in some 48 hours in full co-operation with the army, a high military ability which earned the favourable recognition of no less a commander than General Guderian. In October 1938, the Leibstandarte participated in the occupation of the Sudetenland, and again the whole event proceeded smoothly.

All elements of the Leibstandarte, except for the ceremonial Guard Battalion and a replacement unit, were to take part in the opening stages of the Second World War. As the first armed SS unit, the LAH was destined to hold a proud place as the oldest and smartest formation in the Waffen-SS, and was to earn itself a formidable fighting record at the front.

At the same time as the infant Leibstandarte was being formed to protect Hitler, other small groups of armed SS men were set up all over Germany as a means of bolstering the new régime in the event of civil unrest or counter-revolution. As a general rule, each SS Abschnitt recruited its own Kasernierte Hundertschaft of 100 or so barracked troops, and several of these were amalgamated in key areas to become company- or even battalion-sized Politische Bereitschaften, or PBs, Political Reserve Squads. The entire country was eventually covered by a network of PBs, some of which played a significant part in the 'Night of the

A Leibstandarte battalion parades past Hitler on his forty-ninth birthday, 20 April 1938. Note the white leather gauntlets worn by the officers in the colour party.

Long Knives'. On 24 September 1934, Hitler announced that the Politische Bereitschaften were to be brought together and expanded into a new force to be called the SS-Verfügungstruppe or SS-VT, political troops at the special disposal of the Nazi régime. The SS-VT would be formed on the basis of three Standarten modelled on army infantry regiments, each to comprise three battalions, a motorcycle company and a mortar company. In addition, an SS-VT signals battalion would act in a supporting role. The new formation was to be under the command of the Reichsführer-SS for internal security duties, except in time of war when it would be at the disposal of the army.

The picture of a new and élite force attracted many ex-officers into the ranks of the Verfügungstruppe. SA-Standartenführer Paul Hausser, a former Reichswehr general, was recruited by Himmler to organise the SS-VT and instil some military know-how into the fledgling SS soldiers. In October 1934 a cadet school was opened at Bad Tölz, and early the following year Hausser took personal charge of a second officer training establishment at Braunschweig. Hausser's solid groundwork attracted a sufficient number of ex-army and police officers, redundant Reichswehr sergeant-majors and young military enthusiasts to form the officer and NCO cadres of the future Waffen-SS.

A battalion of the SS-VT Standarte 'Deutschland' marching past Hitler in 1937. Swallow's nests distinguish the regimental bandsmen in the foreground.

The cadres were distributed to the scattered SS-VT battalions and these were gradually formed into regiments. In Munich, three Sturmbanne amalgamated to become SS-Standarte 1/VT, organised and equipped as a horse-drawn infantry regiment. It was given the honour title 'Deutschland' at the Nürnberg Rally in September 1935. Members subsequently wore the SS runes alongside the number '1' on the right collar patch, and a 'Deutschland' cuff title. In Hamburg, another three Sturmbanne duly came together to constitute SS-Standarte 2/VT, which was named 'Germania' at Nürnberg in September 1936. The regimental uniform was characterised by an 'SS 2' collar patch and 'Germania' cuff title.

On 1 October 1936, Hausser was appointed Inspector of Verfügungstruppe with the rank of SS-Brigadeführer. He created a divisional staff to supervise the equipping and training of his troops and avidly welcomed newcomers who brought the promise of a certain dynamism to the SS-VT. Foremost among these was SS-Sturmbannführer Felix Steiner, an ex-Reichswehr officer whose experiences on the western front in the First World War had turned him against the conservative doctrines of Hausser and the army. He favoured the tactics of assault detachments, shock troops and mobile battle groups, to escape from the deadly immobility of trench warfare with one mass army facing another in a mutual battle of attrition. Steiner was given command of the SS-VT Standarte

Hilmar Wäckerle, commander of Sturmbann I, SS-VT Standarte 'Germania', as depicted by Wolfgang Willrich in 1936. Note the 'SS/small 2' collar patch. Wäckerle had formerly been the guard commander at Dachau concentration camp, and in 1938 transferred to the 'Der Führer' regiment to lead its 3rd battalion. He was later killed in action while commanding 'Westland' on the eastern front.

'Deutschland', and he tried out his reforms with one of its battalions, the training of which centred on sports and athletics. Officers, NCOs and men competed in teams against each other, to promote a spirit of comradeship and eliminate differences in rank. Experiments were carried out with camouflage clothing, and Steiner replaced the army's regulation rifle with handier and more mobile weapons, primarily submachine-guns and hand grenades. Soon even the Wehrmacht's eyebrows rose as

Steiner's troops covered almost two miles in twenty minutes in battle order, for such a thing was unheard of. Steiner implanted in his men the idea that they were a military élite, and the success of his modernisation was so obvious that the Verfügungstruppe began to look upon him as their real commander. According to a somewhat jealous Hausser, Himmler considered Steiner to be 'his very favourite baby'.

After the annexation of Austria in March 1938, in which 'Germania' participated alongside the Leibstandarte, Hitler ordered that a new SS-VT Standarte be formed entirely from Austrian personnel, either newly recruited or transferred from other SS units. The resultant regiment was given the honour title 'Der Führer' at the Nürnberg Rally in September that year, and members were distinguished by an appropriately named cuff title and 'SS 3' collar patch.

During the mobilisation preceding the occupation of the Sudetenland in October 1938, 'Deutschland' and 'Germania' were placed under the command of the army and took part in the operation. All the SS-VT Standarten became motorised regiments at the end of the year, and in the spring of 1939 were used to fill the gaps in a number of armoured divisions which invaded Czechoslovakia. In May, 'Deutschland' went on exercise at the Münsterlager training area where it carried out extremely tough and hazardous manoeuvres using live ammunition. Hitler, who was present together with the Reichsführer, was so impressed that he gave his permission for the expansion of the SS-Verfügungstruppe into a full division. The idea was temporarily postponed, however, as units of the SS-VT were integrated with those of the army in preparation for the attack on Poland. By the outbreak of the Second World War, the SS-VT comprised not only the 'Deutschland', 'Germania' and 'Der Führer' Standarten, but

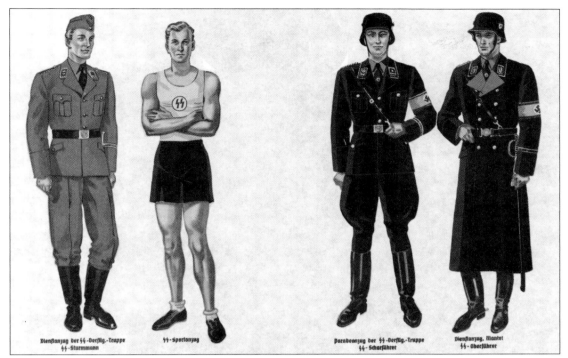

Styles of SS-VT uniform in 1937. From left to right: field service uniform for SS-Sturmmann; sports kit; parade uniform for SS-Scharführer; parade uniform with greatcoat for SS-Oberführer. (Reproduced from the *Organisationsbuch der NSDAP*, 1937 edition.)

NCOs and men of Sturmbann III, SS-VT Standarte 'Germania', outside their barracks at Radolfzell in 1938.

also an artillery regiment; SS-Regiment z.b.V. 'Ellwangen' for special deployment; a signals battalion; a pioneer battalion; the so-called SS-Sturmbann 'N' which was garrisoned at Nürnberg and provided a guard at the annual Nazi party rallies; a reconnaissance battalion; an anti-aircraft machine-gun battalion; and an anti-tank battalion. There were also a number of replacement units, or Ersatzeinheiten, whose purpose was to make good any wartime losses suffered by the SS-VT.

The SS-Verfügungstruppe provided valuable military experience for many SS officers who were later to become prominent personalities in the divisions of the Waffen-SS.

Alongside the Leibstandarte and SS-VT grew a third militarised branch of the SS with a somewhat darker purpose. In March 1933, Himmler set up the first SS-run concentration camp at Dachau to accommodate 5,000 of the 27,000 potential 'enemies of the state' arrested by the SA and SS after the Reichstag fire. Men of the local Allgemeine-SS from Munich were seconded to a new SS-Wachverbände, or Guard Unit, under SS-Oberführer Theodor Eicke to supervise the inmates of Dachau, who were to be incarcerated on a long-term basis. By the summer of 1934, most of the semi-official and often ad hoc SA detention camps throughout Germany had been closed, and as a direct result of the 'Night of the Long Knives', during which Eicke personally killed Ernst Röhm, the remaining camps were removed from the jurisdiction of the SA and civil authorities and were permanently taken over by the SS.

At first, the SS-Wachverbände staffing the concentration camps were lightly armed and were used by the Allgemeine-SS as depositories for poor quality and unwanted personnel. Eicke, however, turned Dachau into a model camp, and in July 1934 he was promoted to SS-Gruppenführer and made Inspector of Concentration Camps with the task of improving the discipline and morale of the SS-Wachverbände. This he accomplished with some considerable success. By March 1935, with new camps opening up on a regular basis to accommodate more and more prisoners, the Wachverbände had expanded to incorporate the following company-sized units, each assigned to a particular camp:

SS-Wachtruppe 'Oberbayern' at Dachau
SS-Wachtruppe 'Ostfriesland' at Esterwegen
SS-Wachtruppe 'Elbe' at Lichtenburg
SS-Wachtruppe 'Sachsen' at Sachsenburg
SS-Wachtruppe 'Brandenburg' at Oranienburg and Columbia-Haus
SS-Wachtruppe 'Hansa' at Hamburg-Fuhlsbüttel

During 1935, these formations were completely removed from the control of the Allgemeine-SS and reorganised into five independent battalions, namely:

SS-Wachsturmbann I 'Oberbayern' at Dachau
SS-Wachsturmbann II 'Elbe' at Lichtenburg
SS-Wachsturmbann III 'Sachsen' at Sachsenburg
SS-Wachsturmbann IV 'Ostfriesland' at Esterwegen
SS-Wachsturmbann V 'Brandenburg' at Oranienburg and Columbia-Haus

By December 1935, Eicke was somewhat prematurely styling himself as 'Führer der Totenkopfverbände', or Commander of Death's Head Units. It was not until 29 March 1936 that the Wachsturmbanne, with a strength of 3,500 men, were officially renamed the SS-Totenkopfverbände, or SS-TV, and allocated distinctive new collar patches bearing the death's head. On 1 July 1937, they were regrouped into the following three regiments, comprising 4,500 men:

Himmler, Hitler and Hausser view the 'Deutschland' regiment on exercise at Münsterlager, May 1939. The officer on the right is Jochen Peiper, then serving as aide-de-camp to the Reichsführer.

SS-Totenkopfstandarte 1 'Oberbayern' at Dachau

SS-Totenkopfstandarte 2 'Brandenburg' at Sachsenhausen

SS-Totenkopfstandarte 3 'Thüringen' at Buchenwald

In 1938 a fourth regiment, SS-Totenkopfstandarte 4 'Ostmark', was formed in Austria to staff the new concentration camp at Mauthausen.

Eicke, a former paymaster of the imperial army, had an undying hatred of the professional officers whom he saw in command of the SS-Verfügungstruppe and one of his primary objectives was to turn the Totenkopfverbände into a sort of brutal working-class counterforce to the SS-VT. Himmler had given him almost complete autonomy in his appointment as Inspekteur der Konzentrationslager, and Eicke kept a jealous watch to ensure that no senior ex-officers infiltrated his organisation to threaten his position. While his troops were heavily armed on army lines, albeit with rather outdated weaponry, Eicke continually warned them against any attempt to ape a military organisation, and he frequently impressed upon them that they belonged neither to the army, nor to the police, nor to the Verfügungstruppe. Their sole task was to isolate the 'enemies of the state' from the German people. Eicke drummed the concept of dangerous subversives so forcefully and convincingly into his men that they became firmly convinced of their position as the Reich's true guardians. They were the only soldiers who even in peacetime faced the enemy day and night . . . the enemy behind the wire.

The regulations governing the Totenkopfverbände became ever stricter. Any member allowing a prisoner to escape would himself be handed over to the Gestapo, and would probably end up being incarcerated in a concentration camp. Prisoners who tried to escape could be shot without warning, as could any inmate who assaulted a guard. The main forms of punishment in the camps were beatings, hard labour and tying prisoners to trees, and there were several instances of inmates being killed by SS-TV guards, whose hatred of the prisoners was consciously cultivated. Eicke made a point of recruiting 'big sixteen-year-olds' direct from the Hitler Youth, and most Totenkopf men were under twenty years of age. Almost 95 per cent of them were unmarried, with few or no personal ties. They were ideally suited to be moulded according to Eicke's doctrines for the SS-TV.

By 1939, the SS-Totenkopfverbände had grown to include SS-Totenkopfstandarte 5 'Dietrich Eckart'; a medical battalion; an anti-tank demonstration company; a motorised signals platoon; and a semi-motorised engineer unit. Whatever Eicke may have intended, his SS-TV had developed into a truly military organisation, and on 17 August Hitler recognised that fact by ordering that in the event of war the Totenkopfstandarten should be used as police reinforcements (Totenkopf-Polizeiverstärkung) within the framework of the Wehrmacht. In other words, they were to be deployed as occupation troops. Their task of guarding the concentration camps would be taken over by older Allgemeine-SS reservists formed into new SS-Totenkopf-Wachsturmbanne. The third battalion of SS-Totenkopfstandarte 4 had already taken up a defensive position as a Home Guard unit in Danzig, the so-called SS-Heimwehr Danzig, and it was bolstered by a reserve battalion, SS-Wachsturmbann Eimann. At the same time, 10,000 younger officers and men of the Allgemeine-SS were called up for service with the Death's Head units. Himmler estimated that 50,000 Allgemeine-SS men would eventually be made available for call-up as Totenkopf-

SS-Gruppenführer Albert Forster, Gauleiter of Danzig-West Prussia, reviewing the SS-Heimwehr Danzig in August 1939. The officer on the left is SS-Obersturmbannführer Friedmann Götze, commander of the Heimwehr, who was killed by a British sniper at Le Paradis on 28 May 1940 while serving with the SS-Totenkopf-Division. Götze's death came the day after 100 unarmed British prisoners of the 2nd Royal Norfolks were murdered by Totenkopf troops under Fritz Knöchlein.

Polizeiverstärkung. The link between the SS-Totenkopfverbände and concentration camp guard duties was all but being dissolved.

When the Second World War broke out the following month, the plan to use Eicke's men as occupation troops was quickly modified. Dachau was cleared of inmates and the Totenkopfstandarten, augmented by the young Allgemeine-SS conscripts and some police personnel, were mustered there and formed into the SS-Totenkopf-Division for combat service alongside the Leibstandarte and SS-VT. The guarding of concentration camps now fell to the older men, unfit for front-line duty, and to 'green' SS recruits and non-German auxiliaries. Death's Head troops, on the other hand, entered a new phase in their unit's story and were soon to gain a reputation as some of the hardest and most ruthless soldiers of the war.

Conditions of service in the armed SS were distinct from those applicable to other SS formations. Volunteers to join the prewar SS-VT and SS-TV had to be between the ages of sixteen and twenty-two, at least 5 ft 11 in tall and of the highest physical fitness. Entry requirements for the Leibstandarte were even more stringent, with a minimum height of 6 ft 1 in, and it was no idle boast of Himmler's that until 1936 even a filled tooth was adjudged a sufficient deformity to disqualify a young man from entry into the Führer's Guard. Needless to say, as with ordinary members of the Allgemeine-SS, Aryan pedigree had to be spotless. From 1935, membership of the Leibstandarte and SS-Verfügungstruppe counted as military service, and rates of pay corresponded to those of the Wehrmacht. However, terms were hard. Enlisted men had to sign up for a minimum of four years, NCOs for twelve years and officers for twenty-five years. Moreover, they were all subject to the SS legal system and discipline code, and were obliged to secure the Reichsführer's permission before they could marry. Membership of the Totenkopfverbände, while similarly demanding in terms of service conditions, did not count as fulfilment of military duty until the spring of 1939. Before that time, SS-TV volunteers had to complete their statutory term of military conscription either in the Wehrmacht or in the SS-Verfügungstruppe. Eicke preferred his men to do their service in the army, navy or air force, as he was concerned that if they were to join the SS-VT they might want to remain in that branch of the SS rather than return to what he called the 'onerous and demanding task of guarding concentration camps'.

Once in the armed SS, recruits were moulded into very adaptable soldier-athletes capable of much better than average endurance on the march and in combat. Great emphasis was placed upon ideological indoctrination, physical exercise and sports, which were made integral parts of the training programme and daily life. More time was spent in the field, on the ranges and in the classroom learning the theory of tactics than was the practice in the army, while considerably less attention was given to drill, even in the Leibstandarte after 1938. This resulted in a standard of battlefield movement and shooting that was appreciably higher than that of the Wehrmacht.

Manoeuvres were made as realistic as possible, with the use of live ammunition and heavy artillery barrages, so that every SS-VT man became fully accustomed to handling a variety of weapons and also to being within 100 yards of explosions from his own artillery fire. The end product was a higher standard of soldier, a man who was a storm trooper in the best traditions of the term.

Unlike their counterparts in the army, SS rank-and-file were taught to think for themselves and not rely too heavily on the issuance of orders from above. Consequently, they became very self-reliant. Every SS man was looked upon as a potential NCO, and every NCO as a potential officer. Officer cadets, irrespective of background or social standing, had to serve eighteen months in the ranks before being commissioned. A very tough training programme was run by the military academies, or Junkerschulen, at Bad Tölz and Braunschweig, and by 1938–9 around 500 officers were being produced annually. The average SS-VT officer was considerably more aggressive in combat than his Wehrmacht colleagues, which is highlighted by the fact that nearly all of the first fifty-four cadets who passed out of Bad Tölz in 1934 were killed in battle between 1939 and 1942. A significant factor which contributed to the unique nature of the armed SS was the atmosphere of camaraderie and 'heroic realism' which permeated its ranks. Soldiers of the SS were taught to be fighters for fighting's sake, and to abandon themselves to the struggle if so required for the greater good. The traditional soldierly concept was turned into one of pure belligerence, with the cultivation of a fatalistic enthusiasm for combat which far exceeded the normal self-sacrifice that might be expected of a soldier. That ethos went a long way to explaining the particularly heavy casualties later suffered by the Waffen-SS during the war, and the determination of its survivors.

Soldiers of the Leibstandarte, SS-VT and SS-

TV were eligible for the whole range of military orders, medals and awards created by the Nazi régime. In addition to these national honours, a series of decorations was instituted specifically for the militarised formations of the SS. The SS Dienstauszeichnungen, or SS Long Service Awards, first announced on 30 January 1938 and modelled on their Wehrmacht equivalents, comprised medals for four and eight years' service and large swastika-shaped 'crosses' for twelve and twenty-five years'. The latter two grades bore SS runes embroidered into their cornflower-blue ribbons. The Dienstauszeichnungen were produced in some quantity during 1939 by Deschler of Munich and Petz & Lorenz of Unterreichenbach, but they were not widely distributed since the Waffen-SS became eligible to receive the Wehrmacht long service awards instead from early 1940. Most Waffen-SS officers and men during the 1940–5 period sported army eagles, not SS runes, on their service ribbon bars. Indeed, photographic evidence reveals only one prominent Waffen-SS officer, Otto Kumm, consistently wearing the runic ribbon of the twelve-year decoration during the war. Runic ribbons were never seen on the tunics of any other Waffen-SS generals, Dietrich, Hausser and Steiner included, although they must have been entitled to wear them, particularly as service before 1933 and after 1939 counted as double for the purposes of presentation. No photographs at all are known to exist showing the four- or eight-year SS medals

militarisation of large sections of the SS? The reason was a simple one. The SS was primarily a civil police force which Hitler hoped would eventually maintain order not only in Germany but throughout Nazi-occupied Europe. To do so, however, it would first have to win its spurs on the battlefield. Only then could the SS possess the moral authority necessary for its future role in the New Order. As early as 1934, Hitler told Himmler:

> In our Reich of the future, the SS and police will need a soldierly character if they are to have the desired effect on ordinary citizens. The German people, through their past experience of glorious military events and their present education by the NSDAP, have acquired such a warrior mentality that a fat, jovial, friendly police such as we had during the Weimar era can no longer exert authority. For this reason, it will be necessary in future wars for our SS and police, in their own closed units, to prove themselves at the front in the same way as the army and to make blood sacrifices to the same degree as any other branch of the armed forces.

In this way, it could be said that the whole relationship between the Allgemeine-SS, the Waffen-SS and the police, as integral parts of the projected Staatsschutzkorps, epitomised the earliest concepts of policing, as voiced by the British philosopher Herbert Spencer in 1851: 'Policemen are soldiers who act alone; soldiers are policemen who act in unison'.

All members of the Allgemeine-SS were subject to the normal term of military conscription into the Wehrmacht, which swallowed up the majority of SS men after the outbreak of war. However, it was the actions of the Leibstandarte-SS 'Adolf Hitler', the SS-Verfügungstruppe and the SS-Totenkopfverbände which personified the early battlefield accomplishments of the SS in the eyes of the German public.

At the end of the eighteen-day Polish campaign, Hitler visited German troops at the battlefront, accompanied by his hand-picked SS bodyguard detachment, the so-called Führerbegleitkommando. Here one of the high-speed escort vehicles is passing a Wehrmacht convoy, forcing a local farmer into the side of the road. The car registration plate is covered for security reasons, and the machine-gunner is a Leibstandarte Untersturmführer.

THE WAFFEN-SS AT WAR

When German troops marched into Poland on 1 September 1939, the armed SS units were split up among regular army formations dispersed along the invasion front. The SS-Heimwehr Danzig immediately secured that city, while other Totenkopf personnel cut through the 'Polish Corridor'. The Leibstandarte, supported by the SS-VT pioneer battalion, was attached to General von Reichenau's 10th Army. The SS-VT Standarte 'Deutschland', together with the SS artillery regiment and the SS reconnaissance battalion, joined Generalmajor Kempf's 4th Panzer Brigade, while 'Germania' became part of the 14th Army under General List. The 'Der Führer' Standarte was not yet fully trained and consequently did not participate in the fighting. Although 'Germania' remained in reserve for

most of the four-week campaign, 'Deutschland' was heavily engaged in the Battle of Brest Litovsk. The Leibstandarte also had a particularly hectic time, taking part in the drive on Warsaw and the encirclement of Bzura with the 4th Panzer Division.

Despite the obvious fighting commitment of the SS, their disproportionately heavy casualties were criticised by the army which claimed that the losses resulted from poor leadership. Hausser countered these accusations by indicating that, in order to operate efficiently, the armed SS would need to be organised into full divisions. The army bitterly opposed such a development, but Hitler was persuaded to allow it in time for the western campaign. At the end of 1939, the term 'Waffen-SS' began to be used in official correspondence when referring to the armed SS, and in February 1940 it became a recognised title. About the same time, army designations such as 'Bataillon' and 'Regiment', which had been used by the Leibstandarte since 1934, generally replaced 'Sturmbann', 'Standarte' and the other SS formation titles throughout the Waffen-SS. In some units of the SS-VT, army rank terms, for example Oberleutnant instead of SS-Obersturmführer, were even utilised for a short period, but that was quickly forbidden by Himmler. The purpose of all this was to assimilate the new force and make it easier for the army to accept the Waffen-SS as a legitimate fourth branch of the Wehrmacht, and one completely separate from the Allgemeine-SS.

The consolidation of the Waffen-SS during the so-called 'phoney war' brought 'Sepp' Dietrich's Leibstandarte up to the strength of a superbly equipped armoured regiment, and the three SS-VT regiments were formed into the first full SS division, the SS-Verfügungsdivision or SS-V, under the command of Paul Hausser. The SS-Totenkopfstandarten amalgamated to become the SS-Totenkopf-Division or SS-T, under Eicke, and a third combat division, the Polizei-Division led by SS-Brigadeführer Karl Pfeffer-Wildenbruch, was created almost overnight by a mass transfer of uniformed police personnel strengthened by cadres of SS-V and SS-T troops. The Polizei-Division was, however, intended to be very much a second-line security unit, and it was organised on the basis of horse-drawn infantry equipped with outdated Czech weapons.

The campaign in the west established beyond doubt the fighting reputation of the

Assault engineers and artillery of the SS-Totenkopf-Division crossing La Bassée canal, 23 May 1940. Camouflage clothing had not been widely distributed to SS-T troops at this early stage in the war, and field-grey army pattern tunics with matching death's head collar patches were the order of the day.

An assault squad of the 'Germania' regiment in France, May 1940. Collar patches have been removed for security reasons, and the men carry smocks folded underneath their belts. A variety of equipment and weaponry is in evidence, including the short-lived SS pattern webbing supporting straps worn by the man in the centre, who has attached foliage to his steel helmet.

Waffen-SS. When the Blitzkrieg began in May 1940, the Leibstandarte and 'Der Führer' were deployed on the Dutch frontier and had little difficulty in sweeping through Holland, securing many vital river crossings as they went. On 16 May, SS-T went into action in support of Rommel's 7th Panzer Division in southern Belgium and eastern France, duly committing one of the first recorded SS atrocities when 100 unarmed British prisoners of the 2nd Royal Norfolks were machine-gunned at Le Paradis by in-experienced and panicky Totenkopf troops who had been thrown into disarray by the ferocity of a recent British counter-attack.

The German advance soon divided the Allied forces into two, with large numbers of British, French and Belgian soldiers separated from the main bulk of the French army to the south of the 'panzer corridor'. The Leibstandarte, SS-V and SS-T were in the forefront of the sweep, and 'Deutschland' distinguished itself particularly well in some fiercely contested canal crossings. The northern Allies quickly became compressed into an ever-decreasing defensive pocket centring around Dunkirk. The Leibstandarte was heavily engaged in desperate fighting at the nearby village of Wormhoudt, where Dietrich was trapped in a burning ditch for several hours as the battle raged around him, before being rescued by an assault squad. A company of his men under Wilhelm Mohnke retaliated by killing eighty British prisoners-of-war in cold blood. After the Dunkirk evacuation, the Waffen-SS was redeployed against the main body of the French army which was holding a line along the River Somme. While the slow-moving Polizei-Division successfully slogged it out through the Argonne Forest, other motorised SS units had little difficulty in smashing through enemy lines on 6 June and within a week the Leibstandarte had linked up with army panzers as far south as Vichy. The SS-Totenkopf-Division advanced on Bordeaux and the SS-Verfügungsdivision raced towards Biarritz. On 17 June, the French sued for peace and five days later the war in the west was over.

In recognition of their bravery and leadership during the western campaign, seven SS men including Dietrich and Steiner received the coveted Knight's Cross of the Iron Cross, at that time the supreme German military award. Many others were decorated with lower grades of the Iron Cross, wound badges and associated combat awards. In September, the Leibstandarte was presented with a new standard by Himmler at their

A Leibstandarte machine-gun team marching through the French countryside, June 1940. By this time, the camouflage helmet cover had become a distinctive mark of the Waffen-SS.

An Untersturmführer of an SS-V ancillary unit, denoted by his lack of a regimental cuff title, during a lull in the western Blitzkrieg, May 1940.

totally incorporated the 'Germania' regiment of SS-V. Initially adopting the name SS-Division 'Germania', the new unit was retitled 'Wiking' ('Viking') at the end of 1940 and placed under the command of Felix Steiner. It was to become one of the finest divisions in the SS Order of Battle.

To make up for the loss of the 'Germania' regiment, the SS-Verfügungsdivision was assigned a Totenkopfstandarte and in January 1941 it was renamed SS-Division 'Reich'. The other Totenkopfstandarten were reorganised to play a more active role as independent formations. Two Death's Head regiments, plus artillery and support units, were formed into SS-Kampfgruppe 'Nord', and another Standarte was sent to Norway for occupation duty as SS-Infantry Regiment 9. The five remaining Totenkopfstandarten went to the Waffen-SS training ground at Debica in Poland, where they were re-equipped and designated as SS-Infantry Regiments. Finally, the existing Death's Head cavalry units amalgamated to become SS-Kavallerie Regiments 1 and 2.

During the spring of 1941, Germany prepared for the impending invasion of the Soviet Union. When Mussolini's surprise attack on Greece went disastrously wrong, and a new anti-German régime seized power in Yugoslavia, Hitler ordered immediate action to secure his southern flank. On 6 April, a Blitzkrieg was unleashed on Yugoslavia and Greece. SS-Division 'Reich' was in the forefront of the attack and a small assault detachment under SS-Hauptsturmführer Fritz Klingenberg audaciously captured the Yugoslavian capital, Belgrade, on 13 April. By using a motor boat, Klingenberg and his men were able to slip through the city defences and force its surrender from a confused and bewildered mayor. In Greece, the Leibstandarte was engaged in a series of more hard-fought battles against not only the Greeks but also

barracks in Metz, and Hitler told them: 'You, who bear my name, will have the honour of leading every German attack in the future'. The Waffen-SS had won its spurs in convincing style.

Germany's success in western Europe opened up a new reservoir of pro-Nazi Volksdeutsche and Germanic peoples whom the Wehrmacht had no authority to conscript and whom Gottlob Berger's SS Hauptamt set about recruiting into the Waffen-SS. With the consequent increase in SS numbers, the Leibstandarte was upgraded to a brigade and a completely new division was authorised, the bulk of its personnel being Nordic volunteers from Flanders, Holland, Norway and Denmark. The leadership of the new division was drawn from existing formations, and it

SS-Totenkopf troops celebrate after the fall of France. The man on the right wears the white 'Hilfs-Krankenträger' armband of an auxiliary stretcher-bearer, and a typical mixture of clothing and insignia is evident from the appearance of the others. One soldier even wears contradictory rank insignia, i.e. the blank left-hand collar patch of an SS-Schütze in conjunction with the arm chevron of an SS-Sturmmann. Anomalies such as this were usually the result of field promotions.

British and New Zealand troops. After suffering heavy losses at the Klidi Pass, the LAH reconnaissance battalion commanded by SS-Sturmbannführer Kurt Meyer took the strategically crucial Klissura Pass and almost 11,000 prisoners into the bargain. On 20 April, General Tsolakoglu of the Greek III Army Corps surrendered to 'Sepp' Dietrich and a week later Athens fell to the German forces. By the end of the month, the Balkan campaign was effectively over. It had been another victory for the Waffen-SS. Klingenberg, Meyer and Gerd Pleiss, commander of the Leibstandarte's 1st Company which had been most active at Klidi, became the latest recipients of the

Knight's Cross. A propaganda film, *Der Weg der LAH*, extolled their exploits.

At dawn on 22 June 1941, Hitler ordered his forces into Russia to begin the epic conflict of ideologies which became a war of extermination and was to change forever the hitherto generally chivalrous character of the Waffen-SS. The rigours of the eastern front, encompassing everything from bitterly cold winters to sweltering summers, and from endless steppes and swamps to mountains and forests, brought out the very best, and the very worst, in Himmler's men. The German deployment for Operation Barbarossa extended from the Baltic to the Black Sea and was organised into three Army

The Leibstandarte-SS 'Adolf Hitler' took part in the Berlin victory parade on 19 July 1940. Some participating soldiers were already wearing collar patches without the black/aluminium twisted cord piping, which was officially abolished the following month.

Groups designated North, Centre and South. The SS-Totenkopf-Division, the Polizei-Division and Kampfgruppe 'Nord' were assigned to Army Group North, SS-Division 'Reich' to Army Group Centre and the Leibstandarte and SS-Division 'Wiking' to Army Group South. The latter two formations particularly impressed their army counterparts by their aggression and skill in attack. 'Reich' was heavily engaged at Minsk, Smolensk and Borodino, where Hausser was severely wounded and lost his right eye, and the division came within a few kilometres of Moscow at the end of the year. The only real SS failure occurred on the Finnish front when the second-rate troops of Kampfgruppe 'Nord' were thrown into a mass panic and

ignominiously routed on 2 July. The unit had to be withdrawn and completely overhauled, and it was thereafter reinforced with seasoned veterans from the Totenkopf-Division to become SS-Division 'Nord'.

At the end of 1941, the great German offensive came to a halt, totally exhausted. Blitzkrieg techniques had met their match in the vast expanse of the Soviet Union and the stamina and apparently endless manpower reserves of the Red Army. The force of the Russian counter-offensive during the winter of 1941–2 shocked the German Army High Command, which argued for full-scale withdrawals. Hitler overruled the generals, however, taking personal command of the army, and the Wehrmacht and Waffen-SS had their first opportunity to exhibit their steadfastness in defence. German troops began to find themselves cut off in isolated pockets, the most notable being that at Demjansk which contained six divisions, including 'Totenkopf'. The winter campaign was so harsh, with temperatures regularly falling below -40°C, that a special medal was later authorised for participants. The honour of designing it fell to SS-Unterscharführer Ernst Krause, an artist serving as a war correspondent with the Leibstandarte.

In the spring of 1942, the Germans opened a new offensive in the south, to reach the oil-rich Caucasus region. During the course of the year the Waffen-SS divisions, still suffering from the battles of the previous winter, were withdrawn in turn and refitted with a strong tank component plus assault guns and armoured personnel carriers. In May, the upgraded SS-Division 'Reich' was renamed 'Das Reich', and in September the SS-Kavallerie-Division was activated for anti-partisan duties behind the lines. November saw 'Das Reich', 'Totenkopf' and 'Wiking' officially redesignated as SS-Panzergrenadier Divisions, now equal in terms of equipment to many full panzer divisions of the army.

Himmler and SS-Brigadeführer Knoblauch reviewing Totenkopf cavalrymen in Russia, July 1941. At this stage of their development, the Waffen-SS Reiterstandarten were mounted on bicycles as often as they were on horses! The officer behind Himmler, wearing a steel helmet, is Hermann Fegelein, later commander of the cavalry division 'Florian Geyer'.

Himmler greeting Waffen-SS cavalry officers on the eastern front, 24 July 1941.

The face of the SS at war: troops of the 6th SS-Totenkopf Infantry Regiment operating a captured Czechoslovakian ZB53 machine-gun in Russia during the autumn of 1941, when German spirits were still high.

The Leibstandarte achieved similar status, with the new division being entitled 'Leibstandarte-SS Adolf Hitler' in commemoration of Hitler's bodyguard, which was its nucleus. The Führer was increasingly impressed with the combat performance of the SS, and in December ordered the formation of two completely new Waffen-SS divisions, named 'Hohenstaufen' and 'Frundsberg'. By the end of the year, Waffen-SS troops in the field numbered around 200,000.

The Soviet offensive of December 1942 proved disastrous for the Germans. All attempts to capture Stalingrad failed and by early 1943 General Paulus' 6th Army was totally isolated and forced to surrender. Other

German forces in the Caucasus also faced the grim possibility of being cut off by the speed and depth of the Soviet penetration. Field Marshal von Manstein, commander of Army Group South, managed to withdraw his forces from the Russian trap, however, and sensing that the Soviet thrust had become dangerously over-extended he launched a rapid counter-attack in the Kharkov region. Kharkov was a prestige target, a prewar showcase for communism, and to spearhead the assault to retake the city an SS-Panzer-Korps comprising the Leibstandarte, 'Das Reich' and 'Totenkopf' was formed under the overall command of Paul Hausser, who had now gained something of a celebrity status on the eastern front as 'the SS general with the

Heavily armed Totenkopf troops take a meal break during the invasion of the Soviet Union.

eye-patch'. For the first time, a substantial body of Waffen-SS troops fought together under their own generals and the result was a resounding victory. The Soviets were thrown into disarray, their 1st Guards Army was destroyed, Kharkov was recaptured and the Germans were able to restore order in the south. The SS suffered 12,000 casualties in the process. To Hitler, who was becoming increasingly disillusioned with army failures, it was proof of the capabilities of the Waffen-SS. Decorations were showered upon the victors of Kharkov, and no less than twenty-six Knight's Crosses, four Knight's Crosses with Oakleaves, and one Knight's Cross with Oakleaves and Swords went to the men of the SS-Panzer-Korps. The city's Red Square was

renamed 'Platz der Leibstandarte' in honour of Hitler's guards. Moreover, the Führer arranged for his old favourite, Theodor Eicke, who had been killed during the early stages of the offensive, to be buried in the style of the ancient Germanic kings, with all the attendant pagan ritual.

The period after the German recapture of Kharkov was relatively quiet, as both sides prepared to resume hostilities in the summer. The Soviet salient around Kursk became the focus of events, and when battle commenced on 5 July Hausser's SS-Panzer-Korps, with 340 tanks including 'Tigers' and 195 assault guns, was deployed on the southern flank. The Germans made reasonable progress in the first few days, but the nature of the war

A Leibstandarte motorcycle combination moves through a burning Russian town, July 1941. The divisional emblem of a skeleton key or 'Dietrich', clearly a pun on the name of the LAH commander, was introduced at the suggestion of Wilhelm Keilhaus and can be seen on the rear of the sidecar.

had changed and greatly improved Red Army forces held the enemy at bay before successfully counter-attacking. The SS-Panzer-Korps, ultimately reduced to 200 tanks, again fought well, despite being weakened by the removal of the Leibstandarte which was transferred to bolster the German army in Italy following the Allied invasion of Sicily on 10 July. Kursk was a strategic failure for the Germans. They lost their chance to gain the initiative and from then on were forced to react to Soviet moves. For the rest of 1943, the Germans fell back westwards across the Soviet Union. The three élite SS divisions, now redesignated as full panzer divisions, spent these hard months acting as Hitler's 'fire brigade', being sent from one flashpoint to another as the situation demanded. The decisiveness with which both 'Das Reich' and 'Totenkopf' threw back Russian assaults

SS soldiers lie where they fell, killed in the Soviet counter-offensive which took place during the horrendous winter of 1941–2. It is likely that the Russians staged this shot to show as many SS insignia as possible, thereby indicating that the Waffen-SS was not the invincible force which Nazi propaganda had portrayed.

Alfred Wünnenberg wearing the police litzen collar patches used by the Polizei-Division between 1939 and 1942. This photograph is also interesting for its portrayal of the common wartime press ploy of 'touching up' old pictures to update them for propaganda reasons. Wünnenberg won the Knight's Cross on 15 November 1941 as a police Oberst at Leningrad, and that is when this photograph was originally taken. On 23 April 1942 he was awarded the Oakleaves as an SS-Brigadeführer, and for the purpose of an immediate press announcement the old photo was dragged out of the files and had the Oakleaves painted on. This type of alteration can often be seen on surviving press pictures, and extends to rank badges as well as decorations.

earned them repeated praise from those army generals who were fortunate enough to have them under their command. In November, the Leibstandarte returned to the eastern front re-equipped with large numbers of the latest 'Panther' tanks, and together with army panzer divisions it crushed a Soviet armoured corps in the Ukraine and retook Zhitomir.

While the Waffen-SS was locked in battle on the eastern front, Hitler continued to authorise the formation of new SS divisions, including 'Hitlerjugend'. The German position in Russia underwent a drastic deterioration on 14 December 1943, when the Soviets launched another massive offensive in the Ukraine. The battle lasted for four months and culminated in the expulsion of the German forces from the south. The speed of the Russian advance led to the encirclement of large numbers of Wehrmacht

A motorised column of the Leibstandarte entering Kharkov, 14 March 1943.

IM NAMEN
DES DEUTSCHEN VOLKES
VERLEIHE ICH
DEM SS-OBERGRUPPENFÜHRER
UND GENERAL DER WAFFEN-SS
SEPP DIETRICH
DAS EICHENLAUB MIT SCHWERTERN
ZUM RITTERKREUZ
DES EISERNEN KREUZES
FÜHRERHAUPTQUARTIER
DEN 14. MÄRZ 1943
DER FÜHRER
UND OBERSTE BEFEHLSHABER
DER WEHRMACHT

On the same day as the SS-Panzer-Korps retook Kharkov, 'Sepp' Dietrich became the first SS recipient of the Knight's Cross with Oakleaves and Swords. The decoration was accompanied by this elaborate citation, signed by Hitler.

troops. 'Wiking', now under the command of SS-Gruppenführer Herbert Gille, and Léon Degrelle's Belgian SS Brigade 'Wallonien' were caught in the Korsun-Cherkassy pocket in a scene reminiscent of Stalingrad, but managed to smash their way out suffering 60 per cent casualties in the process. Degrelle received the Knight's Cross, and Gille the Knight's Cross with Oakleaves and Swords, for this action. In a similar engagement, the Leibstandarte and elements of 'Das Reich' were trapped around Kamenets Podolsky and had to be rescued by 'Hohenstaufen' and 'Frundsberg'. Worn down and exhausted, the Waffen-SS formations were now increasingly unable to stem the advancing Russian tide.

In the spring of 1944, the battered Leibstandarte and 'Das Reich' battle groups were sent westwards to refit and prepare for the expected Anglo-American invasion. The

A motorcyclist of the 5th Reconnaissance Company, 'Das Reich', on the Mius front in August 1943. The twin bar emblem on the front of the sidecar was used as a divisional emblem by 'Das Reich' during the Battle of Kursk, while the Leibstandarte used a single bar and 'Totenkopf' a triple bar. Hausser had devised these temporary formation signs with the intention of confusing Russian intelligence in the lead-up to Kursk.

Totenkopf personnel watching Russian positions on the southern sector of the eastern front, October 1943. The man with the binoculars wears the recently introduced Einheitsfeldmütze, while the panzer officer still sports his black version of the M40 Schiffchen with aluminium piping. Note also the unofficial sheepskin overjacket and fur cap used by the soldier on the right.

hardened experience of their officers, shocked the Allies. However, the latter's command of the air prevented proper deployment of the SS division and the attack ground to a halt. Two months of bloody fighting ensued. The Leibstandarte and 'Hitlerjugend' were grouped together to form a new corps, the 1st SS-Panzer-Korps under 'Sepp' Dietrich, and were immediately assigned the task of defending key positions around Caen. 'Götz von Berlichingen' was hindered by constant air attacks on its journey north from its base in the Loire Valley, and did not reach the invasion front until 11 June. 'Das Reich', travelling from Gascony, took even longer, being subjected to a series of ambushes carried out by the French Resistance. Frustrated at the consequent delays and loss of life, the division wreaked havoc upon the local population, whom it suspected of sheltering the partisans. The village of Oradour-sur-Glane was systematically destroyed and 640 of its inhabitants were shot, and the little town of Tulle was also devastated. 'Das Reich' eventually reached its positions north of St Lô at the end of June, to join up with Willi Bittrich's 2nd SS-Panzer-Korps, comprising 'Hohenstaufen' and 'Frundsberg', which had been hurriedly transferred from the east.

Throughout July, the six SS divisions struggled ceaselessly to contain the Allies in their beachhead, taking a heavy toll of British and American armour. In one notable engagement, SS-Obersturmführer Michael Wittmann and his Leibstandarte 'Tiger' crew destroyed twenty-one British tanks and twenty-eight other armoured vehicles in a single hour. However, the Germans were overpowered by the sheer weight of Allied numbers and were frequently reduced to operating as ad hoc battle groups. By the middle of August, nineteen German army divisions had become trapped around Falaise, and only determined efforts by 'Das Reich', 'Hitlerjugend' and 'Hohenstaufen' kept open

former went to Belgium while the latter went to southern France. They were joined by 'Hitlerjugend' and the 'Götz von Berlichingen' division, which had been formed in France a few months earlier. 'Hohenstaufen' and 'Frundsberg' were relocated in Poland in anticipation of another Soviet attack, along with the emaciated 'Wiking', while the long-suffering 'Totenkopf' remained in front-line service in the east.

When the Normandy landings took place on 6 June, 'Hitlerjugend' was the first SS formation to engage the enemy. The ferocity of the SS assault, combining the youthful enthusiasm of the troops with the battle-

The PzKpfw III command tank of 1st battalion, 3rd SS-Panzer Regiment, 'Totenkopf' Division, in southern Russia during November 1943. The officer on the left is Hauptsturmführer Erwin Meierdrees, holder of the Knight's Cross with Oakleaves, who was killed in action near Dunaalmas, Hungary, on 4 January 1945.

A soldier of the Belgian SS Assault Brigade 'Wallonien' under shellfire at Cherkassy, December 1943. Of the 2,000 Walloons trapped in the Korsun-Cherkassy pocket, only 600 survived unscathed.

In a scene reminiscent of the First World War, an SS-Schütze shelters in his trench dugout on the eastern front, spring 1944.

a gap long enough for them to escape. Increasingly, while ordinary German soldiers were prepared to surrender to the Allies, it was left to the Waffen-SS to fight on.

Meanwhile, in the east, the Red Army had struck again on 13 July and ripped Army Group Centre apart. Once more, the SS panzer divisions were thrown into the breach. 'Wiking' and 'Totenkopf', grouped together as the 4th SS-Panzer-Korps under Herbert Gille, repulsed the Soviet attack on Warsaw during August, while in the Balkans the backbone of the German defence was provided by 'Prinz Eugen', 'Handschar' and other nominally second-grade formations of SS-Obergruppenführer Artur Phleps' 5th SS-Gebirgs-Korps, which had been diverted from their usual anti-partisan duties.

In September, the British airborne assault at Arnhem was countered and defeated by

SS panzergrenadiers entrenched in a village on the eastern front, October 1944.

'Hohenstaufen' and 'Frundsberg' in a battle noted for the mutual respect held by each side for the fighting abilities and fair play of the other. This victory, and the general slowing down of the Allied advance across France due to over-extended supply and communications lines, persuaded Hitler to launch a major offensive in the west, in an attempt to repeat the successes of 1940. Two panzer armies were assembled to spearhead the attack, the 5th Panzer Army under General Hasso von Manteuffel, and the 6th SS-Panzer Army, the larger of the two forces, under 'Sepp' Dietrich. The nucleus of the latter army comprised the Leibstandarte, 'Das Reich', 'Hohenstaufen' and 'Hitlerjugend', now equipped with some of the latest 'King Tiger' tanks. On 16 December the offensive began in the Ardennes, but the hilly and wooded terrain naturally favoured defensive action and after only five days the German advance ground to a halt. SS frustration again translated itself into the committing of atrocities, this time the massacre of seventy American prisoners by men of Joachim Peiper's battle group at Malmédy. A subsidiary offensive in Alsace, led by 'Götz von Berlichingen', also came to nothing and the division ended up trapped in Metz. With a virtual stalemate in the west, Hitler pulled his SS divisions out and sent them eastwards, where the situation had once more become desperate.

On 12 January 1945, a great Soviet offensive was launched across Poland in preparation for the final assault on Berlin. Even so, Hitler's main concern was to safeguard the tenuous hold he still maintained over the Hungarian oilfields. The SS cavalry divisions 'Florian Geyer' and 'Maria Theresa' were besieged in Budapest, and in an effort to relieve them 'Totenkopf' and 'Wiking' were transferred from their key positions on the German–Polish border. A month-long battle failed to save the city,

'Sepp' Dietrich at the time of the Ardennes offensive, wearing his collar patches as SS-Oberst-Gruppenführer und Panzer Generaloberst der Waffen-SS, the senior active tank man at the front. Although promoted to this rank on 20 April 1942, Wehrmacht pressure prevented him from using it or adopting the appropriate insignia until he had secured command of a suitably large force, which he did in the autumn of 1944 with the formation of the 6th SS-Panzer Army.

however, and it fell to the Russians on 13 February, with only 785 German soldiers escaping from the original garrison of 50,000 men. The 6th SS-Panzer Army was immediately moved in from the west and on 6 March a German counter-attack began. It was conducted by the largest aggregation of Waffen-SS forces ever witnessed during the war, comprising the Leibstandarte, 'Das Reich', 'Totenkopf', 'Wiking', 'Hohenstaufen', 'Hitlerjugend' and 'Reichsführer-SS', the latter division having been transferred from northern Italy. At first the SS did well, but there were insufficient back-up resources and by mid-March their advance had been halted.

The failure of the Waffen-SS in Hungary, following on from the collapse of the Ardennes offensive, had a devastating psychological effect on Hitler, who had come to expect the impossible from them, and he openly accused Dietrich and his subordinates of betrayal. Despite that, SS troops carried on fighting as loyally as ever as they slowly retreated into Germany, bowed under the weight of superior Allied numbers and equipment. By now, thousands of grounded Luftwaffe personnel and 'beached' sailors from the Kriegsmarine had been pressed into an infantry role alongside the Waffen-SS. During the last week in April, when Soviet forces broke into Berlin, Felix Steiner led a battle group of hard-core Waffen-SS including elements of the 'Polizei', 'Frundsberg', 'Nordland', 'Wallonien', 'Charlemagne' and 'Nederland' divisions, as well as some 600 men from Himmler's personal escort battalion, in a life and death struggle to defend the Führerbunker. However, most other SS units had by then accepted the reality of the situation and were pushing westwards to surrender to the Anglo-American Allies, rather than risk capture by the Russians.

It is estimated that some 180,000 Waffen-SS soldiers were killed in action during the Second World War, with about 400,000 wounded and a further 70,000 listed 'missing'. The entire establishment of the élite divisions, Leibstandarte, 'Das Reich' and 'Totenkopf', were casualties several times over, with only a few battle-hardened veterans surviving to train the continual injections of young Germans and Volksdeutsche fed in as replacements via the divisional training battalions. A close comparison between the number of men recorded killed, wounded or missing in the 'Totenkopf' division (60,000) and 'Wiking' division (19,000) gives a startlingly different loss ratio. Since both divisions served for the most part alongside each other, the only reason for such horrendous losses must have been the mishandling, or at least rough handling, of 'Totenkopf' troops by their commanders. Certainly, Eicke and his successors were not renowned as humanitarians and it is known that 'Totenkopf' had more requests for 'transfers out' than any other Waffen-SS division. A large proportion of the men who volunteered for service in the SS paratroop forces were 'Totenkopf' transferees, and it was widely recognised that the paratroop battalion was virtually a suicide squad. The fact that many hardened soldiers chose to escape from 'Totenkopf' by signing up with the paras gives an indication of the severity and long-term nature of the suffering which 'Totenkopf' troops had to endure. Among other Waffen-SS men, Death's Head units became known colloquially as 'Knochenstürme' (Bones Companies), or 'that lost lot'.

By 1944–5, SS soldiers were normally in their late teens, and the average age of a Waffen-SS junior officer was twenty, with a life expectancy of two months at the front. Moreover, it was not uncommon for divisional commanders to be in their early thirties, men like Kraas, Kumm, Meyer, Mohnke, Wisch and Witt who had joined the LAH or SS-VT around 1934 and progressed through the ranks. The combination of youthful enthusiasm, political indoctrination and hard-bitten experience was a winning one, and goes a long way to explaining how a division such as 'Hitlerjugend' could suffer 60 per cent casualties over a four-week period in 1944 and yet still retain its aggressive spirit, thereby gaining for the entire Waffen-SS the admiration of friend and foe alike.

The Flemish SS-Sturmmann Richard 'Remi' Schrijnen of 3rd Company, SS-Freiwilligen Sturmbrigade 'Langemarck', being paraded before his fellow soldiers near Prague after receiving the Knight's Cross on 21 September 1944. He is accompanied by Konrad Schellong, the brigade commander, and adjutant Willy Teichert.

Ultimately, more than half the membership of the Waffen-SS comprised non-Germans. In line with Himmler's intention that the SS should develop as a Germanic, rather than a German, organisation, small numbers of suitable foreign nationals had been admitted to the armed SS even before the war, including at least one soldier of dual German/British nationality who served with the SS-VT Standarte 'Deutschland'. Documentary proof of Aryan descent was initially a prerequisite for acceptance, but with the rapid expansion of the Waffen-SS after 1940 the racial rule became something of a dead letter. During the war, the hard-pressed RuSHA authorities were content to accept a signed declaration of Aryan descent from enlisted German and west European Waffen-SS men, which could be investigated later when necessity demanded or when the opportunity presented itself.

With the German conquest of western Europe, the door to a huge pool of manpower which the Wehrmacht had no authority to conscript was opened to Berger's recruiting officers. Large numbers of pro-Germans, anti-Bolsheviks, members of local pseudo-Nazi political parties, adventurers and simple opportunists were only too eager to throw in their lot with the winning side. The first complete unit of foreign volunteers to be raised by the SS was the Standarte

Léon Degrelle and men of his Walloon Division in Pomerania, 9 March 1945. Degrelle wears the Close Combat Clasp in Gold and his unique 'Wallonien' cuff title hand-embroidered in Gothic script. The SS-Unterscharführer in the foreground is a Frenchman, Jean Lejeune. When Belgium was liberated at the end of 1944, Degrelle was sentenced to death in absentia as a collaborator. In May 1945 he flew from Oslo to Spain in Albert Speer's private aircraft. He was protected by General Franco, became a wealthy industrialist and was granted Spanish citizenship in 1954, taking the new name of Léon José de Ramirez Reina. In the 1960s he attended his daughter's wedding wearing the full uniform of an SS-Standartenführer! Degrelle, who dubbed himself the world's last Fascist leader, died on 1 April 1994, aged 87.

the recruiting of further so-called 'foreign legions' was the impending invasion of the Soviet Union, and in order to attract sufficient numbers of these troops the Germans reluctantly accepted that they would have to co-operate with the pro-Nazi political parties in each country, and that the new units would have to retain some of their own national characteristics. The idea of national legions was quickly extended from the Germanic countries to those ideologically sympathetic to Germany, such as Croatia. However, during the early stages of the war at least, Himmler was not prepared to accept racially dubious volunteers into the SS and so the eastern legions, such as the French, Walloon Belgians and Spaniards, were assigned to the army.

During 1940–1, the SS-sponsored legions 'Flandern', 'Niederlande', 'Norwegen' and 'Freikorps Danmark' were raised. Their troops were distinguished from those in the German SS proper by special national badges and by their oath, which committed them solely to the war against communism. The legions were categorised as being 'attached to' rather than 'part of' the Waffen-SS, and were designated by the new title of 'Freiwilligen' or 'Volunteer' units. The recruitment programme soon ran into difficulties, however, when the legionaries found that many of their German colleagues held them in low regard. Despite promises of free land in the conquered east for all victorious SS soldiers, and the bestowal of full German citizenship upon every foreign volunteer after the war, morale plummetted, particularly when 'Flandern' was decimated in Russia early in 1942 and had to be disbanded. The other three legions were reinforced and, at the end of 1942, amalgamated to form the 'Nordland' division. A year later the Dutch contingent was sufficiently strong to be removed and given the status of an independent brigade,

'Nordland', from Norwegians and Danes. It was soon joined by the Standarte 'Westland', comprising Dutchmen and Flemings, and in December 1940 these two formations combined with the SS-VT Standarte 'Germania' to become SS-Division 'Wiking', a truly European force. The main impetus to

which eventually developed into the 'Nederland' division. Both 'Nordland' and 'Nederland' fought well on the eastern front, particularly in defence of the Baltic states, and, together with the rest of Felix Steiner's 3rd (Germanic) SS-Panzer-Korps, they took part in the celebrated 'Battle of the European SS' at Narva in July 1944 before being destroyed in the final struggle for Berlin the following year. Other western SS formations of note included the 'Wallonien' Division, which was transferred from the army as a brigade in 1943 and fought with distinction under the Belgian fascist leader Léon Degrelle; and the French 'Charlemagne' Division, again transferred from the army, which was one of the most redoubtable defenders of Berlin. A fifty-eight-strong 'British Free Corps' was drawn from former British Union of Fascists members and other disaffected individuals in British prisoner-of-war camps, but was of propaganda value only.

Despite the good fighting reputation quickly gained by the western volunteers, they were simply too few in number to meet SS requirements for replacing battle casualties and so Berger turned to the Volksdeutsche scattered throughout central and eastern Europe. In just three countries, namely Romania, Hungary and Yugoslavia, it was estimated that there were some 1,500,000 Volksdeutsche in 1939, and this was clearly a rich source of potential manpower. Recruitment of Romanian Volksdeutsche began as early as the spring of 1940, but a sudden influx of volunteers from Yugoslavia after the invasion of April 1941 led Berger to suggest to Himmler the formation of an entire division of Yugoslavian Volksdeutsche. The result was the raising in the summer of 1942 of the SS-Gebirgs Division 'Prinz Eugen', designed for anti-partisan duties against Tito's mountain-based resistance movement. Later that year, faced with an

SS-Obergruppenführer Artur Phleps, founder of the 'Prinz Eugen' division and commander of the 5th SS-Gebirgs-Korps in 1944. Phleps was an ethnic German from Romania who had served on the General Staff of the Imperial Austro-Hungarian army during the First World War and later as an instructor at the Bucharest Military Academy. Unlike most of his Volksdeutsche subordinates, Phleps was granted full SS membership as indicated by the runes worn below the left breast pocket. He was captured and subsequently killed by Russian soldiers on 21 September 1944, near Arad.

ever-worsening manpower crisis, Hitler gave the SS formal authorisation to conscript the Volksdeutsche, who fell outwith the remit of the Wehrmacht as they were not German nationals. In that way, an impressive numerical level of recruitment was maintained, but many of the conscripts were poor in quality and consequently Volksdeutsche units tended to be second rate. They soon earned for themselves the reputation for being specialists in perpetrating massacres against civilian populations and other soft targets. The

Himmler inspecting Bosnian Muslims of the 'Handschar' artillery regiment being trained in the use of a Pak 38 anti-tank gun at Neuhammer in Silesia, October 1943.

In May 1944, Haj Amin al-Husaini, the self-styled Grand Mufti of Jerusalem and spiritual leader of Bosnia's Muslims, reviewed troops of the 'Handschar' division, who were kitted out with their distinctive field-grey fez.

associated policy of recruiting Croatian and Albanian Muslims into the 'Handschar', 'Kama' and 'Skanderbeg' Divisions, to take on the Christian Serbs from whom many of Tito's partisans were drawn, was a total disaster and all three divisions had to be disbanded in order to free their German officers and NCOs to fight elsewhere.

In the Soviet Union, the Germans made better use of local nationalist groups opposed to Stalin's government, successfully persuading large numbers of the native population to enrol in the Schutzmannschaft for counter-guerrilla operations. The breakthrough for the Waffen-SS recruiters came in April 1943, when no less than 100,000 Ukrainians volunteered for a new SS division, of whom 30,000 were duly accepted. Over 80 per cent of them were killed the following year when the Ukrainian division was trapped in the Brody-Tarnow pocket. In the summer of 1944, after the failed July bomb plot against Hitler, Himmler was given unprecedented military powers as Commander-in-Chief of the Home Army, which effectively gave him control over all reserve and replacement forces in the Reich. He took the opportunity to enhance his personal status still further by transferring many Armenian, Baltic, Caucasian, Cossack, Georgian and Turkestani volunteers from the hastily mustered foreign legions of the German army into the Waffen-SS. However, while the wide range of nationalities involved undoubtedly had some propaganda value, the actual performance of the eastern troops in combat left much to be desired. The Baltic SS divisions, grouped together under SS-Obergruppenführer Walter Krüger as the 6th Waffen-Armeekorps der SS, lived up to modest expectations and were particularly ferocious when defending their homelands, but the remainder were poor at best and at worst a complete rabble. Himmler regarded them merely as racially inferior auxiliaries, in

effect expendable cannon-fodder. They were never considered for SS membership proper, and were prohibited from sporting the SS runes. Although they wore a sort of diluted SS uniform for convenience, they had their own series of distinctive badges so that there would be absolutely no possibility of their being mistaken for 'real' SS men. Not surprisingly, the loyalty of the easterners was always in question, and their horrific behaviour when set loose among the civilian population of Poland during the Warsaw uprising of autumn 1944 led to frequent demands for their withdrawal, even from other SS commanders. Several units had to be disbanded, and some of their leaders were tried by SS courts martial and executed for looting and other excesses.

Non-German nationals ultimately made up the greater part (57 per cent) of the Waffen-SS. It is estimated that 400,000 Reich Germans served in the Waffen-SS during the war, as opposed to 137,000 pure west Europeans, 200,000 pure east Europeans and 185,000 Volksdeutsche. A detailed breakdown of non-Germans by nationality is shown below:

West Europeans

Dutch	50,000
Flemings	23,000
Italians	20,000
Walloons	15,000
Danes	11,000
French	8,000
Norwegians	6,000
Spaniards/Swiss/Swedes/ Luxembourgers/British	4,000

East Europeans

Cossacks	50,000
Latvians	35,000
Ukrainians	30,000
Estonians	20,000
Croatians	20,000

Pro-Nazi Cossack volunteers riding under the flag of the death's head, 1944.

Serbians	15,000	China		3
Byelorussians	12,000	South-West Africa		3
Turkestanis	8,000	South-East Africa		2
Romanians	5,000	South America		2
Albanians	3,000	Spain		2
Bulgarians	1,000	Palestine		2
Finns	1,000	Japan		2
		Sumatra		2
Volksdeutsche		Mexico		1
(by country of origin)		Australia		1
Hungary	80,000	India		1
Czechoslovakia	45,000	New Guinea		1
Croatia	25,000			
Western Europe	16,000			
Romania	8,000			
Poland	5,000			
Serbia	5,000			
Scandinavia	775			
Soviet Union	100			
France	84			
Great Britain	10			
USA	5			
Brazil	4			

While the majority of Waffen-SS men were non-Germans, the wartime Waffen-SS officer corps consisted almost entirely of German nationals, who held all of the most senior posts. The vast majority of non-German officers in the foreign divisions of the SS had their ranks prefixed by 'Legions-' or 'Waffen-' rather than 'SS-' (e.g. 'Waffen-Standartenführer der SS') and they, like their men, were not classed as SS members. Because of this, even 'heroic' figures such as Léon Degrelle, holder of the Knight's Cross with Oakleaves and first recipient of the Close Combat Clasp in Gold, did not merit inclusion in the *Dienstaltersliste*.

The summer of 1941 saw the Waffen-SS officer corps in its best condition, and witnessed an influx of recruits from the police, transferred Wehrmacht officers, party and state officials, doctors, lawyers and youth leaders eager to serve with the new élite before the anticipated victorious cessation of hostilities. However, the subsequent blood-letting in Russia destroyed the cream of the early graduates of Bad Tölz and Braunschweig, and their replacements bore scarcely a token resemblance to them. By 1 July 1943, the officer corps numbered 10,702. Even so, only 4,145 were designated as career or professional officers, with about 1,000 of them holding ranks of SS-Sturmbannführer and above. Himmler observed at that time that the 'Führerdecke', or 'officer cover', for many front-line SS units was lamentably thin, and that the state of the officer corps had deteriorated drastically since the invasion of the Soviet Union.

Three times as many SS officer dossiers survived the war as there were numbers of SS officers in 1941. The great bulk of the remainder related to battlefield commissions granted to Waffen-SS NCOs who had proved themselves at the front between 1942 and 1945. Many thousands of officers were thus added to the corps in a fairly short period, men whose ties with the NSDAP and prewar SS were tenuous or even non-existent. The 'military élite' commanding the European SS of 1944 was, therefore, far removed from the politically motivated SS-VT officer corps of the late 1930s. During the last year of the war, Waffen-SS senior officers' conferences saw elderly former Wehrmacht and police officers standing shoulder to shoulder with the younger generation, many of whom had been NCOs or

subalterns in 1939 and were now hard-bitten and highly decorated colonels and brigadiers. The members of this new officer corps were dubbed by the SS Old Guard as 'Nur-Soldaten', or 'only soldiers', men whose responsibilities were limited to fighting and whose remit did not include the eventual policing of a conquered Europe. The result was a fragmentation of the officer corps between the 'politicals' and the 'fighters', a split which grew ever wider as the war drew to a close. The Waffen-SS uniform never supplanted the Allgemeine-SS membership card in Himmler's mind, and by 1944–5 the typical Waffen-SS officer at the front identified far more with his bloodied Wehrmacht colleagues, and even with his long-suffering enemies, than with his bureaucratic SS seniors in Berlin and Munich.

Although given suitably heroic names from an early date, Waffen-SS divisions were not numbered until 15 November 1943. Unit titles and designations were frequently altered, either to acknowledge a change in status or, particularly late in the war, to camouflage a formation's true identity and confuse enemy intelligence. The 'Das Reich' Division was a typical example, and had its nomenclature altered no less than eleven times:

September 1939	Panzerverband Ostpreussen
September 1939	Panzer Division 'Kempf'
10.10.39	SS-Verfügungstruppe-Division (Motorised)
4.4.40	SS-Verfügungsdivision
1.12.40	SS-Division 'Deutschland'
28.1.41	SS-Division (Motorised) 'Reich'
May 1942	SS-Division (Motorised) 'Das Reich'
May 1942	Kampfgruppe 'Ostendorff'
14.11.42	SS-Panzergrenadier Division 'Das Reich'
15.11.43	2nd SS-Panzer Division 'Das Reich'
24.2.45	Ausbildungsgruppe 'Nord'

Divisions staffed by Germans were known as 'SS-Division', while those comprising mainly Volksdeutsche or Germanic personnel, whether volunteers or conscripts, were called 'SS-Freiwilligen Division'. Units composed primarily of east Europeans or Russians came into the category of 'Waffen Division der SS', a term of inferiority which denoted attachment to, rather than actual membership of, the Waffen-SS.

All the Waffen-SS divisions which had been mustered, at least on paper, by 1945 are listed in the table below. Many divisions numbered above 20 were merely upgraded regiments, flung together in a hurry using any 'spare' personnel available and given grandiose titles. The number of Knight's Crosses awarded is a good indication of the effectiveness and battle experience of each division.

WAFFEN-SS DIVISIONS, 1939–45

Title (and Divisional Strength at Beginning of 1945)	Granted Divisional Status	Primary Composition	Knight's Crosses Awarded
1st SS-Panzer Division 'Leibstandarte-SS Adolf Hitler' (22,000)	1942	German volunteers with Hitler's SS bodyguard regiment as the nucleus	58
2nd SS-Panzer Division 'Das Reich' (18,000)	1939	German volunteers with the SS-Verfügungstruppe as the nucleus	69
3rd SS-Panzer Division 'Totenkopf' (15,400)	1939	German volunteers with the SS-Totenkopfverbände as the nucleus	47
4th SS-Polizei Panzergrenadier Division (9,000)	1939	German police transferees	25
5th SS-Panzer Division 'Wiking' (14,800)	1940	German/west European volunteers	55
6th SS-Gebirgs Division 'Nord' (15,000)	1941	German volunteers with Totenkopf regiments as the nucleus	4
7th SS-Freiwilligen Gebirgs Division 'Prinz Eugen' (20,000)	1942	Yugoslavian Volksdeutsche volunteers	6
8th SS-Kavallerie Division 'Florian Geyer' (13,000)	1942	German volunteers with SS-Kavallerie regiments as the nucleus	22
9th SS-Panzer Division 'Hohenstaufen' (19,000)	1943	German volunteers and conscripts	12

Title (and Divisional Strength at Beginning of 1945)	Granted Divisional Status	Primary Composition	Knight's Crosses Awarded
10th SS-Panzer Division 'Frundsberg' (15,500)	1943	German volunteers and conscripts	13
11th SS-Freiwilligen Panzergrenadier Division 'Nordland' (9,000)	1943	West European volunteers, many from the disbanded SS foreign legions 'Niederlande', 'Norwegen' and 'Freikorps Danmark'	25
12th SS-Panzer Division 'Hitlerjugend' (19,500)	1943	German Hitler Youth volunteers	14
13th Waffen Gebirgs Division der SS 'Handschar' (12,700)	1943	Yugoslavian Muslim volunteers	4
14th Waffen Grenadier Division der SS (22,000)	1943	Ukrainian volunteers	1
15th Waffen Grenadier Division der SS (16,800)	1943	Latvian volunteers, many transferring from the Schutzmannschaft and Police Rifle Regiments	3
16th SS-Panzergrenadier Division 'Reichsführer-SS' (14,000)	1943	German/Volksdeutsche volunteers and conscripts, with Himmler's escort battalion as the nucleus	1
17th SS-Panzergrenadier Division 'Götz von Berlichingen' (3,500)	1943	German/Volksdeutsche volunteers and conscripts	4
18th SS-Freiwilligen Panzergrenadier Division 'Horst Wessel' (11,000)	1944	Hungarian Volksdeutsche volunteers and conscripts	2
19th Waffen Grenadier Division der SS (9,000)	1944	Latvian volunteers, many transferring from the Schutzmannschaft and Police Rifle Regiments	12
20th Waffen Grenadier Division der SS (15,500)	1944	Estonian volunteers, many transferring from the Schutzmannschaft and Police Rifle Regiments	5

Title (and Divisional Strength at Beginning of 1945)	Granted Divisional Status	Primary Composition	Knight's Crosses Awarded
21st Waffen Gebirgs Division der SS 'Skanderbeg' (5,000)	1944	Albanian Muslim volunteers	0
22nd SS-Freiwilligen Kavallerie Division 'Maria Theresa' (8,000)	1944	German/Hungarian Volksdeutsche volunteers and conscripts	6
23rd Waffen Gebirgs Division der SS 'Kama' (disbanded late 1944 and number '23' given to next division)	1944	Yugoslavian Muslim volunteers	0
23rd SS-Freiwilligen Panzergrenadier Division 'Nederland' (6,000)	1945	Dutch volunteers, many formerly of the SS foreign legion 'Niederlande'	19
24th Waffen Gebirgs Division der SS (3,000)	1944	Italian fascist volunteers	0
25th Waffen Grenadier Division der SS 'Hunyadi' (15,000)	1944	Hungarian volunteers	0
26th Waffen Grenadier Division der SS (13,000)	1945	Hungarian volunteers	0
27th SS-Freiwilligen Grenadier Division 'Langemarck' (7,000)	1944	Flemish volunteers, many formerly of the SS foreign legion 'Flandern'	1
28th SS-Freiwilligen Grenadier Division 'Wallonien' (4,000)	1944	Walloon volunteers, many formerly of the German army's Wallonische Legion	3
29th Waffen Grenadier Division der SS (disbanded late 1944 and number '29' given to next division)	1944	Russian convict volunteers	0
29th Waffen Grenadier Division der SS (15,000)	1945	Italian fascist volunteers	0
30th Waffen Grenadier Division der SS (4,500)	1945	Russian volunteers, many transferring from the Schutzmannschaft and Police Rifle Regiments	0

Title (and Divisional Strength at Beginning of 1945)	Granted Divisional Status	Primary Composition	Knight's Crosses Awarded
31st SS-Freiwilligen Grenadier Division (11,000)	1945	Czechoslovakian Volksdeutsche volunteers and conscripts	0
32nd SS-Freiwilligen Grenadier Division '30 Januar' (2,000)	1945	German conscripts and SS training school personnel/Volksdeutsche volunteers and conscripts	0
33rd Waffen Kavallerie Division der SS (destroyed soon after formation, and number '33' given to next division)	1945	Hungarian volunteers	0
33rd Waffen Grenadier Division der SS 'Charlemagne' (7,000)	1945	French volunteers, many of them formerly of the German army's Französisches Legion or LVF	2
34th SS-Freiwilligen Grenadier Division 'Landstorm Nederland' (7,000)	1945	Dutch volunteers, many formerly of the Landwacht Nederland	3
35th SS-Polizei Grenadier Division (5,000)	1945	German police transferees	0
36th Waffen Grenadier Division der SS (6,000)	1945	German/east European volunteers, including a large number of convicted criminals from the Dirlewanger Brigade, a terror unit used against civilians	1
37th SS-Freiwilligen Kavallerie Division 'Lützow' (1,000)	1945	Hungarian Volksdeutsche conscripts and remnants of the 'Florian Geyer' and 'Maria Theresa' divisions	0
38th SS-Grenadier Division 'Nibelungen' (1,000)	1945	German volunteers, conscripts and SS training school personnel	0

During the latter part of the war, it was not uncommon for ad hoc SS battle groups to be drawn together from divisional troops, or for smaller units to be absorbed by larger ones which just happened to be located nearby.

There were also hundreds of replacement formations, such as the Latvian SS Ersatzbrigade which alone accounted for forty full companies of men under training, and some very obscure units such as the

Indische Freiwilligen-Legion der SS, made up of anti-British Indian prisoners-of-war who had been captured in North Africa and Italy. One of the strangest of all was the Osttürkischer Waffen-Verband der SS, composed of three Muslim Waffengruppen der SS recruited from Caspian and Black Sea Tartars under the command of the Austrian SS-Standartenführer Wilhelm Hintersatz. He had been converted to Islam during service alongside the Turks in the First World War and took the name of Harun-el-Raschid Bey, under which he was listed in the *SS Dienstaltersliste*! It was all a far cry from the racial élite of the 1930s.

WAFFEN-SS UNIFORMS

The perennial interest in the Waffen-SS tends to be concentrated on its uniforms and insignia, and for that reason these merit detailed coverage.

The manufacture of Waffen-SS uniform clothing was undertaken either by private firms or, increasingly after 1941, by the SS-owned economic enterprises operating under the auspices of the SS Wirtschafts- und Verwaltungshauptamt. The first SS clothing factory, or SS-Bekleidungswerke, was established in Dachau concentration camp, where the main Waffen-SS clothing depot was also located. In 1939 a training school for tailors and seamstresses opened at Ravensbrück, and after the occupation of Poland and Russia the SS Eastern Industries Ltd, or Ostindustrie GmbH (Osti), used local Jews to manufacture winter uniforms and various items of equipment from property and raw materials seized by the Germans. Civilian clothing confiscated from concentration camp inmates was commonly reprocessed and dyed for transformation into Waffen-SS uniforms. By 1944, the vast majority of SS and police clothing was being manufactured in-house at the following establishments:

Bayreuth labour camp, in Bavaria
Dachau concentration camp, in Bavaria
Oranienburg concentration camp, near Berlin
Poniatowa labour camp, near Lublin in Poland
Posen labour camp, in Poland
Radom labour camp, in Poland
Ravensbrück concentration camp, near Fürstenberg
Schröttersburg concentration camp, near Plock in Poland
Straubing prison, in Bavaria
Trawniki labour camp, near Lublin in Poland

Their products sometimes bore the stamp 'SS-BW', followed by a code number allocated to the particular bench or workshop concerned. Many items manufactured at the SS-Bekleidungswerke were, however, completely unmarked.

During 1944–5, shortages of raw materials created such a crisis in the uniform industry that even the concentration camps could not meet the clothing needs of the Waffen-SS. The result was that newly recruited front-line SS soldiers ended up wearing captured uniforms, particularly Italian items taken after the fall of Mussolini. Older veterans tended to retain their better quality early issue tunics, caps and boots for as long as possible, often until they quite literally fell apart, and there were at least three fully motorised platoons, the so-called SS-Bekleidungs-Instandsetzungszüge 500, 501 and 502, whose sole job it was to travel from unit to unit repairing uniform clothing.

Each Waffen-SS formation regularly submitted requisition forms to the SS Führungshauptamt ordering specific uniform needs. If approved, the SS-FHA would instruct the SS Wirtschafts- und Verwaltungshauptamt to make the necessary issue. The SS-WVHA in its turn then arranged despatch of the material to the unit, either direct from the factory or via one of its twelve main supply depots, the Hauptwirtschaftslager. Alternatively, the uniform items could be made available to the unit at the nearest convenient SS-WVHA sub-depot, or Truppenwirtschaftslager, of which there were twenty spread out across the Reich. On the eastern front, SS supply commands or Nachschubskommandantur were established at Bobruisk, Dnepropetrowsk, Oulu and Riga as links between the SS-WVHA and the local sub-depots. Each supply command was empowered to place contracts with, or make purchases from, private firms in its area. Moreover, where field formations of the Waffen-SS were likely to be operating in a particular zone for a prolonged period, for example 'Prinz Eugen' in the Balkans, special ad hoc supply bases or Stützpunkte were set up at convenient points.

All Waffen-SS officers were expected to purchase their own uniform items, and newly commissioned officers received a special grant of between 350 and 800 Reichsmarks to that end. Once in possession of his clothing grant the officer was supposed to buy his uniform from one of the SS clothing counters, or Kleiderkasse, at Berlin, Kiev, Lublin, Munich, Oslo, Paris, Prague, Riga and Warsaw. These establishments carried extensive stocks of top quality tailor-made items, including tunics by Mohr & Speyer and Holters, boots by Breitspecher and caps by Robert Lubstein, whose trade mark 'EREL' was famous worldwide. However, both the means and opportunity for front-line officers to kit themselves out with expensive uniforms were somewhat limited during the second half of the war, and most relied on their unit stores to provide them with items of field uniform against payment. Standard issue tunics were generally worn unaltered by most officers, although some had them modified to suit individual taste. The most common alterations were to pocket flaps and collars,

replacing them with smarter ones. From August 1943, second-hand tailor-made articles began to be collected and re-sold to officers at three times the listed price of their standard issue equivalents. In that way, those who still retained a desire to look 'a cut above the rest' could do so.

When a Waffen-SS soldier was killed or invalided out of the service, all issued items of uniform clothing and equipment had to be returned to his unit. Those pieces still suitable for use were retained intact, and slightly worn items were re-issued to replacement and training units. Any old or damaged clothing was sent to the concentration camps to be pulped down for reworking. Broken metal articles such as belt hooks and buckles were dismantled and sent to the armaments industry for smelting. In that way, the SS maintained a complete cycle of manufacture – issue – wear – pulping – re-manufacture – re-issue in respect of uniform clothing.

The development of the main components of Waffen-SS uniform, namely headgear, tunics, equipment and insignia, gave the SS soldier his own unique appearance, and this development is now covered in detail.

The standard headgear of the armed SS formations continually evolved from 1933 until the end of the Second World War, with every year seeing either a new pattern being introduced, an existing style being modified or an outdated item being withdrawn. In March 1933, members of the SS Stabswache Berlin were issued with heavyweight 1916 and 1918 model ex-army steel helmets, hand-painted or sprayed black, for wear when on guard duty. These plain Stahlhelme, which did not bear any SS insignia at that time, were the first distinguishing items of headgear to be sported by the armed units, and set the latter apart from the Allgemeine-SS. During the summer of the same year, field caps of the peakless 'pork pie' type, known as 'Krätzchen', were purchased from army

Men of the Sonderkommando Zossen enjoying a break from their training at Essenfassen, summer 1933. All wear black 'krätzchen' field caps and the grey cotton drill fatigue uniform.

surplus storage, dyed black, and distributed to men of the SS Sonderkommando Zossen and SS Sonderkommando Jüterbog for wear during training and fatigues. Standard SS badges were pinned to these extremely unpopular and short-lived caps.

At the end of 1933, it was suggested that the 1916 and 1918 model steel helmets were unnecessarily heavy for the armed SS, whose main role was then one of internal security rather than open warfare. A small number of the army's experimental 1933-pattern vulcanised fibre helmets were duly distributed, but were excessively ugly and immediately rejected. Consequently, during the early part of 1934, the Reichs-zeugmeisterei der NSDAP, or RZM, the Nazi party's contracts office, placed an order for

the supply of new SS helmets which were slightly different in form, weight and appearance from their army counterparts. The RZM-pattern helmet was made of a lighter steel alloy, had standardised 'one size' ventilation lugs and a wider quick-release chinstrap. There were two inspection marks die-stamped inside the neck of the blue-black helmet, i.e. SS runes on the left side and the RZM symbol on the right, and the liner generally bore the unit property stamp in ink, an example being 'II/SS 2' for the 2nd Sturmbann of the 'Germania' Standarte. The RZM helmet was popular, and was distributed for parade and guard duty until 1939.

On 23 February 1934, special insignia were introduced for wear on all SS steel helmets, hand-painted at first and then in decal form. The Leibstandarte, with its unique status, was authorised to use white SS runes on a black shield (soon replaced by black SS runes on a silver shield) on the right side of the helmet, and an army-pattern shield bearing the national colours of black, white and red in diagonal bars on the left side. Troops of the Politische Bereitschaften, and their successors in the SS-VT, wore white-bordered black runes within a white double circle on the right side of the Stahlhelm, and a white-bordered black swastika on the left side. On 15 December 1934, steel helmets began to be painted in so-called 'earth-grey', a grey-brown shade, for military manoeuvres, and at the same time a new other ranks' field cap in an identical colour was introduced to replace the black Krätzchen. The 1934-pattern cap was again intended for drill use only and was shaped like an upturned boat, hence its nickname 'Schiffchen', or little ship. Its design was based on the army forage cap, with a scalloped front and side panels which could be lowered to protect the wearer's ears in cold weather. The first Schiffchen were issued with a machine-embroidered version of the 1929-pattern eagle on the left side and a plain white metal button to the front. Soon after its introduction, however, the plain button was changed to one featuring an embossed death's head.

In March 1935, troops of the SS-Wachverbände were authorised to wear a large silver-painted Prussian Totenkopf on the left side of the steel helmet, to distinguish them from the Leibstandarte and SS-VT. This insignia was short-lived however, for on 12 August 1935 a new set of standardised helmet badges was introduced for all SS units, to replace those previously worn. The new insignia, designed by Professor Hans Haas, comprised black SS runes on a silver shield to be worn on the right side of the helmet, and a red shield bearing a white disc containing a

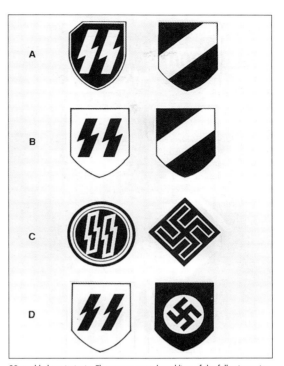

SS steel helmet insignia. These were worn by soldiers of the following units: A – Leibstandarte-SS 'Adolf Hitler' (23.2.34 to autumn 1934); B – Leibstandarte-SS 'Adolf Hitler' (autumn 1934 to 11.8.35); C – Politische Bereitschaften and SS-VT (23.2.34 to 11.8.35); D – all SS formations (12.8.35 to 1945).

black swastika to be worn on the left side. The original order decreed that these badges were to be painted on, but on 14 August it was announced that they would be available in decal form from the firm of C.A. Pocher of Nürnberg, at a cost of 25 Reichsmarks per 1,000 pairs. SS units were instructed to have the decals applied to all their helmets in time for the NSDAP rally that September.

Towards the end of 1935, an earth-grey version of the black SS peaked cap was introduced for officers of the Leibstandarte and SS-VT, to be worn on all occasions when a steel helmet was not required. The new Schirmmütze had an earth-grey top with a black velvet band and white piping for all

An NCO of the Leibstandarte wearing the M35 steel helmet outside Kharkov, March 1943. The SS runes decal is clearly shown.

officers up to and including SS-Standartenführer. Higher ranks had silver piping. Officers acting as judges and umpires at military exercises wore detachable white cloth bands on their caps. On 1 November the same year, a supply of the new lighter model army steel helmet, with shallow neck guard, less protruding visor and simple ventilation holes instead of protruding lugs, was set aside by the War Ministry for distribution to the armed SS. The Leibstandarte and 'Deutschland' received theirs on 11 May 1936, and the other SS-VT formations followed suit. Nevertheless, the traditional 1916 and 1918 models still continued to be worn for some considerable

time, particularly by officers and during parades.

On 31 March 1936, the other ranks' field cap began to be manufactured in a black version for wear with the black service uniform when walking out, and in 'earth-brown' for SS-TV personnel on duty within concentration camps. Insignia remained the same, although the 1929-pattern eagle was replaced by the distinctive SS type later in the year. A new field-grey combat uniform was generally distributed to all branches of the armed SS in 1937, with consequent changes in headgear. The earth-grey and earth-brown Schiffchen were replaced by a ubiquitous field-grey version, and the officer's peaked cap also began to be made with a field-grey top.

On 25 February 1938, a new field cap was created for NCOs. It was similar in appearance to the Schirmmütze, but the peak was made of the same cloth material as the top of the cap and there was no chinstrap or crown stiffener. It could be folded for storage in the back-pack or in a tunic pocket, hence its nickname 'the crusher'. Many NCOs who later became officers continued to wear this very popular cap throughout the war, and some individuals hired private tailors to make variants of it with leather peaks, velvet bands and silk linings. The regulation SS badges in white metal were prescribed for the NCO's field cap, but photographic evidence illustrates a wide variety of insignia, both metal and cloth, being worn with it.

In 1939, a less elaborate version of the field-grey peaked cap was authorised for wear by NCOs in the vicinity of their barracks. It was only after the black uniform had ceased to be worn as walking out dress that other ranks were issued with, or allowed to purchase, the field-grey peaked cap for walking out. It was similar to the officer's Schirmmütze, but had a black leather chinstrap rather than aluminium chincords, and a simple cloth band instead of a velvet one. In June 1939, officers were permitted to purchase a non-regulation white-topped peaked cap for wear with the new summer uniform.

The outbreak of war in September 1939 witnessed the first use by some rear echelon SS units of the so-called Edelstahlhelm, which had previously been issued only to police and firemen and was manufactured from a thin gauge steel. Soon afterwards, following army practice, an inverted chevron or *soutache* of braided piping in the appropriate branch of service colour began to be worn on the front of the other ranks' field cap, above the death's head button, which was thereafter

SS-Gruppenführer Gille was the first Waffen-SS recipient of the Knight's Cross with Oakleaves, Swords and Diamonds. For this presentation photograph, taken on 20 April 1944, he wore a fine example of the SS general's Schirmmütze, with aluminium piping.

painted field-grey. Armed SS officers still had no regulation field cap of their own, and during the first few months of the war many of them purchased the 1938-model army officer's forage cap and replaced or covered the national cockade with either a metal SS death's head or a small silver one removed from an army panzer collar patch. This obvious shortcoming in SS headgear was remedied in December 1939, however, when a new field cap was authorised specifically for Waffen-SS officers. It was again boat-shaped but did not have a scalloped front, and the side panels were gently sloping in the style of the Luftwaffe Fliegermütze. The top of the flap was piped in aluminium cord, and insignia consisted of the SS eagle and Totenkopf machine-woven in aluminium wire on a black ground. A Waffenfarbe *soutache* was worn over the death's head. All officers were instructed to equip themselves with the new field cap by 1 January 1940.

On 21 March 1940, the gaudy black, white and red swastika decal was ordered to be removed from SS steel helmets for the duration of the war, for camouflage reasons. At the same time, helmets began to be painted in a darker shade of field-grey and given a rough surface texture which was less prone to reflecting the light. In June, an order prohibited further manufacture of the white-topped summer peaked cap. On 15 October 1940, the other ranks' 1934-pattern field cap was replaced by a new style Schiffchen identical in cut to the officers' version. It became known as the 'Feldmütze neuer Art', or new model field cap, and featured a machine-woven eagle and death's head on the front of the cap instead of the Totenkopf button and side eagle. On 1 December the same year, the fledgling Waffen-SS alpine units received a field-grey Bergmütze, or mountain cap, to be worn instead of the Schiffchen. It was of basic ski-cap design, with a short peak to provide sufficient shade from the glare of the sun and snow. The scalloped side flaps could be lowered to cover the ears, and fastened at the front by means of two small buttons. Officers' caps had aluminium piping around the crown. Insignia comprised a woven death's head on the front of the cap and an eagle on the left side.

In February 1941, the manufacture and retailing of Waffen-SS peaked caps was freed from RZM control, and from then on the Schirmmütze could be made to individual order by private hatters. Four weeks later, the

1916, 1918 and RZM model steel helmets, and any old stocks of earth-grey cloth headgear still in use, were ordered to be withdrawn from service, and sent to the concentration camp and prison workshops for processing and re-issue to Wehrmacht reserve units. The winter of 1941–2 saw the first widespread use of fur caps, particularly captured Russian *ushankas*, by the Waffen-SS. An almost indescribable range of official, semi-official and unofficial winter caps quickly developed, and the insignia utilised was entirely dependent upon what was available at the time. Metal Schirmmütze badges, cloth Feldmütze insignia, sleeve eagles and even death's heads cut from SS-Totenkopf-Division collar patches have been observed in photographs.

On 1 August 1942, the smooth inward crimping of the steel helmet rim was abandoned for economic reasons, giving the model 1942 helmet a much sharper silhouette. The next month, the *soutache* was dropped and no longer featured on field caps. By 1943, practical experience at the front had shown the Schiffchen to be almost useless in comparison to the Bergmütze. On 1 October that year, therefore, a new field cap was introduced to replace all its predecessors. Known as the Einheitsfeldmütze, or standard field cap, it was very similar to the mountain cap but had a longer peak and lower crown. On 1 November 1943, the SS runes helmet decal was discontinued for the duration of the war. The year 1943 also saw the introduction of the fez, or Tarbusch, for wear instead of the field cap by members of the Muslim SS units. The fez was made from heavy field-grey felt, with a dark-green silken tassel and standard woven insignia. The unlined interior had a thin leather sweatband. A version in maroon was sometimes sported by officers when walking out or on parade, but this was an unofficial variant, obtained by converting the standard civilian fez, and

On 7 October 1944, Himmler spent his birthday visiting Waffen-SS units on the western front. Most of the young SS soldiers in this photograph wear the Einheitsfeldmütze.

was a temporary expedient pending issue of the field-grey type. Albanian Muslims had their own conical fez. In 1944, Italian SS formations made widespread use of former Italian army field caps, peaked caps and steel helmets, with the addition of appropriate insignia, and in 1945 some Indian volunteers transferred from the Wehrmacht wore turbans with Waffen-SS uniform. For Himmler, that must have been the 'final straw' in the development of SS headgear!

As with SS uniform in general, the aforementioned dates in the story of headgear can be invaluable in dating period photographs of Waffen-SS troops. The same can be said of tunics, so they also merit some

detailed coverage. Members of the first armed SS units wore the 1932-pattern black service uniform on all occasions. It was identical to the outfit issued to the Allgemeine-SS, but while it was impressive when worn on parade or when walking out, it proved totally impractical for use in the field or when performing general barrack duties. In order to protect the black uniform in such circumstances, tunics and trousers manufactured from a lightweight grey-white cotton drill were produced in the summer of 1933. Officers and NCOs subsequently wore a drill jacket which was cut very much like the black tunic, although sometimes with concealed buttons, and on which collar

The floppy, battle-worn appearance of the 'crusher' cap made it a popular item of headgear right up until the end of the war. Here it is worn by two NCOs of SS-Panzer-Aufklärungs-Abteilung 1 at Kaiserbarracke in the Ardennes, 17 December 1944. The schwimmwagen driver has kitted himself out with a civilian leather motoring helmet.

patches and a shoulder strap were worn. Other ranks had a less attractive, shapeless, badgeless tunic with a standing collar.

At the beginning of 1935 a new earth-grey uniform, identical in style to the black service outfit, began to be distributed to soldiers of the Leibstandarte and SS-Verfügungstruppe, although it was not referred to in official orders until 25 November of that year. Enlisted men's tunics had five buttons down the front instead of four, and could be worn closed at the neck. Since the standard SS armband with its bright colours was clearly unsuitable for field use, it was replaced on the left arm of the earth-grey tunic by an eagle and swastika. In March 1936, an earth-

brown version of the uniform was produced for everyday work wear for SS-Totenkopfverbände personnel on duty within the confines of concentration camps. It was not to be worn by sentries at the main gate, who were on view to the public, or as a walking out dress. The earth-brown tunic sported collar patches, a shoulder strap and the SS armband.

In 1937, the earth-grey and earth-brown uniforms of the SS-VT and SS-TV were replaced by a new standardised field-grey uniform. It was based on that of the army, but the Feldbluse retained the typically SS features of slanting slash side pockets and a black- and silver-piped collar which was the

Three SS-Hauptsturmführer attached to the 'Handschar' division at the end of 1943. Their decorations indicate that they are German nationals. The officer in the middle, a veteran of the SA/SS rally at Brunswick in 1931, wears the blank right-hand collar patch sported by some 'Handschar' personnel prior to the introduction of the divisional scimitar and swastika patch. Note also the early use of maroon fezzes and Styrian gaiters.

A Leibstandarte Obersturmführer is dwarfed by two recruits wearing the lightweight fatigue uniform, autumn 1934. The officer has a tailored grey drill jacket, used in conjunction with the cap and breeches of the black service uniform. Note also the 2nd pattern LAH helmet decals.

same colour as the rest of the tunic. The following year, the Leibstandarte began to be issued with army tunics, distinguished by their unpiped dark-green collars and pleated patch side pockets, for wear during training.

At the end of 1939, the sudden formation of the SS-Totenkopf-Division and the Polizei-Division necessitated the widespread and general use of army-issue tunics since there were insufficient quantities of the SS-style field-grey uniform to go round. Because of the basic differences in cut between the two patterns, and Himmler's desire for uniformity of dress, various contradictory orders were issued during the winter of 1939–40, prescribing which outfits should be worn by officers as opposed to NCOs and other ranks,

when they should be buttoned or unbuttoned at the neck, and so on. These orders were generally ignored by all concerned, and the result was a fair mixture of dress worn simultaneously within even the smallest units.

By May 1940, army tunics had begun to make their inevitable appearance in the ranks of the SS-Verfügungsdivision, and they soon became universal throughout the Waffen-SS. During the course of 1940, their dark-green collars were phased out in favour of field-grey ones, and that August the black and silver collar piping was discontinued. From 1942, purely for reasons of economy, patch pockets were made without pleats and in 1943 the lower edges of the pocket flaps were straightened. The wool content of the model

LAH, SS-VT and SS-TV officers on parade outside the Führer Building in Munich, 9 November 1938. During this period, the black uniform was still used by the armed SS on ceremonial occasions, here being worn with the aluminium wire aiguillettes and brocade belt of commissioned rank. Most of these men have been issued with the M35 steel helmet, although a few still retain the traditional M16/18 pattern.

1943 tunic was also drastically reduced, which resulted in poor thermal insulation and a low tensile strength. On 25 September 1944, an entirely new style of field service tunic based on the British army battledress blouse was introduced for wear by all German ground combat units, including members of auxiliary formations such as the RAD and NSKK. This uniform required considerably less cloth than the earlier models, and the normal triple or double belt hook location holes were reduced to only one position. Moreover, the internal field dressing pocket was omitted. A universal colour called 'Feldgrau 44', which was more slate-grey-green than field-grey, was devised for the new outfit in an effort to standardise the various military and paramilitary uniform colours hitherto seen on the battlefield. However, in reality, many different shades of it emerged. The 1944 field uniform was very unpopular, and was not issued in sufficient quantities to change the appearance of the Waffen-SS radically.

The victors of Kharkov: Rolf Möbius, 'Sepp' Dietrich, Rudolf Lehmann and Hubert Meyer in April 1943. Möbius wears a standard issue army pattern field blouse, which is rougher in appearance than the privately tailored outfits of Dietrich and Lehmann. Meyer's tunic is a converted prewar 'Rock', and still bears the 1936–8-style SS arm eagle.

The uniform regulations for Waffen-SS officers differed somewhat from those for other ranks. Until 1939, officers in the Leibstandarte and SS-VT had only one field-grey tunic, the 'Rock', which was identical in cut to the black SS service tunic and was always worn open at the neck with a brown shirt and black tie. At the beginning of the war, some SS officers avoided the expense of

having to buy a field blouse for combat wear by having their existing tunics converted, with the addition of stand-and-fall collars which could be closed at the neck. Others had dark-green open-necked collars fitted, even though that was expressly forbidden by Himmler. A number of similar stop-gap measures were taken until the issue of a general order in December 1939, which stipulated that officers' field tunics were henceforth to be identical in style to those of other ranks. Throughout the remainder of the war, Waffen-SS officers generally wore either privately tailored field blouses like those of their army colleagues, or basic issue tunics purchased from their unit stores. White summer versions were also produced, although these were officially prohibited in June 1940, and the olive-green waterproof cotton duck from captured Soviet groundsheets was often made up into lightweight unlined field tunics for hot weather use on the eastern front.

A captured SS-Sturmmann of the Leibstandarte is questioned regarding Russian banknotes found in his possession, autumn 1944. He wears the model 1943 tunic with straight pocket flaps, and a late war round-headed arm eagle.

Three Waffen-SS medical officers assist personnel of the 15th (Scottish) Division after the liberation of Neuengamme concentration camp, April 1945. The Untersturmführer on the left wears the 1944 field uniform, which bears a striking resemblance to the British army battledress also shown in the photograph. The man in the centre, with the M42 tunic, has contradictory rank insignia, i.e. the collar patch of an Untersturmführer and shoulder straps of an Obersturmführer. The Einheitsfeldmütze worn by the third SS officer sports the rarely seen triangular one-piece eagle and death's head insignia.

As tunics developed, so too did their matching trousers. The 1937-pattern SS field trousers, or Feldhose, had straight legs for wear with jackboots, whereas the Keilhose, or wedge trousers, of July 1942 had tapered bottoms designed to fit inside the new ankle boots and gaiters. Officers on duty in the field generally wore riding breeches, with grey buckskin reinforcements on the seat and inside leg. In August 1944, however, they were ordered to wear only long trousers, to show a degree of uniformity with their men. Needless to say, that order was seldom adhered to.

While most Waffen-SS units were issued with one or more of the foregoing series of uniforms, depending upon their dates of formation, the Italians alone were not. At the end of 1943, SS-Obergruppenführer Karl Wolff, the HSSPf in Italy, successfully bargained with the army's Quartermaster-General for the supply of 100,000 captured Italian army uniforms for wear by his SS and police anti-partisan forces. Many of these items were subsequently used to kit out the 24th and 29th SS divisions, whose members duly sported a hodge-podge of Italian garb in grey-green, colonial khaki and Mediterranean camouflage, with their own unique insignia.

The creation of standardised camouflage clothing was the most significant contribution of the Waffen-SS to the history of military uniform development, and had a profound effect on the appearance of all modern soldiery. In February 1937, SS-Sturmbannführer Wilhelm Brandt, who was a Doctor of Engineering and commander of the SS-VT reconnaissance battalion, began work on the design of camouflage clothing and equipment for use by his troops. He shared his task with the Munich professor Johann Georg Otto Schick, and their prototype camouflage groundsheets and helmet covers were successfully tested by the SS-Standarte 'Deutschland' in field manoeuvres the

following December, during which it was estimated that they would reduce battle casualties by 15 per cent. In June 1938, patents in respect of these items were granted to the Reichsführer-SS, so that they could not be copied by the army, and by 1 November contracted production was under way using the firms of Warei, Forster and Joring. By January 1939, despite great difficulties in obtaining sufficient quantities of waterproof cotton duck and the fact that printing had to be done by hand, 8,400 groundsheets and 6,800 helmet covers had been supplied to the SS-Verfügungstruppe. Smocks were also in the course of distribution, and Hausser instructed that at least twenty of these should be held by each company for the exclusive use of assault troops.

Camouflage clothing was not widely worn during the Polish campaign, but even so the revolutionary SS groundsheets and helmet covers earned high praise from Generalmajor Kempf, who sent samples of them to the Army High Command in Berlin for evaluation. By June 1940, hand-printing had been superseded by a much faster machine process using 'Anthrasol' and 'Indanthrene' dyes, which allowed the mass production of 33,000 smocks for delivery to all field units of the Waffen-SS. The ever-present problem, however, even at that early date, was the shortage of raw materials. It was calculated that over 42,000 metres of waterproof cotton duck would be required every month to produce sufficient numbers of groundsheets, helmet covers and smocks, and by January 1943 supplies had all but run out, resulting in its replacement by drill material which had no waterproof qualities.

Many styles of camouflage were ultimately manufactured simultaneously, including the so-called 'oak leaf', 'plane tree', 'palm tree', 'burred edge', 'flower' and 'clump' patterns. Four colours were generally used, and the tendency during the war was towards increasingly spotted designs in lighter shades. Most garments made from waterproof cotton duck were printed on both sides and were reversible, with one side predominantly green and the other brown for use as local and seasonal variations dictated. The later drill outfits were printed on one side only and could not be reversed. All of these patterns were issued indiscriminately throughout the Waffen-SS.

The groundsheet, or Zeltbahn, was the first item of camouflage uniform to see widespread distribution among SS units. It was triangular in shape, measuring 203 cm × 203 cm × 240 cm, and could be worn as a cape or poncho, or buttoned together with three others to form a four-man tent. In fact, any number could be combined to make even larger shelters. When attaching Zeltbahnen in such circumstances care had to be taken to use identical, or at least similar, pattern groundsheets to maintain the camouflage effect, and to that end identifying numbers were printed along their bases. Even when combining shelter quarters of different designs, 'paving slabs' of colour were provided along the edges at regular intervals so that the various camouflage patterns would merge into each other. In December 1943, it was decided not to issue any more groundsheets to men on the eastern front for economic reasons, and by September 1944 their production had ceased completely.

The steel helmet cover was produced from segments of Zeltbahn material, and consequently occasionally featured the identifying printed pattern number. It was designed to conform to the shape of the model 1935 Stahlhelm and was attached by means of three spring-loaded blackened steel clips held on by bare aluminium rivets, one at each side and one at the rear. The 1937 prototype also had a fourth frontal clip, but that was later replaced by a simple fold of material and was never subsequently adopted

SS assault troops wearing newly issued camouflage smocks and helmet covers, May 1940.

for field use. Covers made from 1942 onwards had loops sewn on to hold foliage.

The camouflage smock was a reversible pullover garment gathered at the neck by means of an adjustable cord and at the wrists and waist by elastic. It had no collar and the

A captured SS-Unterscharführer being searched in February 1945. His lack of collar tresse indicates that this man was probably recently promoted in the field. The undyed grey-white interior of the camouflage drill tunic is clearly visible.

first pattern had no pockets, only two vertical openings at the front which gave the wearer access to his tunic underneath. During the war, various modifications were made to it including the adoption of a longer 'skirt', foliage loops sewn in threes to the shoulders and upper sleeves, and the addition of two side pockets with buttoned flaps. However, all smocks conformed to the standard manufacturing process, being cut out from a long strip of Zeltbahn material, with a central hole for fitting over the head. Production ceased in January 1944, although smocks continued to be worn widely until the end of the war.

On 15 April 1942 a camouflage face mask, which had initially been rejected by Hausser during prewar trials, was issued for use in conjunction with the helmet cover and smock. It comprised a series of strings fitted to an elasticated strap and hung like a curtain over the face. The mask was very effective when used in bushy or grassy terrain, and was much prized by snipers. On 1 June the same year, a camouflage field cap, again made from waterproof Zeltbahn material, was introduced. It was shaped like the Bergmütze and was generally unlined and reversible. From December 1942, special insignia woven in green and brown artificial silk were produced for wear on the cap, but they do not appear to have been widely adopted.

On 1 March 1944, a camouflage version of the drill uniform was introduced for both field and working dress. It comprised a tunic

230

Waffen-SS infantry advancing through the Ardennes, December 1944. The man in the foreground, armed with an MP40, wears the camouflage drill jacket on top of a standard field-grey tunic.

and trousers in the same cut as the model 1943 field uniform, but made from lightweight unlined herringbone twill with a standardised spotted or 'pea' pattern camouflage printed on one side only. It could be worn on its own during the summer, or on top of a standard field uniform in cold weather, and was designed to replace the smock and, ultimately, the normal field and drill uniforms. Only the eagle and swastika and special rank badges were intended to be worn on the left sleeve of the tunic, but shoulder straps and other insignia were also occasionally seen. Between 1 November 1944 and 15 March 1945, distribution of the camouflage drill uniform was suspended because of intolerable losses during the winter months. In effect, it was never re-issued.

While the vast majority of Waffen-SS troops wore one or more of the foregoing camouflage garments, there were many instances of non-regulation items being adopted. It was not uncommon for tunics to be tailor-made in the field using spare Zeltbahn material, and large quantities of caps, tunics and trousers in German cut were manufactured from captured Italian camouflage cloth in 1944. There were also isolated cases of Waffen-SS personnel, particularly members of the 14th SS Division, wearing German army-pattern camouflage smocks. A photograph even exists apparently showing the capture of an SS sniper in

On 9 July 1940, the reconnaissance battalion of the SS-Verfügungsdivision crossed the Hendaye Bridge on the Franco-Spanish border to form a guard of honour at a meeting between Hitler and General Franco. These men are from the armoured car platoon, and wear the SS panzerjacke and the ill-fated Baskenmütze, which was discontinued shortly thereafter.

Normandy who is wearing the one-piece camouflage overall issued to US troops serving in the Pacific theatre. However, that may well have been a propaganda shot staged by the Allies. By the spring of 1945 it had become apparent that both the Wehrmacht and Waffen-SS should ideally have one common camouflage pattern. After various tests and trials carried out by Schick and three SS officers from the Bekleidungswerke at Dachau, a new design incorporating carbon-black segments which had the effect of protecting the wearer against infra-red detection was introduced. It never saw

distribution during the Third Reich, but was to form the basis of the camouflage patterns adopted by most post-1945 armies.

SS-VT armoured troops received their own black panzer uniform in 1938. Its special headgear took the form of a floppy woollen beret, or Baskenmütze, fitted over an internal crash helmet, the Schutzmütze, which comprised a heavily padded liner. A large embroidered SS eagle and a uniquely designed Totenkopf, not unlike the army's panzer death's head but with a lower jaw in the SS style, was sewn on to the front of the beret. The Baskenmütze was discontinued in 1940

SS-Untersturmführer Michael Wittmann and his Leibstandarte Tiger crew after being decorated in January 1944. They were killed near Caen seven months later, but not before they had become the most successful team of tank soldiers in history, destroying over 270 enemy vehicles. Only the gunner, Balthasar Woll (second from left), survived the war.

after proving impractical in combat. It was replaced by a black version of the Schiffchen field cap, which in turn was superseded by a black Einheitsfeldmütze in October 1943. The Waffen-SS tank tunic, or Panzerjacke, was a short, tight-fitting double-breasted black jacket fastened with concealed buttons. It differed from its army counterpart in that the front was cut vertically instead of being slanted, the lapels were smaller and there was no central seam down the back. The collar of the jacket was piped in silver for officers but was unpiped for other ranks, and only NCOs of the Leibstandarte were permitted to sport their regulation collar tresse.

In the spring of 1941, a field-grey version of the panzer uniform was issued to members of the Leibstandarte's Sturmgeschütz-Abteilung. By August 1942 this outfit had been distributed to other assault gun units, and four months later its wear was extended to all Waffen-SS anti-tank formations.

On 15 January 1943, SS panzer crews received a one-piece combination work uniform made of camouflage waterproof cotton duck, identical to the material used in the manufacture of the smock and Zeltbahn. At the same time, a winter combination made from two thicknesses of cloth, white on one side and field-grey on the other, was introduced and was worn widely during the Battle of Kharkov. These coverall combinations were never very popular, simply because of the difficulty of getting in and out of them. That fact, allied with the success of the denim gear then on issue and the extreme shortage of waterproof cotton duck, led to the decision being made in January 1944 to discontinue the camouflage combination and produce instead a lightweight version of the panzer uniform in camouflage herringbone twill. It duly appeared two months later, at the same time as the camouflage drill uniform introduced for all other Waffen-SS units, and it was in the same standardised spotted 'pea' pattern, unlined and printed on one side only. The camouflage panzer uniform saw widespread service, particularly on the western front. On 1 November distribution ceased for the winter, and the camouflage outfit was never re-issued.

While the clothing of Waffen-SS armoured personnel remained fairly standard, there was one major initiative at divisional level which drastically altered the appearance of many panzer crews participating in the Normandy campaign. During the autumn of 1943, the Leibstandarte had been involved in disarming capitulated Italian forces and in fighting partisans in northern Italy. In the process, the division had confiscated huge quantities of abandoned Italian motor transport and uniform equipment to supplement its own limited supplies. Among the uniform items seized were large numbers of German U-boat leather jackets and trousers, originally sold by Hitler to Mussolini's navy, and vast stocks of Italian army camouflage material. The latter was quickly used to produce caps, tunics and overalls in the German style, which were distributed to soldiers of the Leibstandarte and 'Hitlerjugend' in France. The U-boat clothing went almost exclusively to the young tank crews of 'Hitlerjugend', and duly protected many of them against serious burns.

Waffen-SS paratroopers also had their own order of dress. SS-Fallschirmjäger Bataillon 500 was formed for 'special duties' at the end of 1943, in the wake of SS-Hauptsturmführer Otto Skorzeny's much-vaunted liberation of the deposed Mussolini that September, which had had to rely on Luftwaffe glider and paratroop support. Contrary to widespread belief, the battalion was not a penal unit. It was composed entirely of volunteers, fully trained in a paratroop role, and all its officers and NCOs were professional soldiers with a great deal of front-line experience. This expertise, combined with the Waffen-SS ethos, produced paratroopers of outstanding ability.

The first major action in which the battalion was deployed, Operation 'Rösselsprung', or 'Knight's Move', involved its being dropped by glider right on top of Marshal Tito's vast partisan headquarters complex at Bastasi, near Drvar in Yugoslavia, where Winston Churchill's son, Major Randolph Churchill, was head of the British military mission. The plan was to capture Tito on his birthday, 25 May 1944, and hold him until support could arrive from the 'Prinz Eugen' Division and other nearby conventional ground formations. However, the SS paras were too small a force to take on the partisan brigades entrenched in the mountain fortress, and they were surrounded in Drvar cemetery and almost wiped out. The survivors were reformed as SS-Fallschirmjäger Bataillon 600, under Skorzeny's command, and trained for a drop on Budapest to capture the son of the recalcitrant Hungarian leader Admiral Horthy, who duly capitulated to the Germans. Some SS paratroopers were later involved in the Ardennes offensive and the remainder fought as infantry on the eastern front, going into captivity at the end of the war.

Of all the branches of the Waffen-SS, least

SS paratroopers entrenched in the defensive positions around Schwedt on the eastern front, February 1945. All wear Luftwaffe Fallschirmjäger helmets, and the men in the foreground have standard Waffen-SS field-grey tunics.

is known about the clothing and equipment of the parachutists. No official uniform orders have come to light, and almost total reliance has to be placed on a few extant wartime photographs. It appears that the Luftwaffe assumed responsibility not only for the training and transportation by air of the SS paras, but also for supplying them with specialist dress and equipment. When Skorzeny and his small joint SS and Luftwaffe commando force rescued Mussolini from his imprisonment at Gran Sasso, they all wore regulation air force tropical clothing with full Luftwaffe insignia. At a celebratory rally held in the Berlin Sports Palace soon afterwards, however, the SS men reverted to their normal field-grey uniforms. The members of the SS-

Fallschirmjäger Bataillone 500 and 600 wore 1940-pattern SS Schiffchen field caps, SS belt buckles and standard Waffen-SS field-grey tunics with the insignia of their previous units, since there were no specialist SS paratroop badges. The Luftwaffe supplied all their protective clothing, which comprised: the normal paratroop steel helmet, with or without the air force eagle decal and geometric 'splinter'-pattern camouflage cover; the 'splinter'-pattern camouflage paratroop smock, with or without Luftwaffe breast eagle; blue-grey or field-grey paratroop trousers; canvas gaiters; and ankle boots. One surviving photograph shows two German paratroopers wearing standard SS-issue camouflage smocks, but these are thought to be Luftwaffe Fallschirmjäger personnel in Italy, who would have had the opportunity of obtaining SS smocks from the 'Hermann Göring' Panzer Division, which was kitted out with them. Another unique picture illustrates an SS paratrooper apparently wearing the 'pea' pattern camouflage drill tunic and trousers while fulfilling an infantry role on the eastern front near the end of the war.

While Waffen-SS troops never served in North Africa, there was a special SS tropical uniform. A number of units, primarily the Leibstandarte, 'Wiking', 'Prinz Eugen' and 'Reichsführer-SS', saw action in the Balkans, southern Russia and Italy, where the sweltering summer conditions made the wearing of conventional uniform items very uncomfortable indeed. The demand for hot weather clothing was usually localised and temporary, however, so the development of a tropical uniform for the Waffen-SS was gradual and on an ad hoc basis.

The first requirement for tropical clothing was voiced in April 1941, during the hastily organised invasion of Greece, but on 15 April Himmler specifically prohibited his officers from using the recently introduced army tropical outfit. Consequently, troops of the Leibstandarte and 'Reich' completed their race through the country wearing heavy regulation tunics and headgear, which proved far from ideal. Some members took to wearing the basic SS sports kit, comprising vest and shorts, when not engaged in combat, while others went bare-chested. A short-term partial solution was achieved by the issue of German, Italian, Dutch and captured British pith helmets, or Tropenhelme, diverted from the army's 5th Light Division. However, these items were generally unpopular and were not worn in any great numbers. When sported by the SS, they bore no insignia.

During the autumn of 1942, SS-Division 'Wiking' advanced deep into the Caucasus region and the real need for hot weather clothing again became apparent. Following upon Himmler's prohibition on the wear of the army's olive-green tropical uniform, some 'Wiking' personnel adopted the Luftwaffe's version instead. It was made from light tan cotton drill and comprised an unlined four-pocket tunic, Schiffchen field cap and baggy trousers. All Luftwaffe insignia were removed and replaced by standard SS badges from the field-grey uniform. On 15 February 1943, SS chevrons in tan-brown on black were created for wear with the tropical tunic by personnel of the ranks of Sturmmann and Rottenführer. At the same time, the use of collar patches with the tropical tunic was forbidden.

In September 1943, a wholly new and, for the first time, formalised Waffen-SS tropical uniform was introduced and distributed on an entire unit basis to the Sturmbrigade 'Reichsführer-SS' on Corsica. The uniform was a strange hybrid and may, in fact, have been made by converting Italian clothing which had recently been seized by the Germans. The tunic had pleated patch pockets in the army style, was coloured light tan in the Luftwaffe style, and featured a caped effect across the upper section in the Italian Sahariana style, the peaks of the 'cape' forming the upper pocket flaps. Insignia was officially restricted to shoulder straps, tropical sleeve chevrons and a special tan-brown woven version of the SS arm eagle, but normal collar patches were also occasionally seen. An SS tropical field cap, to accompany the new tunic, was in the same shape as the Einheitsfeldmütze, but without the flaps and buttons. Cut like the SS camouflage field cap, it was again light tan in colour and sported a tan-brown woven eagle and death's head. Photographic evidence suggests that the 1943-pattern Waffen-SS tropical tunic was only ever issued in quantity to the Sturmbrigade 'Reichsführer-SS', and even then was not worn by members of that formation after they left Corsica to become the nucleus of the 16th SS-Panzergrenadier Division. The Sturmbrigade, a force of around 2,000 men which grew from Himmler's escort battalion, appears to have been chosen to field-test and evaluate the new tunic on an experimental basis. Whether it was reported upon adversely, or whether economies and the lack of tropical campaigns after 1943 dictated that no more stocks of the tunic would be manufactured, is unknown. In any event, it was never issued in large numbers again, although a few jackets were used by officers of the 'Skanderbeg' Division and by men of the 8th SS-Panzergrenadier Regiment in Greece. The SS tropical field cap, on the other hand, was widely distributed among various units fighting in Italy during 1944–5, and was a popular item of dress.

During the last year of the war, members of SS formations fighting in Italy, Austria and the Balkans reverted to wearing a mixture of Wehrmacht and Italian tropical clothing, as availability and climate dictated. Luftwaffe items were most prized, particularly the tunic and Schiffchen, and the latter could often be seen sporting metal SS badges removed from the peaked cap. Moreover, despite the versatility of the camouflage helmet cover, it was not uncommon for Waffen-SS men to paint their steel helmets sand-yellow while serving in the Mediterranean area.

Various items of protective clothing were widely distributed to Waffen-SS personnel, irrespective of their branch of service. As early as July 1935, the Leibstandarte was issued with an earth-grey double-breasted greatcoat, or Mantel, which bore collar piping and full insignia. This item was superseded by a field-grey version in 1937, and with the military development of the SS-VT and SS-TV there was a tendency to follow closely army greatcoat fashions, which led to the gradual adoption of a dark-green collar and the ad hoc removal of collar patches. By

'Sepp' Dietrich's field-grey leather greatcoat, with SS-Obergruppenführer shoulder straps. It bears the maker's label of 'Schuchart & Tschach, Dresden'.

the outbreak of war, the situation as regards greatcoat insignia was muddled and various orders were issued in an attempt to clarify the position. The dark-green collar was officially approved in December 1939, only to be cancelled a few months later. Collar piping for other ranks became obsolete in August 1940, and all surviving examples of the old earth-grey coat were recalled in March 1941. Officers with the rank of SS-Oberführer and above were permitted to wear the greatcoat with the top three buttons undone, in order to expose their distinctive silver-grey lapels, and from 1941 holders of the Knight's Cross or any other neck award were also allowed to do so, for the purpose of displaying their decorations. As the war progressed, many officers countered the declining quality of the issue Mantel by having greatcoats tailor-made

A soldier of the 51st (Highland) Division with two Waffen-SS captives in Normandy. The officer in the middle wears the regulation motorcyclist's coat. Note also the unofficial attachment of cords to his 'crusher' field cap.

to their own specifications. These items incorporated such refinements as removable blanket linings, reinforced buttons, extra pockets and detachable sheepskin or fur collars. The result of all this was that dozens of variations on the basic Waffen-SS greatcoat came to be produced and worn side-by-side, many of them in contravention of regulations. Moreover, a massive version of the Mantel, called the surcoat or Übermantel, was designed to be worn on top of the ordinary greatcoat by drivers of open motor vehicles or those on static sentry duty.

Officers had the option of purchasing a field-grey leather greatcoat, but this item was extremely expensive and few subalterns could afford it. There were several variants, both in cut and in the use of insignia. As an alternative to the Ledermantel, many junior officers and NCOs bought the much cheaper 1938-pattern field-grey raincoat, the so-called Regenmantel, made of rubberised cotton twill with a leather-like appearance. Others used the regulation motorcyclist's coat, or Kradschutzmantel, which was first introduced for army despatch riders and eventually came to be widely worn by a variety of Wehrmacht, Waffen-SS and police personnel during inclement weather. Early examples had a dark-green cloth collar, but after 1940 the whole coat was made from rubberised fabric. The skirt could be divided and buttoned around the legs for ease of use on the motorcycle.

Following the disastrous winter campaign of 1941–2, when no adequate warm clothing was provided for German soldiers fighting on the Russian front, preparations were made to design and supply appropriate uniform items with a view to averting a similar crisis. Various fur, sheepskin and lambswool waistcoats and caps were issued in the short term, and snow anoraks originally intended for mountain troops in Norway were diverted and shipped east. Wherever shortages were still apparent, captured Soviet winter clothing was issued, augmented by civilian items collected in Germany. Throughout 1942, the Waffen-SS developed its own winter combat uniform, or Winter-Sonderbekleidung, independent of the Wehrmacht. It consisted of a heavy, fur-lined parka-type coat in a waterproof cement-grey gabardine, with matching overtrousers. When snow lay on the ground, an undyed white cotton hooded smock and trousers were issued. These were designed to be worn on top of the parka and overtrousers and were readily washable. At the end of the year, a padded reversible parka in a waterproof rayon, white on one side and tan or reed-green on the other, was distributed for use as a windcheater.

The definitive Waffen-SS winter uniform did not enter service until 1943–4, and comprised a hood, jacket, trousers and mittens all made from two layers of windproof material with a wool-rayon interlining. The whole outfit was reversible, being white on one side and SS autumn camouflage on the other, and was designed to be worn over the normal field uniform. The white side tended to get filthy very quickly, which defeated its purpose, so troops were ordered to wear the uniform with the camouflage side out unless they were actually fighting in snow-covered terrain. During 1944, a small number of similar garments

Totenkopf troops in Kharkov, March 1943. The tank commander (whose cap's death's head has almost fallen off!) sports an unofficial sheepskin waistcoat, while his colleagues have been issued with the fur-lined cement-grey parka.

were made utilising stocks of captured Italian camouflage material. The manufacture of fur-lined items for the Waffen-SS was generally undertaken by the Ostindustrie GmbH, and was a speciality of the SS-Bekleidungswerke in the Lublin area, primarily at the Poniatowa and Trawniki labour camps. Fur garments removed from concentration camp inmates throughout the Reich were ordered to be collected and forwarded to Lublin for reprocessing. It is a sad fact that many Waffen-SS soldiers wore winter uniforms lined with fox-furs and stoles taken from old women who had died at Auschwitz, Majdanek, Sobibor and Treblinka.

Away from the front line, the basic SS sports kit comprised a white vest, black

Even the fur-lined winter combat uniform could not always provide sufficient warmth. This miserable-looking Waffen-SS machine-gunner on a static position in the Toropez Forest at the end of 1943 has had to resort to wrapping a blanket around his legs and feet.

shorts, white socks and black shoes. The front of the vest bore a large black woven badge featuring the SS runes within a circle. A black vest with reverse insignia colours was also available as an alternative for wear during team events where the opponents would be in white. Members of the Leibstandarte had their own shield-shaped sports vest badge, comprising an eagle's head surmounted by the 'LAH' monogram. A two-piece black tracksuit with white SS runes was issued for 'warming up' exercises, while SS fencers had silver runes within a black diamond stitched to the upper left sleeve of the padded fencing jacket. Sportswear was

not generally issued to the Waffen-SS after 1941, for reasons of economy, and was thereafter reserved for members of sports teams and for wounded soldiers engaged in exercises and physiotherapy associated with their recuperation.

The standard footwear of the early armed SS troops comprised two pairs of high marching boots or 'jackboots', one of which was for daily use and the other for parades. From 1934, Leibstandarte non-commissioned personnel were also issued with a pair of the shorter army field service marching boots, the so-called Knobelbecher, or 'dice-shakers', and a pair of lace-up ankle boots for barrack duties. Officers generally wore high black riding boots which were privately purchased and so were not of a standard pattern. The first wartime economy measure to hit SS footwear was the reduction in the height of the marching boot in November 1939. The distribution of Knobelbecher to replacement and reserve units ceased completely in November 1940, and from July 1942 a standard lace-up ankle boot was issued to most Waffen-SS personnel instead of the marching boot. However, the very concept of short boots and gaiters was hated by the majority of German soldiers, who spoke of 'retreat gaiters' and retained their traditional high marching boots for as long as possible. In fact, the latter made the wearer very prone to developing varicose veins, and many a Waffen-SS infantryman had cause to curse his prized jackboots in later life.

The boots issued to mountain troops had a specially designed lace-up ankle and thick studded soles to aid climbing and skiing. In the summer of 1943, the Waffen-SS developed its own style of mountain gaiters based on the old Austrian army 'Styrian' pattern. These were made from various types and colours of leather and canvas, covered the top of the boot like spats, and laced on the outside. Styrian gaiters were widely distributed to the 'Prinz Eugen' and 'Handschar' Divisions in the Balkans during 1943–4. A number of heavy duty items of footwear, including overboots in compressed and moulded felt, leather or thick layers of plaited straw, were devised to combat the sub-zero temperatures which regularly prevailed on the eastern front. During 1944–5, the quality of issue footwear declined dramatically, and by the end of the war it was not uncommon to see Waffen-SS soldiers wearing captured enemy boots.

While Waffen-SS uniforms were in many ways distinct from those of the other Wehrmacht forces, the Waffen-SS was issued with the same weapons and equipment as the German army during the Second World War. This equipment encompassed everything from belt leathers, straps and small arms, to mortars, armour and heavy artillery. Initially, ordnance and vehicles were painted field-grey or slate-grey, but by 1943 these shades had proved impractical when used on fronts with different terrains. Consequently, a dark sand-yellow was universally adopted throughout the Wehrmacht as the standard base colour for metal equipment. During the remainder of the war, tanks, assault guns, Panzerfausts and even hand grenades left the factory painted dark yellow, the idea being that a secondary coat of any appropriate camouflage paint could be applied locally as required.

A 42 mm-wide black leather waist belt, or Koppel, with 1931-pattern SS 'box' buckle in nickel-plated steel or matt grey alloy, was issued to all Waffen-SS NCOs and other ranks and was worn with all orders of dress. Since the belt was traditionally removed for safety reasons when a soldier was placed under close arrest (in case he hanged himself with it), its absence came to be regarded as a degradation, and the only non-commissioned personnel allowed out of barracks without wearing their belts were those in military hospitals or convalescing. The SS officer's

buckle, which was circular in shape, was devised for peacetime use and tended to break or come undone in action. However, all attempts to modify it were rejected outright by Himmler on the grounds that it had been 'designed by the Führer himself, and based on his own sketches'. As a result, many officers adopted either the sturdier rectangular other ranks' SS buckle or the basic two-pronged open-face army buckle when in the field.

Most enlisted personnel in front-line SS units were armed with 7.92 mm Kar.98k rifles and M84/98 bayonets, while NCOs and assault squad leaders had MP38 and MP40 submachine-guns. Other semi-automatic and automatic weapons on common issue to the Waffen-SS included the MP28, MG34, MG42, MP43, MP44 and StG44. Entrenching tools, gas masks, bread bags, back-packs, fighting knives, map cases and binoculars were standard army issue, albeit some items of field equipment were made for the SS in their own concentration camp and prison factories. Pistol holsters were usually bought or issued with their accompanying weapons. The service pistols of the Waffen-SS were the 9 mm 'Luger' Parabellum PO8 and the Walther P38, although at the beginning of the war large numbers of obsolete weapons such as the 'broomhandle' Mauser and captured Czech and Polish pistols were frequently carried as well. The preferred officers' side-arm was the handy 7.65 mm Walther PPK, which could be purchased from the local SS Kleiderkasse on presentation of the officer's identity papers. According to an order issued by Himmler on 1 January 1943, the pistol had to be worn on the left hip, barrel facing to the back, when in the operational zone and on the right hip, barrel facing to the front, when on home territory (i.e. when the sword or chained dagger might be worn on the left side). In October 1944, SS officers were instructed to carry loaded pistols at all times when in public, and reminded to take extra care to ensure that they were not stolen when frequenting railway stations, dance halls and the like.

In addition to these, there were several other items of personal equipment commonly carried by the Waffen-SS, including field torches, goggles, compasses, pencils, maps, prescribed spectacles and sundries such as tobacco and army condoms. On a cord around his neck, every SS soldier wore an oval zinc identity disc which was divided in half by perforated holes and bore details of his service number, unit and blood group (the latter also being tattooed under his arm). In the event of his death in action, the disc was broken in half, the portion on the cord remaining with the body and the other half being taken away for recording purposes.

While the majority of wartime Waffen-SS uniforms were made by SS-owned economic enterprises, the insignia attached to them tended to be manufactured by long-established German private companies. That arrangement necessitated strict standardisation and quality control, the administration of which was entrusted to the Reichszeugmeisterei, or RZM, a body which had been set up as early as 1 April 1929 to supervise the production and pricing of all Nazi party uniform items. The basic functions of the RZM were to see that NSDAP contracts went to Aryan firms and to ensure that final products were of a high standard yet priced to suit the pocket of the average party member. It also acted as a 'clearing house' between manufacturers on the one hand and wholesalers and retailers on the other. On 16 March 1935, contract numbers were introduced and awarded to every RZM-approved company, and after that date RZM numbers replaced makers' marks on all NSDAP accoutrements. Thus the buttons, belt hooks and so on of the Allgemeine-SS, which always remained an organ of the Nazi party, consistently featured

RZM marks. Those of the Waffen-SS, however, which was in effect a state arm during the war, very seldom did.

Waffen-SS insignia, like that of the SS in general, fell into several distinct categories according to manufacture. Metal badges such as eagles and death's heads for the peaked cap, Totenkopf buttons for the 1934-pattern field cap, shoulder strap ciphers and rank pips were made in a variety of materials, dependent primarily upon date of production. The most common combinations were:

1. Plated brass or Tombakbronze (1933–6)
2. Copper-plated aluminium with a surface wash (1936–45)
3. Bare aluminium (1936–45)
4. Plated or painted steel (1939–45)
5. Plated or painted zinc (1942–5)
6. Bare zinc (1944–5)

In general terms the quality of metals used declined as the war progressed, but despite that a good standard of overall finish and appearance was always maintained.

Cap eagles and death's heads, which were common to both the Allgemeine-SS and Waffen-SS, normally bore RZM marks, either individually stamped on to the badge reverse or embossed into it as part of the die-striking or casting process. Typical examples were 'RZM M1/52' (Deschler & Sohn of Munich) and 'RZM M1/167' (Augustin Hicke of Tyssa bei Bodenbach). Some items also bore the 'VA' inspection stamp of the SS Verwaltungsamt. During the war, the format of RZM codes used on metal SS insignia changed, deleting the 'M1' prefix and adding a year suffix, e.g. 'RZM 499/41'. No list of these later codes is known to have survived, and so they have never been deciphered.

The earliest SS cloth badges were hand-embroidered, and this form of insignia was worn by soldiers of the armed SS during 1933–5. Hand-embroidery could be in white

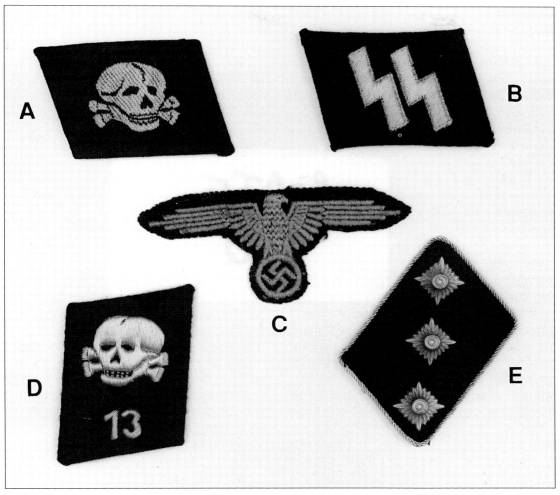

A selection of Waffen-SS cloth insignia: A – 1943-pattern horizontal death's head collar patch, BEVO machine-woven in silver-grey cotton thread; B – SS runes, or Sig-Runes, collar patch machine-embroidered in silver-grey cotton; C – 1938-pattern SS arm eagle with curved head, machine-embroidered in silver-grey cotton c. 1942–3; D – vertical 'death's head/13' collar patch, hand-embroidered in aluminium wire; E – rank collar patch for an SS-Untersturmführer.

or silver-grey cotton thread, fine aluminium wire or heavy silver bullion, with the latter two styles normally being reserved for officers. However, in September 1934 non-commissioned and enlisted ranks of the LAH and SS-VT were also authorised to wear aluminium wire insignia with the black uniform, to set them apart from their colleagues in the Allgemeine-SS. No two hand-embroidered badges were ever identical, since they were individually made. Badge companies generally employed women to do this work, or farmed it out to local seamstresses.

In 1936, by which time the RZM had become effectively organised under Reichszeugmeister Richard Büchner, machine-embroidered insignia began to be produced

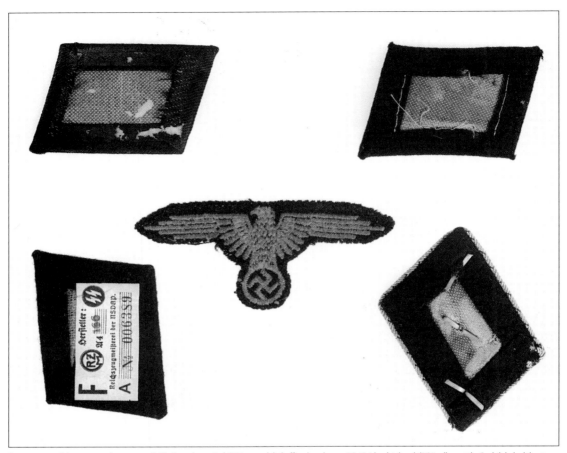

Reverse view of the insignia shown on p. 243. Note the typical RZM paper label affixed to the pre-1940 'death's head/13' collar patch. Such labels did not appear on later wartime pieces.

and widely distributed for wear by SS enlisted men and NCOs. This form of embroidery was cheap and quick to execute, and had a tightly formed and raised appearance. The producers of machine-embroidered insignia were normally fairly substantial firms, as only they could afford the expensive equipment involved in the manufacturing process. Such companies were rigidly controlled by the RZM, and their products had to carry labels bearing the relevant contract numbers. In addition to the standard RZM paper tags used by all NSDAP formations, a system of small black and white woven labels was devised specifically for SS items. Each bore the RZM symbol and SS runes together with the maker's contract number and year date, an example being 'RZM 21/36 SS'. Where a firm was engaged only in embroidery work, the letters 'St', denoting 'Stickerei' or 'embroiderer', were incorporated into the label, for example 'RZM St 459/36 SS'. It was not uncommon for two such labels to be attached to a single badge, particularly a cuff title, if two separate firms were involved in its manufacture due to sub-contracting. One label would refer to the maker of the backing cloth, and the other to the embroiderer. It was also quite common to find the addition of another tag reading 'Vom Reichsführer-SS befohlene Ausführung', indicating that the item in question was made in accordance with SS uniform regulations. Because of all the foregoing, machine-embroidered insignia has come to be known as the 'RZM style'.

Machine-woven badges were produced from 1939, using artificial silk and either cotton or fine aluminium wire. They had a very flat appearance and the manufacturing process, which could result in hundreds of identical insignia being run off on a single continuous strip of ribbon-like material, allowed for the incorporation of very fine detail into the design. The principal producer of these badges was the Wuppertal-Barmen firm of Bandfabrik Ewald Vorsteher, whose trade mark 'BEVO' has become synonymous with machine-woven insignia.

The use of silk-screen printing in the manufacture of certain Waffen-SS badges was introduced in 1944, but was primarily restricted to foreign volunteer shields, war auxiliary armbands and the special rank insignia for camouflage clothing. Low production costs were more than outweighed by the poor quality of the finished article, and printed badges were very unpopular.

The procedures governing the approval and manufacture of Waffen-SS insignia were very complicated. Various SS departments, particularly the SS Hauptamt, the SS Führungshauptamt and the SS Wirtschafts- und Verwaltungshauptamt were continually at each other's throats over who was responsible for this matter, and the process by which new badges were proposed and introduced was not settled until May 1944, when the following was agreed:

1. The SS-HA became primarily responsible for the design and proposal to the Reichsführer-SS of 'political' SS insignia, i.e. national emblems, collar patches, arm shields and formation badges. However, the SS-HA had first to get the opinion of the SS-FHA before submitting samples to Himmler.

2. The SS-FHA became primarily responsible for the design and proposal to the Reichsführer-SS of 'non-political' insignia, i.e. rank badges, cuff titles, qualification badges, branch of service insignia and specialist badges. If political considerations arose in respect of any of these, the SS-FHA had to obtain the opinion of the SS-HA before submission to Himmler.

3. The SS-HA would, after obtaining the approval of the Reichsführer-SS, cede badges listed at 1. above to the SS-FHA. The SS-FHA was then responsible for the execution and issue of the badges in co-operation with the SS-WVHA. The SS-FHA and SS-WVHA would collaborate until the completion of final samples of these badges.

4. The method of wearing new types of badges would be decided in relation to the method of wearing existing badges. If changes in the method of wear were necessary, the SS-FHA was responsible for making them. However, if insignia under 1. above were involved, the SS-FHA had to obtain the opinion of the SS-HA first. Such was the case in 1944, when it was decided to move foreign volunteer shields from their traditional location 1.5 cm above the cuff title to a new position further up the left sleeve, 1.5 cm below the SS arm eagle. The SS-HA was besieged with complaints from foreign volunteer units whose members regarded this as a slur, subordinating their national flags and coats of arms to the Nazi eagle!

To complicate the issue still further, Himmler himself also suggested the introduction of special badges, such as cuff titles for as yet unnamed SS regiments and divisions. He was personally responsible for some designs, and often consulted with two artists on his Persönlicher Stab, namely SS-Oberführer Prof. Benno von Arent and SS-Oberführer Prof. Karl Diebitsch. Once a design had been approved by the Reichsführer it would pass to the SS-WVHA which would in turn authorise the RZM to supply the required quantity. The RZM then placed a contract with one of its approved firms and the finished badges were delivered to one of the SS clothing depots, usually Dachau, from where they would finally be supplied to the unit concerned. So, in the production of a single new badge, no less than four departments, the SS-HA, SS-FHA, SS-WVHA and Pers. Stab RfSS might, and probably would, be involved!

By September 1944, pressures on the RZM had developed to such an extent that it was forced to terminate its involvement in the supply of insignia to the Waffen-SS. The following December it announced that Waffen-SS eagles, death's heads, collar patches, shoulder straps and cuff titles could henceforth be manufactured, without a contract, for direct sale to authorised wholesalers and retailers for the duration of the war. By that stage, no less than twenty-four firms were producing cloth insignia for the Waffen-SS:

Gebrüder Auerhammer, Weissenburg
Albrecht Bender, Weissenburg
Max Dörfel, Eibenstock
Lothar von Dreden & Co., Wuppertal-Elberfeld
Oskar Frank, Eibenstock
Geissler & Hast, Ansbach
August Göbels Söhne, Gross-Schönau
E. Günther, Eibenstock

Hensel & Schuhmann, Berlin
Hinterleitner, Brunnacker & Co., Weissenburg
E. Köhler, Annaberg
Kruse & Söhne, Wuppertal-Barmen
Sigmund Lendvay, Vienna
Lucas & Vorsteher, Wuppertal-Barmen
F. Müller, Rossbach
R. Nitzsche, Eibenstock
J.F. Rieleder, Heilbronn
Julius Riess, Erfurt
Franz Rönnefahrt, Brandenburg
Hermann Schmuck & Co., Weissenburg
Thiele & Steinert, Freiberg
Tröltsch & Hanselmann, Berlin
Ewald Vorsteher, Wuppertal-Barmen
Ferdinand Winter, Treuchtlingen

In common with other Third Reich military formations, the Waffen-SS employed certain colours in the design of its uniforms and accoutrements as a means of unit identification. These colours appeared on tunic shoulder straps, cap piping, and so on and were known as branch of service colours, or 'Waffengattungsfarben', normally referred to in the abbreviated form 'Waffenfarben'. Before the outbreak of the Second World War, all armed SS piping was white, silver or twisted black and silver, like that of the Allgemeine-SS. However, in December 1939, due to the increasing militarisation of the Waffen-SS and its new-found associations with Wehrmacht forces, shoulder straps piped in army Waffenfarbe were introduced. A few officers also began to equip themselves with Waffenfarbe-piped peaked caps and long trousers, made to order through their local SS Kleiderkasse, but Himmler immediately forbade that practice, instructing that the piping on these items was to remain white. Some confusion then ensued, for in May 1940 the Reichsführer backtracked by indicating that peaked caps could thereafter be piped in Waffenfarbe, although all walking out dress trousers were now to be piped in grey. The following November Himmler changed his mind yet again, directing that Waffenfarbe was once more to be restricted to shoulder straps and the *soutache* on the field cap, with all other piping reverting to white or aluminium depending on rank. It is clear that the Reichsführer wanted his soldiers to retain their own unique appearance, distinct from that of the army, but a number of Waffen-SS officers and men continued to wear Waffenfarbe on their peaked caps until the end of the war, in defiance of Himmler's orders.

The Waffenfarbe colours officially authorised for use by the Waffen-SS branches are shown in the table below. However, it should be noted that a few shades were withdrawn, reallocated or even renamed from time to time, and in any case the differences in some colours were so slight as to be almost indistinguishable, a situation compounded by variations in manufacturers' dyes, the bleaching effect of the sun and the general weathering of piping under field conditions.

SS WAFFENFARBEN

Waffenfarbe	*Waffen-SS Branch of Service*
1. Black	Construction units Engineers
2. Dark ('cornflower') blue	Medical units
3. Light blue	Field post office (from February 1943) Motor Technical School (until July 1942) Supply units Transport units (until August 1944)
4. Sky blue	Administration
5. Copper brown	Reconnaissance units (until June 1942)
6. Light brown	Concentration camp staff
7. Dark green	Reserve officers (discontinued 1942) Specialist personnel (until June 1942)
8. Grass green	Mountain troops (from May 1942) Police-Division (discontinued 1942)
9. Light grey	General officers Himmler's Personal Staff (until June 1942)
10. Dark grey	Himmler's Personal Staff (from June 1942)
11. Orange	Military police units Garrison troops Motor Technical School (from July 1942 to August 1944) Recruiting units Technical units Welfare personnel

Waffenfarbe	*Waffen-SS Branch of Service*
12. Light pink	Motor Technical School (from August 1944) Transport units (from August 1944)
13. Rose pink	Panzer units Anti-tank units
14. Salmon pink	Military geologists
15. Bright red	Artillery units Flak units Rocket units
16. Claret ('Bordeaux') red	Legal personnel
17. Crimson red	Veterinary personnel
18. Red & grey twist	Specialist personnel (from June 1942)
19. White	Infantry units
20. Golden yellow	Cavalry units Reconnaissance units (from June 1942)
21. Lemon yellow	Field post office (until February 1943) Signals units War correspondents

The Waffen-SS rank structure was very similar to that of the Allgemeine-SS, with a few specific exceptions. The lowest Waffen-SS rank was that of SS-Schütze, or Private, while a Private with six months' service was known as an SS-Oberschütze. The senior NCO rank was SS-Sturmscharführer, or Company Sergeant-Major, and any man holding Unterführer rank could be appointed to serve as his unit's SS-Stabscharführer or Duty NCO, who fulfilled various administrative and reporting functions and was nicknamed 'der Spiess', or 'the spear', a traditional term dating back the to pikemen of the Middle Ages. The ranks from SS-Untersturmführer to SS-Hauptsturmführer were known as company officers, with those from SS-Sturmbannführer to SS-Oberführer being termed field officers. Higher ranks were classed as general officers. All Waffen-SS

generals were awarded their corresponding army rank titles in 1940, and were thereafter designated as follows:

SS-Brigadeführer und Generalmajor der Waffen-SS
SS-Gruppenführer und Generalleutnant der Waffen-SS
SS-Obergruppenführer und General der Waffen-SS
SS-Oberst-Gruppenführer und Generaloberst der Waffen-SS

Non-German nationals from Germanic countries serving in foreign legions raised by the Waffen-SS replaced the rank prefix 'SS-' with 'Legions-' (e.g. 'Legions-Hauptsturmführer'), while those in non-Germanic units used the prefix 'Waffen-' (e.g. 'Waffen-Hauptsturmführer der SS'). These denoted attachment to the Waffen-SS, rather than membership of the SS proper.

The regular Waffen-SS officer candidate, or Führerbewerber (FB), distinguished by a double lace bar on his shoulder straps, underwent four months' basic training after which he became an officer cadet, or Führeranwärter (FA), and received the title of SS-Junker with the equivalent rank of SS-Unterscharführer. He then attended a six-month military leadership course which culminated in his promotion to SS-Standartenjunker, equal to an SS-Scharführer. At the end of a further six months' officer training he was elevated to the position of SS-Standartenoberjunker, equating to an SS-Hauptscharführer, and was allowed to wear officer's cap cords, belt buckle and aluminium collar patch piping. He was then sent back to his unit where, after a minimum period of two months, he received promotion to SS-Untersturmführer. Officers who did not plan a military career and intended to serve in the Waffen-SS only for the duration of the war were given reserve commissions and were known as Reserve-Führerbewerber (RFB), Reserve-Führeranwärter (RFA), SS-Junker der Reserve, SS-Untersturmführer der Reserve, and so on.

Potential NCOs, or SS-Unter-führerbewerber, were generally trained at a company level, progressing to SS-Unterführeranwärter and then to SS-Unterscharführer. During their training, they wore a single lace bar on their shoulder straps if they had signed up for twelve years or more, and a thin twisted cord in the appropriate Waffenfarbe if they had signed up for less than twelve years.

The Waffen-SS also employed civilian specialists (interpreters, doctors, lawyers, and so on) known as Sonderführer, and later Fachführer, who were given appointments in relation to their tasks. They could hold the ranks of:

SS-Gruppenführer Walter Krüger, commander of 'Das Reich' in September 1943. He wears the heavily embroidered collar patches and shoulder straps of an SS general.

SS-Unterscharführer	(S) or (F)
SS-Hauptscharführer	(S) or (F)
SS-Untersturmführer	(S) or (F)
SS-Hauptsturmführer	(S) or (F)
SS-Sturmbannführer	(S) or (F)

The SS-Fachführer wore a blank right collar patch and shoulder strap piping in dark-green until June 1942. After that date, piping was in a red and grey twist. If a specialist showed that he was capable of commanding a military unit corresponding to his Fachführer rank, the latter ceased and he continued in his duties as a full officer or NCO of the Waffen-SS.

Waffen-SS ranks were indicated by a combination of collar patches and shoulder straps. The earliest armed SS units were technically on the local Abschnitt staff, and as such members wore blank right collar patches. In May 1933, officers' patches began to be piped in a black/aluminium twisted cord, and those of other ranks in white cord. With the rapid expansion of the militarised SS formations, it soon became clear that some kind of distinctive collar insignia was required for the Leibstandarte and Politische Bereitschaften, and towards the end of the year patches bearing double Sig-Runes, hand-embroidered in silver bullion for officers and white or silver-grey cotton for other ranks, were issued to soldiers of the LAH. In June 1934, the SS PBs attached to Oberabschnitte Süd, Südwest and Mitte were authorised to wear runic 'SS 1' 'SS 2' and 'SS 3' patches, respectively, with the numbers as large as the runes, and three months later non-commissioned ranks in the LAH and SS-VT were further distinguished by being allowed to use aluminium wire embroidery on their collar patches. In October, the piping on officers' patches was changed to the definitive plain aluminium cord, with the black/aluminium twist now being adopted by other ranks.

The rest of the prewar period witnessed the introduction of machine-embroidered collar patches for the field uniform, death's heads and other designs for SS-TV and specialist units, and the adoption of the 'SS 1', 'SS 2' and 'SS 3' patches, this time with small numbers, by the 'Deutschland', 'Germania' and 'Der Führer' Standarten.

When army-pattern shoulder straps were introduced for the armed SS in March 1938, it was apparent that the wearing of dual rank badges on both the left collar patch (SS rank) and shoulder straps (army equivalent) was unnecessary. However, Himmler decreed that SS ranks should still be displayed. The situation was exacerbated at the outbreak of war, with the LAH, SS-VT and SS-TV being given specific roles alongside the Wehrmacht. The ordinary German soldier was bemused by the SS rank system, and was at a loss to know which SS men he was supposed to salute and whose orders he was obliged to obey. It therefore became absolutely essential, for practical and disciplinary reasons, that Waffen-SS rank badges should correspond to those in the armed forces and be easily recognised as such. Consequently, during the formation of the first SS field divisions in the autumn of 1939, it was decided that their personnel should not wear SS rank patches. Instead, they received matching collar patches with the runes or death's head on both sides. Their ranks were indicated solely by shoulder straps, in the army style. However, prewar Waffen-SS officers and men jealously retained their existing collar patches, showing their SS ranks.

The increased use of camouflage smocks, which covered the shoulder straps and, indeed, all insignia except the collar patches, led Himmler to rescind the matching collar patch order on 10 May 1940, and reintroduce the SS rank patch for all Waffen-SS members. At the same time, the need for security during the invasion of the Low Countries and France rendered obsolete all SS-VT and SS-TV collar patches bearing numerals or letters, which were ordered removed. The result was that for a short time during the western campaign-personnel in the SS-Verfügungsdivision wore no collar patches at all. From then on, the basic SS runes collar patch became standard for all German and Germanic Waffen-SS formations except Totenkopf units, whose members continued to wear the death's head, now produced in a horizontal version more suitable for use on the closed-neck field tunic. In August 1940, the black/aluminium twisted cord bordering other ranks' patches was abolished, leaving these patches unbordered for the rest of the war.

With the increasing recruitment of non-Germans into the Waffen-SS after 1940, Himmler became concerned about the use of the SS runes insignia by those not racially suitable for full SS membership, and he instructed that such recruits should wear some other form of badge on the right collar patch. The SS thereafter designed and issued a range of appropriate (and sometimes inappropriate) collar patches for its foreign units, and pending the distribution of these insignia blank patches were often worn in new units as an interim measure. German SS officers and NCOs serving in foreign formations were still entitled to wear the SS runes collar patch and, from July 1943, if they chose to identify with their men by wearing the distinctive unit patch, they were obliged to sport the SS runes embroidered below the left breast pocket instead. The latter insignia was identical to that worn by SS men in the German police.

The wearing of collar patches did not always conform to regulations. Matching patches and vertical death's heads, although prohibited in 1940, continued to be worn well into 1942, and officers often used other ranks' patches in the field, or removed the cording from their own patches. In 1943, machine-woven versions of the SS runes and horizontal death's head patches were produced, but the earlier embroidered examples were still being issued at the end of the war. Recruits under training often wore no collar patches at all.

The table on p. 253 lists all SS-VT, SS-TV and Waffen-SS unit collar patches which have been confirmed by contemporary photographic or documentary evidence as having been worn. They were produced in embroidered versions only, unless otherwise indicated.

A number of other strange patches were designed for foreign SS formations, primarily the eastern divisions, but these were never

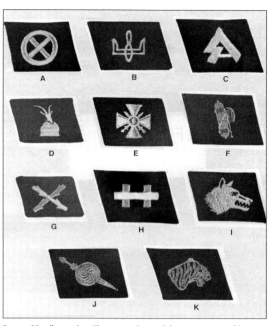

Foreign SS collar patches. These were designed, but never approved by Himmler or issued to the units concerned: A – Danes in 'Nordland'; B – 14th Division/30th Division; C – 'Horst Wessel'; D – 'Skanderbeg'; E – 29th Division (Russian); F – 29th Division (Italian); G – 'Wallonien'; H – 30th Division; I – Tartars; J – Caucasians; K – Indian Legion.

approved by Himmler or worn by the personnel concerned.

Members of the armed SS wore standard Allgemeine-SS shoulder straps on the right side only until 1935, when the earth-grey uniform was introduced. In July of that year, SS-VT officers were ordered to wear their Allgemeine-SS straps on both shoulders of the grey uniform. Other ranks received army-pattern straps made of plain earth-grey material, or earth-brown for SS-TV troops. In 1936, these enlisted men's shoulder straps were replaced first by a round-ended black version piped in black/aluminium twisted cord, then by an unpiped black type with pointed ends. None of these early straps identified the wearer's rank, as that was shown by his collar patches.

In March 1938, army-pattern straps with

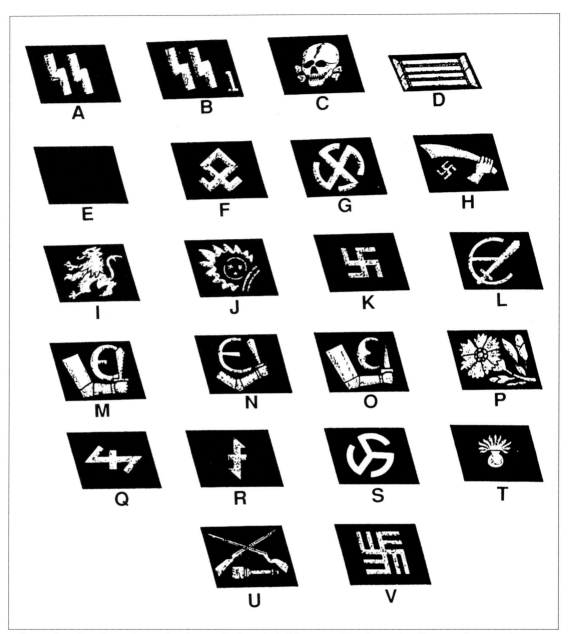

Waffen-SS collar patches. These are known to have been issued and worn by the following units during the Second World War: A – all German and Germanic Waffen-SS formations; B – SS-VT Standarte 'Deutschland'; C – Totenkopf units; D – SS-Polizei-Division and police regiments; E – specialists and foreign units not allocated other patches; F – 'Prinz Eugen'; G – 'Nordland'; H – 'Handschar'; I – 14th Division; J – 15th Division; K – Latvian Legion/15th and 19th Divisions; L – 20th Division (official patch dating from June 1944); M – 20th Division (unofficial patch dating from October 1943); N – 20th Division (official patch dating from October 1944); O – 20th Division (unofficial patch made in Tartu, February 1944); P – 'Maria Theresa'; Q – Dutch Legion/'Nederland' (official patch dating from November 1941); R – Dutch Legion/'Nederland' (unofficial patch); S – 'Nordwest'/Freikorps Danmark/Flemish Legion/'Langemarck'; T – 'Landstorm Nederland' (unofficially continued from the Landwacht Nederland); U – Dirlewanger Brigade/36th Division; V – Non-SS concentration camp guards.

WAFFEN-SS COLLAR PATCHES

Design	Period Used	Unit/Worn By
Blank	1933–45	Specialists/departmental or HQ staff/units not yet allocated patches
SS	1933–45	LAH, then from 1940 all German and Germanic units not allocated other patches
SS/large 1	1934	SS PB 'Süd'
SS/large 2	1934	SS PB 'Südwest'
SS/large 3	1934	SS PB 'Mitte'
D	1934–7	Dachau Guard Battalion
K	1934–7	Concentration camp staff
Ü	1934–7	Dachau training camp
SS/T	1934–40	Bad Tölz officers' school
SS/pick & shovel	1934–40	SS-VT Pioneer Battalion
SS/lightning bolt	1934–40	SS-VT Signals Battalion
SS/small 1	1935–40	'Deutschland'
SS/B	1935–40	Braunschweig officers' school
SS/V	1935–40	Administration school
Vertical death's head	1936–42	Totenkopf units
Vertical death's head/I–V	1936–7	SS-TV Battalion staff
Vertical death's head/1–26	1936–40	SS-TV Companies
Vertical death's head/S	1936–40	SS-TV Medical Battalion
SS/small 2	1936–40	'Germania'
SS/S	1936–40	SS-VT Medical Battalion
SS/N	1936–40	'Nürnberg'
Vertical death's head/K	1937–40	Concentration camp staff
SS/small 3	1938–40	'Der Führer'
Police litzen	1939–42	Police-Division
Police litzen (woven)	1939–42	Police-Division
Horizontal death's head	1940–5	Totenkopf units
Lion with axe	1941–3	Norwegian Legion
Lion with axe (metal)	1941–3	Norwegian Legion
Wolfsangel	1941–5	Dutch Legion/'Nederland'
Trifos	1941–5	'Nordwest'/Freikorps Danmark/Flemish Legion/'Langemarck'
Lyre	1941–5	Music school
Danish flag	1942	Freikorps Danmark
Odal-Rune	1942–5	'Prinz Eugen'
Open sonnenrad	1943–5	'Nordland'
SS (woven)	1943–5	All German and Germanic units not allocated other patches
Horizontal death's head (woven)	1943–5	Totenkopf units
Scimitar & swastika	1943–5	'Handschar'

Design	Period Used	Unit/Worn By
Lion rampant	1943–5	14th Division
Swastika	1943–5	Latvian Legion/15th Division/19th Division
Sun & stars	1944–5	15th Division
E & mailed arm/sword	1944–5	20th Division
Cornflower	1944–5	'Maria Theresa'
H	1944–5	'Hunyadi'
Crossed rifles & grenade	1944–5	Dirlewanger Brigade/36th Division
Three lions passant	1944–5	British Free Corps
Double-armed swastika	1944–5	Non-SS concentration camp guards
Flaming grenade	1945	'Landstorm Nederland'
Flaming grenade (metal)	1945	'Landstorm Nederland'

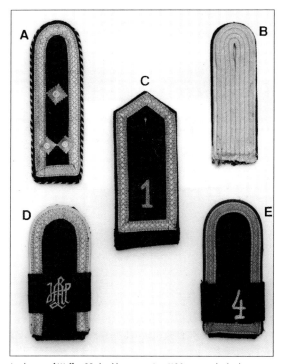

A selection of Waffen-SS shoulder straps: A – M38 strap with obsolete black/aluminium twisted cord piping, for an SS-VT Sturmscharführer; B – M39 strap with white waffenfarbe piping, for an SS-Untersturmführer; C – M38 strap with chain stitch '1', for a Scharführer in SS-Totenkopfstandarte 1 'Oberbayern'; D – M40 strap with white waffenfarbe piping and machine-embroidered 'LAH' slip-on tab, for an Unterscharführer in the Leibstandarte; E – M40 strap with chain stitch '4' slip-on tab, for a Scharführer in the 4th SS-Totenkopf Infantry Regiment.

black underlay and gilt stars were issued to all armed SS officers, and NCOs began to wear aluminium lace, or Tresse, and white metal 'pips'. Rank was thereafter clearly indicated by the straps. From December 1939, officers sported coloured Waffenfarbe piping between the aluminium braid and black underlay, and other ranks received their definitive Waffenfarbe-piped black straps with rounded ends. A large number of unit identification insignia were worn on the shoulder straps. For officers, these numerals and ciphers were initially in gilt metal, then bronze after 1940. Other ranks had them embroidered directly on to their straps or on to removable slip-on tabs from 1940. The table on p. 255 lists the various identification badges known to have been used on Waffen-SS shoulder straps.

In October 1943, Himmler cancelled the use of these ciphers for the duration of the war, on security grounds. In any case, units and specialist personnel were still readily identifiable by other badges. The only exception was the Leibstandarte, whose members were permitted to retain their LAH monogram as an honorarium.

Cuff titles, woven black tapes about 28 mm in width and 49 cm in length which were

WAFFEN-SS SHOULDER STRAP BADGES

Badge	Unit
A	SS-VT Artillery Regiment
A (Gothic)	SS-VT Reconnaissance Battalion
AS/I	Artillery School I
AS/II	Artillery School II
Cogwheel	Technical units
D	'Deutschland' Standarte
DF	'Der Führer' Standarte
E/Roman numeral	Recruiting Offices
Fl	SS-VT Anti-Aircraft Machine Gun Battalion
G	'Germania' Standarte
JS/B	Junkerschule Braunschweig
JS/T	Junkerschule Tölz
L	Motor Technical School
L (Gothic)	Training establishments
LAH	Leibstandarte-SS 'Adolf Hitler'
Lyre	Bands
MS	Musikschule Braunschweig
N	'Nordland' Standarte
P (Gothic)	SS-VT Anti-Tank Battalion
Serpent	Veterinary units
Serpent & staff	Medical units
SK/D	Dachau garrison
SK/P	Prague garrison
US/L	Unterführerschule Lauenburg
US/R	Unterführerschule Radolfzell
W	'Westland' Standarte
1–17	Totenkopf Standarten

worn on the lower left sleeve of the tunic and greatcoat, became very distinctive features of SS uniform and, apart from identifying the unit of the wearer, were partly responsible for the remarkable *ésprit de corps* of the Waffen-SS. All prewar regiments and most ancillary formations of the SS-VT and SS-TV had their own cuff titles, which were handed over as part and parcel of the clothing issue. Each man received four, one for each of his uniforms, and they were expected to last him nine months. These early cuff titles were embroidered in Gothic lettering with the exception of the Leibstandarte's 'Adolf Hitler' insignia, which featured the old German form of script known as Sütterlin, officially reserved for the Führer's guards from 1936. This archaic handwriting style had been promoted by Berlin graphics teacher Ludwig Sütterlin (1865–1917) and was widely taught in German schools until 1941.

On 1 September 1939, the Gothic 'SS' used on certain cuff titles was replaced by a runic version, and three months later all Gothic

finally the 'Das Reich' title from September 1942.

As the war progressed, cuff titles took on a new significance and were presented at solemn ceremonies during which unit commanders would remind recipients of the great honour being bestowed upon them and that they should do nothing to disgrace the names which their cuff titles bore. The exact criteria for awarding names and cuff titles are not known, but what is certain is that many SS divisions, such as the 14th and 15th, were never named, while some of those which were, such as 'Handschar' and 'Maria Theresa', never received cuff titles. Himmler apparently judged every application on its own merits, refusing some new units on the grounds that a cuff title had to be earned on the field of battle, and turning down others because they had been formed as a temporary wartime expedient from personnel considered racially unsuitable for SS membership.

Any Waffen-SS soldier transferring from one unit to another had to remove his old cuff title and replace it with that of his new unit. However, if the latter had not been awarded a cuff title, the man was permitted to continue to wear the title of his former unit. That explains why 'Adolf Hitler' and 'Der Führer' cuff titles featured among the officer cadre of the 24th SS Division in northern Italy at the end of the war, and why miscellaneous cuff titles were worn by SS paratroopers. On occasion, two cuff titles could be worn together. Officer cadets being trained at Bad Tölz, for example, were initially allowed to wear the 'SS-Schule Tölz' cuff title above their own regimental or divisional titles, while war correspondents and military policemen often wore the 'SS-Kriegsberichter' and 'SS-Feldgendarmerie' titles below those of the regiment or division to which they were attached. The wearing of more than one cuff title in this fashion was forbidden in August 1943.

The Leibstandarte's 'Adolf Hitler' cuff title, hand-embroidered in Sütterlin script. This photograph of a captured tunic was taken by a British war correspondent in 1945. The Crimea campaign shield has been placed for effect only, and would normally be sewn on to the upper sleeve.

script was discontinued in favour of standard Latin lettering. In May 1940, the cuff titles worn by ancillary Waffen-SS units, for example 'SS-Pioniersturmbann' and 'SS-Nachrichtensturmbann', were abolished because they constituted a security risk. Regimental titles such as 'Deutschland' continued to be used, however, even after the introduction of divisional titles. The latter did not materialise until 1942, and were worn by divisional personnel not entitled to regimental cuff titles. So a member of the signals battalion of the SS-Verfügungsdivision would wear the 'SS-Nachrichtensturmbann' title until May 1940, then no cuff title at all, and

Cuff titles fell into four categories according to their method of construction:

1. *Hand-embroidered in aluminium wire or thread*
   Produced from 1933 until June 1942. For wear by all ranks until 1936, and thereafter by officers only.
2. *Machine-embroidered in white or silver-grey cotton thread*
   The so-called 'RZM style'. Produced from 1936–43 for wear by other ranks only.
3. *Machine-woven in aluminium thread*
   Produced from 1939–43 for wear by officers only.
4. *Machine-woven in flat grey cotton or silken thread*
   The so-called 'BEVO' pattern. Produced from 1943–5 for wear by all ranks.

While the foregoing details the intended recipients of the various manufacturing styles, it was not uncommon for officers to use other ranks' cuff titles on their field uniforms, or for NCOs to acquire officer quality titles for wear on their dress tunics. Moreover, old stocks of some early cuff titles continued to be worn long after they had been officially discontinued. A few rare or even unique styles are also known to have existed, one example being 'Sepp' Dietrich's wartime 'Adolf Hitler' cuff titles, which he had embroidered in gold bullion in the manner of a Wehrmacht general officer.

The table on p. 262 lists all SS-VT, SS-TV and Waffen-SS cuff titles which have been confirmed by contemporary photographic or documentary evidence as having been authorised and worn.

A small number of unapproved localised cuff titles, such as the 'Narwa' and 'Estland' titles worn by some members of the 20th SS Division, have also been confirmed from photographs.

The cuff titles in the table below were authorised during the war, but were never issued for a variety of reasons.

The SS arm eagle also came to be a distinctive part of Waffen-SS uniform. The eagle and swastika was established as the national emblem, or Hoheitsabzeichen, of the Third Reich on 7 March 1936, but the first SS tunic eagles were sported by 'Sepp' Dietrich and others as early as the summer of 1935, with the newly introduced earth-grey uniform. The use of eagles on the right breast was restricted by law to the army, navy and air force, so members of the LAH and SS-VT took to wearing theirs on the upper left arm,

UNISSUED CUFF TITLES

Title	Authorised For
Artur Phleps	Gebirgs Rgt. 13, 7th SS Division
Charlemagne	33rd SS Division
Finnisches Frw. Bataillon der Waffen-SS	Finnish Volunteer Battalion
Hinrich Schuldt	Grenadier Rgt. 43, 19th SS Division
30 Januar	32nd SS Division
Landstorm Nederland	34th SS Division (n.b. this title already existed for the Dutch Germanic-SS unit of the same name)
Latvija	2nd Brigade, 19th SS Division
Osttürkischer Waffen-Verband der SS	Tartar SS Regiment
Woldemars Veiss	Grenadier Rgt. 42, 19th SS Division

ISSUED WAFFEN-SS CUFF TITLES

Title	Year Introduced	Unit/Worn By
Adolf Hitler	1933	Leibstandarte/1st SS Division
Brandenburg	1937	SS-Totenkopfstandarte 2
British Free Corps	1944	British Free Corps, 11th SS Division
Danmark	1943	Grenadier Rgt. 24, 11th SS Division
Das Reich	1942	2nd SS Division
Death's head (insignia)	1938	SS-Totenkopfstandarte 1
Den Norske Legion	1941	Norwegian Legion
Der Führer	1938	'Der Führer' Standarte
De Ruiter	1943	Grenadier Rgt. 49, 23rd SS Division
Deutschland	1935	'Deutschland' Standarte
Elbe	1937	SS-Wachsturmbann II
E SS/TV	1939	SS-TV training units
Florian Geyer	1944	8th SS Division
Freikorps Danmark	1941	Freikorps Danmark
Frundsberg	1943	10th SS Division
Frw. Legion Flandern	1941	Flemish Legion
Frw. Legion Nederland	1941	Dutch Legion
Frw. Legion Niederlande	1941	Dutch Legion
Frw. Legion Norwegen	1941	Norwegian Legion
General Seyffardt	1943	Grenadier Rgt. 48, 23rd SS Division
Germania	1936	'Germania' Standarte
Götz von Berlichingen	1943	17th SS Division
Hermann von Salza	1944	Panzer Battalion 11, 11th SS Division
Hitlerjugend	1943	12th SS Division
Hohenstaufen	1943	9th SS Division
Horst Wessel	1944	18th SS Division
Kdtr. Ü.L. Dachau	1935	Dachau training camp
Kurt Eggers	1943	War Correspondent Regiment
Langemarck	1942	Infantry Rgt. 4, 2nd SS Division; and 27th SS Division
Legion Niederlande	1941	Dutch Legion
Legion Norwegen	1941	Norwegian Legion
Michael Gaissmair	1944	Gebirgs Rgt. 12, 6th SS Division
Nederland	1944	23rd SS Division
Nordland	1940	11th SS Division; and Grenadier Rgt. 'Nordland', 5th SS Division
Nordwest	1941	'Nordwest' Standarte
Norge	1943	Ski Battalion, 6th SS Division; and Grenadier Rgt. 23, 11th SS Division
Oberbayern	1937	SS-Totenkopfstandarte 1

Title	Year Introduced	Unit/Worn By
Ostfriesland	1937	SS-Wachsturmbann IV
Ostmark	1938	SS-Totenkopfstandarte 4
Police eagle (insignia)	1942	4th SS Division
Prinz Eugen	1942	7th SS Division
Reichsführer-SS	1943	16th SS Division
Reichsführung-SS	1940	SS high command staff
Reichsschule-SS	1943	School for female SS auxiliaries
Reinhard Heydrich	1942	Gebirgs Rgt. 11, 6th SS Division
Sachsen	1937	SS-Wachsturmbann III
Sanitätsabteilung	1936	SS-VT and SS-TV Medical Battalions
Skanderbeg	1944	21st SS Division
SS-Ärztliche Akademie	1939	Medical Academy
SS-Feldgendarmerie	1942	Military Police
SS-Heimwehr Danzig	1939	SS-Heimwehr Danzig
SS-Inspektion	1936	SS-VT Inspectorate
SS-KB-Abt	1941	War Correspondent Battalion
SS-Kriegsberichter	1940	War Correspondents
SS-Kriegsberichter-Kp	1940	War Correspondent Company
SS-Musikschule Braunschweig	1941	Braunschweig Music School
SS-Nachrichtensturmbann	1937	SS-VT Signals Battalion
SS-Pioniersturmbann	1937	SS-VT Pioneer Battalion
SS-Polizei-Division	1942	4th SS Division
SS-Schule Braunschweig	1935	Braunschweig officers' school
SS-Schule Tölz	1934	Bad Tölz officers' school
SS-Totenkopfverbände	1937	SS-TV Staff and Police Reinforcements
SS-Übungslager Dachau	1937	Dachau Training Camp
SS-Unterführerschule	1940	NCO School
SS-Verwaltungsschule	1935	Administration School
Theodor Eicke	1943	Grenadier Rgt. 6, 3rd SS Division
Thule	1942	Grenadier Rgt. 5, 3rd SS Division
Thüringen	1937	SS-Totenkopfstandarte 3
Totenkopf	1942	3rd SS Division
Wallonien	1944	28th SS Division
W.B. Dachau	1935	Dachau Economic Enterprises
Westland	1940	Grenadier Rgt. 10, 5th SS Division
Wiking	1942	5th SS Division

in lieu of the gaudy Allgemeine-SS armband which was clearly unsuitable for field use. The pattern of sleeve eagle officially adopted by the armed SS in May 1936 was that introduced simultaneously for the railway police, with a right-facing eagle with dipping wings. It was discontinued after only two years, but was still being worn by some SS veterans as late as 1943. The second and definitive pattern of SS national emblem, with a left-facing eagle and straight wings tapering to a point, was devised in 1938 and was eventually produced in several variations. The commonest manufacturing method was machine-embroidery, in white or silver-grey cotton thread on black, and these RZM-style eagles came in the following three types, depending upon period of production:

Type 1   with a pronounced square head (1938–41)
Type 2   with a less pronounced curved head (1942–3)
Type 3   with a shallow round head (1944–5).

Photographs confirm these types time and time again as period, rather than manufacturers', variations. The square-headed 'Type 1' eagle can regularly be seen in prewar shots and pictures taken during the western and Balkan Blitzkriegs of 1940–1, while the round-headed insignia never features in these photographs. Conversely, the round-headed 'Type 3' eagle is consistently seen on camouflage drill tunics during the Normandy and Ardennes battles, with the 'Type 1' badge being conspicuous by its absence at that stage of the war.

In 1939, a BEVO machine-woven version of the 1938-pattern SS sleeve eagle began to appear, in flat grey cotton or silken thread for other ranks and fine silver wire for officers. It was widely worn on all types of Waffen-SS uniform throughout the war, and was even used as a cap badge by female SS auxiliaries. The BEVO eagle was also produced in tan-brown from 1943, for the tropical uniform.

The BEVO machine-woven version of the SS arm eagle for other ranks.

An Obersturmführer of the SS-TV Medical Battalion temporarily seconded to the army for training purposes in 1939. In addition to the standard SS sleeve eagle, he wears the army eagle above his right breast pocket. This is the only known photograph showing both of these insignia being worn simultaneously.

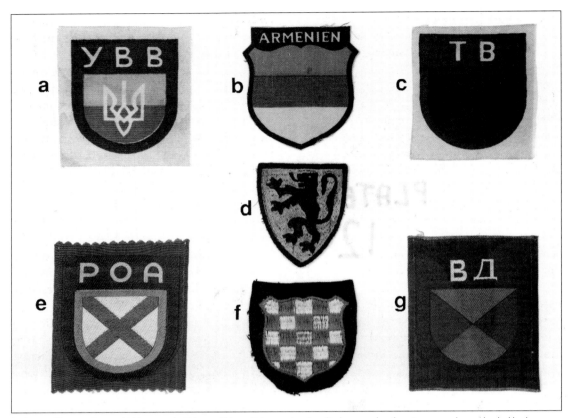

A selection of foreign volunteer shields, many of which were Wehrmacht issue and continued to be worn when the units concerned were absorbed by the Waffen-SS during the last year of the war. Those shown identified: (a) – Ukrainians; (b) – Armenians; (c) – Terek Cossacks; (d) – Flemings; (e) – Russians; (f) – Croats; (g) – Don Cossacks.

Officers frequently had their arm eagles hand-embroidered in silver bullion, and 'Sepp' Dietrich again highlighted his unique status by having his insignia executed in gold wire.

In addition to the various regulation types of the 1938-pattern SS Hoheitsabzeichen, other eagles were sometimes worn on the left arm of the Waffen-SS tunic. A number of ex-army officers who transferred to the Waffen-SS, and foreigners who had previously served in Wehrmacht legions, wore the army breast eagle on the sleeve, either to emphasise their origins or simply because the army eagle was more readily available to them. The use of army eagles was particularly common during the rapid expansion of the Waffen-SS in 1939–40, when SS eagles were in short supply and army-style Waffenfarbe piping and matching collar patches were the order of the day. A few SS-VT and SS-TV men on secondment to army units even wore the army eagle on the right breast while still sporting the SS eagle on the left arm! The Italian SS had their own version of the sleeve eagle, which was right-facing and clutched a *fasces* instead of a swastika, and between August 1942 and October 1944 the German police eagle in orange thread was worn by members of the SS-Feldgendarmerie.

In addition to the foregoing insignia, which were common to most Waffen-SS personnel, a number of related badges existed which merit only brief coverage. A range of arm shields was created for foreign volunteers in the Waffen-SS, and generally took the form of machine-embroidered national flags on a black cloth ground measuring around 60 mm × 50 mm. These were standardised in 1943, and most were produced by the Berlin firm of Tröltsch & Hanselmann. The shields were at first worn above the cuff title, and later beneath the arm eagle, and gradually replaced the army versions hitherto worn by many foreigners. The flags of Belgium, Denmark, Estonia, France, Great Britain, Holland, Latvia and Norway featured on these shields, while the badges for Albanian, Croatian, Finnish, Flemish and Ukrainian volunteers bore suitable heraldic motifs.

A series of trade badges to identify skills and specialities was designed in the shape of black cloth diamonds for wear on the lower left sleeve. Each badge was awarded after the successful completion of the relevant SS training course, and those who graduated from army schools were obliged to wear the army trade badge in lieu of the SS one. From October 1943, mountain troops sported a machine-embroidered edelweiss on the left side of the Bergmütze and on the right tunic sleeve, above the Honour Chevron of the Old Guard if the latter was also worn. Uniformed female SS auxiliaries had a unique badge consisting of a black oval containing silver SS runes, which was sewn to the left breast pocket. Other civilian employees were given embroidered, woven or printed armbands bearing the wording 'Waffen-SS' or 'Im Dienste der Waffen-SS' when on duty, and brassards featuring national colours were worn by the young SS flak helpers from the east.

During the Second World War, Waffen-SS soldiers were eligible for the whole range of Nazi military decorations, including the Iron Cross, the German Cross, the War Merit Cross, and so on. Participation in the Crimea, Demjansk and Kurland battles earned the appropriate campaign distinctions for men of the Leibstandarte, SS-Totenkopf-Division and 6th Waffen-Armeekorps der SS, while troops of all units wore Infantry Assault Badges, General Assault Badges, Flak and Panzer Battle Badges, Wound Badges, Tank Destruction Awards and the Close Combat Clasp. Among the plethora of Third Reich combat decorations, however, only the Guerrilla Warfare Badge was singled out as being of specific relevance to the activities of the Waffen-SS, and for that reason it deserves some detailed coverage.

Hitler's invasion of the Soviet Union in June 1941 soon resulted in the Wehrmacht facing an entirely new type of enemy, professionally organised partisans who attacked in large groups capable of taking on and defeating German units of battalion or even regimental strength. The partisan movement stemmed from the presence in German-occupied territory of whole Red Army units which had been cut off by the rapidity of the German advance. As early as July 1941 the Central Committee of the Communist Party called upon Soviet citizens to join these units and take up arms, and the following year the Soviet High Command took steps to co-ordinate guerrilla activity by establishing the Central Staff of the Partisan Movement. Liaison officers, wireless equipment, weapons and supplies were provided in ever-increasing numbers and partisan operations were fully integrated into Red Army strategy. In addition to widespread attacks on German communications, partisans made specific efforts in support of Soviet offensives, notably at Kursk, and were able to ease the progress of conventional forces by securing bridges and key

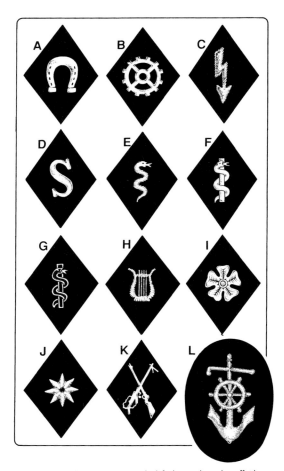

SS trade badges. These were worn on the left sleeve, above the cuff title, and denoted the following specialist appointments or qualifications: A – Farrier; B – Technical Officer; C – Signaller; D – Transport NCO; E – Veterinarian; F – Medical Officer; G – Medical orderly; H – Musician; I – Legal Officer; J – Administrative officer; K – Armourer NCO; L – Coxswain.

installations in the path of their advance. The vastness of the area behind the German lines and the terrain of forests, mountains and marshes lent themselves to guerrilla attacks and the partisans went from strength to strength. They eventually numbered around 400,000 in Warsaw, 390,000 in Yugoslavia, 230,000 in the Baltic states, 150,000 in Byelorussia, 50,000 in northern Italy, 40,000 in the Ukraine, 40,000 in Greece and 35,000

in Albania. The largest German anti-partisan sweep of the war, 'Operation Cottbus', which took place in Byelorussia in June 1943, involved nearly 17,000 German troops and was conducted so brutally and ruthlessly that nothing, human or animal, was left alive in the zone of operations. Nevertheless, as was typical in this sort of warfare, 'Cottbus' failed to trap its quarry and was a major setback for the Germans. The struggle between the Nazis and the partisans was always one where no quarter was asked or given. Atrocities committed against captured German soldiers were met with a policy of extermination on the part of the occupying forces. On entering Taganrog, for example, the Leibstandarte found the mutilated remains of six of its men who had been killed and thrown down a well. During the next three days, Dietrich's troops shot some 4,000 Russian prisoners as a reprisal. Anti-partisan duties increasingly tied down large numbers of German soldiers from all the fighting services, and vast tracts of German-occupied territory soon became virtual no-go areas, allowing even better co-ordination of partisan activity.

The campaign against this 'invisible enemy' took a significant turn when Himmler was made responsible for all anti-partisan operations in October 1942. In a speech given shortly afterwards, he stated that the new enemy did not deserve the title 'partisans', which had patriotic connotations, as they were simply members of what he called outlaw gangs, or 'Banden'. He ordered that in every case these gangster guerrillas were now to be rooted out and executed without trial. Himmler appointed SS-Obergruppenführer Erich von dem Bach as his counter-guerrilla chief, a man who was such a pathological Slav-hater that he had dropped 'Zelewski' from the end of his name in November 1940 because he felt it sounded 'too Polish'. Himmler and von dem Bach arranged for the formation of large numbers of SS-Police regiments, police rifle regiments and Schuma battalions to combat the partisans, thus releasing the army for front-line service. In August 1944, the partisan 'Polish Home Army' rose up in Warsaw, in anticipation of approaching Red Army assistance which never materialised. The rebels initially gained control of two-thirds of the city, but the ferocity of the SS and police response, which levelled Poland's capital, forced the guerrillas underground, into the sewers, where they were gradually reduced and defeated by forces equipped with armour and flamethrowers, supported by Luftwaffe Stuka squadrons. Among the SS troops most active in Warsaw were the Kaminski and Dirlewanger Brigades, terror units composed of convicted criminals specially selected for their brutality and expendability. The crushing of the Warsaw uprising was the most notable anti-partisan victory achieved by the Germans during the war. Von dem Bach, who personally commanded a battle group in the action, received the Knight's Cross after the successful conclusion of the fighting.

The ferocity of the war waged against the partisans eventually necessitated the creation of a new decoration to reward those who had been engaged upon it for a prolonged period. On 30 January 1944, Hitler instituted the Bandenkampfabzeichen, literally 'Bandit Battle Badge' but more accurately 'Guerrilla Warfare Badge'. It was officially designated as a 'Kampfabzeichen der Waffen-SS und Polizei', or 'Waffen-SS and Police Battle Badge', and was the only military decoration of the Third Reich attributed specifically to the SS. Award of the badge was not made in the name of the Supreme Commander of the Wehrmacht, as was usually the case with military decorations, but in the name of the Reichsführer-SS. An order issued from Himmler's field headquarters on 1 February 1944 laid down the following:

1. The Guerrilla Warfare Badge recognises the bravery and meritorious conduct of the recipient.
2. It is awarded in three grades, Bronze, Silver and Gold.
3. The Guerrilla Warfare Badge can be awarded to all officers, NCOs and men engaged in anti-guerrilla operations.
4. The qualification for award is:
   (a) Bronze – 20 combat days
   (b) Silver   – 50 combat days
   (c) Gold   – 100 combat days.
5. A combat day is reckoned to be one during which the recipient has taken part in close combat (man against man) with guerrillas.
6. Combat days may be reckoned as from 1 January 1943.
7. The Guerrilla Warfare Badge may be worn on the left breast pocket of all SS, police and NSDAP uniforms.
8. The Badge is awarded with a citation.
9. Posthumous presentations of awards in respect of those who have qualified for them prior to being killed in action will be made to their next-of-kin.

Qualification for award was therefore very high, making the Bandenkampfabzeichen far more difficult to achieve than similar decorations such as the Infantry Assault Badge.

The design of the Guerrilla Warfare Badge was based on that of the insignia of the Silesian Freikorps of 1919 and featured a wreath of oakleaves enclosing a sword with sunwheel swastika (representing the German and auxiliary forces) plunging into a hydra (the partisans). The Hydra was a fabulous multi-headed sea serpent of Greek mythology, and was almost impossible to destroy since its heads grew quickly again if they were cut off. The parallel with the partisan forces, which sprang up vigorously time and time again, is obvious. At the sword's point was a death's

The Guerrilla Warfare Badge in Bronze. The first awards of this rare decoration were made to SS officers and men during the second half of 1944.

head, which was doubly appropriate since it symbolised both the SS involvement and the deadly nature of the struggle which was being carried on.

Himmler reserved the right to award the gold badge personally, which is not surprising since it was the equivalent of winning the prestigious Close Combat Clasp in Gold twice. The *Völkischer Beobachter* of 21 February 1945 reported that: 'The Reichsführer-SS yesterday presented the first Guerrilla Warfare Badges in Gold to four members of the Waffen-SS engaged in the fighting on the Adriatic Coast'. The first recipient was SS-Obersturmführer Erich Kühbandner of the 24th SS Division, which had been raised specifically to combat partisans in the Carso and Julian Alps. Given the late stage in the war, and the time taken to process award applications and arrange presentation ceremonies, it is unlikely that any further awards of the gold badge were made. Even the bronze and silver badges were highly prized by the Waffen-SS and police, and were seldom bestowed since the chances of surviving more than a few days' close combat with partisans were slim indeed.

In many ways, the design and story of the Guerrilla Warfare Badge represent the desperate and friendless straits in which the Waffen-SS found itself in the last year of the war. It is still difficult to reconcile the substantial battlefield achievements of the SS with the undoubted atrocities which some of its units committed against soldiers and civilians alike.

266

EPILOGUE

By the autumn of 1944, the Black Order had secured almost total political, military and economic power in Germany, and there were only two men who really mattered in the whole of the Reich – Adolf Hitler and Heinrich Himmler. The Swedish press was already referring to Himmler as 'Dictator of Germany', and with Göring long since disgraced it seemed to many that the Reichsführer-SS was merely waiting for Hitler's death to place himself at the head of the Nazi régime. As Commander-in-Chief of the Home Army, it was Himmler who drew up plans for the last-ditch defence of the Fatherland and threatened that every deserter would be punished not only by his own execution but also by that of his entire family. Flying Waffen-SS courts martial swung into action right across the country, and began hanging shirkers and lead-swingers from trees and lamp-posts as a warning to others. Allgemeine-SS men serving in the Wehrmacht and with the Volkssturm increasingly kept their ears to the ground for defeatist talk, and reported whether the sentences passed on offenders by regular military courts martial measured up to Himmler's severe standards. In November, the Reichsführer's power reached its peak, for on the 9th of the month he was granted the unique and symbolic privilege of taking Hitler's place for the delivery of the traditional beer hall speech commemorating the Munich putsch.

In the background, however, lurked a shadowy rival in the power struggle. Martin Bormann, Head of the Party Chancellery and Hitler's closest NSDAP adviser, wore the Blood Order not because of any involvement in the Munich putsch, but because he had served a year in prison as a political murderer. He was an SS-Obergruppenführer, but felt only jealous hatred towards Himmler and longed for his downfall. Bormann knew that the Reichsführer was no military tactician, and in a wily effort to discredit him persuaded Hitler to nominate the SS chief to the vacant post of Commander of Army Group Upper Rhine in early December. This, in effect, gave Himmler the responsibilities of a Wehrmacht Field Marshal at the critical time when the armed forces were collapsing on all fronts. As expected, Himmler

The Reichsführer-SS in November 1944, by which time he had become accepted as Hitler's heir-apparent.

Hitler greeting 'der treue Heinrich' at Führer Headquarters, while Martin Bormann lurks in the background. On his left breast pocket, Himmler wears the Pilot Observer Badge in Gold with Diamonds, which was a personal gift from Hermann Göring.

the arch-policeman completely buckled in his new soldierly role and did no better when reassigned to take charge of Army Group Vistula in January 1945. Haunted by the spectre of defeat, unable to cope with his now massive personal responsibilities, and no longer sure of Hitler's favour in these volatile times, Himmler went on extended sick leave with 'severe influenza' and took refuge in the SS hospital at Hohenlychen run by his old friend Karl Gebhardt. On 20 March, a disillusioned Führer relieved him of his army command on the Vistula. Bormann's scheme had worked perfectly, and had made him the new favourite to succeed Hitler as head of the NSDAP.

Having suddenly lost face, and consequently all realistic hope of the succession, Himmler now determined to save his own skin and that of his SS comrades by opening secret peace negotiations with the western Allies, using important concentration camp inmates as bargaining counters. At the beginning of April, Count Folke Bernadotte, Vice-President of the Swedish Red Cross and agreed intermediary in the talks, paid his second visit to Himmler at Hohenlychen to discuss the possibilities of arranging a German capitulation on the western front. Bernadotte was prepared to appeal to Eisenhower only if Himmler would declare himself Hitler's successor, dissolve the NSDAP and release all Scandinavian prisoners held in Germany. Himmler, however, was unable to make up his mind. He dreamed of himself as the new saviour of Nazi Germany, but still could not wrench free from Hitler's overpowering psychological influence to which he had been subject since 1923. As late as 13 April 1945, Himmler personally denounced his old adjutant Karl Wolff as a traitor when Wolff opened up his own independent peace

The abandoned Waffen-SS recruiting office at Calais, 12 October 1944. Over 8,000 Frenchmen joined the Waffen-SS during the Second World War.

negotiations with the Allies in Switzerland. The situation worsened dramatically when other notable SS leaders panicked and began to abandon the sinking ship in considerable numbers. Three SS-Obergruppenführer, namely Felix Steiner, Curt von Gottberg and Richard Hildebrandt, seriously considered a plan to assassinate Hitler as a means of swiftly putting an end to the war, and even Ernst Kaltenbrunner of the RSHA plotted the surrender of Austria to the Americans. The general consensus among the SS was that their postwar interests would be best served if Himmler was Head of State and able to negotiate on their behalf.

On 19 April, SS-Brigadeführer Walter Schellenberg, Kaltenbrunner's subordinate, implored Himmler for the last time, on behalf of a growing section of the SS leadership, to depose Hitler and make peace. The Reichsführer wavered, but his courage evaporated once more. The following day, he journeyed to the Chancellery Bunker to pay his respects on his master's birthday, and tried unsuccessfully to persuade Hitler to quit the capital and continue the battle from an alpine redoubt in southern Germany. After the meagre birthday celebrations, Himmler bade a final farewell to Hitler and left Berlin for his field headquarters at Hohenlychen. On 28 April, news was relayed to the Führerbunker that Schellenberg, supposedly acting on behalf of the Reichsführer-SS, had offered the western Allies the conditional capitulation of Germany, which they had duly rejected. Himmler had probably never officially sanctioned

Schellenberg's offer, but Hitler was none the less paralysed by the apparent revelation of 'der treue Heinrich's' betrayal. He immediately ordered SS personnel in the room to leave his presence and thereafter issued Bormann with instructions for Himmler's arrest, simultaneously expelling the Reichsführer from the NSDAP and all his government offices. Hitler then appointed SS-Obergruppenführer Karl Hanke, Gauleiter of Lower Silesia, as the new Reichsführer-SS. However, Hanke never received word of his promotion, having already abandoned his post

in the besieged city of Breslau and flown off in one of the few helicopters then in operation.

Forty-eight hours later, Hitler was dead and the Third Reich was at an end. In its stead, confusion and chaos reigned. Grand Admiral Dönitz, head of the rump Nazi government, confirmed that he had no place for Himmler in his short-lived administration. SS officers and men from all branches of the organisation, fearful of the reprisals which they were sure would be directed against them, burned their uniforms, files and identity papers, cast aside their daggers, swords and death's head rings, gathered what loot and

One of the veteran Totenkopf NCOs at Belsen being searched by British soldiers after the liberation of the camp, 17 April 1945.

SS officers and men clearing dead bodies at Belsen, 17 April 1945. At the end of 1944 and beginning of 1945, the prisoners at Auschwitz, Majdanek and the other extermination camps were marched westwards in front of the Russian advance and deposited at concentration camps in Germany. These were the 'human skeletons' whom the British and Americans freed at the end of the war.

booty they could, and fled into hiding. Those captured were put to work clearing up the mess, then herded into Dachau and other camps pending a de-Nazification process and possible criminal proceedings. The dreaded day of reckoning had arrived.

For Himmler, the cease-fire concluded by Dönitz on 5 May 1945 marked the end of the road. All the Wehrmacht officers who had hastily gathered around the Grand Admiral, desperate to avoid charges of war crimes being levelled against them, now shifted the

SS-Standartenführer Walther Rauff (left), head of the security police in Milan, surrenders to the Americans on 30 April 1945. Rauff was also a Korvetten-Kapitän der Reserve in the navy, and took part in Kriegsmarine actions in North Africa, for which he received the 'Afrika' campaign cuff title, seen here being worn on the sleeve of his SS uniform.

blame for Nazi Germany's conduct totally on to the SS and the person of the Reichsführer. On 6 May, Himmler mustered his remaining faithful entourage including his brother Gebhard, Hans Prützmann, Léon Degrelle, and various Hauptamt chiefs, police generals and Waffen-SS leaders, and gave a final farewell speech. He ended by handing out prepared false identity documents, and advised his followers to 'submerge in the Wehrmacht'. Each then went his own way. Himmler furnished himself with the papers of a former military police sergeant named Heinrich Hitzinger, who had earlier been executed by the SS for defeatism. He also carried a phial of cyanide, and had a hole

drilled in one of his molars to accommodate it. There was no doubt in his mind about his fate and that of his chief accomplices should they fall into enemy hands.

On 10 May, Himmler set out on foot from Flensburg to Bavaria. He was escorted by SS-Obersturmbannführer Werner Grothmann and SS-Hauptsturmführer Heinz Macher, both in army uniform. Grothmann, only twenty-nine years old, had been the Reichsführer's personal aide-de-camp since 1943, and was one of his most loyal subordinates. Macher, although four years younger, was a hardened combat veteran and had won the Oakleaves to his Knight's Cross in 1944 while serving with 'Das Reich' in

Leibstandarte and 'Der Führer' officers attached to the 24th SS Division surrender to the British near Treviso in northern Italy, 7 May 1945. The Obersturmführer on the left, with the tropical field cap and shorts, wears the Guerrilla Warfare Badge in Silver above his other awards.

Russia. It was Macher who had blown up Wewelsburg Castle the previous month on Himmler's direct instructions, to prevent its capture by the Allies, and he had also been charged with the task of burying the castle's treasures, including over 9,000 death's head rings held in the shrine to commemorate SS men killed in action. Protected by these two stalwarts, Himmler intended to join the many other SS and NSDAP leaders who had fled south-east to the Alps. On 21 May, however, the three men were arrested by the British at a routine check-point between Hamburg and Bremen. Two days later they arrived at an interrogation centre at Barfeld, near Lüneburg, where the former Reichsführer's identity was confirmed. As his elated captors

began to question him, Himmler bit on the cyanide capsule and was dead within minutes, thus escaping the humiliation of a show trial and the certain fate of a hangman's noose. He was subsequently buried in an unmarked grave on Lüneburg Heath, and his false identity disc, spectacles and few other meagre possessions were distributed among the attendant Allied intelligence personnel as souvenirs.

Only a small number of SS leaders followed Himmler's example by committing suicide. Among them were Hans Prützmann, Philipp Bouhler, Herbert Backe, Leonardo Conti, Odilo Globocnik, Friedrich-Wilhelm Krüger and Ernst-Robert Grawitz, the latter blowing both himself and his family up with

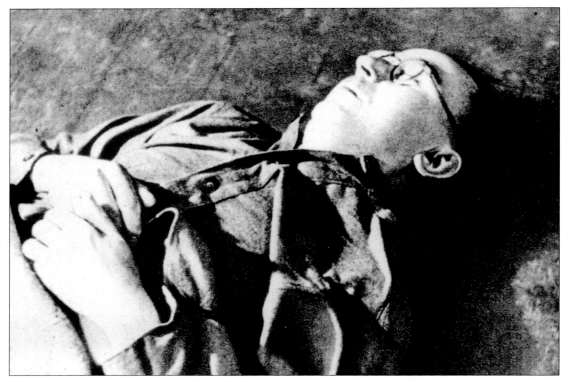

Himmler after his suicide, 23 May 1945.

hand grenades. Christian Weber, the old Stosstrupp veteran, was killed in action in Bavaria at the end of the war and Karl Hanke, the last Reichsführer-SS, was beaten to death by Czechs a couple of months later. Many SS officers, including the Gestapo chief Heinrich Müller, the Concentration Camp Inspector-General Richard Glücks, and the infamous Dr Josef Mengele, simply disappeared underground as Himmler had recommended.

During the second half of 1945, the victorious Allies engaged upon a concerted effort to root out and round up all former members of the SS, which they declared had been an illegal and terrorist organisation. Their primary objective was to put the leaders before a military tribunal, to answer charges of war crimes. Mass arrests followed and 32,000 ex-SS men were incarcerated at Dachau alone by the end of the year. Franz Breithaupt died at Prien soon after being taken into British custody, and Maximilian von Herff suffered a similar fate at Cornshead Priory POW camp on Lake Windermere in September, the same month in which Walter Schmitt expired in Dablice as a captive of the Czechs. Those who were duly put on trial at Nürnberg and elsewhere during 1946–7 received a variety of sentences. Ernst Kaltenbrunner, Oswald Pohl, Arthur Greiser, Karl Hermann Frank, Kurt Daluege, Karl Gebhardt, Friedrich Jeckeln, Karl Brandt and Albert Forster, along with a further eighteen less well-known SS and police generals, were condemned to death

A chart depicting the organisation of the RSHA is displayed at Nürnberg during the trials of SS and SD men, 20 December 1946.

and executed for their involvement in the Nazi extermination policy. Large numbers of more junior personnel who had staffed concentration camps, served in Einsatzgruppen or taken part in Waffen-SS atrocities were similarly dealt with. Gottlob Berger was sentenced to twenty-five years' imprisonment, Werner Lorenz and Hans Lammers each received twenty years in jail, Wilhelm Keppler got ten years, and Walter Buch was condemned to five years' hard labour before committing suicide. Gustav-Adolf Scheel and Walter Schellenberg were each given five years' imprisonment, and Otto Dietrich one year. Erich von dem Bach, a prime candidate for the death sentence,

saved his neck and avoided extradition to Poland by acting as a witness for the prosecution at Nürnberg. The majority of these men served out their terms of imprisonment, which were often reduced on appeal or for good behaviour, and went on to enjoy comfortable lives in postwar West Germany. Indeed, for years thereafter, Allied intelligence agencies frequently sought the advice of Schellenberg and his former RSHA colleagues, and paid handsomely for the benefit of their expertise in espionage and interrogation techniques.

As for the other former SS commanders and notable personalities, Franz Xaver Schwarz succumbed to ill-health in

Otto Ohlendorf pleading 'not guilty' at Nürnberg, 15 September 1947. Behind him sit his former RSHA colleagues Heinz Jost, Erich Naumann, Werner Braune and Walter Hänsch. As one-time commander of Einsatzgruppe 'D' in Russia, and chief of the SD in Germany, Ohlendorf was sentenced to death.

Regensburg internment camp in 1947, while Ulrich Greifelt died in February 1949 at Landsberg, also after a long illness. Ulrich Graf perished a pauper in Munich in March 1950, followed by Richard Hildebrandt in 1951. Richard Walther Darré expired from liver failure two years later, Rudolf Diels accidentally shot and killed himself during a hunting expedition in November 1957, and Max Amann died in poverty the same year having had all the wealth which he accrued from publishing *Mein Kampf* confiscated by a de-Nazification tribunal. Heinz Reinefarth, the first SS member to win the Knight's Cross and commander of police units involved in crushing the Warsaw uprising, was luckier, taking up a career in local government and rising to the post of Bürgermeister of Westerland in 1958. His close police associate, Alfred Wünnenberg, died in Krefeld in 1963. Karl Wolff, always a 'smooth talker', built up a successful public relations business until he received a belated ten-year prison sentence in 1964, following revelations at the Eichmann trial. Hans Jüttner died at Bad Tölz in 1965, and in 1966 four former Waffen-SS generals, namely 'Sepp' Dietrich, Georg Keppler, Herbert Gille and Felix Steiner, all succumbed to various illnesses and were buried after funeral services openly attended by hundreds of Waffen-SS veterans. Julius Schaub pursued his profession as a Munich chemist until his demise in 1967, while Karl Fiehler and Jakob

Grimminger both died in obscurity in 1969. Emil Maurice, the part-Jewish holder of SS membership number 2 (Hitler held number 1) lived until 1972, the same year as ninety-two-year-old Paul Hausser, the revered 'Father of the Waffen-SS', was laid to rest in the presence of his old comrades. Werner Lorenz died in 1974, Gottlob Berger in 1975, and August Heissmeyer in 1979. The last surviving Hauptamt chief, Karl Wolff, gave up the ghost at Rosenheim in 1984. With his death, the former top-ranking SS leadership and the lingering Old Guard of the organisation were finally extinguished.

However, while the majority of the very highest SS leaders were too well known to avoid detection and arrest by the Allies at the end of the war, there were many more anonymous and rather faceless individuals who quite easily evaded capture. Prominent among such men were Heinrich Müller, Richard Glücks and Dr Josef Mengele, whose associations with the extermination programme earned them death sentences 'in absentia' from the Nürnberg tribunal. Hundreds of junior SS officers and NCOs from concentration camp guard units, policemen who had served with Einsatzgruppen in the east, and foreign volunteers such as Léon Degrelle who were regarded as arch-traitors in their own countries, managed to flee to the safety of sympathetic nations and set up new and comfortable lives for themselves after 1945. Their ability to do so was due almost entirely to the assistance provided by a vast and typically efficient escape network organised by the SS in its terminal stages.

At the end of 1944, Himmler ordered the RSHA to prepare false identity documents and passports bearing fictitious names which were subsequently distributed to selected leading members of the SS and NSDAP. After the surrender was signed, many top Nazis went into hiding or operated openly under their new pseudonyms. In front of the very eyes of the Allied administration, valuable contacts were established between high-ranking Nazis in prison and new underground groups outside, using secret codes devised by the SD before the collapse of the Third Reich. The initial overall organisation which co-ordinated these activities was called 'Spinne', or 'Spider', and was restricted to operating within Germany itself. Most important ex-SS men did not want to hang around the Homeland for too long, however, and by 1946 they decided that the time had come to set up a worldwide escape network. As a result, the ODESSA (Organisation der SS-Angehörigen, or Organisation of SS Members) came into being the following year.

In a surprisingly short time, using the expertise of its RSHA veterans, ODESSA built up an efficient system of couriers who managed to smuggle wanted SS men and other Nazis out of the country. A few enterprising individuals even secured jobs driving US Army trucks on the Munich–Salzburg autobahn, and hid fugitives in the backs of the vehicles, which were seldom searched by the American military police, to get them safely across the Austrian border. Every forty miles or so, an ODESSA Anlaufstelle, or reception centre, was established, run by at least three but not more than five people, who knew only the Anlaufstellen on either side of them along the route. These relay points covered the entire German–Austrian frontier, with the most important ones being situated at Ostermiething in Upper Austria, Zell-am-See in the Salzburg District, and Igls near Innsbruck in the Tyrol. Many SS men on the run ended up at either Bregenz or Lindau, both on Lake Constance, from where they crossed into Switzerland and thereafter boarded civil airline flights to the Middle East or South America. ODESSA also ran a so-called Monastery Route, between Austria and Italy, where sympathetic Roman Catholic clergy, particularly Franciscan friars, passed hunted SS men down a long line of religious 'safe houses'. Moreover, the organisation had connections with professional smugglers in all frontier areas, and cultivated valuable contacts in the Spanish, Egyptian, Syrian and numerous South American embassies in various European capitals. One of the main organisers was Obersturmbannführer Franz Roestel, formerly of the Waffen-SS division 'Frundsberg'. Although not on the 'wanted' list himself, he operated under the assumed name of Haddad Said, and found places for many of his ex-colleagues as military advisers to the governments of developing Arab states.

All this cost money, a resource which ODESSA conveniently had in virtually unlimited supply. The huge profits amassed through the SS economic enterprises, the substantial donations received over many years from members of the Freundeskreis RfSS and the Fördernde Mitglieder, and the cash raised by the sale of confiscated Jewish property and art treasures looted from the occupied territories had filled the wartime coffers of the SS to the point of overflow. Early in 1945, the WVHA and RSHA conspired to liquidate all remaining SS assets and transfer the bulk of its money into bank accounts opened in neutral countries. These were subsequently used to establish and finance over 750 SS-sponsored companies which sprang up all over the world, including 112 in Spain, 58 in Portugal, 35 in Turkey, 98 in Argentina, 214 in Switzerland and 233 in other countries. Trusted former SS officers suddenly and unexpectedly had substantial sums deposited into their personal bank accounts, which explains how so many of them became 'successful businessmen' in later life. One ex-Obersturmbannführer paid a visit to his bank in 1947 to discover that his account, which had stood at a modest 12,000

Marks the previous week, had risen abruptly to over 2,600,000 Marks! He had no idea where the additional money had come from, until he recalled a mysterious visit he had had in the autumn of 1944 from two senior SS officers, who wanted to know the number of his bank account and asked for a specimen of his signature on two blank sheets of paper. Although no explanation had been given at the time, they had evidently been preparing the groundwork for the distribution of SS funds after the war.

It has been estimated that between 1945 and 1948 the SS managed to hide the present-day equivalent of around £1,000,000,000 in money and assets in various parts of the world. The six lists of the people authorised to dispose of, and benefit from, these funds are probably the most important undiscovered documents of the Third Reich. Two were in the hands of the men who organised ODESSA in 1947, two are said to be in the safe-keeping of banks, and one of the remaining two is believed to be lying at the bottom of Lake Töplitz in Austria, where a large quantity of Nazi loot was hurriedly sunk in 1945. The vast majority of those named on the lists are now dead, but their children live on. There can be little doubt that many respected family businesses currently operating successfully across the globe owe their origins and continued existence to ODESSA and the funds of the SS.

While ODESSA was always a secret network, geared towards securing the escape of SS war criminals and the continuance of Nazi ideology, a second well-publicised organisation for ex-SS men was established at about the same time. It was the Hilfs-gemeinschaft auf Gegenseitigkeit der Soldaten der ehemal Waffen-SS, or HIAG, the Welfare Association of Former Soldiers of the Waffen-SS. HIAG consistently denied any connection with ODESSA, but the latter undoubtedly financed it in the early days. Its avowed purpose was to campaign for and achieve the payment of state benefits to ex-servicemen of the Waffen-SS, particularly the war-wounded, who did not qualify for regular Wehrmacht disability pensions. In that aim, it was moderately successful. Over the years, as its original membership progressively died off, HIAG dwindled in importance to become only a pale shadow of its former self, devoted almost entirely to the running of a small publishing house, Munin-Verlag GmbH of Osnabrück, which produced literature celebrating the combat achievements of SS field troops during the Second World War. The dismemberment of HIAG in the early 1990s saw the end of the last acknowledged active remnant of the SS.

However, while the SS may now be consigned to the history books, interest in the story of the organisation, and its regalia, has never been greater. The Waffen-SS in particular continues to hold a position of unique interest, with recent analyses setting aside the atrocities and reappraising the Waffen-SS as an élite multi-national fighting force, even a forerunner of NATO, whose soldiers earned the respect not only of their Wehrmacht comrades but also of their enemies.

A veritable multi-million pound business has grown up around the buying and selling of SS militaria and other memorabilia. Indeed, the collecting of SS regalia began even before the cessation of hostilities in May 1945. As German towns and cities, and concentration camps, fell to the Allies, SS items rapidly discarded by their owners were just as quickly 'snapped up' by souvenir-hunting British and American troops. Like their counterparts in armies throughout history, the victors of the Second World War eagerly traded in and bartered with the spoils taken from the vanquished. Large stockpiles of SS uniforms at Dachau were liberated *en masse*; SS stores and military retailers had their premises

stripped; prisoners-of-war had their badges confiscated; and so on. Such was the availability of SS effects that no great value was put on any of them. Soldiers might exchange an SS general's peaked cap for an Iron Cross 2nd Class, a death's head ring for a belt buckle or a Reichsführer's sword of honour for a steel helmet. Few knew exactly what was passing through their hands: they merely swapped things according to individual preferences. When the Allied troops returned home with this booty they found a ready market for their acquisitions. With some elementary research into the subject, a more discerning breed of collector soon evolved and the whole business took off.

During the 1950s and 1960s, such was the demand for all manner of National Socialist regalia, both military and civil, that several unscrupulous dealers began to have it reproduced and passed their fakes off as genuine articles. The 1970s and 1980s witnessed an even bigger boom in the trade and a resultant explosion in the creation of improved fakes to meet the ever-increasing demand. While the collecting of SS items will always be distasteful to many, for quite understandable reasons, the fact remains that these are now the most sought after pieces of Nazi regalia. Not an insignificant number of Jewish businessmen have 'had the last laugh' by dealing in fake SS militaria for which they charge exorbitant prices, making considerable profits as a result. The cash benefit of selling SS items was brought to a head during the late 1980s, when the official in charge of the German archives storing wartime SS personnel records amassed a fortune by removing documents signed by Himmler, Heydrich and the like and selling them on the open market. He subsequently received a lengthy jail sentence for his efforts, and collectors throughout the world were obliged to return to the authorities in Germany items which they had bought in good faith.

Among the SS pieces now in greatest demand are peaked caps, tunics, camouflage clothing and insignia of all types. Originals are hard to find, and to meet the demand the fakers have turned to producing 'fantasy' items which had no authentic counterparts during the Third Reich! Foremost among these are the following 'fantasy' cuff titles, none of which existed before the end of the Second World War:

Berlin
Böhmen-Mähren
Britisches Freikorps
Dachau
Dirlewanger
Galizien
Junkerschule Tölz
Kaminski
KTL der SS
Leibstandarte
Lettland
Lützow
Nibelungen
Otto Skorzeny
Schill
Seelager
SS-Fallschirmjäger
SS-Kavallerie-Division
SS-Polizei
Totenkopf I
Totenkopf II
Totenkopf III
Ungarn
Wallonie

While the fakers have always tended to concentrate on the lucrative areas of collar patches, shoulder straps, arm eagles and so on, every type of SS badge has been copied. Reproductions include sports vest insignia,

unit ciphers, the whole range of foreign volunteer arm shields, mountain troop edelweisses, Old Campaigner's chevrons, breast runes and the rank insignia for camouflage clothing. Copy piping and Tresse for collars and shoulder straps are available by the metre, and even RZM labels have been faked for sewing on to bogus uniforms and badges. Moreover, dozens of other SS collectables have been reproduced. Belt buckles, cap cords, tunic buttons, sword knots, identity papers and discs, flags, pennants and rings are just a small selection. Waffen-SS recruiting posters, driving licences and even song books have been reprinted. Convincing new fakes regularly appear with plausible 'pedigrees' designed to assist their acceptance. In 1992, for example, a 'batch of SS uniform thread' was allegedly 'found in the former East Germany' and rolls of it, complete with RZM labels attached, circulated widely on the collectors' market. Suspicions were soon aroused by the sheer quantities of thread available, however, and these suspicions were duly justified when one buyer cut open his newly acquired roll to reveal the words 'Made in Pakistan' stamped inside. Yet another 'Eastern bloc find' had been exposed!

The point of all this is that there would be no purpose in producing such fake trash if there were not a vast and lucrative market for it. Most buyers think they are acquiring true relics of the SS, and are still captivated by the death's head and runes, even with the full knowledge of what these came to represent during the Second World War. It therefore becomes all the easier to understand how Himmler's Black Order could hypnotise so many ordinary Germans in the 1930s and set them eagerly along the road to perpetual damnation.

BIBLIOGRAPHY

PRIMARY SOURCES

Archiv der Reichsführer-SS und Chef der Deutschen Polizei. Presently stored within the National Archives, Washington D.C.

Das Schwarze Korps: Zeitung der Schutzstaffel der NSDAP, Organ der Reichsführung-SS. (Zentral Verlag der NSDAP, Munich, 1935–45.) The official newspaper of the SS.

Der Dietrich. (Various issues.) The bulletin of the Leibstandarte-SS 'Adolf Hitler'.

Dienstaltersliste der Schutzstaffel der NSDAP. (SS Personalhauptamt, Berlin, various editions.) The SS Officers List.

FM-Zeitschrift: Monatschrift der Reichsführung-SS für Fördernde Mitglieder. (Zentral Verlag der NSDAP, Munich, 1935–45.) The journal of the SS Patron Members Organisation.

Organisationsbuch der NSDAP. (Zentral Verlag der NSDAP, Munich, various editions 1934–45.) Includes the development of SS uniforms and insignia.

Schutzstaffel der NSDAP: Kleiderkasse Preisliste. (SS Verwaltungsamt, Berlin, various dates.) The official SS uniform and equipment price list.

SS Personnel Files and Records. Several million of these are preserved by the Bundesarchiv, Berlin.

The General SS. (SHAEF Counter-Intelligence Sub-Division, 1944.) Comprehensive Allied intelligence report on the Allgemeine-SS.

SUGGESTED FURTHER READING

d'Alquen, G., *Die SS.* Berlin, 1939. Official pamphlet produced by the Reichsführung-SS, detailing the origins and functions of the SS organisation. German text.

Angolia, J.R., *Cloth Insignia of the SS.* Bender, San Jose, 1983. Lavish illustrative history of the development of SS badges.

Barker, A.J., *Waffen-SS at War.* Ian Allan, Shepperton, 1982. Good coverage of Waffen-SS battles during the Second World War.

Beaver, M.D. and Borsarello, J., *Camouflage Uniforms of the Waffen-SS.* Schiffer, Pennsylvania, 1995. Detailed photographic study of SS camouflage patterns.

Bender, R.J. and Taylor, H.P., *Uniforms, Organisation and History of the Waffen-SS, Vols 1–5.* Bender, San Jose, 1969–83. A good reference on unit histories and insignia, for the first twenty Waffen-SS divisions.

Borsarello, J. and Lassus, D., *Camouflaged Uniforms of the Waffen-SS, Vols 1 & 2.* ISO, London, 1986–8. Photographic study of SS camouflage.

Buss, P.H. and Mollo, A., *Hitler's Germanic Legions.* McDonald & Jane's, London, 1978. An illustrated history of the western European legions of the Waffen-SS, 1941–3.

Cooper, D.J., *Using the Runes.* Aquarian Press, Wellingborough, 1987. A comprehensive introduction to the ancient art of runecraft.

Davis, B.L., *Waffen-SS.* Blandford, Poole, 1985. A basic photographic history.

Eelking, Freiherr von, *Die Uniformen der Braunhemden: SA, SS, Politische Leiter,*

Hitlerjugend & BDM. Zentral Verlag der NSDAP, Munich, 1933. Illustrates early SS uniforms. German text.

Frutiger, A., *Der Mensch und seine Zeichen*. Weiss Verlag, Dreieich, 1978. The designs and meanings of signs and symbols. German text.

Gilbert, A., *Waffen-SS*. Bison, London, 1989. An excellent illustrated history.

Hamilton, C., *Leaders and Personalities of the Third Reich*. Bender, San Jose, 1984. Mini-biographies of all the main Nazi leaders.

Harms, N. and Volstad, R., *Waffen-SS in Action*. Squadron/Signal, Texas, 1973. A general pictorial account.

Hayes, A. (ed.), *SS Uniforms, Insignia and Accoutrements*. Schiffer, Pennsylvania, 1996. A photographic study of SS regalia.

Höhne, H., *Der Orden unter dem Totenkopf*. Verlag der Spiegel, Hamburg, 1966. The standard history of the SS. German text.

Holzmann, W.K., *Manual of the Waffen-SS*. Bellona, Watford, 1976. Basic reference on Waffen-SS uniforms and equipment.

Hunt, R., *Death's Head*. Hunt, Madison, 1979. A combat record of the SS-Totenkopf-Division in France, 1940.

Jurado, C. and Hannon, P., *Resistance Warfare, 1940–45*. Osprey, London, 1985. Includes coverage of the Germanic-SS and associated units in the west.

Krausnick, H. and Broszat, M., *Anatomy of the SS State*. Paladin, London, 1970. A scholarly account of the concentration camp system and the persecution of the Jews.

Kumm, O., *Vorwärts Prinz Eugen!* Munin-Verlag, Osnabrück, 1978. An illustrated history of the SS division 'Prinz Eugen'. German text.

Lehmann, R., *Die Leibstandarte*. Munin-Verlag, Osnabrück, 1977. An illustrated history of the Leibstandarte-SS 'Adolf Hitler'. German text.

Littlejohn, D., *Foreign Legions of the Third Reich, Vols 1–4*. Bender, San Jose, 1979–87. Includes sections on the non-German units of the Waffen-SS.

Littlejohn, D., *The Hitler Youth*. R.L. Bryan, Columbia, 1988. Good coverage of the relationship between the SS and the Hitler Youth.

Lucas, J. and Cooper, M., *Hitler's Elite*. McDonald & Jane's, London, 1975. The story of the Leibstandarte-SS 'Adolf Hitler'.

Lumsden, R., *Third Reich Militaria*. Ian Allan, Shepperton, 1987. A collector's guide.

Lumsden, R., *Detecting the Fakes*. Ian Allan, Shepperton, 1989. How to spot reproduction Nazi regalia.

Lumsden, R., *The Black Corps*. Ian Allan, Shepperton, 1992. A collector's guide to the history of the SS.

Lumsden, R., *The Allgemeine-SS*. Osprey, London, 1993. A general history of the Allgemeine-SS and its uniforms.

Lumsden, R., *The Waffen-SS*. Ian Allan, Shepperton, 1994. A collector's guide.

Lumsden, R., *SS Regalia*. Bison, London, 1995. Photographic record of the uniforms and insignia of the SS.

Mollo, A., *A Pictorial History of the SS, 1923–45*. McDonald & Jane's, London, 1976. Excellent photographic record of the SS.

Mollo, A., *Uniforms of the SS, Vols 1–7*. Historical Research Unit, London, 1969–76. The standard books on SS uniform.

Mund, R., *Der Rasputin Himmlers*. Vienna, 1982. The story of SS-Brigadeführer Karl-Maria Wiligut-Weisthor. German text.

Munoz, A., *Forgotten Legions*. Paladin, Colorado, 1991. The tale of the obscure combat formations of the Waffen-SS.

Padfield, P., *Himmler: Reichsführer-SS*. Macmillan, London, 1990. The ultimate biography of Heinrich Himmler.

Page, R.I., *Runes*. British Museum Press, London, 1987. The story of runic writing in Dark Age Europe.

Pallud, J.P., *Ardennes 1944: Peiper and Skorzeny*. Osprey, London, 1987. The Waffen-SS involvement in the Battle of the Bulge.

Passmore, M., *SS Porcelain Allach*. TLO, Oxford, 1972. A history of the SS porcelain and ceramics industry.

Peterson, D., *Waffen-SS Camouflage Uniforms and Postwar Derivatives*. Windrow & Greene, London, 1995. A reconstruction of Waffen-SS camouflage uniforms in wear.

Pia, J., *SS Regalia*. Ballantine, New York, 1974. Includes good colour illustrations of SS collectables.

Quarrie, B., *Waffen-SS in Russia*. PSL, Cambridge, 1978. A photographic account of the Waffen-SS on the eastern front.

Quarrie, B., *Hitler's Samurai*. PSL, Cambridge, 1983. A history of the Waffen-SS.

Quarrie, B., *Hitler's Teutonic Knights*. PSL, Cambridge, 1987. A history of the Waffen-SS panzer divisions.

Quarrie, B., *Weapons of the Waffen-SS*. PSL, Cambridge, 1988. Covers all types of small arms and heavy artillery.

Quarrie, B., *Waffen-SS Soldier, 1940–45*. Osprey, London, 1993. A history of the tactics, actions and uniforms of the SS infantryman.

Reider, F., *L'Ordre SS*. Editions de la Pensée Moderne, Paris, 1980. A good general account of the SS. French text.

Reitlinger, G., *The SS: Alibi of a Nation*. Heinemann, London, 1956. The first detailed history of the SS.

Russel, S. and Schneider, J., *Heinrich Himmlers Burg*. Heitz & Höffkes, Essen, 1989. A chronicle of Wewelsburg Castle, 1934–45. German text.

Schneider, J., *Their Honour Was Loyalty*. Bender, San Jose, 1977. An illustrated and documentary history of the Knight's Cross holders of the Waffen-SS and police.

Simpson, K., *Waffen-SS*. Bison, London, 1990. Photographic history of the Waffen-SS.

Smith, J.H. and Saris, W., *Headgear of Hitler's Germany, Vol 2*. Bender, San Jose, 1992. Covers Waffen-SS headdress.

Stein, G., *The Waffen-SS: Hitler's Elite Guard at War*. Cornell, New York, 1966. A scholarly account of the Waffen-SS.

Stephen, A. and Amodio, P., *Waffen-SS Uniforms in Colour Photographs*. Windrow & Greene, London, 1990. Imaginative reconstructions of Waffen-SS uniforms in wear.

Stöber, H., *Die Sturmflut und das Ende*. Munin-Verlag, Osnabrück, 1976. Illustrated history of the SS division 'Götz von Berlichingen'. German text.

Sydnor, C., *Soldiers of Destruction*. Princetown University Press, Princeton, 1977. The story of the SS-Totenkopf units, 1933–45.

Thomas, N. and Abbott, P., *Partisan Warfare, 1941–45*. Osprey, London, 1983. Includes coverage of SS anti-partisan engagements on the eastern front.

Time-Life Books (various authors), *The SS*. Time-Life, Alexandria, 1988. An illustrated history of the SS.

Weidinger, O., *Division 'Das Reich'*. Munin-Verlag, Osnabrück, 1979. An illustrated history of the SS division 'Das Reich'. German text.

Williamson, G., *The SS: Hitler's Instrument of Terror*. Brown, London, 1994. A history of the SS.

Williamson, G., *Loyalty is My Honour*. Brown, London, 1995. Recollections of former members of the Waffen-SS.

Wilson, K., *SS Headgear: A Collector's Guide*. Reddick, Texas, 1990. Colour photographs of Waffen-SS headdress.

Windrow, M., *The Waffen-SS*. Osprey, London, 1982. A general history of Waffen-SS units, uniforms and campaigns.

INDEX